ITALIAN
CUISINE

ITALIAN CUISINE

THE NEW ESSENTIAL REFERENCE
TO THE RICHES OF THE ITALIAN TABLE

TONY MAY

ST. MARTIN'S PRESS ❧ NEW YORK

www.stmartins.com

Library of Congress Cataloging-in-Publication Data

May, Tony, 1937–   .
     Italian cuisine / Tony May.—3rd ed.
        p. cm.
     ISBN 0-312-30280-0
     EAN 978-0-312-30280-1
        1. Cookery, Italian.

TX723.M38 2005
641'.5945—dc21

                        2002031881

First published in the United States by Tony May Group, Inc.
First St. Martin's Press Edition: June 2005

10   9   8   7   6   5   4   3   2   1

*I dedicate this book to the two women in my life,
my wife, Halima, and my daughter, Marisa*

CONTENTS

PREFACE

This book was first published fifteen years ago as a resource for those in the restaurant industry. Several years ago, a second edition updated the contents to reflect changes in the evolution of Italian eating habits. Now, four years later, the third edition has been updated again in answer to many individuals who are not in the restaurant industry but who want to prepare authentic Italian dishes in the home.

In order to do so, several recipes have been simplified and measurements standardized to those found in most kitchens. In addition, several ingredients, native to Italy but not readily found in American shops, have been replaced without compromising the quality of the food.

Perhaps a distinction should be made between the styles of cooking of Italian and American cooks. Italian cooks read recipes to get the general idea of what is needed. The quantities usually are flexible, depending on individual taste and the availability of certain products. American cooks are more methodical. Directions are followed carefully, so ingredients should be listed sequentially, that is, in order of use. Aside from "a pinch of salt," exact measurements are important.

This new edition closes the gap between the two styles. To accommodate the growing audience of American cooks, measurements have been converted to teaspoons, tablespoons, and cups for liquids and ounces and pounds for solids wherever possible. In addition, the amount of herbs is indicated more exactly.

This should not inhibit cooks from varying the ingredients, the amounts, or the use of mechanical aids for kneading dough for bread or pasta to match their own style and taste. After preparing a particular dish, the creative cook will individualize the recipe to match personal preferences.

Some recipes require ingredients, especially meats, which are not found ordinarily in the local supermarket. Most meat purveyors will be happy to order some of these meats such as heart, liver, and kidneys (from goats or lambs or calves), tripe, sweetbreads, brains, rabbit or hare, capon, and other less common foods.

In order to familiarize the reader with the diversity and use of many foods, the recipes in each chapter are preceded by a section giving historical, regional, and culinary information. It describes some methods of making certain standbys, discusses the qualities and differences among various products such as oils and cheeses, and gives general directions for cooking techniques. Finally, the book includes an extensive glossary of words and expressions currently in use in Italian cuisine.

—Tony May

HISTORICAL NOTES

This volume is not meant for coffee-table exposure but rather as a comprehensive reference book, a reliable consultation tool aimed not only at those who operate in the restaurant industry but also at lovers of Italian cuisine who wish to learn the basics of cooking Italian. Three hundred and fifty recipes may not seem many compared to the bulk of recipe books currently available on the market, but they were in fact accurately selected to provide the very essential structures of the fantastic architecture of Italian cookery.

Italy boasts a thousand-year-old gastronomical tradition enriched by the contribution and the expertise of all the populations that ruled over Italian territories before and after the fall of the Roman Empire: from the Arabs in Sicily to the Spaniards in Naples, from the Lombards coming from the north to the Saracens, who landed on the western shores of the peninsula. The gastronomical culture we can call Italian cuisine today is a result of the cultural integration of these populations with the culinary habits derived from the local traditions of single regions.

We must not forget that today's Italy is the result of the reunification of the many small states it had been divided into over the past centuries, which in turn were divided into regions with different dialects and cultural traditions. In 1861 when the Italian kingdom was officially instituted, out of a population of twenty-five million inhabitants, no more than six hundred thousand citizens could speak the national language; everyone else spoke regional dialects. The same is true for eating habits. Pasta, which was introduced by the Arabs in Sicily in the tenth century, was the staple food all over the South, whereas people from the north preferred polenta (cornmeal mush) and rice, which, although introduced in Europe by the Arabs, was actually brought to Italy by the Spaniards. There was already a kind of "noble" cuisine, which had developed inside the palaces of the Renaissance aristocracy and had almost disappeared as a consequence of the fall of such classes.

Rural traditions, which were centered around the consumption of local agricultural products, obviously bounced into the city culture. The restaurant industry was two-sided: on the one hand the famous grand hotels boasting French chefs or Italian chefs trained in France; on the other hand the family-managed restaurants, which were often little more than dignified country inns where the innkeepers' wives prepared the same dishes they would make for their families.

The first book listing a systematic collection of Italian recipes was *La Scienza in cucina e l'arte di mangiar bene*, in which the author, Pellegrino Artusi, had gathered all the typical dishes of the average Italian household. Only around the second half of the twentieth century, when the ancient Renaissance texts (those of Platina, Bartolomeo Scappi, Bartolomeo Stefani, and Cristoforo di Messisburgo, *Il Cuoco galante* of Vincenzo Corrado) were rediscovered, did the great Italian cuisine of the past centuries really come back to life again. Still, the most radical changes occurred after the 1960s. The development of transportation made it possible for fresh fish to be delivered to inland cities rather than being available only at seaside towns. This resulted in the amazing spread of excellent fish restaurants in the main cities. All this happened alongside the consumers' growing demand for lighter eating, using olive oil instead of butter, lard, or other animal fats. Cooking times have remarkably shortened and, generally speaking, Italian cooking has become more and more oriented toward respecting typical foods' original flavors and smells, thus topping them less and less with the heavy sauces used in the past.

The results of all these changes are collected in this book as clear descriptions and step-by-step instructions. The volume does not go into detail as to the thousands of recipes that make up today's Italian cuisine but, rather, it provides detailed information that will enable the reader to re-create and interpret at his or her own leisure—depending on what inventiveness suggests and what is available on the market—the immense heritage of the Italian culinary tradition. This book is surely meant for anyone who wants to approach Italian cuisine the sensible, practical way.

—GIORGIO MISTRETTA
JOURNALIST AND FOOD HISTORIAN

ACKNOWLEDGMENTS

No book of this kind can be compiled by any one man, and whatever its value as a comprehensive and authoritative repository of informed opinion, it is due to the many people who have helped me pull all the elements together into a volume. I hope it is as readable as it is useful to all. My gratitude to the following people is outweighed only by my respect for their knowledge, enthusiasm, and energies in helping me bring this book out.

I wish first to thank Fernanda Gosetti, noted cookbook author, who helped me write the first edition in 1990.

For his dogged research into the origins, history, curiosities, and regional differences of Italian cooking and for his review of the second edition, I thank journalist and food writer Giorgio Mistretta, who passed away in an untimely fashion in 2001. I miss him tremendously. And for their encouragement and help at every turn, I shall not soon forget the input of noted cookbook writer and television personality Vincenzo Buonassisi and journalist and food expert Stefano Milioni, and my good friend, anthropologist Alessandro Falassi. When it came to compiling the recipes, chefs both in Italy and the United States, Valentino Marcattilii, Paul Bartolotta, Angelo Paracucchi, Carlo de Gaudenzi, Sandro Fioriti, Pierangelo Cornaro, and Odette Fada offered enormous help and resources. From there, it was first taken over by John F. Mariani, whose editorial direction, from asking the simplest of questions to making the most insightful demands, has made what I once thought unmanageable into a work of authoritative cogency.

The new edition of this volume was then thoroughly revised and edited by Louise Matteoni, Ph.D., whose common-sense approach has made this edition a better cookbook by reading through the recipes and adding consistent terminology and easy reading. I also wish to thank Arthur Golden, the technology guru, for his help in watching over the computer rewrite to get it all done on time, Ferdinand Metz for his continued support, and Tim Ryan and Mark Erickson of the Culinary Institute of America for their early help with recipe testing.

I hope the readers of this book and future generations enjoy this work and learn from it as much as I have in putting it all together.

—TONY MAY

A NOTE ON ITALIAN USAGE

In Italy, the language of food incorporates dozens of regional dialects that may or may not conform to standard Italian grammar, spelling, and usage. A single food term may take more than one regional name: *fettuccine,* for example, is the word used in Rome to describe the flat noodles known more commonly as *tagliatelle* in the rest of Italy. These regional terms enrich Italy's culinary language as devil's food, dirty rice, and hush puppy enrich American English.

Italian is an inflected language. The standard rules for singular and plural forms, however, are based on gender, though only a thorough knowledge of the language will help to sort out why some words are masculine and others feminine. In general, masculine nouns in the singular end in -*o* and feminine nouns in -*a*. Masculine nouns in the plural end in -*i* and feminine nouns in -*e*.

Here are some examples:

Masculine		Feminine	
Singular	*Plural*	*Singular*	*Plural*
scampo	scampi	quaglia	quaglie
piatto	piatti	linguina	linguine
sorbetto	sorbetti	fettuccina	fettuccine

There are exceptions to these rules, especially singular nouns ending in -*e,* which can be either masculine or feminine (e.g., il padre, "the father," and la madre, "the mother"). In both cases the plural ending is -*i (i padri, le madri).* There are even Italian masculine nouns ending in -*o* that become feminine in the plural (e.g., *l'uovo,* "the egg," *le uova,* "the eggs").

The Italian definite article for the English word "the" is "il" for masculine nouns *(il piatto, il sorbetto)* if singular; if plural, *i (i piatti, i sorbetti). Lo* (singular) and *gli* (plural) are also used in special cases *(lo scampo, gli scampi).* For feminine singular nouns, "the" is *la (la quaglia);* if plural, *le (le quaglie).*

Usage for referring to a food item in the singular or plural is, as in English, very much a matter of common sense. Just as in English, for example, the words "oats" and "French fries" are always used in the plural, in Italian *spaghetti, gnocchi,* and *tagliatelle* are always used in the plural. In this book, therefore, the plural for Italian dishes and ingredients has been used whenever it makes sense to do so.

—JOHN F. MARIANI, PH.D.

PANE
Italian Bread

Bread has always been the basic nutrient for the entire Mediterranean basin. Unjustly undermined for a while, bread has returned to take its rightful place as man's basic nutrient, according to a study conducted by Ancel Keys, Professor of Physiological Hygiene at the University of Minnesota. The study reports on the importance of the Mediterranean diet, based on olive oil and wine, and claims that bread occupies the first place in order of nutritional value.

In Italy the traditions of bread making are very old indeed. Still today, we find several types of bread, very different from each other. The most representative perhaps are *michetta, rosetta, banana, biova, bovolo, ciabatta, ciriola, manina ferrarese*, and, of course, *pane casareccio*, the traditional large-sized, thick-crusted bread which is still a favorite from Tuscany to Sicily.

It is clear that every name given to an individual bread represents a historic or geographical event that in reality or fantasy has played a major role in the tradition of regional bread making. A typical example is Tuscan bread. Tuscan bread, made without salt, is a classic example of enduring traditions.

During the period of papal dominance, an extremely high salt tax was imposed. So, as a form of protest, the Tuscan bakers decided to abolish salt in the preparation of their bread, a tradition that has been perpetuated until today out of a taste preference rather than as historical imperative. Consequently, the Tuscan prosciutto is much saltier than its Parma or Friuli counterparts, the additional salt making up for the blandness of the bread, which generally accompanies prosciutto.

In the panorama of Italian bread, we cannot forget *grissini*, the famous breadsticks from Torino, known the world over thanks to the many commercially produced versions. Legend has it that *grissino* was invented by the personal doctor of the Savoia family, rulers of the Piedmont and Valle d'Aosta regions in the seventeenth century. While caring for the Duke's health, the doctor instructed a baker to bake some *gherse*, a word from Piedmontese dialect that indicates a very long, thin kind of bread.

In 1643, another episode occurred, noted by the Florentine monk Vincenzo Rucellai. During one of Rucellai's trips, he stopped at an inn in Chivasso (Piedmont) and was served a bread *"lungo quanto un braccio e sottile sottile,"* as long as an arm and very, very thin.

Bread baking is based on a biological process that can be partially controlled by the baker. The quality of bread is based on optimal conditions of several factors: flour, water, weather, fermentation, and, finally, baking.

These are the most popular breads in Italy:

Biova or *biovetta*, a round-shaped, slightly elongated white loaf with fat *(strutto)* added. Only the size distinguishes the two names. The *biova* may weigh up to 12 ounces while the *biovetta* is generally 1 to 2 ounces.

Also typical of the North is *montasù*, a name which means "climbing up," because of the bread's shape, triangular and rising in a spiral. It is made of wheat flour. Oil is added to the dough and so it is fairly compact. Its weight varies from 7 to 10 ounces.

Michetta in Milan and *rosetta* in Rome are the same bread with two names. *Michetta*, perhaps, is a little more doughy. This roll may weigh from 2 to 5 ounces; it is round in shape, prepared with white flour, and very crusty on the outside, almost completely devoid of a doughy inside because of the forced fermentation (achieved with the help of a mechanical mixer) that puffs up the bread while it bakes. The same dough, made into a roll, takes the name of *modenese*.

Banana is softer, richer, and more widely used for sandwiches. It is made from a strip of dough rolled into an oblong shape similar to the fruit from which it takes its name.

Miccone, another characteristic bread from Lombardy, has a compact, yet soft center, and the loaf is made in different shapes, which may easily exceed 2 pounds and which can be kept relatively fresh for at least a week. It is bread that should be used sliced.

In the most northern regions where there is a decided Austrian-German influence, the most common bread is called *chifel*. Weighing about an ounce, it is shaped like a half moon, much like a croissant. It takes its name from the pastry chef Chiffering, who came to Italy to the court of the Duke of Parma as part of the retinue of Maria Luisa of Austria. It was Chiffering who first produced the croissant in Italy as a mock reminder of the battle of Vienna and the Turkish symbol of the half moon. By eliminating the sugar from the dough used in a croissant, we get *chifel*.

Not only in Trentino but also throughout the northeast and Venezia Giulia as well, the common, crusty bread is called *salino,* which refers to the rock salt on its crust. Weighing approximately 1 to 2 ounces, it is sprinkled with salt or cumin seeds and customarily eaten with beer and with fresh, dry, grilled sausages. Larger rye and whole wheat loaves are also spread with cumin seeds and weigh about 1 pound. Using the same kind of dough, a flat bread about 5 inches in diameter is eaten fresh with *speck,* a cured pork belly typical of the area. This bread may also be dried out and crumbled in soups and rich gravies.

Similar to the Piedmontese *montasù*, the *bovolo*, a Venetian dialect name for snail, which describes its shape, has a firm dough with a delicate, soft crust and weighs about 4 to 5 ounces.

The most characteristic bread in Emilia-Romagna, made with hard dough, is called *ferrarese*. The best example is called *manina ferrarese*, shaped like a hand with thin strips of finger-like dough that remains soft inside while crusty outside after baking.

Heading south to Tuscany and Umbria, one more frequently finds *pane casareccio*, or "country bread," a large, round or oblong-shaped bread, weighing 1 to 3 pounds and up (meant to last more than one day). It is made of white or whole-wheat flour, plus no more than water and natural yeast, rarely animal or vegetable fats. In the past, because the bread was baked only once a week, it was made of sufficient size to accommodate a large family. Because women baked the bread in a communal oven, the loaves had personalized, distinctive cuts for easy recognition.

The *ciriola*, from Rome, is a long loaf, 3 to 4 ounces, with a sharp cut in the center and a golden, crispy crust.

Apulia has three definite bread traditions: *barile*, a 4-pound loaf made with hard durum wheat with a thick, dark crust and a compact, porous dough; *schiacciata*, 4 pounds, is allowed only a single rise before being placed into the oven, and therefore remains a flat bread with soft, porous dough; and *frisedda*, a type of bread from Apulia shaped like a large doughnut. After an initial baking, *frisedda* is cut into two disks and baked again until the bread becomes *biscottato* (dry and crumbly). It keeps for several months. *Frisedda* is made with white or whole-wheat flour, water, and natural yeast. It is usually eaten for breakfast or as an afternoon snack, softened with cold water, or used as a base for mixed salads, or served in a bowl with boiling hot broth and grated cheese.

In Sicily the tradition of *pane casareccio* (country bread) is prevalent. There are remarkable local differences in its preparation, such as using a pinch of saffron in the dough (of Arabic origin) or covering the dough with sesame seeds before baking. Even small loaves for average use run 8 to 10 ounces. *Mafalda* is a typical Sicilian bread, made with white flour and shaped like a braid. Another Sicilian bread is *ferro di cavallo*, made with hard dough shaped like a horseshoe.

The traditions of the island of Sardinia are exemplified in breads like *carta da musica* (music paper) or *carasau*, a very thin sheet of bread made without yeast and left to dry before it is eaten in small pieces. *Carasau* is simply flavored with a bit of olive oil. It is an essential ingredient in a very famous soup of the area called *pane frattau*. The bread is placed at the bottom of a bowl and covered with boiling broth, a fresh egg, and grated cheese. Sardinia also produces the largest bread in Italy, made from the semolina of the area near Sanluri and Cagliari, called *civraxiu*; prepared with natural yeast, it can be as large as 10 pounds.

In addition to the better-known regional breads, there are also *pan frizze* from Friuli, made with flour, eggs, cracklings of pork, butter, and salt; *ramerino*, from Tuscany, with dough enriched with filtered, warm olive oil strongly scented with rosemary; *pagnotta di Santa Chiara*, from Naples, a stuffed, warm bread made with potato and wheat flour, yeast, lard, and pepper, shaped into two disks stuffed with tomatoes and anchovies, then rolled and baked. Typical of the Naples area is *casatiello*, usually made over Easter: ring-shaped, it is prepared with white flour, yeast, pork fat, *pecorino* and *Parmigiano,* and small bits of salami. Before baking, a few eggs are placed raw into cavities made on the surface, to be cooked directly in the oven together with the bread.

BASIC DOUGH FOR BREAD

MAKES 1 LOAF

7 cups bread flour (high-gluten flour)
1 ounce brewer's yeast or natural yeast
2 cups lukewarm water
Pinch of salt

Method 1

Place the flour on a wooden board and make a well in the center. Dissolve the yeast in a cup of lukewarm water and pour in the middle of the flour. Work the mixture with the tips of your fingers, adding the rest of the lukewarm water a little bit at a time and the salt until the dough no longer sticks to your fingers. Knead the dough for an additional 15 minutes. Form a ball; make a cross-shaped cut with a sharp knife on the top. Wrap the ball in a dry cloth and let it rest in a warm place for half an hour, or until doubled in size.

Start kneading the dough again, energetically, for another 15 minutes. Make a ball, cover it, and let it rest for 6 hours. It should again double in size and become elastic. It is now ready for baking, in any desired shape. (To obtain a darker color, there is an old-fashioned custom of adding a teaspoon of sugar to the flour before mixing.)

Preheat the oven to 400°F. Bake for 30 minutes.

Notes:

All professional bread baking ovens are equipped with steam; for baking at home, place a pot of water in the back of the oven.

It is desirable to bake bread in a wood-burning oven. A wood-burning oven may be imitated by placing tiles in the oven and baking bread directly on the tiles.

Always rest the finished bread for at least one hour before using it.

Method 2

There is also another, more elaborate, method of preparing the dough. Dissolve the yeast in a cup of lukewarm water and work with a few teaspoons of flour until it forms a soft, preliminary dough. Allow it to rise in a warm place. When the dough has doubled in size, work in the rest of the flour with more lukewarm salted water, kneading continually until the dough has a smooth, even texture. Allow to rise until doubled in size once more, and work again, allowing it to rise a third, final time.

Preheat the oven to 350°F. Bake for 30 minutes. In the bakery, but also at home, when people made bread regularly, beer yeast was substituted with a special bread leavening agent consisting of a small piece of fermented dough watered down with lukewarm water to a fluid paste, which was then used to make the preliminary dough. This method takes much longer for the bread to rise, but the result is particularly soft, fragrant, and aromatic bread.

PANE INTEGRALE (Whole-Wheat Bread)

MAKES 1 LOAF

Use the same quantities as in the basic recipe, but use half whole-wheat and half white flour. (For better rising, dissolve the yeast in lukewarm water with a few teaspoons of flour as in Method 2.) Mix together and form a small ball. Let rest, covered, in a warm place for 20 minutes. Prepare the flour on a wooden board with a center well. Add the dough prepared in advance and knead the dough energetically for 15 minutes. Once you have obtained a smooth, soft dough, shape it into a ball; wrap it in a cloth, sprinkle with flour, and let rest for 1 hour in a warm place. Place the dough on a greased sheet pan sprinkled with fine breadcrumbs.

Preheat the oven to 500°F. Bake for 20 minutes. Lower temperature to 350°F and keep baking until the bread is golden brown and crusty on the outside, approximately 60 minutes in all.

GRISSINI (Breadsticks)

1 ounce brewer's yeast or natural yeast
2 cups lukewarm water
8¾ cups all-purpose flour, divided
2 tablespoons salt

Dilute ½ ounce of yeast in 1 cup of lukewarm water, combine with ½ cup of flour, and let it rest in a warm place for 1½ hours, or until the volume doubles. Add to the fermented dough 2 cups of flour, the remainder of the yeast, the salt, and enough lukewarm water to make the dough soft and elastic. Knead the dough until it comes away easily from your hands. Shape the dough into a large ball, make a cross-like incision on top, and cover with a towel. Let it rest in a warm place for 5 hours, or until the dough doubles in size. Knead the remainder of the flour and the water into the fermented dough until you obtain a smooth and elastic dough. Cut small pieces of dough and roll on a wooden board to form long, thin sticks and place in a greased baking pan. Let the dough sticks rest in a warm place until they double in size.

Preheat oven to 550°F. Bake for 10 minutes.

Note:
With the same dough, you can make the classic *michetta* or *rosetta*.

BRUSCHETTA (Garlic Bread)

MAKES 4 SLICES

Bruschetta was originally created in the regions of central Italy (Lazio and Tuscany in particular). Today, it has come to be of common consumption as an antipasto or as an afternoon snack.

4 slices country bread, cut ½ inch thick
1 garlic clove
2 tablespoons extra virgin olive oil
Salt and pepper, to taste

Make a few shallow cuts across the surface of the bread slices, then place the bread on the grill to toast (or use a toaster). The slices should be golden and uniformly toasted. As soon as they are ready, rub the surface with the garlic clove, drizzle with olive oil, salt, and pepper, and serve immediately.

A variation of this recipe is to top the bruschetta with a chopped fresh ripe tomato and basil.

CASATIELLO (Neapolitan Lard Bread)

MAKES 1 LOAF
8 ounces soft lard
2 ounces brewer's or natural yeast
1 tablespoon salt
7 cups all-purpose flour
8 ounces diced salami
2 tablespoons cracked peppercorns
6 whole eggs, unshelled

Combine 6 ounces of the lard, the yeast, salt, and flour with as much water as needed to achieve a smooth, soft dough. Place the dough in a bowl previously dusted with flour, cover with a cloth, and let rise in a lukewarm place. After 1½ hours, place the leavened dough on a pastry board and flatten it by pressing it down into a 12 by 24-inch flat sheet ½ inch thick. Grease the flattened dough and sprinkle one third of the salami and one-third of the pepper. Fold the dough over lengthwise and repeat the operation 2 more times.

You now have a seasoned rolled dough 24 inches in length. Grease a baking savarin mold twelve inches in diameter. Place the dough into the pan, making sure the 2 ends adhere well together. Place the baking pan in a warm place to leaven for 3 hours.

Preheat the oven to 350°F. The *casatiello* is now ready for baking. Just before placing it in the oven, arrange the 6 eggs on top by gently pressing them halfway down into the dough at an even distance from each other.

Bake for 1½ hours. Let cool thoroughly before serving.

CONDIMENTI
Condiments

In the following paragraphs, we will look at the various Italian cooking fats, along with vinegars, which are also essential.

OLIO D'OLIVA (Olive Oil)

Olive oil is undoubtedly the most used vegetable fat in Italian cuisine. If it is used raw to flavor salads and other dishes, extra virgin olive oil is preferred. If it is used for frying, sautéing, or other cooking processes, less expensive extra virgins or regular olive oil can be used.

Olive oil is the authentic and most important base for the vast majority of sauces and condiments in Italian cooking and often replaces butter, lard, or *strutto*. Olive oil is the best for sautéing onions, garlic, or other herbs and spices *(soffritto)*—the very first step in preparation for sauces and many other recipes that are typical of Italian cooking.

Olive oil is obtained by crushing olives, the fruit of a tree *(Olea europaea sativa* of the family *Oleaceae)*, originally from Asia Minor and cultivated in the Mediterranean basin since ancient times.

How Olive Oil Is Made

There are different methods of olive oil extraction. The most classic is that of crushing *(frangitura)* the olives with traditional large granite wheels and then, after stirring *(gramolatura)*, distributing the olive paste on filtering panels placed in a column subject to hydraulic pressing *(estrazione)*. Crushing methods can vary from one producer to another.

The liquid extracted is called must *(mosto)*. This is then passed through a centrifugal machine in order to separate the oil from the vegetable waters. The solid remnants are called *sansa*. These are sent to refineries to produce lesser-quality oils. All virgin oils are clarified to rid them of small vegetable residues and emulsions in order to avoid bad fermentation and oxidation.

There are two clarification methods: filtering through cotton or paper or periodically transferring the oil into different containers (this method offers more guarantees because it shortens the contact with the air and no pressure takes place).

Bottling

After clarifying, the oil can be bottled. The bottles should be made of thick, dark glass or covered with a special material to shield the oil from the light. It is very important to store extra virgin oil in a cool, dark place.

Color

The color of extra virgin olive oil ranges from light yellow and golden yellow with shades of green, to deep green, depending on the maturation of the olives and the processing method.

Quality Standards

The quality of extra virgin olive oils depends on several factors:

- the olives' varieties, integrity, degree of ripeness, and harvesting method
- the time and type of processing
- the level of other accessory operations
- the level of professionalism and experience of the olive oil maker

For an olive oil to be classified as extra virgin, the oil must have no organoleptic defects and must contain a given amount of acidity and antioxidant elements (see chart on page 9).

Current Italian laws refer to the European Community rules for the general classification and to strict regulations for the oils designated as DOP (*Denominazione di Origine Protetta*, Denomination of Protected Origin). DOP oils must clearly show on the label the olives' production area and the special symbol of the European Union.

Today, many producers seek the additional HS (High Standard) quality certification, controlled and guaranteed by CSQA (*Certificazione Sistemi Qualità Agroalimentare*), a certification body, the only one in Italy recognized by IQ Net (International Quality Network).

This new important certification is promoted by the Mastri Oleari Association, whose aim is to preserve and protect the quality of extra virgin olive oil.

The DOP and High Standard, "HS" along with the Mastri Oleari seal on the label, are a guarantee of high quality.

How Extra Virgin Olive Oil Is Classified

Each area of production or each consortium or association names a panel of certified tasters to classify the quality level of extra virgin olive oil. Tasters must follow strict judging criteria, established by the Italian government and by the European Community. For an international certification like High Standard and for the Mastri Oleari seal, the panel must be recognized also by the International Olive Oil Council. The chart below shows the standards established by the Italian government and the European Community versus the standards established by CSQA.

	EC	CSQA
Polyunsaturated Acid	3.5–22%	5–12.9%
Oleic Acid (Monounsaturated)	55%	70%
Free Acidity	1%	0.5%
Anti-Oxidant Activity (Vitamin E)	not prescribed	1 gr./4 kg.
Judge Taste Mark	6.5	7

Tasting Extra Virgin Olive Oil

High organoleptic quality is determined by the absence of defects and by the number of positive attributes (see below). Excellence is attained by the harmony of the attributes. Note that color does not count in establishing quality.

The taster first looks for defects. Once it is established that the oil is defect free, the taster goes on to rate the positive attributes. Taste must be rated above 6.5 or 7 or that olive oil cannot be rated as extra virgin.

Taste defects are: rancid, fusty, muddy, sediment, mustiness, metallic, rough, sour, winey, vinegary, and other unallowable attributes.

Positive taste attributes are: fruity, bitter, pungent, grassy, ripe fruit, rounded.

Expiration

Always note the expiration date on the label. But remember that there is no expiration date fixed by law. Rather, the date is indicated by the producer in relation to the levels of perishability of the product. An expired extra virgin oil, provided it has no bad smell or rancid taste, can be used for cooking but not consumed raw. In any case, it is better to use young oils. Buy extra virgin olive oil in small quantities, replenishing your supply frequently.

Different Extra Virgin Olive Oils by Region

Except for Piedmont and Valle d'Aosta, every Italian region produces olive oils. Because of differences in olive varieties, types of soil and climate, altitudes, and processing, each production area has its own peculiarities, and each olive oil is unique. Although olive oils don't always taste different in relation to their origin, it is true that the ones from northern areas like Liguria and Lake Garda, for example, are generally lighter and more delicate, whereas olive oils produced in Tuscany and Umbria gain in intensity, color, and taste. In southern regions, olive oils have a stronger taste and more intense texture and color.

How to Use Olive Oil

The richness and variety of high-quality olive oils have led many Italian restaurants to offer their customers an extra virgin olive oil list from various regions aimed at suggesting the best match for salads or other dishes for which a dash of extra virgin olive oil is recommended.

The choice of the most suitable olive oil depends on the dish. A light preparation of vegetables or fish may require light, fragrant olive oil, whereas dishes with definite, strong flavors call for more decisive, stronger oils. Extra virgin olive oils used raw best enhance their characteristics.

Olive oil is often flavored with herbs, cloves of garlic, or *peperoncino*. Flavored olive oils are used to dress salads or vegetables or as toppings for *minestre, minestrone,* and *zuppe*.

Olive oil is excellent for frying because it contains many anti-oxidant elements that reduce the oxidation process. For this purpose, regular (non-virgin) olive oil can be used. Olive oil can be reused several times, provided that it is always filtered after frying. It is not advisable to add fresh oil to old oil.

OTHER OILS

Oils from sources other than olives must be extracted by adding mechanical and chemical solvents. These oils can be made from peanut, corn, sunflower, and flax seeds and other vegetables. They can be used as a condiment for various raw and cooked vegetables as well as in the preparation of sauces. They are generally used for frying; however, since they require a lower temperature, the food will be lighter in color and will absorb more fat than if olive oil were used. Frying with other oils at excessively high temperatures can be harmful because high temperatures release the toxic elements contained in the solvents used to prepare the product. These oils contain mostly polyunsaturated acids (linoleic and linolenic), which speed up the oxidation process, thus causing damage to human cells.

ANIMAL FATS

BURRO (Butter)

Among animal fats, butter is the least important ingredient in Italian cuisine, used mainly for the preparation of risotto and desserts. Good butter should have a whitish-yellow color (more yellow if produced in the summer); an aromatic flavor; and a delicate, slightly sweet taste. When heated, it should melt into an oily yellow liquid with whitish residues underneath (which can be discarded). In order to be preserved adequately for a week or so, butter must be kept in the refrigerator, wrapped in wax paper or aluminum foil. It can also be frozen.

GUANCIALE (Hog Jowl)

Guanciale is the jowl and the cheek of the hog. These pieces are placed in a corrosion-proof container, then covered with a mixture of salt and pepper and left in a cool place to cure for a month. They are turned once a week. The pieces are then hung in a dry, airy place for another month before being used. *Guanciale* can be used like lard or *pancetta*. It is most common in central Italy.

LARDO (Lard—Commonly Known as Fatback in the United States)

Lard is prepared from the layer of fat located along the back and underneath the skin of the hog. Hog butchers prepare it during the slaughtering process and preserve it in salt. Of particular standing in Italian cuisine is *lardo di Colonnata*, produced only in a tiny village of the Alps by the marble caves of Carrara. It owes its quality to the fact that it is left to season in brine inside marble tubs. The calcareous geological structure of marble interacts with the salt in the brine and extracts most of the toxic chemicals from the pork fat. *Lardo di Colonnata* is eaten raw, very thinly sliced, on toast or warm *focaccia*.

MARGARINA (Margarine)

Margarine is not a typical Italian condiment, but it has become popular since the 1950s as a less expensive substitute for butter in many dishes. It is an industrial product obtained through chemical and physical processing of vegetable and animal fats, mostly of poor quality. Contrary to popular belief, margarine has the same amount of fat as butter and seems lighter only because it has a neutral taste.

PANCETTA (Cured Pork Belly)

Pancetta is one of the most popular kinds of cured meats. It is made with the layer of fat and flesh located along the stomach, directly underneath the skin of the hog. The various versions of *pancetta* are all prepared with salt and pepper; some, such as round and stuffed *pancetta,* are prepared with cloves, cinnamon, and other spices in addition to salt and pepper. *Pancetta* has a distinctive bright red color and is aged for 2 months; smoked *pancetta* (better known as bacon) is smoked for at least 2 days with beech, oak, or, less frequently, juniper wood. *Pancetta* can be used for dressing beef or game; it can be barbecued or baked. It can also be eaten sliced, with country bread or roasted *polenta*.

RIGATINO (Lean Pancetta)

This is a Tuscan term for a type of pancetta with more meat and less fat than typical pancetta. As with *pancetta, rigatino* can be used for *soffritto* and to dress various types of meat. It can also be sliced and consumed as a cold cut. *Rigatino* should not be sliced too thinly.

STRUTTO (Reconstituted Pork Fat)

Strutto is melted and reconstituted pork fat. When completely melted, it is strained through a large and sturdy cloth and collected in a container underneath. The remaining strips of fatty meat are put through a masher to squeeze out the excess fat and then refrigerated to be later consumed with bread or *polenta*. These very flavorful pieces of crispy fat are called *ciccioli*.

    Strutto is primarily used for frying or to prepare crusts for savory pies. It can also be called *sugna*.

Note:
In the United States pork products must be certified by the U.S.D.A. prior to marketing and consumption.

ACETO (Vinegar)

Vinegar is the product of the acetic fermentation of wine under the action of a fungus called *Mycoderma aceti*. Vinegar first appears in the form of a light "veil" that penetrates the liquid more and more, forming a thick, folded, sticky skin called in French *mère de vinaigre*, in Italian *madre dell'aceto*, and in English the mother. Good vinegar must be clear and transparent, colorless if made from white wine, pinkish if it comes from red wine. It must have a distinctly acidic taste and an aroma recalling that of the wine from which it is made.

    Vinegar may be made of any kind of alcoholic liquid. Alcohol vinegar is colorless, unless it has been tinted with caramel. Cider vinegar is yellowish, and always less acidic than wine vinegar. Vinegar should be kept in dark, securely closed bottles or in a special vinegar cask, at room temperature: not too hot, not too cold. If kept too long, vinegar may become cloudy: if this happens, simply filter and pour it into a clean bottle.

    Italian vinegar is classified into various types:

ACETO ORDINARIO (Common Vinegar)

This vinegar is produced from non-vintage wine that is already slightly turned, or from grape must with an alcohol rate of less than 80. Fermentation is fast and finished within 2 to 6 months. Common vinegar is clarified and filtered before going on sale and has a moderately short life.

ACETO DI VINO (Wine Vinegar)

This vinegar is produced from quality vintage wines. Fermentation is rather slow. The vinegar is left to stand for about 8 months in special wooden casks before being transferred into bottles, where it remains for another 8 months. When matured, this vinegar has a wine flavor and a clear color.

ACETO DECOLORATO (Decolored Vinegar)

This is common vinegar that has been decolored and de-tanninized. It is mainly used for pickling vegetables, since it does not alter their color.

ACETO AROMATICO (Aromatic Vinegar)

This is a quality vinegar with the addition of aromatic herbs. To make it, boil the vinegar, slowly reducing the quantity by half. Remove from the heat and pour into a container with the desired herbs or spices such as rosemary, garlic, raspberry, etc. Cover and let marinate for a few hours. Filter and save in sealed bottles.

ACETO BALSAMICO (Balsamic Vinegar)

A specialty of Emilia, particularly from Modena and its surroundings, this rare product is a culinary symbol of that region. It is made from *Lambrusco Salomino*, a full-bodied red grape, although in some areas outside of this region, *Sangiovese* or *Trebbiano* grapes may be used. The wine is reduced by two thirds and then aged for years in special barrels, in fact several barrels, each of a different wood. The aging of balsamic vinegar is obtained by transferring it into a different barrel each year so that it may absorb the flavor of each of the woods from which the barrels are made. Balsamic vinegar is brown in color, more or less dark depending on its age, with an aromatic scent and sweet-and-sour taste.

Authentic balsamic vinegar takes at least twelve years to make, sometimes as many as thirty. The wood from which the barrels are made and the sequence of the barrels are very jealously kept family secrets, which may only be passed from one family member to another. The wood used for the barrels may be oak, chestnut, cherry, ash, mulberry, and others. The balsamic vinegar one finds in the market today is mostly a commercial, pasteurized product. Some of it is excellent but it does not compare with the true *Aceto Balsamico Tradizionale*.

True balsamic vinegar must be packaged in 100-gram bottles, and must be at least ten years old. The label must bear the words *Aceto Balsamico Tradizionale* and must be stamped by the *Consorzio ABTM*, the word *Tradizionale* being the key word. If the word *Tradizionale* is not on the label, it is a commercially produced balsamic vinegar.

In recent years, balsamic vinegar has become widely used in Italian cooking to enhance flavors. It can be used straight or as an addition to sauces, in salad dressings, or even with fruit. In ancient times, it was also used as a digestive. Balsamic vinegar is very strong and must be used sparingly.

ACETO DI MIELE (Honey Vinegar)

This is a typical product of Monteu Roero, in Piedmont—not far from Alba, the capital town of white truffles. Honey vinegar is made from acacia honey diluted in water and then put through an acetic fermentation process. The result is a light-colored, clear vinegar with a distinctive scent, though less strong than that of wine vinegar. It is used both for salad dressing and as an ingredient for various sauces made from braising the cooking juices of many dishes such as rabbit, veal rib, mullets, and more.

ERBE AROMATICHE
Herbs

AGLIO (Garlic)

The pungent, segmented bulb of the perennial plant *Allium sativum*, a member of the lily family, is closely related to the onion. Among the oldest known cultivated plants and most universally popular cooking herbs, garlic appears extensively, both raw and cooked, in the cuisine of southern Europe and is considered essential to many dishes in Italy. The peeled cloves can be preserved for short periods in jars of oil.

ANETO (Dill Seeds)

Pungent and slightly bitter, dill seeds come from an aromatic herb *(Anethum graveolens)* with feathery foliage. In addition to being used to flavor salads, stuffings, and sauces, they may also be used to flavor desserts and vinegar.

BASILICO (Basil)

An annual herb *(Ocimum basilicum)* of the mint family, this is the distinguishing ingredient of the Ligurian specialty *pesto*. Its glossy, aromatic leaves are used to add tangy flavor and a mildly spicy bouquet to many dishes and sauces, especially preparations in which tomatoes play a prominent role.

CAPPERI (Capers)

The pickled or salted flower buds of the spiny, trailing Mediterranean shrub *Capparis spinosa*, capers add a tart flavor and mild astringency to uncooked sauces and cold dishes such as *vitello tonnato*.

CERFOGLIO (Chervil)

The scientific name is *Anthriscus cerofelium*, and it is a very aromatic plant. Chervil has been used since the Roman Empire and is still widely used today. There are various varieties, the most common being the curly type used to decorate dishes. Chervil has a very pleasant aroma and should always be used fresh.

CORIANDOLO (Coriander Seeds)

Coriander seeds come from an Old World herb *(Coriandrum sativum)*, originating in the Middle East. The seeds are small and spherical and have a strong, aromatic flavor. Coriander has many uses; it may be coated with sugar in confectionery or may be used in the preparation of salami and sauces.

CUMINO (Cumin)

Cumin is a low plant *(Cuminum cyminum)*, long cultivated for its aromatic seeds. It is a classic flavoring used for sweets and to make the famous *kummel* liqueur.

DRAGONCELLO O SERPENTARIA (Tarragon)

Artemisia dracunculus is a herbaceous plant used to flavor salads and various sauces. Its leaves are thin, tapered, and very fragrant; they are also used to flavor oils and vinegar. In Siena, it is also coated in batter, deep-fried, and served as a side dish with fried meat entrées.

ERBA CIPOLLINA (Chives)

A perennial plant *(Allium schoenoprasum)* of grass-like appearance and a mild onion flavor, chives are usually finely minced and used to flavor salads and some sauces.

FINOCCHIELLA (Wild Fennel Seeds)

Known as wild fennel *(Foeniculum vulgare)*, this is a plant that grows wild in central Italy. The plant grows up to 4 feet and produces a flower with seeds. The flower is combed, and the seeds are then dried and peeled. They are dark yellow in color and have an intense, fennel-like aroma. These seeds are called *finocchiella*. Highly aromatic, they are used for roasting the traditional *porchetta romana* as well as other preparations (see *Porchetta* in Glossary).

FINOCCHIETTO SELVATICO (Fresh Wild Fennel Herb)

This wild herb grows in the south of Italy, and it is widely used in Sicilian cookery (like *pasta con le sarde*). If this herb is left to grow, it produces seeds called *semi di finocchio*, fennel seeds, which are used to top breads or to flavor meats and sausages.

GINEPRO (Juniper)

Juniper is an evergreen shrub or tree that grows in wooded areas. *Juniperus communis* in Latin, its berries are fleshy, very aromatic, blue-black in color, and used to flavor or marinate various kinds of meat, especially game. It is also the base for the production of gin.

LAURO (Bay Leaves)

The bitter, spicy, pungent leaves of *Laurus nobilis*, bay leaves are usually dried before use. Extensively used as a flavoring agent for vinegar and in pickling and marinating mixtures, they enhance stocks, soups, sauces, and almost any poached, braised, or stewed dishes.

MAGGIORANA (Sweet Marjoram)

The scientific name is *Origanum majorana*. It is a variety of oregano. Its leaves, with white flowers and tiny seeds, have a more distinctive aroma than fresh oregano. They are used to flavor various dishes and in marinades for game.

MENTUCCIA (Wild Mint)

Scientifically known as *Melissa officinalis*, wild mint looks and smells similar to lemon leaves, but unlike the latter it grows wild in meadows. It is used in the Roman specialty *carciofi alla romana* and for marinades.

NEPITELLA (Catmint)

The scientific name is *Calaminta repeto*. It belongs to the same family as mint. It grows wild and is commonly used to flavor white meats or roasts. The aroma is similar to mint with scents of sage. It should not be confused with wild mint.

ORIGANO (Oregano)

Origanum vulgare is a wild aromatic herb that is generally used dried. It has a characteristic sauerkraut flavor, bitter and very aromatic. Very common in the south of Italy, it is used in many tomato-based preparations, *pizza,* various salads, and sauces such as *pizzaiola.*

PEPERONCINO (Chili Pepper)

Peperoncino's generic Latin name is *Capsicum*. Widely used, especially in the south of Italy, *peperoncino* can be green or red, round or long, and more or less hot. Fresh peppers are used to add character to many dishes: soups, sauces, marinades, or pickles. To preserve them for long periods, they should be dried. They can then be kept whole, finely chopped, ground, or placed in a jar and covered with oil. The small red ones are often threaded on a string by their stalks and hung, because they are very spicy. The term *diavolicchio* is used in Abruzzese dialect, referring to the heat associated with the devil in the popular imagination.

PINOLI (Pine Nuts)

Pine nuts, *Pinus pinea*, are the edible kernels of several varieties of pines, used in sweets as well as in stuffings for various dishes. They are a traditional ingredient in *pesto* and commonly used in desserts.

PISTACCHIO (Pistachio Nuts)

Pistachios are the greenish, edible seeds of a small tree *(Pistacia vera)* of the Sumae family. They are used in sweets, ice cream, galantines, and *mortadella di Bologna*.

PREZZEMOLO (Parsley)

Scientifically known as *Petroselinum crispum*, parsley is an aromatic, herbaceous garden plant with smooth leaves. It has many varieties. The curly type is less common and is particularly suitable for garnishing. Parsley is excellent to neutralize garlic odor.

RAFANO (Horseradish)

A large fleshy root, *Nasturtium armoracia* is pungent in fragrance as well as in taste. It stimulates the eyes to tears. It is grated to prepare sauces or cut straw-like and served with cocktail sauce to be added at will. It is also known as *cren* or *barbaforte*.

ROSMARINO (Rosemary)

Scientifically known as *Rosmarinus officinalis*, rosemary is a bushy plant with needle-like leaves and a fresh piney fragrance. It is used to flavor grilled roast meats, as well as sauces. It may also be used to prepare aromatic vinegar in Tuscany, where it is also known as *ramerino*.

SALVIA (Sage)

Salvia officinalis has rough, silver-green leaves that are extremely fragrant. It is often mixed with rosemary to flavor roasts. It is also used to flavor sautéed fish and particular cuts of meat such as veal, pork, and liver. Butter and sage make a particularly good condiment for fresh stuffed pasta such as *ravioli* and *cappelletti,* and it is an essential herb for *saltimbocca alla romana* (see page 223). The broader leaves are often dipped in a light batter, fried in oil, and served as an *antipasto* or side dish. Sage can also be used to prepare aromatic oils and vinegar.

SEMI DI FINOCCHIO (Fennel Seeds)

See *Finocchietto selvatico.*

SEMI DI SESAMO (Sesame Seeds)

Sesame is a plant that grows wild in Africa and India. The scientific name is *Sesamum orientale.* In Italy, it grows in small quantities in Calabria and Sicily. The main producer is China. Sesame seeds are used in the preparation of bread and biscuits. In the kitchen they may also be used for sesame seed oil, which is often cut with olive oil.

TIMO (Thyme)

Thymus vulgaris grows wild in the arid areas of the Mediterranean. It can also be grown organically and is widely used in cooking. Thyme has very small leaves, which are used dried to flavor sauces, marinades, certain roasts, and varieties of fish.

SPEZIE
Spices

CANNELLA (Cinnamon)

This popular spice is from the family of *Cinnamomum zeylanicum* and it is the center part of a tree called *cinnamomo (cinnamomus)*. More precisely, it is the layer between the outer part and the wood of the tree. Cinnamon has a pleasant, aromatic taste and can be bought in sticks or powder. It is used to flavor various savory dishes as well as desserts.

CHIODI DI GAROFANO (Cloves)

Cloves *(Eugenia caryophillata)* are stalks, petals, and centers of flowers that grow on a plant native to the Moluccan Islands in the East Indies and the Philippines. They are used to flavor stews, fish preparations, sauces, desserts, cooked fruit, marinades, and brines.

MACIS (Mace)

Mace is the lacy fiber that grows on the outside of the nutmeg. It is used to flavor fruits and desserts.

NOCE MOSCATA (Nutmeg)

The solid kernel of the fruit of a tree that grows in Indonesia, *Myristica fragrans*, is about half the size of a walnut, buff in color with a ridged exterior. It is pleasantly aromatic. Nutmeg is used dried and grated in small quantities to flavor stuffings, main courses, and desserts.

PEPE—BIANCO O NERO (Pepper—White or Black)

A small and spherical fruit of the Orient, *Piper nigrum* kernels are first green, then become red as they mature. Eventually they turn black as they dry. White pepper is the kernel picked as it is maturing. Still red, bathed in salted water and peeled, it is then dried. Pepper is considered to be one of the oldest spices known to man. It is best when used freshly ground.

SENAPE (Mustard)

These seeds come in three varieties: dark ones *(Brassica nigra)*, white ones *(Sinapsis alba)*, and the Indian variety called *Brassica juncea*; the strongest is the dark type and the mildest the white. The characteristic pungent flavor is released when the powdered seeds come in contact with water, which must be cold in order to promote good mustard. Warm water would give the substance a bitter taste. Commercially prepared mustard sauce is used to season meat and as a flavoring for other sauces.

VANIGLIA (Vanilla)

The vanilla bean is the fruit of a tropical climbing orchid plant. Dried, the fruit of this plant forms a pod, dark brown in color, about 4.6 inches long. It has a very pleasant flavor that blends easily with any ingredient to which it is added. It is used mainly in desserts such as custards and ice cream.

ZAFFERANO (Saffron)

Crocus sativus is the stamen of a flower, originally from Asia Minor. In Italy it grows in the region of Abruzzo. It comes either powdered or in threads and is used in various dishes, both to flavor and color the food, for example, *risotto alla milanese*. It should be used in very small quantities because if too much saffron is used it gives a medicinal taste. Generally, 1 gram can flavor approximately 1 pound (2 cups) of rice. Saffron is one of the most expensive food ingredients in the world.

ANTIPASTI
Antipasto

The term *antipasto,* usually translated as appetizer in English, literally means "before the meal" and denotes a relatively light dish designed to stimulate the palate before the service of more substantial courses. In the hands of a creative cook or chef, the antipasto course can play much the same role in the presentation of the meal as that of the overture in an opera. It can set the tone of—and heighten anticipation for—what is to follow, while establishing the author's style and outlook and the quality that may be expected of the whole performance. *Antipasti*, however, are not essential to the Italian table; a formal Italian dinner without *antipasti* would not betray the traditions of Italian gastronomy. Still, today it is difficult to imagine a formal dinner that would not include some dishes classified as *antipasti*. In regional Italian cuisine, *antipasti* are an important element of meals served at festivities and special occasions.

Over the years, some dishes served as accompaniments to main courses became thought of as too rich for such use. Many of these dishes have been adapted to serve as antipasto. *Antipasti* take full advantage of all kinds of different foods not generally regarded as being substantial enough to be served as main courses. Cleverly used, they produce a wonderful variety of flavorful and unusual items.

When considering recipes presented later in the book for the *antipasti* course, don't consider the serving size of each individual dish. Rather, consider that a number of these dishes should be presented all on a large platter to serve the number of people sitting down to dine. Each of the individual elements should complement each other in flavor, color, and texture, providing a well-orchestrated prelude to the main part of the meal.

BREAD AND BISCUITS IN SALADS

Stale and re-baked bread as well as unleavened biscuits can be toasted, soaked, and chopped together with vegetables, fish, greens, and so on to make delicious first courses and salads.

CHEESE

Cheese leftovers can be very cleverly used as appetizers. Cheese such as *mozzarella* or *ricotta* is best served as *antipasto* when very fresh but is also excellent cooked when a few days old.

EGGS AND OMELETS

Eggs, either cooked soft, hard, stuffed, or *frittate* (flat omelet), accompanied by or with the addition of a variety of meats, cheese, or vegetables, can make some interesting starters.

FISH

The Italian coastline provides a rich variety of fish that may not be appropriate as main courses but would be excellent as an antipasto. Among the fish *antipasti*, one can list *bottarga* (air-dried tuna or mullet roe); fish *carpaccio*; seafood salads; baked, sautéed, or stewed fish; shellfish and mollusks, which can be served either alone or as a main ingredient in a famous Ligurian recipe called *cappon magro* (see pages 107–9).

FOCACCIE AND FRITTERS

Focaccie and fritters, as well as savory pies and *sformati,* can be served, like *pizza,* as starters, though these too can be heavy.

FRIED FOODS

From vegetables to organ meats, frying is one of the most widespread forms of using bits and pieces of leftovers. The skill of frying should not be underestimated, as it requires perfect timing. Fried food may be served as *antipasti* or as a main course.

LEGUMES

Cooked beans, used as salads or poured over bread or biscuits, are often served as *antipasti.*

MARINADES

The term marinade refers to all types of food flavored with herbs, spices, liquids, or fats, to be consumed raw or to be cooked afterward. At times, certain foods are first cooked, then marinated or preserved. The role marinades play in *antipasti* is very important, because dishes such as *carpaccio*, marinated raw anchovies, and vegetables marinated in vinegar *(sott'aceto)* or marinated in oil *(sott'olio)* fall into this category.

MEATS

Many meat dishes can be served as *antipasti,* generally with light dressings. For example, sliced meats or meat leftovers cut into strips or diced and dressed with various condiments. Organ meats such as chicken livers, tripe, brains, and sweetbreads are often used, too, not to forget the very Roman *coratella* (see page 241), which, along with meat pâtés and galantines, completes the spectrum of typical Italian meat *antipasti*.

MUSHROOMS AND TRUFFLES

Fresh mushrooms may be served as a salad with just oil and drops of lemon juice. White or black truffles can be used to add flavor to cheese, *antipasti*, or as toppings to toast or pâtés.

PIZZA

Regarded more as a snack than as an *antipasto, pizza* has come a long way since its inception as poor people's food in Naples. Toppings can be as varied as your imagination. Because it can be heavy, *pizza* should be used as an *antipasto* only in small amounts.

SALADS

Meat, fish, vegetables, legumes, and starches can all be used as salad for starters, although they may be successfully served as a main course as well. Salads should be served well chilled, although in recent times lukewarm salads are served, often as combinations of legumes or greens with fish or meat.

SALAMI AND SALUMI

Salumi, such as *prosciutto* and *bresaola,* are quite often served as *antipasti,* often with fruit such as melon or figs, or with greens like arugula, or with a condiment of oil and lemon. They can serve as an *antipasto* as part of *affettato misto*, a term which implies that many types of salami and *salumi* are used in the same dish. Salami can also be served as a snack or as stuffing for sandwiches.

VEGETABLES

Many vegetables used as salads, steamed, baked, stuffed, or marinated, were at one time used as side dishes and today are used successfully as *antipasti*.

SALSE E RAGÙ
Sauces

What is a sauce? It is neither a food nor a dish in itself, but rather a condiment meant to add flavor. Centuries ago, sauces were called *savori*, or "flavors," from the Venetian word *saor*, meaning they were used to flavor meat, fish, and other dishes. There are hundreds of Italian sauces. Many start with a *soffritto* made by simply sautéing oil and chopped onions. A good *soffritto* is the base of many Italian recipes: Chop one or more types of vegetables (onions, carrots, etc.) into julienne, add herbs and spices, and lightly fry the mix in extra virgin olive oil, *pancetta,* or lard until it loses its crunchiness. Most Italian sauces are quite simple, some are more complex, but each sauce has its own individuality. Each Italian sauce, with the exception of basic tomato sauce, represents an original creation. *Ragù* is a very typical Italian sauce: It has many variations, but basically it is made by slowly braising beef or fish with *soffritto*, often with tomatoes. There is not a single Italian region that does not have its own *ragù*.

AGLIATA (Garlic Sauce)

Agliata, along with *porrata*, is one of the most interesting condiments in Italian cooking. The former is prepared with garlic, the latter with leeks. Their existence dates back to ancient Rome. The following version of *agliata* is still common today. *Agliata* is recommended on boiled or broiled fish, meat, and vegetables. To make a *porrata*, substitute chopped leeks for the garlic.

SERVES 4

⅓ cup fresh white breadcrumbs
2 tablespoons wine vinegar
10 garlic cloves, smashed
1 cup extra virgin olive oil
Salt and pepper, to taste

Soak the breadcrumbs in vinegar, drain, and squeeze. Add the garlic. Beating constantly, add the olive oil in a very slow, steady stream. Add a pinch of salt and pepper so as to obtain a smooth emulsion.

AGLIO, OLIO E PEPERONCINO (Oil, Garlic, and Hot Pepper Sauce)

One of the oldest ways to dress pasta is with olive oil and garlic. Later, ingredients like *peperoncino* were added.

SERVES 4
4 garlic cloves
½ cup extra virgin olive oil
Peperoncino, to taste
1 pound spaghetti, cooked
1 tablespoon finely chopped parsley
Salt, to taste

Sauté the garlic in a skillet with 6 tablespoons of the olive oil and *peperoncino* until golden brown. Remove the browned garlic, if desired. Mix the cooked *spaghetti* briskly in the same skillet, add the parsley and salt, and the remaining 2 tablespoons of olive oil, toss, and serve.

Note:
Spaghetti should be undercooked before tossing with the sauce. If it proves to be too dry, add a ladleful of the cooking water.

Variations:
Add anchovies (6 fillets, washed and cut into pieces) to the garlic, oil, and *peperoncino*.
Brown 3 to 4 tablespoons of breadcrumbs in oil and garlic just before serving and toss them into the pasta.

BAGNA CAUDA (Anchovy and Garlic Dip)

Literally translated from Piedmontese dialect, *bagna cauda* means "warm sauce." The ingredients suggest it is a country recipe because all the ingredients are garden grown. Even the oil was probably produced on the farm. The exception is salted anchovies, which were widely used as a substitute for salt.

SERVES 4
6 garlic cloves, crushed
8 anchovy fillets, chopped
2 tablespoons extra virgin olive oil
1 cup clarified butter
Pepper, to taste

Sauté the garlic and anchovies in olive oil. Stir constantly until the anchovies disintegrate. Reduce the heat and add butter and pepper to taste. Bring to a simmer and remove from heat. This sauce is served in a pot, for everyone to dip the vegetables in, or in individual terra-cotta bowls. The garlic's flavor becomes somewhat milder if you leave the cloves to soak in milk for a few hours or add a small amount of cream at the last minute. *Bagna cauda* must be placed on warmers, as it must simmer constantly. It is usually served with cardoons, fennel, peppers, celery, and carrots, much like *pinzimonio*.

BESCIAMELLA (Béchamel)

MAKES 2 CUPS
2 ounces butter
4 tablespoons all-purpose flour (sifted)
2 cups milk
Salt and pepper, to taste
1 thyme sprig
4 bay leaves
1 pinch nutmeg

In a high-sided pan, melt the butter. When it simmers, add the sifted flour and stir it into the butter. Add the milk, salt and pepper, thyme, bay leaves, and nutmeg and bring to a simmer. Cook for 15 minutes. The béchamel should not be too thick or heavy. Strain the resulting sauce and use it as desired.

DOLCEFORTE 1 (Sweet Mustard Sauce 1)

This recipe comes to us from the Renaissance; today it is very seldom used. This sauce is similar to *agrodolce*; instead of vinegar, mustard is used, and frequently honey replaces sugar. This sauce is excellent with boiled meats or venison. Unsweetened chocolate may be added for strong meats such as wild boar.

MAKES 1 CUP
1 ounce butter
2 cups red wine
1 pound sugar or honey
Juice of ½ lemon
Salt, to taste
2 tablespoons dry mustard

Melt the butter in a casserole over medium heat. When melted, add the wine. Let simmer for a few minutes, then add the sugar. Combine well and add the lemon juice and salt. When the sauce is reduced by one-third, add the mustard, mix well, and remove from the heat.

DOLCEFORTE 2 (Sweet Mustard Sauce 2)

9 whole walnuts, shelled
2 cups beef broth (see pages 123–24)
1 teaspoon dry mustard
¾ cup honey

Scald the walnuts in boiling water. Peel and pound them in a mortar until you have a paste. Mix the walnuts with the broth, mustard, and honey. Stir until you get a smooth emulsion. This sauce will keep a couple of days in the refrigerator.

FINANZIERA (Chicken Liver and Sweetbread Sauce)

Although it is said that *finanziera* (literally, "the business of finance") is a French sauce introduced in Piedmont two centuries ago, the Piedmontese claim it is one of the most traditional condiments of their regional cuisine. Its curious name comes from a nineteenth-century Piedmontese tradition: Innkeepers and restaurant chefs used to make *finanziera* especially on market days, when traders and merchants would gather round their tables to talk about business. This sauce is usually served with pasta or *risotto*.

SERVES 6

½ pound veal sweetbreads
½ pound chicken livers
½ pound lean veal
1 ounce butter
1 ounce dried mushrooms, reconstituted in warm water
½ cup Marsala
Water or beef broth (see pages 123–24), as needed
Salt and pepper, to taste

Blanch the sweetbreads in a pot with water for a few minutes. Strain, cool, and remove excess skin and veins under cold running water. Dice the chicken livers and veal and brown in butter with the mushrooms. Add the sweetbreads and Marsala and cook on low heat for 20 minutes, adding some water or broth as necessary. Add salt and pepper to taste.

PESTO (Basil Sauce)

Pesto is a very old sauce made especially in cities by the sea that are often hedged in by mountains on one side and the sea on the other, thus presenting tremendous difficulties in getting fresh food. In fact, all ingredients used in *pesto* can be kept for long periods, while the basil could be easily grown on the windowsills and preserved in oil for a long time. *Pesto* is most associated with Genoa, on the Ligurian Sea, where this very popular condiment is said to have originated. The basil there has a particular scent and is not too reminiscent of mint. *Pesto* comes from the verb *pestare*, meaning to crush or to beat.

The preferred pasta with *pesto* is fresh *trenette*. Boil the *trenette* in plenty of salted water with the addition of a very finely sliced potato. *Pesto* may also be used for *minestrone genovese* (see page 131).

SERVES 6

½ pound very fresh basil, preferably leaves from plants not yet in blossom
2 ounces pine nuts or toasted walnuts
6 garlic cloves, peeled
Salt and pepper, to taste
⅔ cup extra virgin olive oil
2 tablespoons Parmigiano
2 tablespoons pecorino cheese
1 pound trenette pasta
1 small potato, peeled and very thinly sliced

Wash the basil leaves and pat dry with a cloth. Place in a mortar. Add the pine nuts, garlic, a pinch of salt, and pepper. Pound these ingredients with a circular motion of the pestle. Continue until you achieve a soft green paste. (A food processor may be used.) Put the paste in a bowl and gradually drip in the oil, while continuously mixing. Use as much oil as necessary. Set aside. Add cheese just before adding to the pasta, and more oil if necessary.

Cook pasta with the sliced potato, drain, and reserve a small amount of the water. In a large serving bowl, away from the heat, toss the pasta with the *pesto* (the potatoes will have disintegrated to form a grainy texture on each string of pasta so the sauce can cling better to it). Add a little cooking water if the pasta is too dry. Toss well and serve immediately.

Note:
One-half cup *pesto* should be enough for 1 pound of pasta.

PESTO ERICINO (Pesto from Erice)

This version of *pesto* comes from the Sicilian town of Erice, near Trapani, and is common in most of western Sicily. *Pesto ericino* is used to dress different types of pasta, especially fresh hand-made pasta like *orecchiette* or *cavatelli* as well as *farfalle* or *spaghetti*. It has almonds instead of pine nuts, breadcrumbs instead of cheese, and tomatoes.

SERVES 6

6 garlic cloves
½ pound basil
½ pound roasted almonds
½ pound tomatoes, peeled, seeded, and chopped

½ cup extra virgin olive oil
Salt and pepper, to taste
2 tablespoons toasted breadcrumbs

In a mortar, pound the garlic with the basil, almonds, and a pinch of salt until you get a creamy texture. Blend in the tomato. When well blended add the olive oil in a continuous stream while stirring. Add salt and pepper to taste. Add the breadcrumbs when tossing the pasta, as they replace the grated cheese.

RAGÙ BOLOGNESE (Meat Sauce)

SERVES 8
3 ounces pancetta or bacon
1 celery stalk, chopped
1 small carrot, chopped
1 small onion, chopped
½ pound ground veal
½ pound ground beef
½ pound ground pork
½ cup dry red wine
2 cups beef broth (see pages 123–24)
1 teaspoon tomato paste
Salt and pepper, to taste
2 tablespoons butter

Prepare a *battuto* by sautéing the *pancetta,* celery, carrot, and onion until they lose their crunch. Add the ground meats, brown well, then add the wine. When the wine has evaporated, add half the broth. Continue to cook until the liquids are reduced, then add the remaining broth. Reduce again and then add the tomato paste. Cover the saucepan and let cook over medium heat for 2 hours or more. Add salt and pepper to taste. Add the butter just before using the *ragù.* The *ragù* is ready to serve over fresh or stuffed pasta.

Note:
This sauce may include *prosciutto, porcini,* or chicken livers.

RAGÙ DI PESCE (Fish Ragù)

The most suitable fish for this *ragù* is octopus, squid, cuttlefish, prawns, clams, or any fish with a firm flesh. This sauce is best used with *spaghetti* or *linguine.*

SERVES 8
2 pounds fish
1 small onion, chopped

1 small carrot, diced
1 small celery stalk, diced
1 garlic clove, minced
1 tablespoon chopped parsley
½ cup extra virgin olive oil
½ ounce dried mushrooms, reconstituted and chopped
½ cup dry white wine
1 pound ripe tomatoes, peeled, seeded, and chopped
Salt and pepper, to taste

Clean the fish carefully and cut into strips or small pieces. Prepare a *battuto* with the onion, carrot, celery, garlic, and parsley. Heat the oil in a saucepan and add the *battuto* and mushrooms. Let brown over medium heat until the vegetables begin to get tender. Add the wine and cook. When the wine has evaporated, add the tomatoes, salt, and pepper and let cook over very low heat for about 20 minutes. Add the fish and cook till done (time varies depending on type of fish used, not to exceed 5 minutes). Stir occasionally, adding spoonfuls of water if the sauce becomes too dry.

Note:
Any fish that requires more than 5 minutes to cook must be precooked before adding with other fish fillets to the *ragù*.

RAGÙ GENOVESE (Braised Onion and Beef Ragù Sauce)

Despite its name, this is a recipe from Naples and is used as a condiment for pasta. The origins seem to go back to the sixteenth century when a group of immigrants from Genoa used to cook meat in this fashion; hence the name *genovese*. This sauce is good for *ziti* or any other type of pasta with a large hole. The meat can be served, sliced, together with the *ragù* or as a separate course.

SERVES 8
6 pounds onion
1 garlic clove
1 celery stalk
1 carrot
2 ounces pancetta, chopped
2 ounces prosciutto
6 tablespoons extra virgin olive oil
1 pound lean beef top round
1 teaspoon tomato paste, diluted in ½ cup warm water
1 cup white wine
Beef broth as needed (see pages 123–24)
Salt and pepper, to taste

Preheat the oven to 325°F. Thinly slice the onion and chop the garlic, celery, and carrot. Coarsely chop the *pancetta* and *prosciutto*. Place everything into a baking pan, with the oil, on top of the stove. Sauté slowly over low heat until the vegetables are soft. Add the beef and brown it. Dilute the tomato paste into ½ cup of lukewarm water and add to the pot together with the wine. Cover pan and place it in the oven. Cook for 3 to 4 hours, adding beef broth as necessary. Add salt and pepper to taste. The final result should be that of a rather dark, glazed onion sauce.

RAGÙ NAPOLETANO (Neapolitan Ragù)

Naples has its own *ragù*, with as many variations as you might imagine. Its nickname is *ragù del guardaporta*, which means "doorman's *ragù*," because a doorman supposedly having nothing else to do but watch the main entrance could watch the slow cooking of the *ragù* as well. Neapolitan *ragù* has been written about in poems, such as the one penned by journalist Giuseppe Marotta:

> *What an aroma . . .*
> *How delicious! And you, Maria, dip your fork in.*
> *No, wait! Let us examine our conscience first!*
> *I love you and I am faithful to you!*
> *What about you, Maria?*
> *Let us think, well . . .*
> *Are we really worthy of this ragù?*

SERVES 8

> *1 onion, thinly sliced*
> *4 tablespoons extra virgin olive oil*
> *2 tablespoons lard, chopped*
> *1 carrot, chopped*
> *1 stalk celery, chopped*
> *1 pound beef top round*
> *1 pound lean veal*
> *½ pound pork short ribs*
> *3 pounds tomatoes, peeled, seeded, and chopped*
> *20 basil leaves*
> *Salt and pepper, to taste*

Sauté the onion in the oil and lard in a skillet. Add the carrot and celery. Sauté them until wilted but not browned. Add the meats and sauté until browned on all sides. Add the tomatoes and 10 of the basil leaves and season with salt and pepper to taste. Stir well and cook, covered, over very low heat for about 3 to 4 hours. When the *ragù* is ready, remove the meat from the casserole, add the rest of the basil, and set aside. Use the sauce as a condiment for pasta and serve the various meats with it or as a second course. *Rigatoni* is the best pasta for this *ragù*.

Note:
Variations of this *ragù* may include fresh pork sausages; *braciola* stuffed with raisins, pine nuts, and spices; and pork skins stuffed in the same manner. These meats may be used in addition to or instead of other cuts; in any event, the less choice cuts are more suitable for this long-cooking *ragù*.

SALMORIGLIO (Olive Oil, Lemon, and Garlic Sauce)

This is probably the most interesting of the Mediterranean sauces inherited from Sicilian cuisine. To achieve a good emulsion it is advisable to whip *salmoriglio* in a double boiler or just combine all the ingredients, mix well, and use as a sauce over grilled fish, meat, or poultry. There are many variations of *salmoriglio*; some replace oregano with parsley, others add crushed tomatoes, and many replace lemon with vinegar.

SERVES 8
> 2 tablespoons fresh lemon juice
> ½ cup extra virgin olive oil
> 2 garlic cloves, minced
> 1 teaspoon oregano

Place the lemon juice in a bowl, add the oil in a slow, steady stream, and whip vigorously. Finish with the garlic and oregano.

SALSA AL POMODORO (Tomato Sauce)

In a well-known book by Pellegrino Artusi, *La Scienza in cucina e l'arte di mangiar bene* (*Science in the Kitchen and the Art of Eating Well*), written in 1891, in a preface to a recipe for tomato sauce, Artusi emphasizes its popularity with this anecdote: "There was a priest of a small village who had the bad habit of sticking his nose into everything and into everybody's family affairs. He was, however, an honest man, and more good than bad came from his meddling, and his people would let him be. But the villagers, sharp as they were, renamed him Don Pomodoro because, just like tomatoes, he could be welcomed everywhere." Good tomato sauce is the basic condiment of many wonderful dishes, including pasta.

SERVES 8
> 2 pounds ripe tomatoes
> 10 fresh basil leaves

5 tablespoons very good extra virgin olive oil
1 garlic clove (optional)
Salt and pepper, to taste

Scald the tomatoes in boiling water. Peel, seed, and either dice or crush them. Wash and tear up the basil leaves and set aside. Heat the oil in a skillet and sauté the garlic, if using. Remove when brown. Add the tomatoes and salt and pepper to taste. Cover and let simmer for about 25 minutes, stirring now and then. Add the basil at the end. The sauce is now ready to be used.

Notes:
If fresh tomatoes are not available, canned, peeled tomatoes may be used, provided they are of good quality.

If the tomatoes are not very ripe, add a small carrot, finely diced, to the *soffritto.* This will help tone down the acidity of the unripe tomatoes.

This basic sauce may be used as a condiment for pasta or for all preparations requiring tomato sauce.

To achieve a creamy consistency, the sauce may be passed through a fine sieve.

If instead of basil, oregano is added, the sauce is called *marinara.*

Add 4 anchovy fillets, *peperoncino,* a spoonful of capers, and 2 tablespoons of chopped Gaeta olives to the basic recipe to make a sauce called *puttanesca* (see pages 145–46).

SALSA AMATRICIANA (Guanciale and Tomato Sauce)

This is used as a condiment for pasta, preferably *bucatini* or *perciatelli. Guanciale* may be replaced with *pancetta* or bacon. When tossing *amatriciana* with pasta, always use grated *pecorino* cheese.

SERVES 4
½ pound guanciale (page 11)
1 onion, sliced
1 pound ripe tomatoes, peeled, seeded, and chopped
Peperoncino, to taste
Salt, to taste
4 tablespoons grated pecorino cheese

Cut the *guanciale* into thin slices and put in a large pan. Let brown slowly, then dispose of all the liquid fat. Add the onion and cook until wilted. Add the tomatoes and the *peperoncino* and salt to taste and cook for about 10 minutes over medium heat. Add *pecorino* after tossing the sauce with pasta.

SALSA DI NOCI (Walnut Sauce)

Walnuts are widely used in Italian cookery in a variety of preparations, the best known being the recipes from Liguria.

SERVES 6
½ pound walnuts, shelled
2 slices crustless white bread
½ cup milk
1 garlic clove, minced
1 tablespoon chopped fresh marjoram
Salt and pepper, to taste
3 tablespoons extra virgin olive oil
1 cup heavy cream

Scald the walnuts and peel off the skins. Dip the bread in milk and squeeze out excess. In a mortar pound the walnuts together with the bread, garlic, marjoram, and salt and pepper to obtain a smooth paste. Place the mixture in a mixing bowl, drip in the olive oil, and whip constantly. Add the cream and continue to stir well till you reach a creamy consistency. The sauce is ready to use. This sauce is very good with *pansotti,* walnut ravioli, or with roasted or boiled white meats.

Note:
In the original Ligurian recipe, soured milk, called *prescinsoeua* in dialect, is added instead of cream if this is the preference. *Prescinsoeua* can be replaced with plain yogurt.

SALSA DI FUNGHI (Mushroom Sauce)

Serve this sauce over any kind of pasta or gnocchi.

SERVES 6
1 tablespoon parsley
1 small rosemary sprig
1 garlic clove
1 pound ripe tomatoes
1 pound fresh porcini mushrooms
4 tablespoons butter
2 tablespoons extra virgin olive oil
2 anchovy fillets
Beef broth as needed (see pages 123–24)
Salt and pepper, to taste

Finely chop the parsley, rosemary leaves, and garlic for a *battuto*. Peel the tomatoes, remove the seeds, and cut into small pieces. Set aside. Clean and slice the mushrooms and set aside. Place the butter and oil in a casserole, add the anchovy fillets and the *battuto*, and let brown, stirring to dissolve the anchovies. Add the tomatoes and a little broth to moisten. Stir well and let cook over a very low heat for about half an hour. Add the mushrooms, which have been previously sliced and browned in a separate skillet, and cook another 5 minutes. Season with salt and pepper.

SALSA PER CARPACCIO (Sauce for Carpaccio)

SERVES 8

> 2 tablespoons minced baby onions
> 2 tablespoons minced gherkins
> 2 tablespoons minced capers
> 2 anchovy fillets
> 2 tablespoons vinegar
> ½ cup extra virgin olive oil
> 6 tablespoons finely chopped parsley
> Salt and pepper, to taste

Combine all the vegetables in a food processor with the anchovies, vinegar, and oil. Bring to a creamy consistency, then add the parsley. Mix and add salt and pepper to taste. Cover thinly sliced raw meat, preferably filet of beef, with the sauce. Serve.

SALSA PEVERADA (Spicy Sauce)

Peverada is a sauce that always contains pepper (*pevere* in Venetian dialect). Since the spice was once rare and expensive, it was fashionable for rich families to use it on or in everything, from soups to sauces to broth. *Peverada* was also referred to as "the water in which beef has been cooked" or "peppered broth." In Ancient Rome, a sauce called *piperatum* was prepared by adding *garum* (fermented fish sauce) to pepper. *Peverada* is a sauce used as a common condiment in today's Italian cookery. It is excellent with duck, poultry, game, and roasted meats. The most popular is the recipe used in the Veneto area.

SERVES 8

> ½ cup olive oil
> 2 garlic cloves, 1 minced, 1 left whole
> 1 bunch parsley, minced
> 1 slice soppressa, minced (about 3 ounces)
> 4 anchovy fillets, minced

1 pound duck liver, chopped
Pinch of salt
1 tablespoon freshly ground black pepper
2 cups beef broth (see pages 123–24)
1 tablespoon lemon juice
1 tablespoon wine vinegar

Heat the oil and the whole garlic clove in a casserole. When brown, add the minced ingredients, except the liver. Stir constantly and, when golden brown, add the liver, a pinch of salt, and the pepper. Sauté briskly for 2 minutes. Add the broth and simmer for 15 minutes. Then add the lemon juice and wine vinegar, reduce for 5 more minutes, and remove from the heat. Cool and pass through a fine sieve. This sauce should be rather thick but fluid. Warm before serving.

SALSA TONNATA (Tuna Sauce)

Tuna sauce has become popular in different regions of Italy and has several variations, some suitable for pasta, others for roast or boiled meats. One of the best-known versions is a Piedmontese tradition: a sliced roast of veal with tuna sauce (see page 226). The following is a recipe for tuna sauce for pasta:

SERVES 6
½ ounce dried porcini
1 small onion, thinly sliced
¼ cup extra virgin olive oil
1 garlic clove, chopped
1 celery stalk, diced
1 small carrot, finely chopped
1 ounce pine nuts
½ pound tuna in oil, crumbled
1 pound tomatoes, peeled, seeded, and chopped
Salt and pepper, to taste
1 pound pasta (optional)
1 tablespoon finely chopped parsley

Reconstitute the dried *porcini* in lukewarm water, chop, and set aside. Sauté the onion in oil with the garlic, celery, and carrot. When the vegetables are wilted but not browned, add the *porcini,* pine nuts, and tuna. Sauté briskly and add the tomatoes, reduce the heat to medium, and cook for 25 minutes. Add salt and pepper to taste. Toss sauce with pasta, if using, add parsley, and serve.

SALSA VERDE (Green Sauce)

Salsa verde was originally known as *bagnet verd* (the Piedmontese word for green sauce), the basic ingredient being parsley. The addition of capers, onion, and hard-boiled egg yolks is optional. *Salsa verde* is used for boiled meats (*bollito misto*) or fish.

MAKES 2 CUPS

3 anchovy fillets
2 slices fresh crustless white bread
2 tablespoons white wine vinegar
2 garlic cloves, minced
4 tablespoons finely chopped parsley
1 cup extra virgin olive oil
Salt and pepper, to taste

Thoroughly wash and cut the anchovy fillets into small pieces. Soak the bread in vinegar, squeeze out excess liquid, and drain. Place the bread and anchovy with the garlic and parsley in a mixing bowl and add the olive oil in a slow, steady stream while stirring continuously until you get a dense sauce. Add salt and pepper to taste.

INSACCATI E SALUMI
Salami and Cured Meats

SALAME (Salami)

The term salami refers to ground meat which has been packed into a casing. The generic term for salami in Italian is *insaccati* (encased). The casing can be natural (intestine) or synthetic.

There are three types of salami: fresh, dry-aged, and precooked. All fresh salami must be cooked before eating. Dry-aged can simply be sliced and served. Precooked and preserved salami must be kept refrigerated and consumed within a limited period. The production of salami is covered by special guarantees and regulatory bodies to check ingredients and procedures followed in making and storing preserved foods.

Making salami has four basic stages: preparing the meat, marinating, packing, cooking (or aging). It is impossible to generalize about the preparation of salami because each type requires a specific method. This holds true for the marinating process as well. Salt is the element common to all kinds of salami; pepper is also frequently used. The list of ingredients may also include cinnamon, nutmeg, cloves, and mace, whose use is recorded in the most ancient treatises on how to make salami.

One of the crucial ingredients is the casing. It must be strong, flexible, and porous enough to allow the meat inside to age without rotting or becoming moldy. The casing must also be heat-resistant. The two types of casings are natural and artificial. Natural casings are obtained by treating certain animal parts, such as the bladder, intestine, and pigskin, in order to achieve adequate strength and texture. Artificially produced casings can be divided into three categories: casings obtained from animal skin, casings made with cellulose fibers, and casings made of polyvinyl. Synthetic casings are mainly used for products that are cooked or smoked.

Of the many varieties of salami for aging (and every pork-consuming region has its own specialties), the choicest varieties are: *salame di Felino, salame di Varzi, salame di Milano, salsiccione, salame di Fabriano, salame toscano, soppressa calabra, salsiccia napoletana stagionata, salame mantovano, salame abruzzese, salsiccia sarda, finocchiona, coppa, cacciatorino, bondiola, salama da sugo ferrarese, mortadella di Bologna,* and *salame cotto.*

These types of salami are all made with pork, mixing three parts of meat and one of fat. Salt is always added; pepper, either ground or in peppercorns, is also usually present. Nitrites and nitrates, necessary preserving agents, are added in quantities allowed by law. Occasionally some coloring agent is also added. Dry-aging is done in well-ventilated, semi-dark, cool rooms, specifically created for this purpose, or in well-ventilated, not too humid cellars or attics. In good quality salami the filling must be compact and the bits of fat must not separate from the bits of meat when sliced.

SALUMI (Cured Meats)

The term *salumi* refers to whole cuts of meat that are either cured in salt and then dry-aged or cured in brine *(salamoia)* and then preserved. Some *salumi* are cooked and later preserved.

All *salumi* can be used as classic appetizers. They must be cut into thin slices shortly before being served. It is best to remove the skin before slicing to prevent the meat from being contaminated by mold, which usually forms on the skin during the aging process.

The following types of cured meat may be included among the aged *salumi: pancetta, guanciale, speck,* and various kinds of *prosciutto.* Another delicacy to mention made with beef, not with pork, is *bresaola,* a specialty of the Valtellina area.

SALAME FRESCO (Fresh Salami)

COTECHINO (Fresh Pork Sausage)

Cotechino and *zampone* make up the most classic fresh salami of the Emilia-Romagna region. *Cotechino* is priced lower than *zampone,* mainly due to its casing, which can be either natural or synthetic. *Cotechino* may be used as an *antipasto* or as a main course, with a starch or a legume, or added to a *bollito misto.*

> *8 pounds pork rind*
> *10 pounds pork shoulder, whole*
> *8 pounds pork jowl or neck*
> *1½ pounds salt*
> *4 tablespoons black pepper*
> *3 ounces saltpeter*
> *1 tablespoon ground cloves*
> *1 teaspoon ground cinnamon*
> *Natural casing, if possible*

Clean the pork rind, pass it over a flame, and scrub it. Grind it together with the rest of the meat and blend the resulting mixture with the other ingredients. Using a funnel, pack the meat into the casings. Take care not to leave air bubbles while stuffing. Avoid pressing too much, however, to prevent the casing from breaking.

Tie the upper end of the casing with several knots, cut the string, and tie a single knot about every 10 inches, leaving 1 loop to hang each *cotechino*. Cut the casing and repeat the operation, creating several *cotechini*. Hang them by their loops and let them dry at least 1 day. When dried, *cotechino* may be stored for up to 1 month in the refrigerator. It is then boiled before eating.

Put the *cotechino* in cold water and let stand for a few hours. Then prick it with a fork all over (so that it does not explode while cooking), change the water, and bring to a boil over medium heat. When it begins to boil, lower the heat, cover the pot, and cook 1 hour for each 10 ounces. Let it stand in its cooking water for about 15 minutes before serving. *Cotechino* can be served sliced as an *antipasto,* with *bollito misto,* or with mashed potatoes or lentils as a main course.

ZAMPONE (Stuffed Pig's Feet)

The ingredients to make *zampone* are the same as those used to make *cotechino,* but instead of intestine casing the skin of the pig's foreleg and foot is used. The boning is done from the top open end, not by cutting the skin down the side. The preparation is also very similar to that of *cotechino,* the difference being that the open end of the hog's foreleg is sewn up with thread.

Soak the *zampone* in water for about 12 hours to soften the skin. Prick the foot with a skewer. Tie well and lay it on a thin wooden board the same size as the *zampone* and wrap with a clean towel or cheesecloth to protect it while cooking. Boil over medium heat without changing the water. When it begins to boil, lower the heat, cover, and cook for about 3 hours. When ready, let stand in the pot for 15 minutes before serving. *Zampone* may be served in the same way as *cotechino*. The classic accompaniment for *zampone* is stewed lentils.

SALAMELLE

Salamelle is a fresh salami originally from the province of Mantova. It is made with hog's meat (shoulder) in a natural or synthetic casing. It is much leaner than most other salami, seasoned with salt and pepper, no wine or garlic. This fresh sausage, consequently, makes for a broth with less fat and acidity. In fact, this broth is generally used to cook *tortelli di Mantova,* typical of this city.

Salamelle are eaten boiled with mashed potatoes or split and grilled.

SALSICCE (Pork Sausages)

The ingredient for *salsicce* is just coarsely ground pork meat with less choice cuts of meat and more fat. The proportions should be 60 percent lean meat and 40 percent fat). Garlic, fennel seeds, and peperoncino can also be added to the mixture for extra flavor. *Salsicce* are one third the thickness of *cotechino*. To make *salsicce*, follow the procedure outlined in the *cotechino* recipe, tying the sausages with knots. Sausages prepared without tying knots between them are called *luganiga* or *salsicca* "by the yard." *Salsicce* may also be consumed fresh, in which case 70 percent pork meat and 30 percent fat is used. For this type of sausage, do not use saltpeter but regular sea salt. The sausages may be pan-fried or cooked in sauce.

SALAMA DA SUGO (Liver and Tongue Sausage)

The epitome of the richness of the food specialties from the town of Ferrara, *salama da sugo* is a special sausage a little like a huge pomegranate, weighing approximately 1 to 2 pounds. According to tradition, the pig's bladder is used to encase it. The filling is made with liver and tongue and bits of mixed lean meats cut with a knifepoint and moistened with red wine, Marsala, or brandy and seasoned with salt, pepper, cinnamon, and cloves. Once tied with a string, *salama* is left to rest for 1 year, hanging in a ventilated room.

Wash the *salama* well, let it soak in cold water for 12 hours, then put it into a cloth bag. Tie the top of the bag to a wooden stick that reaches across the top of the cooking pot, so that the *salama* hangs in the middle of it. Cook the *salama* in a large quantity of warm water over medium heat for at least 4 hours. When ready, cut it open along the seam and remove the meat from the casing with a spoon. Serve with mashed potatoes in winter and melon in summer.

SALAME (Dry-Aged Salami)

Dry-aged salami is made with raw pork (with or without beef), salt, and various spices. The degree to which the meat is ground is different for various types of salami, as is the length of the aging period. The name of a town on the label of salami specialties does not refer to where it was made but to the method of production. Large salami is sliced by machine (*salame di Milano*, for example), whereas the smaller ones are cut by hand (e.g., *salame di Felino* and *cacciatorino*).

Most of the time, the various preparations may differ only in how the sausage is tied, the proportion of lean meat to fat, and the seasonings used. Following is the preparation of the most popular dry-aged *salame*.

CACCIATORINO (Hunter's Salami)

This is rather small salami, usually made with half pork and half beef with the addition of fresh pork fat, black pepper, garlic, and optional spices. *Cacciatorino* is approximately 5 to 7 inches long and weighs about 6 to 8 ounces. It is knotted at each end (just like a regular sausage). It must age for at least 30 days.

SALAME DI VARZI (Varzi Salami)

The name comes from the small town of Varzi in Lombardy. This salami is made strictly with lean pork meat and fresh pork fat, both coarsely ground and seasoned with white wine and salt. No other spice is used. The standard length is approximately 12 inches, and it is knotted lengthwise, then across with intermediate loops. *Salame di Varzi* must age for at least 6 months.

SALAME DI MILANO (Milan Salami)

This is a typical salami from Lombardy, made with very finely ground pork, beef, and fat in equal quantities, spiced only with salt and pepper. The salami can weigh up to 3 pounds and is aged for at least 3 months. It is knotted lengthwise, then across with intermediate loops. *Salame di Milano* should be sliced fairly thin, either by hand or by machine.

FINOCCHIONA (Salami with Fennel Seeds)

Made with finely ground pork, *finocchiona* is seasoned with salt, pepper, and garlic and, as indicated by its name, with *semi di finocchio* (fennel seeds). It is dry-aged for about 3 months. It is rather thick in diameter and is 8 to 10 inches long. *Finocchiona* is knotted lengthwise with intermediate loops across. It should be sliced fairly thick.

SALAM D'LA DUJA (Preserved Salami)

This is small salami made with less choice cuts of lean pork meat seasoned with salt and pepper. *Duja* is a Piedmont dialect word for a terra-cotta jar used to cook or to preserve foods. This salami is typical of the eastern part of Piedmont in the provinces of Vercelli and Novara. It is a rather small salami which is kept soft and fresh in a terra-cotta jar totally filled with liquefied pork fat, then sealed. This particular method of preserving the salami is necessary in this region because the humidity in the air does not allow normal dry-aging. *Salam d'la duja* is kept in its jar for 3 months prior to eating.

SALAME NAPOLETANO (Neapolitan Salami)

This salami is prepared with relatively finely ground lean pork meat mixed with a small quantity of fat and heavily spiced with ground *peperoncino,* which gives it its familiar red color. The mixture is then stuffed into a 1-inch-wide, 20-inch-long casing simply folded in half and tied at each end. There is also a much less peppery version of this salami. *Salame napoletano* is dry-aged for at least 6 months.

SALAME DI FELINO (Felino Salami)

This is made of excellent quality, relatively finely ground pork mixed with a small quantity of pure pork fat and a few spices. It is put in a natural casing, and once it has been stuffed and tied, it is about 15 inches long and bigger at 1 end than at the other. It is knotted vertically with alternate loops across and aged for at least 3 months. Felino is a village outside Parma, on the hills below the Apennines (a chain of mountains that goes all the way from the north to the south of Italy), a few kilometers from Langhirano, the traditional *prosciutto di Parma* area. The dry climate and crisp air allow for exceptional aging; thus, this *salame* is particularly sought for its excellent quality.

SOPPRESSATA (Head Sausage)

Soppressata, not to be confused with *soppressa* (a *salume*), is made with lean meat taken from the head of the pig. This is then coarsely chopped, mixed with lard, pepper, and spices, and stuffed into a natural casing. It is then flattened down (compressed), knotted with intermittent loops across, and pulled very tight so as to form several squares each attached to one another. *Soppressata* is aged for at least 40 days. It should be served rather soft. It is not consumed immediately after its aging period; it must be preserved under melted back fat. It is served sliced by hand.

SALAME COTTI
(Cooked and Preserved Cured Meats)

The term *salame cotto* refers to precooked and then preserved salami. It is mostly prepared with pork meat or beef or a combination of both. The meat is ground rather coarse and flavored with spices that very, depending on the type of salami. The casing is generally synthetic as it adapts better to the heat while cooking. This salami has a limited shelf life and must be kept in cool rooms and refrigerated after being cut.

MORTADELLA DI BOLOGNA (Cooked Salami with Pistachio Nuts)

Mortadella goes back to the Middle Ages, when the seasonings used to include myrtle berries. *Mortadella* is made in different sizes, the choicest being the larger ones. It contains the poorer cuts of meat that cannot be used for any other type of salami. The meat is ground very fine and mixed with coarsely ground fatback plus the usual preserving agents, salt, finely ground white pepper, black peppercorns, coriander seeds, mixed spices, shelled pistachios, and wine. The mixture is packed into a beef bladder for large *mortadella* and into a pig's bladder for smaller *mortadella*. It is then hung in an oven and cooked at about 225°F (2 hours for every 2 pounds). The finished product must be kept in a cool room at all times and refrigerated after being cut. The particular taste of this product is very different from that of any other type of salami.

PROSCIUTTO (Cured Ham)

Prosciutto is made by salting, aging, and dressing a pork leg, and then preparing it according to local usage. The choicest varieties come from Parma, San Daniele del Friuli, and Tuscany. *Prosciutto di Parma* is cut with a short shank or, as the natives say, a *coscia di pollo* (chicken leg). The leg should keep the same shape as when butchered, that is, fairly round. *San Daniele* ham is different in two ways: first, the leg is kept whole up to the hooves; second, the leg is somewhat flattened. Therefore, the leg is worked in such a manner that it remains stiff. It is then salted and placed under weight, a method that allows the leg to discard more moisture and, thanks to the climatic conditions of the area, allows for a particularly sweet-flavored product. *Prosciutto toscano* has a very different production method from *prosciutto di Parma* and *San Daniele*. First of all, Tuscan production is limited to an artisan level. It is much saltier, because traditionally the Tuscans do not salt their bread. Consequently, the additional salt in the prosciutto makes up for the lack of salt in the bread. *Prosciutto toscano*, therefore, is drier and much redder in color. It is traditionally sliced by hand and not by machine.

The basic method of making *prosciutto* is as follows. After having cut and cleaned the leg, let it lie flat for a day in a cool place. Then cover it with salt and let it lie flat on 1 side for 4 days, then, again, for 4 more days on the other side. When the salting period is over, rub it vigorously with fresh salt and let it stand for a few more days without salt. Wash the leg several times with cold water in order to remove the remaining salt and hang in a dry, airy, ventilated place. This stage is very important since the air plays a primary role in the quality of the final product. It is not possible to set the length of this stage in advance; it depends on the local climate. The *prosciutto* will be ready when entirely dry. It generally takes 12 to 18 months to achieve a fine-quality prosciutto. The production is supervised and approved by a local board with the aim of checking and preserving the product's quality.

Notes:

Prosciutto can be made anywhere with a mild climate. The fact that *prosciutto* is so distinctive in terms of aroma and taste is because the Italian climate allows for subtle, slow aging. It is a natural phenomenon that cannot easily be explained or reproduced.

Because of FDA regulations, San Daniele *prosciutto* imported to the United States is also cut with a short shank.

CULATELLO (Homemade Cured Ham)

Culatello is a very particular type of *salame* produced in a small area around Parma in the villages of Soragna, Zibello, Colorno, and Busseto, all located along the river Po.

The most singular aspect of *culatello* is that it has the same characteristics as *prosciutto* but is aged in a casing and preferably aged in a humid climate rather than a dry and ventilated one.

Only the best part of the hog leg is used. It is boned and rubbed immediately following the slaughter with a mix of salt, herbs, and spices. It is then wrapped in a layer of fresh pork fat and stuffed into a natural casing and securely fastened with a strong thread. *Culatello* is hung in the cellar and slowly aged for at least 1 year and, at times, 18 months. When the time comes to use the *culatello*, it is placed in a bath of white wine for a few days. (Some prefer to wrap it in a cloth soaked in white wine.) The thread, casing, and protective fat are then removed and the sausage is eaten sliced like *prosciutto,* though *culatello* tastes much smoother and sweeter. One of the main characteristics of *culatello* is its soft texture, which is due mainly to the climate of the area, particularly the morning mist around the river Po, which favors the slow disintegration of the product's enzymes. *Culatello* has always been homemade and does not lend itself to industrial production. *Culatello* is one of the most prized and expensive cured meats, but it is not easy to find. The production is supervised and approved by a local board with the aim of checking and preserving the product's quality.

COPPA (Cured Pork Neck)

Coppa is known as *capocollo* in the central and southern part of Italy and as *bondiola* in Lombardy. It is made with pork neck trimmed to a desired shape. The whole neck is rubbed and then marinated with a seasoning mixture of salt, black pepper, cloves, and wine. The marinating process takes at least 20 days, since it is done in stages. During every stage (in 5-day intervals) it is rubbed again and again with the seasoning and turned over. Once marinated, the pork neck is rubbed dry with a cloth and wrapped in a casing. It is hung in a warm place for 2 days, then aged in a cool place for at least 3 months. It is sliced fairly thin and eaten with country bread. The best-known *coppa* is prepared in the Piacenza area.

SOPPRESSA (Cured Pork Shoulder or Leg)

This is a specialty of the Veneto region, from Treviso in particular. It is made with lean pieces of meat such as the shoulder or leg and the meat around the neck, following the same method as *coppa*. Red wine is used in addition to the usual seasonings. *Soppressa* is hung to dry in a warm place, and aged in a cool place for over 1 year.

SPECK (Cured Ham)

Speck must not be confused with the German word *Speck* meaning "bacon." Italian *speck* is a specialty of the upper river Adige area prepared by stretching and boning the ham. The specifics of the process to prepare *speck* can only be described in general terms, since this is a homemade delicacy and the methods used vary from family to family. The meat is seasoned with salt, pepper, bay leaves, and juniper berries, then placed on a tilted surface so that the meat juices can be collected and used to moisten the meat daily. *Speck* is then smoked with juniper and other aromatic woods. Traditionally it is sliced in squares one-quarter inch thick and eaten with country bread.

PROSCIUTTO DI CAPRIOLO (Roebuck Ham)

This is deer's leg treated with salt, pepper, finely minced garlic, and *peperoncino*. It ages for about 50 days. It is usually thinly sliced, and served with oil and lemon, salt, and pepper. It is typical of Valle d'Aosta and Valtellina. It is also called *violino* (violin), referring to the elongated shape of the roebuck's leg and to the fact that it is cut by handling it like a violin and moving a long, thin knife like a bow.

PROSCIUTTO DI CINGHIALE (Wild Boar Ham)

Wild boar ham is typical of Tuscany, a region with much wooded land, an ideal habitat for wild boar. Basically the leg of the boar is processed with the same method as for all types of prosciutto, the only difference being that from the shank up to the hoof the skin is kept on. This allows for the dressed leg to absorb all the indispensable quantities of salt and spices only through the skinned portion of the leg, so the final product keeps its game-like taste, without becoming too salty. In the past, wild boar ham was very rare, but today wild boars are grown on farms and are more readily available. This *prosciutto* is rather lean and is thinly sliced by hand.

MOCETTA (Cured Deer Thigh)

This is a characteristic product of Valle d'Aosta made from the thigh of a chamois deer or mountain goat *(stambecco)*. It is made in the same way as roebuck ham, has a very distinctive game flavor, and is served thinly sliced as an *antipasto*.

BRESAOLA (Dry-Aged Beef)

Bresaola is an Italian counterpart to the Swiss specialty called *viande de Grison*. Typical of Valtellina, it is made from beef cuts (generally the filet) treated with a mixture of salt and spices, then wrapped in thin nets, and aged for at least 1 month. When ready for consumption, *bresaola* is a bright dark red color, softer in texture than its Swiss counterpart and more aromatic. It is generally used as an *antipasto,* sliced very thin and briefly marinated in oil, lemon, and pepper.

PROSCIUTTO COTTO (Cooked Ham)

Success in making ham depends entirely on the quality of the meat chosen. Begin with a medium-sized pork leg with the bristles, bone, and fat removed. Put the meat in a container with a brine of heavily salted water, a bit of sugar, bay leaves, cloves, cinnamon, and saltpeter. Let it stand for about 20 days. Wash the ham in cold running water, dry it, and put it in a pan for cooking ham. The meat is pressed into the desired shape. It is sealed in a pot and soaked in water. While cooking, the temperature of the water should be 425°F. Ham should cook 1 hour for each 2 pounds of meat. Let it cool in the cooking water, then keep it in the refrigerator. Leave it to rest for 1 day and then the ham is ready to be eaten. This product must be refrigerated all the time and should be sliced only when ready to eat; otherwise it gets dark.

MARINATE E CONSERVE
Marinades and Preserved Foods

Marinades are known in Italy as *marinate* or *conce*. They are used to preserve, flavor, or tenderize. Marinating time varies according to season and temperature.

There are two main kinds of marinades: quick marinades and long marinades.

MARINATE (Marinades)

MARINATE CORTE (Quick Marinades)

The more delicate the food, the milder the marinade. Quick marinades are suitable for *carpaccio* and small or thinly sliced fish or vegetables served either raw or previously cooked. The ingredients vary from just salt, pepper, and oil to liquids such as lemon juice, vinegar, or wine, as well as herbs and spices, according to the type of food and recipe. Quick marinades are frequently used in preparing dishes for *antipasto*.

MARINATE LUNGHE (Long Marinades)

Long marinades usually contain vegetables and wine. They are suitable for large cuts of beef, hare, rabbit, and other game. A common preparation is as follows.

Coarsely chop carrots, scallions, onions, celery, and parsley (including the stems) and place in a bowl together with some thyme, some crumbled bay leaves, a few peppercorns, and some pounded (not ground) cloves. Add good-quality white or red wine and vinegar (the amount depends on the size of the cut of meat being marinated). Arrange the meat in a bowl and pour the marinade over it, turning the meat over so that the ingredients can spread evenly. Cover the bowl and let stand in a cool place for 2 to 3 days, or as indicated in the recipe. If the meat is in small chunks, 1 day of marinating is enough; if it is a large piece and also tough, it will take longer to marinate. Marinades that take longer than 2 to 3 days must be cooked and then cooled before being used, to avoid fermentation. In this case, bring all the ingredients to a boil and cook them over low heat for 5 minutes. Strain the marinade before using for cooking.

ZUCCHINE IN SCAPECE (Marinated Zucchini with Mint)

SERVES 4

1 pound zucchini
3 tablespoons extra virgin olive oil
1 tablespoon white wine vinegar
2 mint sprigs, finely chopped
Salt and pepper, to taste

Wash, slice across, pat dry, and fry the zucchini in oil. When golden brown, remove from the oil and remove the excess oil on paper towels. Arrange on a serving platter and flavor with olive oil, vinegar, and chopped mint. Add salt and pepper to taste.

SARDELLE IN SAOR (Sardines in Saor)

SERVES 4

2 pounds sardines
3½ cups all-purpose flour
1 cup olive oil
Salt, to taste
1 pound white onions, sliced
1 cup vinegar
2 tablespoons pine nuts
2 tablespoons raisins

Cut and remove the heads and bones of the sardines. Wash and pat dry, coat with flour, and fry in olive oil, reserving 2 tablespoons. Drain, remove the excess oil with paper towels, salt, and set aside.

Prepare a cooked marinade. Fry the onions in the remaining 2 tablespoons olive oil over low heat and, when golden brown, add the vinegar. Keep over low heat for a few more minutes to reduce the vinegar by 50 percent. Remove from the pan and set aside.

Fill a terra-cotta dish with alternate layers of sardines and the marinade and add the pine nuts and raisins. The top layer should be the marinade. Cover and let rest at least 6 hours before eating. This is very good served as an *antipasto*.

PESCE IN CARPIONE (Fish in Carpione)

SERVES 4

2 pounds any firm fish fillet
Olive oil, for frying
1 lemon, sliced
4 tablespoons extra virgin olive oil

1 pound onions
2 garlic cloves, chopped
½ cup white wine vinegar
1 rosemary sprig, chopped
1 parsley sprig, chopped
Sage leaves, chopped
Salt, to taste

Flour and sauté the fish on both sides in hot oil to a golden brown color. Place on paper towels to remove excess oil and arrange on a platter. Cover with some slices of lemon.

Prepare the marinade. Heat the 4 tablespoons of oil in a sautéing pan and add the onions and garlic. When the onions are soft (not browned), add the vinegar and reduce slightly. Remove from the heat, cool, and pour the marinade over the fish fillets. Refrigerate for 1 day before serving. Sprinkle the rosemary, parsley, sage, and salt over the platter. Decorate by adding sliced lemon around the platter just before serving.

INSALATA DI BIANCHETTI (Whitebait Salad)

Bianchetti are tiny fish, the spawn of sardines or anchovies. They can be fished only during certain limited times of the year so as not to endanger the fish population. The fish must be absolutely fresh for this dish.

SERVES 4
1 pound whitebait
Salt and pepper, to taste
2 tablespoons lemon juice
6 tablespoons extra virgin olive oil
1 lemon, sliced

Wash the whitebait well in cold salted water (in Italy, where possible, it is washed in seawater), drain, and season with salt, pepper, and lemon juice. Let stand refrigerated for 1 hour. Remove all the liquids, rinse, place on a serving platter and add olive oil, decorate with lemon slices, and serve.

ACCIUGHE MARINATE (Marinated Anchovies)

SERVES 8
2 pounds very fresh anchovies
Juice of 4 lemons
Salt, to taste
1 cup extra virgin olive oil

1 tablespoon finely chopped parsley
2 garlic cloves, thinly sliced
Pinch peperoncino

Remove the innards and bones from the fish without damaging it too much and leaving the fillets attached along the back. Wash and pat dry. Place on a platter, squeeze 2 of the lemons over the fish, salt, cover, and let sit in the refrigerator for 2 hours.

Drain the anchovies, squeeze the juice from the remaining lemons over them, drain again, and pat dry. Place on a platter and season with the olive oil, parsley, and garlic. Add *peperoncino* to taste. Refrigerate for 1 hour and serve.

LEPRE AL VINO ROSSO (Hare in Red Wine)

SERVES 4

Marinade
2 hares
1 onion
1 carrot, chopped
2 celery stalks, chopped
3 parsley sprigs
1 rosemary sprig
2 bay leaves
4 cloves
5 juniper berries
1 pinch of cinnamon
2 marjoram sprigs
2 bottles good red wine

Cooking
4 ounces lard
2 ounces butter
1 onion, finely sliced
1 garlic clove, finely chopped
Salt and pepper, to taste
Polenta (see pages 175–76), for serving

For the marinade, clean and cut the hares into small chunks. Put the pieces of hare into a large pot with 1 onion, 1 carrot, the celery, parsley, rosemary, bay leaves, cloves, juniper berries, cinnamon, and marjoram. Add enough wine to cover the hare completely and let marinate for at least 12 hours.

For cooking, preheat the oven to 350°F. Pound the lard, put it into a large pan with the butter, and brown a finely sliced onion to make a *soffritto*. Remove the hare from the marinade, reserving the marinade, pat dry, and brown with the *soffritto* on medium heat for 20 minutes. Add 2 cups of filtered marinade liquid and cook in oven for 2 hours, adding more filtered marinade occasionally, as needed. When the hare is tender, add the finely chopped garlic, and salt and pepper to taste. Serve with *polenta* (see pages 175–76), or, if preferred, *pappardelle*.

LINGUA SALMISTRATA (Pickled Tongue)

SERVES 6

Marinade
1 veal tongue
1 pound coarse sea salt
1 teaspoon curing salt
1 cup sugar
1 bunch thyme
1 teaspoon peperoncino
1 carrot
2 celery stalks
½ large lemon
2 leeks
1 garlic head

Cooking
2½ quarts veal broth (see page 124)
1 cup white wine
1 cup vinegar
Same spices, herbs, and vegetables as for the marinade

For the marinade, wash the tongue thoroughly and soak it deep in the marinade with all the spices, herbs, and vegetables for 6 days. Turn over every day.

For cooking, cook the tongue in plain water for 1 hour. Remove tongue, skin it, and cook it again for 2 hours in the veal broth with the wine, vinegar, spices, herbs, and vegetables. Cool and refrigerate. Pickled tongue can be kept refrigerated for up to 1 month.

CONSERVE (Preserved Foods)

Cooked and preserved, marinated in brine or preserved in salt, or air-dried, these foods are meant to be kept for long periods of time. These processes are suitable for meat, fish, vegetables, and fruits as well. Many of these preserved foods may sometimes be served as *antipasto* by simply adding a few drops of oil.

SOTT'ACETI (Marinating in Vinegar)

This preparation is suitable for young onions, carrots, turnips, small cucumbers, peppers, string beans, and celery. The vinegar has to be very good but not too strong and preferably white so as not to change the color of the vegetables or make them too sour.

> 2½ pounds mixed vegetables, such as onion, turnip, celery, cucumber,
>   carrot, and cauliflower
> 6 cups white wine vinegar
> 2 bay leaves
> Pinch of sugar
> 1 garlic clove
> 1 clove
> 5 white peppercorns
> Pinch of salt
> Pinch of tarragon
> 1 cinnamon stick
> 1 teaspoon olive oil
> 6 cups vinegar

Clean, wash, and cut the vegetables according to the various types. Boil half of the vinegar, let cool, and set aside. Bring the remaining vinegar with 6 cups of water to a boil in a large saucepan with 1 bay leaf, a pinch of sugar, the garlic, the clove, the peppercorns, and salt. Add the vegetables and let cook for at least 3 minutes—the vegetables must remain crunchy. Remove the pot from the heat and when the vinegar has cooled drain the vegetables and place them in a deep bowl. Add the remaining bay leaf, the tarragon, cinnamon, oil, and the vinegar that had been set aside. Cover the bowl and keep refrigerated for later use.

SOTT'OLIO (Preserving in Oil)

This preparation is suitable for small artichokes, mushrooms, and eggplants.

Prepare the vegetables in the same way as for *sott'aceti*. Cook them in 3 parts of water to 1 part water with a pinch of salt until they are tender but still crisp. Drain and let dry on a clean towel. Then place in a bowl with few peppercorns, a few bay leaves, and a piece of cinnamon. Cover completely with extra virgin olive oil, cover, and save for later use.

POMODORI ESSICCATI (Sun-Dried Tomatoes)

In Italy, this preparation is best done at the end of July or in the first twenty days of August, when the sun is very hot, so the tomatoes are very dry and perfectly ripe. Tomatoes prepared like this can be served as part of an *antipasto* or as a side dish for boiled and broiled meats. If you cannot dry the tomatoes outdoors because of the weather, you can dry them in a warm oven (preheated and then turned off).

4 pounds ripe, firm, medium-size tomatoes
Salt, to taste
4 ounces basil leaves
Peperoncino, to taste
1 garlic clove (optional)
1 quart extra virgin olive oil

Clean the tomatoes thoroughly and cut them in half lengthwise. Remove the seeds, put them over a wire rack with the open side up, and sprinkle liberally with salt (if they are not salted enough, they will become moldy).

Leave the tomatoes in the sun for 4 to 5 days, turning occasionally and taking them indoors at night. At the end of each day, drain the water they will have oozed. On the last day, wash the basil leaves and let them dry on a cloth in the shade. Put the tomato halves back together, placing a basil leaf in the middle, and press well. Then place them in layers in a clean, dry jar. Press well, add some *peperoncino* and a clove of garlic if you wish, drizzle olive oil over each layer of tomatoes, cover, and refrigerate. They will be ready for consumption in 2 weeks.

OLIVE SCHIACCIATE (Crushed Green Olives)

5 pounds green olives (not too ripe)
5 garlic cloves, sliced
1 bunch basil
Pinch of peperoncino
4 tablespoons oregano
1 red bell pepper, minced
Salt, to taste
1 cup extra virgin olive oil
1 tablespoon vinegar

Pound the olives with a mallet without crushing them completely. Wash and let soak in water for about 10 days, changing the water frequently. Drain the olives, squeeze them, and make layers in a bowl that can be covered.

Cover each layer with a little garlic, basil, *peperoncino,* oregano, and bell pepper, salting each layer. When the bowl is full, push down on the olives to squeeze out as much liquid as possible. Pour off the excess liquid. Fill the bowl with olive oil mixed with a few drops of vinegar and keep refrigerated. The olives will be ready to eat after 2 months.

OLIVE AL FORNO (Baked Black Olives)

5 pounds black olives
2 pounds sea salt
1 teaspoon peperoncino
2 teaspoons oregano
3 cups extra virgin olive oil

Make 2 or 3 small cuts in the olives' pulp. Soak them in cold water for 1 week, changing the water 3 times a day. Drain, let dry, and cover the olives with salt.

Bake at 225°F until wrinkled. When cool, put into a jar with *peperoncino* and oregano, cover completely with oil, and refrigerate for later use.

PASTA DI OLIVE (Olive Pâté)

This is served as an antipasto spread on toast and brushed with olive oil. It can also be used as a sauce for pasta. Olive pâté will keep in the refrigerator for about a month.

1 pound black olives
Grated zest and juice of 1 lemon
1 tablespoon breadcrumbs
5 tablespoons extra virgin olive oil
Salt and pepper, to taste

Pit the olives and chop them very fine or use a food processor so as to make a homogeneous mixture. Add the grated zest and juice of the lemon, the breadcrumbs, and 4 to 5 tablespoons oil. Add salt and pepper and mix thoroughly. Put the mixture into a jar, cover completely with oil, and refrigerate. The pâté can be used immediately.

ACCIUGHE SOTTO SALE (Anchovies Preserved in Salt)

The liquid that results from salting the anchovies is called *colatura.* In some fishing villages, it is used as an additional ingredient in a sauce for pasta.

5 pounds anchovies
5 pounds rock salt

For this procedure you need a wooden barrel or a terra-cotta jar. Remove the heads and gut and clean the anchovies. Cover the bottom of a terra-cotta jar with rock salt, then arrange a layer of anchovies and a layer of salt. Repeat until all the anchovies have been used, finishing with a layer of salt. Put a wooden disk on top. On top of the disk place something to act as a weight. The weight will cause the excess liquid to rise to the surface. Remove the liquid occasionally with a clean cloth. The anchovies will be ready after 2 to 3 weeks.

TONNO SOTT'OLIO (Tuna in Oil)

8 cups water
1 cup white vinegar
1 onion, cut into quarters
4 garlic cloves
Bay leaves
2 pounds fresh tuna, sliced 1 inch thick
1 cup extra virgin olive oil
10 peppercorns

Place the water, vinegar, the onion, 2 cloves of the garlic, and a few bay leaves in a large pot. Let the liquid simmer and reduce by one third. Add the tuna and continue simmering for 45 minutes. Drain, cool, and dry the tuna. Put it in a bowl, cover with olive oil, and add peppercorns and the remaining 2 garlic cloves. Store in a cool place. It will be ready to eat after 20 to 30 days and can be saved for as long as 5 to 6 months.

PIZZA E FOCACCIA
Pizza and Focaccia

This book will not go into detail as to how and where *pizza* originated. Its history is rather controversial, and food experts find it difficult to agree on dates and origins. In Naples' Archaeological Museum, visitors can admire a statue from the Pompeii digs showing a boy holding a pasta disk very much like a modern *pizza*. World-known and eaten practically everywhere on the planet, *pizza* is nevertheless an undeniable Neapolitan specialty.

Pizza always consists of a thin disk of leavened dough covered with various ingredients such as tomato, cheese (especially *mozzarella*), seafood, small fish, mushrooms, and many other toppings. The following recipes refer to specialties within the Neapolitan culinary tradition and others of the various regions of Italy.

Some things to keep in mind:

- Never refrigerate the dough to slow down the fermentation.
- When stretched out, the dough should be slightly thicker at the edges, as is the trademark of a real Neapolitan *pizza*.
- A wood-burning oven should be lit at least 3 to 4 hours in advance; it will be ready for baking when the temperature is about 650°F to 700°F.
- If you do not have a wood-burning oven, cook the *pizza* in an oven preheated to 550°F, on an oiled baking pan or on a preheated sheet pan lined with ceramic tiles.
- All ingredients that go on top of a *pizza* must be raw; if pre-cooked toppings are desired, they should be added to the *pizza* when it is taken out of the oven, making sure they are hot.
- Some *pizzaioli* like to add some fat to the dough, such as olive oil or lard.
- Always drizzle extra virgin olive oil on top of the *pizza* when the *pizza* is placed in the oven.
- When done, the edges of the *pizza* will show burned spots. Remember the oven heat is at 650° to 700°F. It will take just 3 to 4 minutes to cook. That's why it is almost impossible to make *pizza* at home. The homemade *pizza* is more of a crusty pie, since it takes not less than 15 minutes to cook.

PIZZA DOUGH BASIC RECIPE

SERVES 6

1 ounce brewer's yeast
7 cups all-purpose flour
Pinch of salt
Water, as needed

Crumble the yeast in a cup and dilute with several tablespoonfuls of lukewarm water. Pour the flour on the pastry board, add a pinch of salt, and knead with warm water (the dough should not be too soft). Add the diluted yeast and continue to knead vigorously until the dough becomes elastic. Shape the dough into 6 even balls, then place them on a flat wooden board, lightly coated with flour. Cover with a cloth and keep in a warm place until the dough swells to twice its former size.

The dough is now ready to be punched down, made into disks approximately 10 inches in diameter, and used for *pizza* with any topping you wish and always drizzled with 1 tablespoon of extra virgin olive oil.

PIZZA NAPOLETANA (Pizza with Tomato, Garlic, and Basil)

SERVES 6

1½ cups peeled, seeded, and chopped tomatoes
2 garlic cloves, minced
½ cup extra virgin olive oil
12 basil leaves
Salt and pepper, to taste
Pizza dough (see above)

Preheat oven to maximum temperature.

Combine the tomatoes, the garlic, 2 tablespoons of the olive oil, salt and pepper to taste, and set aside. Make the dough.

When ready, punch each of the dough balls into a disk about 8 to 10 inches in diameter. Spread the sauce over the pastry disks. Shove each of the disks onto an edgeless shovel (*pala* in Italian) dusted with flour. Drizzle each *pizza* with 1 tablespoon of olive oil and shove it into a wood-burning oven with a brisk backward move: rotate the disks occasionally to allow for even cooking. Cook a few minutes and remove from the oven with the shovel. Place 2 basil leaves on each *pizza* as you remove it from the oven.

PIZZA MARINARA (Pizza with Tomato, Garlic, and Oregano)

SERVES 6

Follow instructions for *pizza napoletana* (page 59), but replace the basil with 1 teaspoon oregano, and add the oregano to the tomato mixture before baking.

PIZZA MARGHERITA (Pizza with Mozzarella, Tomato, and Basil)

Pizza Margherita was created in 1889 by *pizza* maker Raffaele Esposito as a tribute to the Queen of Italy, Margherita di Savoia, because its ingredients represent the colors of the Italian flag, red, white, and green.

SERVES 6
Pizza dough (see page 59)
1½ cups peeled, seeded, and chopped tomatoes
1 pound mozzarella, diced
½ cup extra virgin olive oil
12 basil leaves
Salt and pepper, to taste

Preheat oven to maximum temperature.

The procedure is the same as in basic *pizza* recipe. Spread the *mozzarella* over the tomatoes. Place 2 basil leaves on each *pizza* as you take it out of the oven and serve.

Note:
There is also a tomato-less version of this *pizza*, called *Margherita bianca*. If you add a few filleted and diced anchovies, it takes the name of *pizza alla romana*.

PIZZA QUATTRO STAGIONI (Four Seasons Pizza)

SERVES 6
1 pound cockles or littleneck clams
1 pound mussels
2 medium artichokes, chokes removed, thinly sliced, and placed in acidulated water
1½ cups peeled, seeded, and chopped tomatoes
2 garlic cloves, minced
Pinch of oregano
½ cup extra virgin olive oil
Salt and pepper, to taste
Pizza dough (see page 59)
24 pitted black olives
6 salted anchovy fillets, chopped up

Preheat oven to maximum temperature.

Steam the clams and the mussels (see recipe for *pizza alle vongole,* below). Sauté the artichokes, cut in julienne, and set aside.

Prepare the tomato sauce as in *pizza marinara.* Flatten the dough into 8-inch disks. Spread the prepared sauce on each disk of dough and then place in oven. Remove when done and place each ingredient (mussels, clams, artichokes, and olives with anchovies) into one of 4 different sections. Drizzle with the remaining oil and serve.

PIZZA ALLE VONGOLE (Pizza with Clams)

SERVES 6

> 3 tablespoons cockles or littlenecks (vongole veraci would be the preferred clam)
> 4 garlic cloves, crushed
> ½ cup extra virgin olive oil
> Pizza dough (see page 59)
> 1½ cups tomato sauce
> Pinch of peperoncino
> 1 tablespoon chopped parsley

Preheat oven to maximum temperature.

Sauté the clams with garlic and olive oil, with the pan covered. When they are all open, remove from heat, cool, then shell. Set the clams aside in their cooking water so they stay moist and hot.

Prepare the dough as in basic recipe. Flatten the dough into 8-inch disks, spread evenly with the tomato sauce, add the *peperoncino,* and bake. When the *pizza* is ready to take out of the oven, evenly distribute the shelled clams, sprinkle with olive oil and parsley, and serve.

Note:
For culinary drama, some clams can be left in their shells and placed on top of the *pizza.*

Variations:
Mussels can be used instead of clams.

Replace the clams with 1 pound of whitebait. Cook the whitebait as follows: Clean, rinse the fish, and let drain. Sauté garlic with 2 tablespoons of olive oil. When the garlic is golden brown, discard it. Add the whitebait, and remove from the heat. Set aside but keep warm.

CALZONE (Stuffed Pizza with Ricotta)

This is a type of pizza in which the dough is folded over and sealed, making a half-moon shape enclosing the filling.

    Pizza dough (see page 59)
    1 pound ricotta cheese
    ⅓ pound mozzarella, diced
    3 ounces salami, diced
    ¼ pound ham, diced
    2 tablespoons grated Parmigiano
    2 tablespoons grated pecorino cheese
    Salt and pepper, to taste
    1 egg
    2 tablespoons extra virgin olive oil

Preheat oven to maximum temperature.

Prepare the dough as in basic recipe and divide into 6 equal balls. Sieve the *ricotta,* letting it fall into a bowl, and mix together the *mozzarella,* salami, ham, and grated cheeses, a little salt, and a pinch of pepper.

Stretch each of the dough balls with your hands (lightly coated with oil) and make a disk 10 inches in diameter.

Cover half the dough with the previously prepared mix, and fold the other half over. Pinch the edges of the 2 halves together and seal thoroughly. Coat with the beaten egg and the oil and bake in a wood-burning oven until it becomes golden. Let it rest for a few minutes and serve.

CALZONE FRITTO (Bite-Size Fried Calzone)

Use the same ingredients and amounts as in the basic *calzone* recipe, but form the dough into 4-inch disks. Fry until they are golden brown. They are served hot either as an *antipasto* or over a very good strained tomato sauce.

FOCACCIA (Focaccia)

This is a type of savory bread that may have various toppings such as onion, rosemary, sage, or simply olive oil. *Focaccia* is generally baked in a flat sheet pan and then served cut in various sizes and shapes.

SERVES 6
    Pizza dough (see page 59)
    6 tablespoons extra virgin olive oil
    1 teaspoon coarse salt

Preheat oven to 450°F. Prepare the dough as in the basic *pizza* recipe. In a well-greased baking pan, flatten out the dough to ½ inch thickness. Drizzle generously with oil, sprinkle with coarse salt, and bake for about 30 minutes, until it is golden brown. *Focaccia* is best eaten warm, but it must rest a little when out of the oven.

PIADINA (Piadina)

This is a specialty from the Romagna region. Made of a disk of unleavened dough that can be substituted for bread, it can be eaten with a soft cheese (*squaquarone*) or with either *prosciutto* or ham. It is served warm. *Piadina* is traditionally cooked on a flat cast-iron pan called a *testo,* on a lively flame.

MAKES 6
   3½ cups all-purpose flour
   1 ounce lard, very finely chopped
   ½ teaspoon baking soda
   Salt, to taste

Pour the flour on the pastry board, forming a cone with a cavity on the top (*fontana* in Italian, that is, like a well). Add the lard and the baking soda and knead the dough, using just enough lukewarm salted water (not hot) so as to obtain a rather firm dough. Knead vigorously for 10 minutes and then divide the dough into 6 pieces to be stretched out by hand to make each *piadina* about 8 inches in diameter. Heat up the *testo* and lay on a disk of dough (do not brush with oil). Prick the top with a fork and repeat when you turn the *piadina* over. Let the *piadina* cook well on 1 side and then turn over; when you notice little charred bubbles forming on the disk, the dough is ready. Continue cooking several disks of *piadina* this way, placing the ones that are ready in a pile so that they keep warm. Serve *piadina* either plain instead of bread or folded over with a filling such as cheese, *prosciutto, mortadella,* or a cooked green vegetable such as chicory or broccoli di rape.

Note:
Piadina can also be roasted in a cast-iron pan.

TORTE SALATE E SFORMATI
Savory Pies and Molds

TORTE SALATE (Savory Pies)

Savory pies are common all over Italy and like many other preparations they developed as a way to use leftover foods. The dough used for the crust is very similar throughout Italy, though certain types of savory pies are made without a crust.

TORTINO DI CICCIOLI (Ciccioli Pie)

Ciccioli are the solid particles that are left when one melts lard or bacon that has been pressed through a potato ricer to remove excess fat. When melting, lard or bacon should always be chopped.

SERVES 6

3½ cups all-purpose flour
1 ounce brewer's yeast
Salt, to taste
8 ounces butter, at room temperature
3 eggs
6 ounces fresh ciccioli

Make a cone of flour on the pastry board with a cavity on the top. Dissolve the yeast in a few tablespoonfuls of lukewarm water, pour into the cavity, and add a pinch of salt, the butter, the eggs, and half of the *ciccioli*. Salt to taste. Knead the ingredients together until the dough is no longer sticky, adding more flour if necessary.

Preheat the oven to 400°F.

Butter an 8-inch baking pan with high sides, stretch out the dough into the pan until it covers the bottom and the sides, then sprinkle with the remaining *ciccioli*. Cover and set in a warm place until risen.

When ready to bake, bake for 30 minutes, or until a golden brown crust has formed on top.

TORTA PASQUALINA (Savory Artichoke Pie)

SERVES 6

7 cups all-purpose flour
6 tablespoons extra virgin olive oil
Salt, to taste
Water, as needed
12 artichokes
1 small onion, chopped
2 tablespoons chopped parsley
1 cup extra virgin olive oil (use as much as needed)
6 tablespoons grated Parmigiano
1 pound ricotta cheese
9 eggs
Salt and pepper, to taste
4 tablespoons butter, flaked

Preheat the oven to 400°F. Make a soft dough with the flour, 6 tablespoons oil, a pinch of salt, and cold water. Knead well until the dough becomes elastic. Divide the dough into 16 balls the size of an egg, keeping each one in a wet cloth, and set aside.

Meanwhile, prepare the stuffing.

Wash and trim the artichokes, remove the chokes, and cut them into thin slices. Sauté the onion and parsley in 4 tablespoons oil, add the artichokes, and cook for 15 minutes. Let cool. Combine 5 tablespoons *Parmigiano* and the *ricotta* with 3 eggs, add salt and pepper, and mix in the sautéed artichokes. Set aside.

Flatten each piece of dough, one at a time, making each a very thin disk, larger than the baking pan (preferably 10-inch round) you are going to use. Place the first circle of dough in the greased baking pan, making sure the dough is about ½ inch wider than the pan, and brush the surface with oil. Place another disk over it and repeat until you have used 8 disks. Pour the stuffing over this and make 6 small cavities in a circle equidistant from one another. Put a raw egg into each cavity and sprinkle each with salt, pepper, *Parmigiano,* and butter flakes. Cover with all the remaining stretched disks of dough, each brushed with oil. Pinch the borders and trim the excess dough. Prick the top of the pie in a few places and then brush with oil. Bake for about 1 hour, or until golden brown. Let cool and serve at room temperature.

Note:

Torta pasqualina can be made with other vegetables instead of artichokes.

ERBAZZONE SCARPAZZONE (Savory Pie with Chard)

This savory pie has a rich double crust, and is most often filled with greens, eggs, or cheese.

SERVES 6

3½ cups all-purpose flour
1 ounce lard, chopped
3 tablespoons extra virgin olive oil
Salt, to taste
2 ounces lard or pancetta
2 tablespoons chopped parsley
1 garlic clove
1 small onion
2 pounds chard leaves
2 eggs
Salt and pepper, to taste
2 tablespoons extra virgin olive oil
6 tablespoons grated Parmigiano

Knead the flour with 1 ounce lard, the 3 tablespoons of oil, warm water, and a pinch of salt to have a rather stiff dough. Knead for about 10 minutes, wrap in a sheet of wax paper, and keep in a cool place for about 1 hour.

Preheat the oven to 400°F. Make a *battuto* with 2 ounces lard, parsley, garlic, and onion. Clean, wash, and drain the chard well and dry thoroughly. Chop the chard very fine. Lightly sauté the *battuto*, and when the lard has melted, add the chard and cook for about 5 minutes. Remove from the heat, put in a bowl, and let cool. Add the eggs and a pinch of salt and pepper. Lightly coat with olive oil a 12-inch springform pan with high sides.

Split the dough into 2 balls, one twice the size of the other. Roll out the bigger ball with a rolling pin and make a disk large enough to line the pan (bottom and sides). Arrange the chard in layers, sprinkling each layer with grated cheese, using all the chard and all the cheese. Roll out the remaining batch of dough, making a disk larger than the diameter of the baking pan. Roll this disk around the rolling pin and unroll it over the chard. Since the top disk is larger than the baking pan, it will have a bumpy surface. Pinch the edges of the 2 disks of dough together, drizzle with a little olive oil, and bake for 40 minutes, or until it is golden brown. *Scarpazzone* can be served either hot or at room temperature.

Note:
In Emilia, lard is sometimes used instead of oil to dot the dough.

TORTINO DI CARCIOFI (Artichoke Pie)

SERVES 4

> 4 artichokes
> All-purpose flour
> 4 tablespoons extra virgin olive oil
> 8 eggs
> Salt and pepper, to taste
> 4 tablespoons grated Parmigiano

Preheat the oven to 375°F. Wash, trim, remove the chokes, and cut the artichokes into quarters. Coat with flour and fry them in the oil in a large skillet over high heat, until browned. Drain off the excess fat and set aside. In a bowl, beat the eggs with salt, pepper, and *Parmigiano* and mix in the artichokes. Grease an 8-inch pie pan and pour in the mixture. Bake for about 20 minutes, or until it has reached the desired doneness (prick it with a fork—when the fork comes out dry it is done, but you may like it more cooked, so use your judgment).

TORTINO DI FUNGHI (Mushroom Pie)

SERVES 4

> 4 slices white bread
> 1 cup milk
> 1 garlic clove, chopped
> 5 tablespoons extra virgin olive oil
> 1 pound mushrooms, sliced
> ½ cup seeded, peeled, and chopped tomatoes
> 6 eggs
> 2 tablespoons grated Parmigiano
> Pinch of oregano
> Salt and pepper, to taste

Preheat the oven to 350°F. Remove and discard the crusts of the bread and moisten it with milk. In a skillet, sauté the garlic with oil, stir in the mushrooms, cook until tender, and then add the tomatoes. Cook for 2 more minutes. Let cool. Whip the eggs, mix in the *Parmigiano* and the moist bread, and combine with two thirds of the sautéed mushrooms and tomatoes. Put this mixture in a buttered baking dish and top with a layer of the remaining mushrooms. Sprinkle with oregano, salt, and pepper. Bake for about 20 minutes, or until a thin crust has formed on top.

SFORMATI (Molds)

A mold is an attractive dish usually made with vegetables, though it can also be made with meat, fish, or many leftovers. *Sformato* should not be confused with soufflé. For more elaborate presentations, various types of sauces (tomato sauce, chicken liver, or beef *ragù,* for example) may be poured in the center of the finished *sformato.*

The Mold

In order to cook any kind of *sformato* you need a shallow, smooth-walled round mold. The mold should have a capacity of 1½ to 2 quarts. Butter the mold well, especially at the bottom, before pouring in the mixture. Small molds, for individual servings, may also be used.

Baking in a Mold

Any good *sformato* should be cooked in a *bagnomaria* (bain-marie), either on the stove or in the oven; in the latter case, it is advisable to cover the *sformato* with aluminum foil halfway through the cooking process, to prevent the surface from drying.

Sformato is ready when firm (but not hard) to the touch. Remove it from the bain-marie, let stand for about 5 minutes, remove from mold, and serve.

Any kind of mild-flavored green can be used to make a *sformato*. The greens must be quite dry; otherwise the *sformato* will turn out too soft (longer cooking cannot correct this). The chopped texture can vary from very fine to rather coarse.

SFORMATO DI VERDURE (Vegetable Mold)

SERVES 8

> 6 ounces green beans
> 1 small bunch asparagus tips
> 3 artichokes, quartered
> 1 small cauliflower
> 2 carrots
> 2 small potatoes
> 2 ounces butter
> Salt and pepper, to taste
> 2 eggs
> 6 tablespoons grated Parmigiano
> ½ pound sliced prosciutto

Preheat the oven to 375°F. Wash and trim all the vegetables. Boil all the vegetables and the potatoes, separately, in boiling salted water to a crunchy consistency. Coarsely cut up all the vegetables and the potatoes. In a large casserole melt the butter. When brown, add the vegetables and the potatoes, add salt and pepper to taste, and cook for 3 minutes. Remove from the heat and let cool. Put the vegetables in a blender and blend to a coarse consistency. Whip the eggs into the vegetable mixture and add the *Parmigiano*.

Line a 2-quart mold with the *prosciutto* slices, pour in the vegetable mix, smooth the surface, and cook in a bain-marie in the oven for 30 minutes, or until firm to the touch. Remove from the oven and serve in its mold.

Notes:
This *sformato* can be served as an accompaniment to meat or fish preparations.

It can also be baked in individual ramekins.

SFORMATO DI FORMAGGIO (Cheese Mold)

SERVES 6
1 cup béchamel sauce (see page 27)
¼ pound mild cheese, diced
¼ pound Parmigiano, grated
1 ounce butter
4 eggs, separated
Salt and pepper, to taste

Preheat the oven to 400°F. While the béchamel is still hot, blend in the 2 cheeses. Let cool. Whip the egg yolks in a bowl, and separately whip the egg whites until stiff but not dry. Fold the egg yolks and egg whites into the béchamel. Adjust for salt and pepper. Pour into a buttered 8-inch mold and bake in a bain-marie in the oven for about 1 hour, or until firm.

SFORMATO DI PORRI IN SALSA DI PATATE (Leek Mold in Potato Sauce)

SERVES 6
4½ pounds leeks
¾ pound ricotta cheese
2 eggs
¼ cup grated Parmigiano
Pinch of nutmeg
Salt, to taste
1¼ cups extra virgin olive oil
1 small onion, chopped
3 medium potatoes, thinly sliced
1 ladleful vegetable broth
Pinch of saffron
Dash of heavy cream

Preheat the oven to 400°F. Remove the green part of the leeks and wash well. Slice the leeks and cook them in boiling water for 20 minutes, or until tender. Remove from the heat and let cool. Combine the *ricotta,* eggs, *Parmigiano,* and the nutmeg. Drain the leeks and add them to the ricotta mix, add salt, then blend in a food processor, dripping in 1 cup of the olive oil until smooth. Pour into a greased 2-quart baking dish; bake for 20 minutes. Then cover the dish with aluminum foil so that the top of the mold will not brown, and bake for another 20 minutes, or until firm. Check doneness with a toothpick—the toothpick should come out clean. *Sformato* can be made in a big round mold or in a number of small individual molds.

For the sauce, slowly sauté the onion in the remaining ¼ cup of oil. When brown, add the thinly sliced potatoes, a ladleful of broth, and salt. Cook for 10 minutes. Add the saffron diluted in a little boiling water, mix, and continue cooking until the potatoes are quite tender. Put the cooked potatoes into a blender to liquefy and then put it back on the heat. If the sauce is too thick, dilute it with a little milk or cream over very low heat (do not boil). The sauce is done when it has reached a creamy consistency. Turn the mold upside down on a platter and serve with the sauce on the side.

IL FRITTO E LE FRITTELLE
Fried Food and Fritters

One of the best-known and most appreciated Italian culinary specialties is an assortment of fried food, although less popular today in home kitchens because of the time it takes to prepare. *Il fritto*, however, is one of the basics of Italian regional cuisine and includes not only the traditional *fritto misto*, which is a platter with a wide variety of fried food, but also various other fritters, which are listed in this chapter.

Successful frying entails cutting, trimming, or shaping the food to be fried into the same form and size so that the cooking is done evenly. The food to be fried should always be dry. Some items are floured so as to remove any trace of humidity, which would prevent a crust from forming and cause the fried food to absorb oil.

Most food can be simply floured and fried. If a thicker crust is desired, it should be dipped in beaten egg and then, if desired, in breadcrumbs. Some foods may also be dipped in a batter; it can add flavor and enclose the flavor of the food being fried. Batter may also be a binding agent when frying food that is rather small and crumbly such as small fish or thinly sliced vegetables. Fillets and larger fish can be breaded. While some vegetables can be boiled first, fish must always be raw before it is fried.

Frying should be done in an iron pan, but a deep fryer is an acceptable alternative. When frying, do not crowd the pan; fry the food (floured, breaded, or dipped in batter) in the oil a few pieces at a time, so that they can be carefully watched and the temperature of the oil remains constant. Turn the pieces 2 or 3 times so that they fry evenly. If it is necessary to add more oil while frying, make sure to wait until it reaches the right temperature before continuing.

Once the fried food is ready, remove it with a slotted spoon and set it on paper towels to drain off the excess fat, then store in a warm, dry place, uncovered, until serving time. Never cover fried food or it will become soggy.

PASTELLA (The Batter)

A good batter (*pastella*) can improve the taste of fried food as well as increase its volume. It can also make it look more appetizing. Small and crumbly food that falls apart easily is more suitable for frying in batter. A soft batter can be prepared as follows.

2 tablespoons all-purpose flour
1 cup lukewarm water, or as much as needed
2 tablespoons extra virgin olive oil
Salt
2 egg whites, beaten stiff

Whisk the flour into the water quickly, so as not to form lumps, bring to a simmer, and cook for 20 minutes. Mix in the oil and salt, remove from the heat, and let cool. Just before using, fold in the beaten egg whites. Dip the pieces to be fried, one at a time.

The Pan

Ideally the pan should be made of light iron and be rather deep, so that it holds a lot of oil. It doesn't need to be very wide because it is better to fry a few pieces at a time. An iron pan should never be washed but should be wiped out with paper towels after each use. Occasionally it should be rubbed with salt, then wiped again with paper towels. An electric frying pan can also produce excellent results, because it cooks evenly and the temperature can be regulated with a thermometer.

The Frying Oil

Most of the frying in an Italian home is done with olive oil. There should always be plenty of olive oil in the pan. The temperature of the oil is very important. If a thermometer is not handy, the frying point can be determined by putting a piece of bread into the oil when hot; when bubbles begin to form around it, the oil is ready for frying.

To ensure thorough cooking and avoid burning, the temperature of the oil must remain constant. It should be lower for vegetables containing a lot of water. For fish and bigger-sized pieces of meat, a low temperature is advisable because these take a longer time to cook. Food that has previously been cooked (such as vegetables and croquettes) should be fried at a medium-high temperature. The oil should be very hot for frying small fish, cheese, and any kind of food in small or thin pieces. If pieces of food or batter collect in the bottom of the pan and turn black, filter or change the oil and clean out the pan with paper towels before continuing.

Raw Frying

This is often used for fish. Cut the fish fillets into the desired size just before frying, dry, flour, and fry in olive oil. The same procedure applies to small fish: clean, dry, flour, and fry.

Batter Frying

This is often used for vegetables. Parboil the vegetables, drain, and let cool. Cut into the desired shapes, pat dry, flour, and coat with batter. Fry in very hot oil. Fish must always be raw if it is to be fried, whether or not in batter.

Bread Frying

This is used for both meat and fish. Breadcrumbs should be made from bread that is not too stale; do not use breadcrumbs that have been oven-dried. The breadcrumbs should be made out of 2 to 3 day-old white bread. If the crumbs are too dry, you can sprinkle them with a little water and rub them between your hands to moisten them evenly. If you wish, you can add a small amount of grated *Parmigiano* to the breadcrumbs.

Dry the meat or fish thoroughly, then dredge lightly with flour, shaking to remove excess. Once coated with flour, the food must be soaked in beaten, unseasoned egg. Some chefs add a teaspoon of oil to the egg to get a crisper crust. When well coated with the egg, cover the food thoroughly with breadcrumbs, pressing with the palm of your hand so that the crumbs adhere well. Do not dip in the egg a second time: The crust would be too thick and the meat would not cook properly.

Either oil or butter can be used for frying—although the crust will turn out tastier using oil, or a mixture of both. Heat the fat in a shallow frying pan and cook the breaded food over medium heat, turning once, so both sides are golden brown. Add salt and pepper to taste after frying.

FRITTO MISTO (Mixed Fried Food)

Speed is of utmost importance in a *fritto misto*, and the amount will vary according to the number of people to be served. A good rule of thumb is always to use one piece of each kind of food for each person. Remember, for speed's sake you can also limit the types of food to include in *fritto misto* and some preparation can be done in advance. The recipes can also vary according to seasonal food availability.

SERVES 6

Meats
6 ounces veal sweetbreads
6 ounces veal brains
6 ounces veal marrow from the spine
6 pair frog's legs, boned

Vegetables
1 sliced eggplant, salted and weighted down, then cut into thick strips
   2 inches long
2 zucchini, cut into thick strips 2 inches long
6 whole zucchini blossoms
6 mushrooms

All-purpose flour, for coating
6 eggs, beaten
1¼ cups breadcrumbs

Chicken Dumplings

6 ounces cooked chicken
1 teaspoon chopped parsley
4 tablespoons breadcrumbs
1 egg

Semolina

2 cups milk
1 teaspoon sugar
1 ounce butter
1¾ cups semolina flour

Olive oil, for frying
Salt, to taste

Clean the meats, vegetables, and frog's legs. Cut the meats into 1-inch pieces. Cut the eggplant and zucchini into thick strips. Keep the zucchini blossoms and mushrooms whole. Flour and dip each piece into the beaten eggs, coat with breadcrumbs, pat the food to get rid of excess crumbs, and set aside.

To make the chicken dumplings, mix the chicken with the parsley, 4 tablespoons of breadcrumbs, and 1 egg. Combine the ingredients in a food processor to get a smooth mixture. Shape into small, slightly elongated, and flat dumplings. Flour, dip in egg, coat with breadcrumbs, and set aside.

For the *semolina*, bring 1 cup of milk and 1 cup of water to a boil with the sugar and butter, gradually sprinkle in *semolina* flour, and cook, while stirring, for 40 minutes, adding more milk if necessary, until cooked. Pour and spread evenly into a flat pan and let cool. Cut the hardened *semolina* into the desired uniform shapes (not too big). Flour, dip in egg, coat with breadcrumbs, and set aside.

Fry each piece of food separately, as they require different cooking times. When golden brown on both sides remove from the frying pan and place on paper towels. When all the frying is finished, arrange the various pieces of food on a serving platter. Salt to taste. Serve very hot.

Note:
To keep hot just place serving tray in a warm area such as in the oven at very low heat (200°F), but never cover fried food or it will get soggy.

CHIZZE (Chizze)

Chizze are small packets of rich dough filled with cheese and fried. They are like hors d'ouevres and are served on a platter.

3½ cups all-purpose flour
Salt, to taste

½ ounce active dry yeast
2 tablespoons strutto or finely chopped lard
1 pound soft cheese, such as ricotta, mascarpone, or robiola
5 ounces butter
Olive oil, for frying

Knead the flour with a pinch of salt. Add the yeast, previously diluted in lukewarm water, *strutto* or lard, and enough lukewarm water (or milk if you wish) and knead until you obtain a rather firm dough. Let the dough rest, covered with a cloth, for 30 minutes.

Roll out the dough with a rolling pin to about ⅛ inch thick. Cut the dough into rectangles 3 by 2 inches. Place a dollop of the cheese in the center of one side together with a curl of butter, fold the dough over the stuffing, dampen the edges, and press the dough firmly around the stuffing to seal the little packets well (if not tightly sealed, the *chizze* will open when frying). Repeat until there is no dough or cheese left.

Deep-fry the *chizze* in olive oil. The frying oil should not be too hot, to allow the dough to cook inside. As they are ready, remove with a skimmer, place on paper towels, and keep in the front of the oven with the door open, set at low temperature so they may keep warm and dry a little.

CHISOLINI (Dough Puffs)

This is a rich, leavened dough that is folded and rolled to create many layers that are then cut into shapes and fried. These can be served with various accompaniments such as *Parmigiano, prosciutto,* salami, and so on. They can also be eaten for breakfast with coffee and milk.

3½ cups all-purpose flour
1 ounce active dry yeast
1 teaspoon salt
2 ounces butter, softened and cut into pieces
1 cup lukewarm milk
Olive oil, for frying

On the pastry board, make a cone of flour with a cavity (*fontana*) on top. Add the yeast, previously diluted in lukewarm water, salt, and butter in the center of the *fontana* and start to knead with enough lukewarm milk to obtain a rather smooth and soft dough. Let the dough rest for 30 minutes.

When ready, roll the dough out with a rolling pin, fold the dough in quarters, then roll out the dough again, and fold it again, repeating the process a total of 5 times. Finally roll the dough out ¼ inch thick and cut into shapes 4 inches long by 2 inches wide (size can be altered if desired.) Always keep the dough, before and after cutting, well floured, so the pieces do not stick to one another.

When you have finished cutting all the dough, heat the vegetable oil in a deep frying pan and start frying the pieces of dough. They will puff up and be an even, golden color. Drain, remove the excess fat by placing on paper towels, and serve hot.

CARCIOFI ALLA GIUDEA (Deep-Fried Artichokes)

This is a very old recipe named *alla giudea* because it was typically made in the Jewish ghetto of Rome.

SERVES 4

    8 tender artichokes
    Juice of 1 lemon
    Salt and pepper, to taste
    2 cups olive oil for frying

Remove the outer leaves of the artichokes and leave about 2 inches or more of stem. Trim off the hard part of the leaves and peel the stem with a sharp knife. Open the leaves and remove the choke from the center. Place in cold water and lemon juice, to avoid discoloration, until ready to cook.

Drain and dry the artichokes and press them upside down until the leaves open up completely. Salt and pepper the inside of the artichokes. Heat the olive oil in a deep terra-cotta or iron pot and fry the artichokes for 18 minutes over medium-high heat, with the pot covered. Remove from the frying pan and place on paper towels to drain excess fat and let cool. Reheat the same oil, this time making sure it is very hot. Place the artichokes in the oil, with the stems up, and press down. Cook until they open up like a sunflower and are very crisp. Remove from the oil, pat dry, and serve hot.

SUPPLI DI RISO (Rice Balls)

MAKES 32

    4 tablespoons butter
    1 pound long-grain rice
    6 cups chicken broth (see page 124), hot
    5 tablespoons grated Parmigiano
    3 ounces mozzarella, diced
    3 ounces prosciutto, diced
    2 tablespoons chopped parsley
    1 egg, beaten
    Pinch of nutmeg
    Salt and pepper, to taste
    1 cup all-purpose flour

3 eggs, beaten
1 cup breadcrumbs
Olive oil, for frying

Melt the butter in a skillet, add the rice, and toast for 1 minute. Add the hot broth slowly, stirring frequently. The rice should be done in 15 minutes. When ready, remove from the heat, mix in half of the *Parmigiano,* and lay the rice out on a flat pan to cool.

Prepare the stuffing. Mix the *mozzarella* and *prosciutto,* the rest of the *Parmigiano,* the parsley, 1 egg, the nutmeg, salt, and pepper. With slightly damp hands, take a handful of rice in one hand and a pinch of stuffing with the other. Push the stuffing into the middle of the rice. Squeeze the rice all around the stuffing and mold it into an egg shape. When you have used up all of the mix, flour the balls, dip in beaten eggs, and roll them in breadcrumbs. Fry in very hot oil until golden brown, remove excess oil, and serve immediately.

Note:
The size of the rice balls can be from ½ ounce to 1 ounce each.

CRISPEDDI (Anchovy and Dill Fritters)

1 ounce brewer's yeast
7 cups all-purpose flour
2 tablespoons extra virgin olive oil
30 to 40 salted anchovy fillets
2 bunches dill
Olive oil, for frying
Salt and pepper, to taste

Dissolve the yeast in lukewarm water and mix in about ¾ cup flour until you get a soft mixture. Cover the dough and put in a warm place to rise for about 1 hour. When the dough has doubled in size, punch it down and knead in the oil, the remaining flour, and enough warm water to make a soft dough similar to bread dough. Shape the dough into a ball, cut a cross on the top with a sharp knife, and leave, covered, in a warm place until the dough has doubled in size. Knead it again briefly and then cut it into pieces the size of walnuts. Stuff each piece of dough with an anchovy fillet and a sprig of dill and seal well.

Flour the dough pieces and place the balls on a clean, floured pan in a warm place for about 30 minutes. Heat the oil, but not to the boiling point. Fry the balls, turning them often so that they expand and brown evenly on all sides. Get rid of excess fat by placing the *crispeddi* on paper towels. Add salt and pepper and serve hot.

BACCALÀ FRITTO (Batter-Fried Salt Cod)

SERVES 4

2 pounds salt cod
Batter, but without egg white (see page 71)
Olive oil, for frying
Salt and pepper, to taste

Let the salt cod soak in cold water for 2 to 3 days, changing the water frequently. Cut into even 1-inch rectangular pieces, removing any fins or bones. Dry well.

Prepare the batter as on page 72, but without the egg white. Coat the cod in the batter and fry in an iron pan with plenty of hot olive oil (but not deep-fried). Fry until golden brown and crispy. Place on paper towels to get rid of the excess fat. Add salt and pepper to taste and serve hot.

ACCIUGHE IN PASTELLA (Batter-Fried Anchovies)

1 pound fresh anchovies, headless, boned, and cleaned
½ cup white wine
1¾ cups all-purpose flour
3 egg whites
Olive oil, for frying
Salt, to taste

Prepare the anchovies, wash, pat dry, and leave them split open on a flat pan. Bring the wine to a simmer and whisk in the flour. Cook for 20 minutes. Remove the batter from the heat and let cool. Beat the egg whites until stiff but not dry. Fold the egg whites into the batter just before frying. Dip the anchovies in the batter and fry in plenty of hot oil, using a cast-iron pan. When golden brown, remove from frying pan and place on absorbent paper to get rid of excess fat. Arrange on a serving platter, salt to taste, and serve hot.

CIECHE FRITTE (Fried Baby Eels)

SERVES 8

1 cup olive oil
6 garlic cloves (do not peel)
Peperoncino, to taste
1 pound baby eels
Salt, to taste

This is an example of an uncoated food fried in oil. Warm the oil in a small terra-cotta pot (preferably one for each person), add garlic and *peperoncino,* and brown. Get the oil very hot, throw the baby eels (previously washed, rinsed, and patted dry) into the hot oil, toss and mix the *cieche* gently, and remove from the heat. Adjust salt and serve in the same pot.

CALAMARI FRITTI (Fried Squid)

SERVES 4

1 pound baby squid
1¾ cups all-purpose flour
2 cups olive oil, for frying
Salt, to taste
2 lemons

Clean, wash, and pat dry the squid. Cut them crosswise into strips to form small rings, leaving the tentacles whole. Make sure they are fairly dry. Roll them in flour and fry in hot oil until golden. Place on paper towels to get rid of excess fat. Place on a serving platter, add salt, and serve, garnished with lemon wedges.

FRITTELLE DI BIANCHETTI (Whitebait Fritters)

1 pound whitebait
2 cups water
3½ cups all-purpose flour
1 ounce active dry yeast
1 tablespoon chopped parsley
4 tablespoons extra virgin olive oil
2 garlic cloves
Salt, to taste

Wash the whitebait, pat dry, and set aside. Make a batter with water, flour, and yeast and let it rise for 1 hour.

When dough has doubled in size, mix the parsley into it. Now combine the white-bait with the batter and mix well. Heat the oil with the garlic. Remove the garlic when brown. When the oil is very hot, take a spoonful of the batter with the fish and fry un-til golden brown. Place on paper towels to get rid of excess fat, adjust the salt, and serve very hot.

UOVA E FRITTATE
Eggs and Omelets

Eggs are particularly suitable for making simple as well as sophisticated antipasti. Boiled eggs may be sliced or cut into wedges and placed on a dish, alternating thin slices of tomato, *mozzarella,* and scallion rings drizzled with extra virgin olive oil. Boiled eggs may also be served with anchovy fillets, capers, pitted green or black olives, chunks of tuna fish in oil, fresh lettuce leaves, celery strips, and peppers preserved in oil.

Another popular way to prepare boiled eggs is to cut them in half, remove the yolks, sieve them together with either tuna in oil or liver pâté, anchovies, capers, and parsley or basil, and fill the whites of the eggs with this stuffing.

Frittata, a savory, flat omelet, is made with beaten eggs mixed with vegetables or other ingredients and cooked in a frying pan. Using no more than six medium-size eggs and a frying pan about 10 inches in diameter will yield a quick cooking process and good results.

Preparing a *frittata* is simple. The most difficult part is turning it. The eggs should be beaten just enough to mix the yolks with the whites. As an *antipasto, frittata* is always prepared with vegetables such as asparagus, artichokes, peppers, onions, mushrooms, and tomatoes, cheese cut into small pieces, or meat such as liver, sweetbreads, kidneys, and sausages. It is served either hot or at room temperature.

The Pan

An aluminum pan with a heavy bottom is ideal for cooking *frittata* so that the temperature of the pan can be easily controlled. The bottom must be completely flat—neither convex nor concave—and quite smooth. It must also be of the proper size; it is preferable to use a slightly larger pan than a smaller one. If the pan is too small for the number of eggs used, the *frittata* will be thick and will consequently take longer to cook, and the result will be too heavy.

For a *frittata* with 3 eggs (and no other ingredients) the frying pan should be 8 inches in diameter. It is best to have a frying pan that is used exclusively for *frittata*. Do not wash it after using, but simply clean it with absorbent paper. Every so often, it is a good idea to clean it thoroughly; the best way to do so is to heat the pan on a flame, rub it with coarse salt, and then wipe it with paper towels.

Beating the Eggs

The eggs, always at room temperature, should be broken into a bowl and beaten with a fork shortly before cooking. They must be beaten just long enough to mix the yolks with the whites, or they will get foamy, thus making the *frittata* heavier. A spoonful of milk or cream may also be added.

Cooking Procedure

You may use either oil or butter: for 3 eggs you will need 2 tablespoons extra virgin olive oil or 1 tablespoon butter. Place the fat in the frying pan and turn the heat on. Break the eggs into a bowl and beat them. When the butter is frothy or the oil is hot (it is important that the fat be hot, otherwise it will mix with the beaten eggs rather than cook them), pour the eggs into the frying pan. Briskly mix the eggs with a wooden spoon, gently bringing the cooked parts to the center. Repeat until the eggs acquire an even, semi-solid texture.

Spread the eggs evenly on the bottom of the frying pan and let cook, shaking the frying pan now and then to prevent the *frittata* from sticking to the bottom. Then flip or turn the *frittata* over to cook the other side. Use a plate, or anything flat that covers the pan, and turn the pan upside down with a very fast movement. Slide the *frittata* back into the pan. Fry as long as necessary to allow it to cook through, but still be moist. Remove from the heat and serve immediately. The thinner the *frittata,* the better it will taste.

How to Serve a Frittata

Generally, *frittata* is served hot for breakfast or lunch, as a second course, or as a light snack. *Frittata* leftovers can also be used in sandwiches or cut into strips and served as part of a country-style *antipasto.*

As a rule, the *frittata* is made with 3 eggs per person, while the additions should not exceed one-third of the volume of the eggs.

FRITTATA DI CIPOLLE (Frittata with Onions)

SERVES 2

Sauté 1 julienned onion in 2 tablespoons butter. Do so slowly over low heat so that the onions get golden brown and not crispy. Let cool. Mix with 6 eggs and cook as described above.

ROGNOSA (Frittata with Cured Meats)

SERVES 2

This is a specialty from Piedmont, probably created to use the leftover bits of cured meats too small to cut and serve as cold cuts but large enough for *frittata*.

Skin and mince 3 ounces of *salam d'la duja* (see page 43). Mix 6 eggs with 3 tablespoons grated *Parmigiano* and salt and pepper to taste. Heat 2 tablespoons butter and 2 tablespoons extra virgin olive oil in a large frying pan and fry the salami. Add the egg mix and cook the *frittata* as described on page 81. The result should be ¾ inch thick and tender. Various types of leftovers may be used for this preparation.

FRITTATA CON ZUCCHINE (Zucchini Frittata)

SERVES 2

Wash, dice, and sauté small zucchini until golden brown. Place on paper towels to get rid of excess fat and set aside. Mix the fried zucchini and 6 eggs in a large bowl. Make a *frittata* as described on page 81.

You can add some sautéed onion and/or grated *Parmigiano*.

FRITTATA CON CARCIOFI (Artichoke Frittata)

SERVES 2

Remove the hard leaves with spiny tips and the chokes from 2 artichokes. Slice the tender leaves and bottoms very thin and place in lemon water. Remove from the water, dry, and sauté the artichokes until they are tender. Set aside. Mix the artichokes with 6 eggs and make a *frittata* as described on page 81.

FRITTATA CON LE RANE (Frittata with Frog's Legs)

SERVES 2

Use 6 small-sized frog's legs and poach them first in broth for 5 to 7 minutes. Remove meat from bone, flour and sauté lightly in butter, and set aside. Mix frog's legs and 6 eggs and make a *frittata* as described on page 81.

FRITTATA CON FIORI DI ZUCCA (Zucchini Blossom Frittata)

SERVES 2

Clean 6 zucchini blossoms, cut into strips, and sauté in oil with a few tablespoons of warm water. When cooked, drain and set aside. Beat 6 eggs, add 2 tablespoons chopped parsley, salt and pepper to taste, and the zucchini blossoms, and make the *frittata* as described on page 81.

UOVA AL TARTUFO BIANCO (Eggs with White Truffle)

SERVES 4

12 eggs
Salt and pepper, to taste
3 tablespoons grated Parmigiano
1 ounce butter
4 tablespoons extra virgin olive oil
1 white truffle

Beat the eggs in a bowl and add salt, pepper, and *Parmigiano*. Brown the butter and oil in a frying pan, pour in the egg mixture, and stir. Lightly scramble the egg, keeping it soft, and add salt and pepper to taste. Dish it out and serve with shavings of white truffle.

UOVA FRITTE CON POLENTA E TARTUFI
(Fried Eggs with Polenta and Truffles)

SERVES 4

8 slices yellow cornmeal polenta
1 ounce butter
4 tablespoons extra virgin olive oil
8 eggs
Salt and pepper, to taste
1 white truffle (1 ounce)

Make the *polenta* (pages 175–76), let cool, and cut into eight ½-inch-thick slices. Grill the *polenta* slices and place in a serving dish.

Brown the butter and oil in a frying pan, then fry the eggs two at a time. Slide 2 eggs onto each serving of *polenta,* add salt and pepper, then cover with plenty of white truffle shavings. Serve immediately.

UOVA AFFOGATE COL POMODORO (IN PURGATORIO)
(Poached Eggs with Tomato)

SERVES 4

> 1 *medium onion*
> 2 *garlic cloves*
> 2 *tablespoons extra virgin olive oil*
> 1 *pound tomatoes, peeled, seeded, and chopped*
> 1 *cup water*
> *Salt and pepper, to taste*
> 8 *eggs*
> 8 *basil leaves*

Use a casserole large enough to poach 8 eggs (at least 16 inches). Sauté the onion and garlic, and remove the garlic when brown. Add the tomatoes and simmer for 15 minutes. Add the water to get a very light, fairly liquid tomato sauce. Add salt and pepper. Bring to a simmer; add the eggs, whole, into the sauce, one at a time. When all the eggs have been added, cover the pot, cook for 4 minutes, remove from the heat, and serve in rimmed plates with 2 basil leaves on each plate. This dish should be accompanied with good country bread.

UOVA TRIPPATE (Eggs in Tomato Sauce)

The name *uova trippate* describes a thin *frittata* cut into strips that resemble the way tripe is cut and then baked with a sauce.

SERVES 4

> 8 *eggs*
> 1 *small onion, sliced*
> 2 *tablespoons extra virgin olive oil*
> ³⁄₄ *pound tomatoes, peeled, seeded, and chopped*
> *Salt and pepper, to taste*
> 4 *tablespoons grated Parmigiano*
> 8 *basil leaves*
> 4 *mint leaves*
> 1 *parsley sprig*

Preheat the oven to 400°F. Prepare 4 very thin *frittate* using a large pan, following the basic recipe on page 81. Cook until the *frittate* are well done. Cool, roll, and cut the *frittate* into strips. Set aside. Sauté the onion in the oil until golden brown. Add the tomatoes, reduce by one third, add salt, pepper, and basil and set aside. Arrange layers of *frittata,* tomato sauce, cheese, basil, and mint in a buttered baking dish. Keep layering until all the ingredients are used. The last layer should be tomato sauce and cheese. Bake for 15 minutes, decorate with parsley, and serve with good bread.

VERDURE E INSALATE
Vegetables and Salads

It is important to choose vegetables that are in season; like every cuisine originating in rural communities, Italian vegetable cookery is based on availability. Vegetables are prominent in *antipasti* and are used in side dishes and in a variety of preparations from raw (for salads) to boiled, baked, braised, sautéed, and pan-fried. The most traditional recipes are offered here.

VERDURE (Vegetables)

ASPARAGI (Asparagus)

Asparagus is a spring vegetable. There are different varieties of asparagus: green, white, and purple; fat and thin. Another less common but excellent variety is that which grows wild in damp woods. The stalks are long, thin, green, and tender. Thin asparagus is called *mangiatutto*—literally eat all, because even the stems can be eaten. For most other varieties, only the tips are edible.

BARBABIETOLE (Red Beets)

Beets are available all year long. They must always be cooked. They are usually an ingredient in salads and can be mixed with boiled potatoes and onions. In dishes like *insalata russa*, beets improve the flavor, and their red color brightens the whole.

BROCCOLI DI RAPE (Broccoli Rape)

This winter vegetable, very common in southern Italy, grows in bunches with slightly indented green leaves that have small green sprouts in the center. For most preparations, blanch the vegetable first to improve its rather bitter taste. It can be included in soups, sautéed with oil and garlic, or eaten just boiled and seasoned with oil, lemon juice, salt, and pepper. As a side dish, bitter broccoli is generally served with pork meat or sausages. The early broccoli rape are called *friarielli* in the Neopolitan region.

CARCIOFI (Artichokes)

Artichokes are available from November through May. They are the flowers (not the fruit) of a plant about 3 feet tall with large, tapered leaves. The best are those that grow at the top of the stem. In late spring, the plant produces the last artichokes, which are only as big as an egg and ideal for canning. Artichokes can be with or without thorns (i.e., either prickly or Roman "unarmed" varieties, respectively). The soft parts can be eaten raw, sliced, with oil, pepper, and salt. If boiled, they can be dipped in a sauce made with oil, garlic, and parsley or stuffed and either baked or braised. They can be used to make *frittata, risotto,* and other dishes. Artichoke hearts without leaves can be boiled, fried, baked, or filled with any stuffing and served either cold or warm.

CARDI (Cardoons)

Available in the fall and throughout the winter, cardoons look like large celery stalks and can reach 3 feet in height. Cardoon is a domestic variety of the wild thistle in the artichoke family. Since only part of the plant is edible, be sure to buy enough for your preparation. Some are hollow (and thus suitable for stuffing), while others are solid. Whatever the final preparation, cardoons should be boiled first. Since they darken easily, it is advisable to keep them in water soured with lemon juice. First separate the stems and then dispose of the woody stalks. Slice the tender stalks and the heart and cook them together. Once cooked, cardoons can be served with one of a variety of sauces, or breaded and deep-fried, or cooked in the *parmigiana* style. Cardoons can also be eaten raw with a sauce such as *bagna cauda* or simply with extra virgin oil.

CICORIA (Chicory)

This salad green is on the market year round but it tastes best in winter. Known variously in Italy as *catalogna, cicoria cimata*, or *cicoriella*, it looks like a big bunch of long, thin green leaves with a large white vein. *Catalogna* must always be cooked.

Puntarelle, a variety of chicory from Lazio, is served as a salad, traditionally with an anchovy dressing. Before dressing *puntarelle*, it is better to split the stems and cover them with ice water until ready to serve. In this way, it will lose a bit of its bitter flavor and will curl.

COSTE (Swiss Chard)

The main season for Swiss chard is the spring. The variety with big leaves and thin veins can be used instead of spinach, while the ones with large veins are normally used to prepare gratin dishes or for frying or stewing.

FINOCCHIO (Fennel)

Available in winter, fennel has a delicate anise flavor and can be eaten raw, either sliced or whole, and seasoned with oil, lemon juice, pepper, and salt or cooked in various ways (e.g., braised, fried, or boiled). Fennel, usually served as a side dish to complement meat courses, is also served as a salad.

FIORI DI ZUCCA E DI ZUCCHINE (Squash and Zucchini Blossoms)

Available in spring and summer, squash blossoms are slightly bigger than those of zucchini. Both are cooked in the same way. They are never eaten raw but can be stuffed and fried, cooked in *fritatte,* and fried in a special batter or simply with flour. Always choose the freshest ones. When cleaning them, remove the pistils and check the insides to make sure that there are no insects.

LAMPAGIONI (Muscari Bulbs)

Also called *lampascioni* or *cipollacci,* these vegetables are often used in southern Italian cuisine, especially in the Apulia region. They are a kind of bulb, similar to an onion, with a rather strong, bitter taste. After cooking, they become reddish. Prior to cooking, the outer leaves must be removed and the bulbs soaked in cool water (which should be changed occasionally) so that they lose some of their bitterness. Otherwise they can be cooked in fresh water until they are done. They are used in salads, fried, and marinated in oil or vinegar.

MELANZANA (Eggplant)

Available in summer, eggplants come in many sizes and colors: they may be different shades of violet or white; they may also be long or round. All are cooked in the same way: fried, stewed, thinly sliced and cooked with oil, garlic, and basil or oregano, or stuffed and baked. Eggplants can also be used in savory pies and cakes. It is advisable to slice, salt, and place a weight on top of them one hour before cooking to remove the bitter water most often found in less mature eggplants. Before cooking, wash off the salt and pat dry.

PEPERONE (Pepper)

Available in summer, there are many kinds of peppers varying in hotness (sweet or hot), color (most often green, yellow, or red), and shade (light to dark). They can also vary in shape (round or long) and in size. They are delicious mixed with tomatoes, olives, and onions. They can also be roasted, peeled, and served in oil.

POMODORO (Tomato)

Tomatoes were imported to Europe from Central and North America. The first mention of tomatoes in Italy dates back to 1544 by Pietro Andrea Mattioli, who gives an accurate description and calls them *pomi d'oro*—succulent gold fruit or golden fruit. At the beginning, the tomato plant was not accepted so readily since it was believed to be poisonous, so much so that in 1820 the State of New York passed a law banning the consumption of tomatoes. This belief was proven to be false by Robert Gibbon Johnson, who took a bagful of tomatoes into a courtroom in Salem, New York, and ate the entire bagful before an incredulous public. Another gentleman, Mr. Michele Felice Corne, did the same thing in Newport, Rhode Island.

In Italy, tomatoes entered popular use in the seventeenth century. In 1773, Vincenzo Corrado published the book *Il Cuoco galante,* in which he listed several recipes with tomatoes. But the boom of tomatoes' popularity in Italy began in 1875 when Francesco Cirio first started tomatoes' industrial production with the famous *Salsa Cirio,* followed later by canned and peeled tomatoes. This success started off botanical experimenting with the tomato plant that has produced today's many different varieties. Among the better-known varieties is the San Marzano, a type of tomato that takes its name from the area of its origin. San Marzano is a farm village in Campania.

PORRO (Leek)

Available almost all year round, leeks belong to the family of garlic and onion. They are a good substitute for onions in soups, *risotto,* and various sauces; they can also be baked.

RAPA (Turnip)

Available from fall to spring, depending on the variety, turnips are very digestible roots with a delicate taste. They can be cooked in various ways: in soups, baked, or *sott'aceto.*

SEDANO (Celery)

Green celery, available all year round, is used to flavor soups and various sauces. The largest varieties are cooked like white celery. Both the stalks and tender leaves can be eaten raw.

White celery, available in fall and winter, comes in sizable bunches. The outside stalks are yellowish while the inside ones are white. White celery can be eaten raw, as an antipasto, seasoned with *pinzimonio* (an oil, salt, and pepper dressing) or with *bagna cauda.* It can also be cooked and served as a side dish.

Celery root or *sedano di Verona* is available in winter. Only the root of this celery is eaten, while the stalks may be used to flavor soups. It can be eaten raw, cut into matchsticks and seasoned with oil, vinegar, pepper, and salt. If served as an appetizer, it may be dressed with a mixture of mustard and mayonnaise or cut into wedges or slices that are sautéed or fried (with or without breading). It is an excellent accompaniment for meat courses.

VERZA E CAVOLO CAPPUCCIO (Savoy Cabbage and Head Cabbage)

These belong to the same family as broccoli and cauliflower and are primarily a winter vegetable. Savoy cabbages have compact heads of wrinkled, curly leaves, dark green on the outside and lighter in the inside. Head cabbages also have compact heads but with smooth, light green leaves; they are more delicate in taste than the Savoy. The leaves of the head cabbage can also be russet or violet in color (known in Italy as *cavolo nero* or Tuscan cabbage). Both varieties may be eaten raw cut into thin strips and seasoned with oil, vinegar, salt, and pepper, or may be stewed or cooked in savory pies and soups.

ZUCCA (Gourd Squash)

The most common Italian squash of this type is *zucca*, a squat, round, very bumpy-skinned squash, whose flesh resembles that of a pumpkin in color and texture. Available in late fall and winter, *zucca* can vary in shape and size. *Zucca* is heavier and much fleshier than the common pumpkin and tastes a lot like pumpkin. It must always be of the best quality, and it may be baked, boiled, steamed, fried, or sautéed. It can also be used in *risotto* or as stuffing for *tortelli* and *gnocchi*.

ZUCCHINE (Zucchini)

Available in the summer, there are many varieties of this vegetable with different sizes and shapes (straight or curved). Choose the small, very firm ones. Choose the shape according to how they are to be prepared (for example, straight ones to make stuffed zucchini). Regardless of shape, they can be fried, steamed, or baked.

BROCCOLETTI ALLA ROMANA
(Braised Broccoli Rape Roman-Style)

SERVES 4

> 2 *bunches broccoli rape*
> 2 *garlic cloves*
> 2 *tablespoons extra virgin olive oil*
> 1 *peperoncino*
> Salt, *to taste*

Wash the broccoli rape, removing the large stems and larger leaves. Cook in salted boiling water for a few minutes, then drain and set aside. Brown the garlic in the oil in a large skillet. Add the *peperoncino* and when the garlic is brown remove it and add the broccoli. Salt to taste and cook until tender but still crisp. Serve as a side dish to any white meat courses such as fowl or pork.

FRIARIELLI ALL'AGLIO E PEPERONCINO ALLA NAPOLETANA
(Broccoli Rape with Garlic and Peperoncino, Neapolitan-Style)

For this preparation you need young broccoli rape, which in Neapolitan slang is called *friarielli.*

SERVES 6
> 2 bunches broccoli rape, young and tender
> 2 garlic cloves
> Pinch of peperoncino
> 6 tablespoons extra virgin olive oil
> Salt

Wash the broccoli, discarding the larger leaves and stems, and put the broccoli in cold water. Sauté the garlic and *peperoncino* with 6 tablespoons of the oil in a large casserole. Remove the garlic when brown. Remove the broccoli from the water but do not dry, place into the casserole with the water clinging to the leaves, cover, and cook over low heat. Let cook until tender. Add salt and serve.

CARCIOFI ALLA ROMANA (Artichokes Braised with Mint)

> 8 small artichokes
> Juice of 1 lemon
> 1 wild mint sprig, chopped
> 2 garlic cloves, chopped
> Salt and pepper, to taste
> ½ cup extra virgin olive oil

Remove the tough outer leaves of the artichokes. Trim off the tips of the leaves and the skin off the stems with a sharp knife. Do not cut off the stems. Open the leaves and remove the chokes from the center. Place the artichokes in cold water and lemon juice to avoid discoloration. Wash and finely chop together the wild mint and garlic. Remove the artichokes from the water, open the leaves, and fill the center with mint, garlic, salt, and pepper.

Place the artichokes upside down (with the stems up) tight against each other in a pot at least as tall as the artichokes. Salt and pepper to taste; sprinkle with olive oil; add as much cold water as needed to just cover the artichokes. Cover and cook over medium heat for about 1 hour or until the artichokes are tender to the fork.

Cool and place the artichokes in a deep dish with the cooking juice (if it is too liquid, first reduce it over high heat). Adjust the salt and pepper to taste. These are best served warm but may also be served at room temperature.

CARCIOFI TRIFOLATI (Sautéed Artichokes)

SERVES 6

12 artichokes, medium size
Juice of 1 lemon
4 garlic cloves, chopped
6 teaspoons extra virgin olive oil
½ cup beef broth, if needed (see pages 123–24)
Chopped parsley
Salt and pepper, to taste

Wash the artichokes, remove the longer leaves and the tips and the chokes, and thinly slice them lengthwise. Immediately dip them in water soured with the lemon juice. Brown the garlic in oil and remove when brown. Add the artichokes and sauté over moderate heat, stirring frequently. Add the broth if necessary. When the artichokes are done, add the chopped parsley and salt and pepper to taste, toss well, and serve.

INVOLTINI DI CAVOLO (Savoy Cabbage Rolls)

SERVES 4

12 large Savoy cabbage leaves
1 pound braised lean meat (beef, veal, chicken, or any leftover meat)
¼ pound mortadella, diced
1 egg
2 tablespoons grated Parmigiano
2 tablespoons chopped parsley
Salt and pepper, to taste
1 small onion, chopped
2 ounces pancetta, diced small
1 garlic clove
1 ounce butter
2 sage leaves
½ cup dry white wine
1 cup chicken or beef broth, if needed (see pages 123–24)

Boil the cabbage leaves for about 3 minutes in salted water, being careful not to break the leaves. Drain, place them in cold water, and let cool. Drain again and lay them on a cloth. Cover with another cloth and let them dry. Meanwhile, finely grind the meat and the *mortadella*. Mix them with the egg, *Parmigiano,* parsley, and salt and pepper to taste. Blend well and top each cabbage leaf with this mixture. Roll tightly and fasten with toothpicks.

Finely chop the onion and the *pancetta* together. In a baking pan, brown the garlic in butter and remove when brown. Add the sage and onion and *pancetta*. Cook over low heat until soft. Add the cabbage rolls, continue browning for a few minutes, then add the wine, reduce a bit, and adjust with salt and pepper. Cover and let cook for about 30 minutes over low heat, adding the broth if needed. Serve hot.

CICORIETTA SALTATA CON PANCETTA
(Chicory Sautéed with Pancetta)

SERVES 4

2 pounds chicory
¼ pound pancetta, diced
2 garlic cloves
4 tablespoons extra virgin olive oil
2 tablespoons chopped parsley
Salt and pepper, to taste

Clean, wash, and boil the chicory. Drain, let cool, and set aside. Sauté the *pancetta* until browned and set aside. Brown the garlic in olive oil in a large frying pan and remove when brown. Add the chicory, sauté briskly, then add *pancetta* and parsley. Stir well and continue to cook to desired doneness. Remove from the heat and add salt and pepper to taste. Serve.

CIPOLLINE AL DOLCEFORTE (Sweet-and-Sour Pearl Onions)

SERVES 6

2 pounds pearl onions
6 ounces butter
2 tablespoons sugar
⅓ cup very good white wine vinegar
Salt and pepper, to taste

Peel the onions. Cook them in boiling water for 3 minutes, drain, and set aside. Melt the butter in a large saucepan and add the onions. Stir in the sugar and allow it to dissolve. Add the vinegar and stir well. Cover and simmer gently over low heat for about 1 hour. If the sauce becomes too thick, add some hot water as needed. Add salt and pepper. Pearl onions prepared in this way can be served with braised meats or venison.

FINOCCHIO CON FONTINA (Fennel with Fontina Cheese)

SERVES 4

4 heads fennel
½ pound fontina cheese
3 ounces butter
Salt and pepper, to taste
Pinch of nutmeg
½ cup beef broth (see pages 123–24)

Preheat the oven to 375°F.

Clean the fennel heads and cut them lengthwise. Boil for 5 minutes in salted water and drain. In a buttered baking dish, alternate a layer of fennel with slices of *fontina* and curls of butter.

Sprinkle with salt, pepper, and very lightly with nutmeg. Add the broth and bake for 20 minutes, or until the cheese has melted. Serve plated or in the baking dish.

INVOLTINO DI MELANZANE (Eggplant Roll)

SERVES 4

4 medium eggplants
Salt
Flour, for dredging
6 tablespoons extra virgin olive oil
8 slices mozzarella
8 fresh basil leaves
Pepper, to taste

Preheat the oven to 375°F. Thinly slice the eggplants, leaving the skin on. Salt and weight them down for 1 hour. Wash the eggplants and pat dry with a paper towel. Dredge the eggplants with flour and brown both sides in a saucepan with some of the olive oil. Remove eggplants from pan, drain on paper towels to get rid of excess fat, and cool. Top each slice with a thin slice of *mozzarella* and basil leaf, salt and pepper, and roll up to make an *involtino*. Fasten with a toothpick. Place in a baking casserole, sprinkle with 1 tablespoon olive oil and pepper, and bake for about 20 minutes. Serve hot with a sprinkle of extra virgin olive oil.

MELANZANE ALLA PARMIGIANA (Eggplant Parmigiana)

SERVES 6

6 medium eggplants
Salt
1 small onion, finely sliced

1 garlic clove, crushed
½ cup extra virgin olive oil
1 pound ripe tomatoes, peeled, seeded, and chopped
½ pound mozzarella, sliced
1¾ cups all-purpose flour
6 tablespoons Parmigiano
12 basil leaves

Preheat the oven to 375°F. Wash the eggplants. Remove the stems and cut lengthwise into slices no thicker than ¼ inches. To rid them of their bitter water, place the slices on a large platter, slightly on an angle. Sprinkle them with lots of salt, place a weight on top, and let stand for about 1 hour.

Meanwhile, brown the onion and the garlic in oil over very low heat, add the tomatoes, and let simmer for about 30 minutes, stirring frequently. When done, pass through a sieve and add a pinch of salt.

Cut the *mozzarella* into very thin slices and let them dry on a cloth. Wash the salt off the eggplants and dry them. Dredge them in flour and fry them in very hot oil. Turn them over to brown and, when both sides are done, lift them out of the pan and drain on paper towels. Coat a deep 10-inch baking dish with olive oil and put in a layer of eggplant. Pour on a layer of tomato sauce, sprinkle with *Parmigiano* and a few basil leaves, and cover with slices of *mozzarella*. Repeat this layering until all the ingredients have been used, cover with tomato sauce, sprinkle with more grated *Parmigiano,* and bake for about 30 minutes. This dish is very good hot or at room temperature and makes a good *antipasto.*

Note:
Zucchine alla parmigiana can be made in the same way, substituting zucchini for eggplant.

MELANZANE AL FUNGHETTO (Sautéed Eggplant)

SERVES 4
4 medium eggplants
½ cup extra virgin olive oil
1 onion, chopped
6 ounces ripe tomatoes, peeled, seeded, and diced
Pepper, to taste

Cut the eggplants into very thick slices and place on a platter. To rid them of their bitter water, cover generously with salt, place a weight on top for 1 hour, then wash, cut the slices into cubes, and set aside. Prepare a *soffritto* with 2 tablespoons olive oil and the onion. When tender, add tomatoes. Cook for about 7 to 8 minutes and set aside. Heat the remainder of the oil, add the eggplants, cook until almost done, then add the *soffritto.* Toss well and continue to cook until the eggplant is tender but still crisp. Add salt and pepper to taste. Serve warm or at room temperature.

CAPONATA SICILIANA (Eggplant and Tomato Stew)

SERVES 4

2 pounds eggplant
Salt
½ cup extra virgin olive oil
1 pound onion, coarsely chopped
2 stalks celery, diced
1 pound ripe tomatoes, peeled, seeded, and diced
3 ounces green olives, pitted
1 teaspoon capers
Basil leaves, chopped

Slice and salt the eggplants. Place a weight on top and let them drain for 1 hour to rid them of the bitter water. Wash, dry, and dice the eggplants and sauté in 4 tablespoons of the olive oil. Cook until tender but still crisp and set aside.

Sauté the onion and the celery in the remaining 4 tablespoons of oil. When golden brown, add the tomatoes, olives, and capers and let cook for 10 minutes. Combine with the eggplant and add the chopped basil and salt to taste. Toss and serve. This dish can be served warm or cold (at room temperature) and as an antipasto.

Caponata is also made in a sweet-and-sour version. Add 1 tablespoon raisins and 1 tablespoon pine nuts to a dressing of 1 cup vinegar and 1 tablespoon sugar and reduce by one third. Add the dressing to the *caponata*, toss well, and serve.

PEPERONATA (Peppers Sautéed with Oil and Capers)

SERVE 4

2 pounds firm sweet peppers
1 small white onion, chopped
1 garlic clove, chopped
½ cup extra virgin olive oil
4 ounces ripe tomatoes, peeled, seeded, and diced
Salt and pepper, to taste

Clean and cut the peppers into strips. Make a *soffritto* by sautéing the onion and garlic in a saucepan with 2 tablespoons of the oil. When golden brown, add the tomatoes. Cook for 5 minutes over low heat. Remove from the heat and set aside.

In a large skillet, heat the remaining 6 tablespoons of oil, and then add the peppers, cooking until the peppers are tender but still crisp. Add the *soffritto*, mix thoroughly, and remove from the heat. Add salt and pepper to taste and serve. *Peperonata* can also be served at room temperature.

Note:
You may add some pitted black olives.

ZUCCHINE AL FORNO (Baked Zucchini)

12 zucchini
2 tablespoons finely chopped parsley
1 tablespoon finely chopped basil
1 garlic clove, finely chopped
¼ cup fresh breadcrumbs
1 tablespoon grated Parmigiano
2 ounces pine nuts, toasted
Salt and pepper, to taste
3 tablespoons extra virgin olive oil

Preheat the oven to 375°F. Split the zucchini in half and cut each half into 2 inch or equal-length pieces. Scoop out and discard the seeded center of each piece. Combine all the other ingredients except the oil. Mix well. Cook zucchini in boiling salted water for a few minutes, or until al dente (undercooked), and then cool in ice water. Drain on paper towels. Fill the zucchini with stuffing, without packing too tightly, and place in a baking pan brushed with olive oil. Bake for 15 minutes.

MELANZANE RIPIENE CON CACIOCAVALLO
(Eggplant Stuffed with Caciocavallo)

Caciocavallo is a semisoft cheese. Sweet *provolone* can be used as a substitute.

SERVES 4

2 pounds medium eggplants
Salt
6 tablespoons extra virgin olive oil
1 garlic clove
1 pound ripe tomatoes, peeled, seeded, and diced
1 tablespoon capers
3 anchovy fillets, chopped
½ onion, chopped
10 ounces caciocavallo or other semisoft cheese, diced
1 tablespoon chopped parsley
10 basil leaves
Pepper, to taste
1 teaspoon oregano

Preheat the oven to 375°F. Cut the eggplants in half lengthwise and salt and weight them down. Let rest for 1 hour. When ready, scoop out the pulp and arrange the eggplants side by side in an oiled baking pan. In a saucepan, heat 2 tablespoons of oil and brown the garlic. Add the tomatoes, the pulp of the eggplant, capers, anchovies, and onion and cook for 10 minutes over medium heat. Next, mix in the *caciocavallo,* parsley, and basil. Adjust for seasoning with salt and pepper. Blend all the ingredients well and fill the eggplants with the mix. Sprinkle with oregano. Bake for about 1 hour or until the top is golden brown. Serve hot.

PEPERONI RIPIENI CON PANE (Peppers Stuffed with Bread)

8 small bell peppers
3 tablespoons extra virgin olive oil
2 cups breadcrumbs, soaked and squeezed dry
1 tablespoon minced parsley
2 garlic cloves, minced
1 tablespoon capers
3 salted anchovy fillets, chopped
¼ cup green olives, pitted
Salt, to taste

Preheat the oven to 400°F. Clean the peppers, removing the stem and the seeds. Prepare a stuffing with 2 tablespoons of the oil, the breadcrumbs, parsley, garlic, capers, anchovies, olives, and salt. Stuff the peppers without packing them too tight, place them in a baking pan, pour over the remaining oil, and bake for about 1 hour or until the top is golden brown.

POMODORI RIPIENI CON RISO (Tomatoes Stuffed with Rice)

SERVES 4

4 large round tomatoes, ripe and firm
Salt
2 tablespoons finely chopped parsley
1 garlic clove, finely chopped
2 tablespoons finely chopped basil
Pinch of oregano
Pepper, to taste
1 cup cooked rice
Extra virgin olive oil
½ cup breadcrumbs

Preheat the oven to 350°F. Wash, dry, and cut the tomatoes in half horizontally. Remove the inside, sprinkle with salt, and set them upside down over a sieve for about 30 minutes. Prepare the stuffing by mixing together the parsley, garlic, basil, oregano, and salt and pepper to taste and add to the rice. Blend all the ingredients well, fill the tomatoes with the mixture, and level off the top with a spatula. Coat the inside of a large baking pan with oil. Place the tomatoes side by side in the pan, cover the surface with bread-crumbs, and sprinkle with a small quantity of oil. Bake for about 30 minutes, or until the top is golden brown. Serve warm, or at room temperature, as a side dish or *antipasto*.

POMODORI RIPIENI AL PANE ED ERBE
(Tomatoes Stuffed with Bread and Herbs)

These are excellent either warm or cold and can be served as a side dish or as an *antipasto*.

SERVES 6

6 round, ripe, firm tomatoes
Salt
1 parsley sprig
8 basil leaves
1 garlic clove
½ cup breadcrumbs
1 tablespoon oregano
1 teaspoon capers, chopped
4 tablespoons extra virgin olive oil

Preheat the oven to 375°F. Cut the tomatoes in half horizontally and remove the seeds. Salt and leave upside down on a towel for 30 minutes. Chop the parsley with basil and garlic. Add breadcrumbs, oregano, and capers. Salt and mix well. Place the tomatoes on a greased baking dish and fill them with the stuffing. Drizzle them with oil and bake for 30 minutes or until a golden crust forms on top.

ZUCCHINE RIPIENI CON FORMAGGIO
(Zucchini Stuffed with Cheese)

SERVES 4

2 pounds zucchini
6 slices white bread
⅓ cup milk
1 cup ricotta cheese
4 tablespoons grated Parmigiano
2 eggs, beaten
Salt, to taste
⅓ cup breadcrumbs
2 ounces butter

Preheat the oven to 375°F. Boil the zucchini in salted water for about 5 minutes (they should still be firm). Let cool and cut lengthwise. Scoop out some of the pulp with a spoon, being careful not to cut into the shell, and set aside. Remove the inside of the bread, soak it in milk, and then squeeze out the moisture. In a bowl, mix *ricotta, Parmigiano,* the pulp of the zucchini, eggs, and the bread and adjust the seasoning with salt. Stuff the zucchini shells with this mixture. Sprinkle with breadcrumbs and thin pats of butter. Place the zucchini side by side in a greased baking pan. Bake for about 30 minutes or until they brown on top.

Note:
You may replace *ricotta* with a different soft or fresh cheese.

INSALATE (Salads)

In Italian culinary terms, an *insalata* is any dish consisting of single or mixed greens; salads with vegetables or legumes, flavored with salt, oil, and vinegar; and salads with meat, fish, rice, and other ingredients. More precisely, in addition to vegetable salads, Italians enjoy egg, meat, fish, seafood, cereal, and even fruit salads.

While a simple green salad is considered a side dish, salads prepared with vegetables are usually served as a cold appetizer, and others are served as a cold main course. For example, a *panzanella* can work as an *antipasto* and a salad with tuna in oil, onions, and potatoes as a light main course.

INSALATA VERDE (Green Salad)

This may refer to either a single kind of green or several types of greens mixed together. Wash the greens repeatedly in plenty of water, then drain well without crushing. If the greens are not to be used immediately after draining, keep in a covered container and refrigerate. When ready to serve, toss with a dressing (see below).

CONDIMENTI (Dressings)

The typical dressing for raw salads is extra virgin olive oil, wine vinegar, salt, and pepper. The standard proportions—adjustable to individual taste—are 3 parts oil to 1 part vinegar. Choose among the various types of oil (see pages 7–10) and vinegar (pages 12–14) to make the most suitable dressing for the type of salad being served. Remember that white vinegar is strong and aromatic, while red vinegar is milder and fruitier in flavor. Aromatic and balsamic vinegar are also popular; the latter is particularly strong and should be measured out drop by drop (see pages 13–14). Lemon is not always a good substitute for vinegar, as its acidity content is less than that of vinegar. Lemon-based dressing is suitable to flavor raw celery, fennel, artichokes, mushrooms, and carrots.

For an emulsified dressing, pour the vinegar in a dish, mix it with the salt and pepper, and slowly add the oil, whisking constantly. If you wish to add a light garlic flavor, rub the garlic on the inside of the bowl in which the salad will be tossed, or pierce a clove of garlic with a fork and use this to mix the dressing.

In addition to vinegar or lemon, oil, salt, and pepper, the following ingredients can be included in dressings to flavor all kinds of salads: finely minced parsley, chopped or shredded basil, finely minced raw scallions or chervil, mustard, oregano, crushed garlic, anchovy paste (made by pounding the anchovy fillets to a paste in olive oil), and capers, (usually together with anchovies).

Another dressing, often used with high-fiber vegetables such as radicchio, is *pancetta* or lard browned to a crisp texture and, together with its melted fat, mixed and boiled for a minute with vinegar. This dressing is served when still slightly warm.

COMMON VARIETIES OF GREENS

CICORIA RICCIA (Curly Chicory)

The leaves, joined together in a bunch, are curly on the edges as well as in the inside. Light green in color, some varieties are slightly brown-rimmed. In salads, curly chicory is always mixed with other greens. It is seldom used for cooking.

DENTI DI LEONE (Dandelion Greens)

Dandelion greens are the long, pointed, dark green leaves of the dandelion plant. The young spring greens are preferable, as they are less bitter in flavor. They can be eaten raw when young or blanched or wilted with a hot dressing.

INDIVIA O CICORIETTA (White Curly Chicory)

These are large bunches of curly, wrinkled, off-white colored leaves, lighter in color around the center of the bunch. They can be served as a salad or boiled and dressed with extra virgin olive oil.

LATTUGA (Lettuce)

Lettuce is the most popular of all greens and includes at least 150 varieties. The most common is the *lattuga cappuccio* (iceberg), with a round shape and leaves that grow one upon the other. *Lattuga romana* (romaine) has long ribbed leaves. *Lattuga bina* is a variety with a fast cycle found mostly during the summer. Its leaves are very tender, light green in color, with red shades occasionally. Its taste is mild.

PUNTARELLE (Roman Wild Chicory)

From the same family as chicory, this very special green is typical of central Italy and only available in the winter months. *Puntarelle* must be washed and the green leaves removed. The white-greenish tips are split with a knife lengthwise and dipped in cold water. This will allow the leaves to curl and lose some of their bitter taste. *Puntarelle* is best eaten with an anchovy dressing.

RADICCHIO (Radicchio)

Radicchio is produced in many regions of northern Italy, but its production is particularly plentiful in Veneto. *Radicchio* is classified according to color and the form of the leaves. The three most common varieties are the following: *Radicchio variegato* has a rounded shape, with large leaves that are cream-colored with streaks that range from violet to lively red. Its taste is sweet to slightly bitter. *Radicchio trevisano* has an elongated form. Its base is white, and the color changes to red at the tips of the leaves. The taste is slightly bitter, and the texture is crispy. *Radicchio di Chioggia* has a spherical, compact form. The base is white, changing to reddish/violet at the tips of the leaves. The taste is sweet and the leaves are rather crispy. Radicchio has very good digestive properties. It is generally used for salad, but is also excellent braised and served as an accompaniment to beef or lamb.

RUCOLA, RUGOLA, RUGHETTA, O ARUGOLA (Arugula)

There are many names for this very popular oak-leafed vegetable with a pungent, radish-like flavor. Because of its definite taste, arugula is most often used in salads mixed with milder greens. Oil and vinegar are the most suitable dressing. Arugula is also served with a pasta dish from Apulia called *orecchiette con rucola e pomodoro*.

PINZIMONIO (Raw Vegetable Salad)

The simplest dressing for raw vegetables is undoubtedly *pinzimonio*, a dipping sauce of extra virgin olive oil, salt, and pepper. *Pinzimonio* is used as a dip for raw celery, artichokes, leeks, scallions, fennel, sweet peppers, asparagus, and the like. The vegetables must be cut rather large so that they may be picked up by the stem and dipped in the dressing at the tip.

BAGNA CAUDA (Bagna Cauda)

Another popular vegetable salad is *bagna cauda* (see pages 26–27).

PUNTARELLE CON SALSA DI ACCIUGHE
(Roman Wild Chicory with Anchovy Dressing)

SERVES 4

2 pounds puntarelle, or two bunches
3 anchovy fillets

2 garlic cloves
⅓ cup extra virgin olive oil
Juice of 1 lemon or 2 tablespoons red wine vinegar
Salt and pepper, to taste

Let the *puntarelle* soak in cold water for 30 minutes. Meanwhile, crush the anchovies and garlic in a mortar until they become a paste. Blend in the oil, the lemon juice, and a pinch of salt and pepper. Drain the *puntarelle*, place in a large bowl, toss with the sauce, and serve.

INSALATA DI RINFORZO (Cauliflower Salad with Pickled Vegetables)

The name for this salad, which is popular in the Naples area, means "nutritious and reinvigorating." It is traditionally served on Christmas Eve, as an accompaniment to fried fish.

SERVES 4
1 cauliflower
¼ pound Gaeta olives, pitted
1 tablespoon capers
8 anchovy fillets
4 ounces vinegar-marinated mixed vegetables
½ cup extra virgin olive oil
Salt and pepper, to taste

Boil the cauliflower in salted water without overcooking. Drain and let cool. Cut the cauliflower or break up the florets from the stem, chop the stem, and place on a large platter. Combine with the olives, capers, and anchovies. Scatter the vinegar-marinated mixed vegetables over the cauliflower and dress with oil, salt, and pepper. Serve cool.

INSALATA DI FAGIOLI BIANCHI DI SPAGNA
(White Spanish Bean Salad)

SERVES 8
2 pounds dried Spanish beans
1 small celery stalk
1 bay leaf
1 small carrot
1 leek, white part only
½ cup extra virgin olive oil
Salt and pepper, to taste
2 tablespoons chopped parsley

1 garlic clove, minced (optional)
1 small onion, sliced (optional)

If using dried beans, soak them overnight. Cook the beans in boiling water (if fresh), or start with cold water (if dried). Tie the aromatic herbs and greens (celery, bay leaf, carrot, and leek) together in a bunch and add to the boiling water just after the beans. Cook the dried beans for 1½ hours, fresh beans for 30 minutes. When done, drain. Remove the vegetables and place the beans in a ceramic (not wooden) salad bowl. Season the beans with oil, salt, pepper, chopped parsley, and, if desired, garlic, or an onion cut in slices.

INSALATA DI TONNO E FAGIOLI (Tuna and Cannellini Bean Salad)

SERVES 4
1 pound dried cannellini beans
6 ounces canned tuna in oil, coarsely crumbled
1 medium onion, finely sliced
¼ cup extra virgin olive oil
Pinch of white pepper
Salt, to taste

Soak the beans overnight and cook for 1½ hours, starting with cold, salted water. Drain and cool. Remove the tuna from the can and discard its oil. Combine the beans, tuna, and onion in a bowl. Add the olive oil, pepper, and salt to taste. Toss well. Serve at room temperature.

INSALATA DI CARCIOFI E PARMIGIANO
(Artichoke and Parmigiano Salad)

SERVES 4
6 artichokes
Juice of 1 lemon
⅓ cup virgin olive oil
Salt and pepper, to taste
2 ounces Parmigiano shavings

Remove the stems, the outer leaves, and all the hard parts of the leaves of the artichokes, leaving only the bottoms and the tender inside leaves. Remove the chokes, cut the artichokes into thin slices, and put them in cold water soured with lemon juice until ready to use. Drain the artichokes, dress with oil, salt, and pepper, and toss well. Cover with *Parmigiano,* sliced thin using a truffle cutter or a potato peeler so that the *Parmigiano* shavings curl up. Serve on a serving platter.

INSALATA DI FUNGHI (Mushroom Salad)

SERVES 4

1 pound ovoli or porcini mushrooms
3/4 cup extra virgin olive oil
Juice of 1 lemon
Pinch of tarragon
Salt and pepper, to taste

Clean and slice the mushrooms very thin. Add olive oil, lemon juice, tarragon, salt, and pepper to taste and toss delicately so that the mushrooms do not crumble. Serve.

Variation:
Add very thin shavings of *Parmigiano* on top and/or white truffles when in season.

INSALATA DI FRUTTI DI MARE (Seafood Salad)

SERVES 12

6 ounces cuttlefish
6 ounces octopus
6 ounces scallops
6 ounces lobster
6 ounces fish fillets
1/2 pound mussels, shelled
1/2 cup plus 2 tablespoons extra virgin olive oil
3 garlic cloves, minced
1/2 cup dry white wine
1 baking potato, boiled and diced
2 celery stalks, diced
2 tablespoons finely chopped parsley
Juice of 2 lemons
Salt and pepper, to taste

Clean, poach, and dice all the fish. Steam the mussels in 2 tablespoons of the olive oil, 1 garlic clove, and the white wine until they open. Shell and mix with the rest of the fish. Add the potato and celery and refrigerate. Combine the parsley and remaining garlic and set aside. Prepare the dressing with the remaining 8 tablespoons of olive oil and the lemon juice, add salt and pepper to taste, whisk well, and set aside. Just before serving, mix the dressing with the fish and toss well, top with a generous sprinkling of the combined parsley and garlic, and serve.

INSALATA DI POLIPETTI (Baby Octopus Salad)

SERVES 4

2 pounds baby octopus
2 garlic cloves, finely chopped
½ cup extra virgin olive oil
2 tablespoons fresh lemon juice
¼ cup chopped parsley
Salt and pepper, to taste

Clean the octopus and boil it in a small amount of salted water for 25 to 45 minutes, depending on the size. Drain and cool. Remove the skin and cut the octopus into small pieces. Season with the garlic, olive oil, lemon juice, parsley, salt, and pepper just before serving. This salad is excellent served warm or cold.

INSALATA DI RISO NOVARESE (Rice Salad Novarese-Style)

SERVES 4

½ pound (1 cup) long-grain rice
1 cup dry white wine
6 tablespoons extra virgin olive oil
1 garlic clove
4 anchovy fillets, chopped
Juice of 2 lemons
Salt and pepper, to taste
1 tablespoon chopped parsley

Cook the rice in a large pot in 3 cups of boiling salted water for 8 minutes. Add the wine and continue to cook until done, approximately another 8 minutes, adding more hot water if necessary. Place the rice in a dish and drizzle with a small amount of oil. Spread the rice out on a tray, let cool, then place on a large platter. Sauté the garlic in oil and remove when browned. Add the anchovies, cook until the mixture becomes well blended, and add the lemon juice and salt and pepper to taste. Remove from the heat and cool. When ready to serve, pour the sauce over the rice. Toss well, add the parsley, and serve at room temperature.

INSALATA DI ARANCE SANGUIGNE (Blood Orange Salad)

Blood orange salad is generally served as a starter.

SERVES 4

6 blood oranges
1 onion, cut into julienne

1 tablespoon finely chopped parsley
3 tablespoons extra virgin olive oil
Salt and pepper, to taste

Peel the oranges and slice into thin disks. Arrange the orange slices on a large platter, place the onion over the oranges, and sprinkle with parsley. Dress with olive oil, salt, and pepper and serve.

SALADS WITH BREAD OR BISCUITS

The most appropriate bread for *antipasti* is usually a large simple loaf called *casareccio*, or country bread. This should be neither too fresh nor too stale (day-old bread is ideal) so it can absorb the juices of whatever is put on it without breaking. Regional specialty breads are often re-baked (that is, *biscottato*, meaning "twice cooked"; after the first baking, the bread is sliced and baked again). *Pane biscottato* lasts a long time and is very tasty when served with a dressing.

Some special dishes such as *cappon magro* are made using *gallette* (sea biscuits), which are made without yeast and shaped like a bagel. Generally, all breads used for *antipasto* are soaked briefly either with water, water and vinegar, or in their own dressing.

FRISEDDA ALLA PUGLIESE (Frisedda with Tomato Salad)

SERVES 4
4 frisedda bread disks
3 ripe tomatoes, sliced
Pinch of oregano
Salt and pepper, to taste
¼ cup extra virgin olive oil

Lightly soften each *frisedda* in water and drain of excess water, taking care not to break them. Lay them on a plate and spread with the sliced tomatoes; add oregano, salt, pepper, and olive oil. Serve.

CONDIGGION (Sea Biscuits with Smoked Fish Salad)

SERVES 4
4 sea biscuits (gallette)
3 tablespoons vinegar
6 tablespoons extra virgin olive oil
4 ounces ripe tomato, thinly sliced
½ bell pepper, cut into julienne
1 cucumber, thinly sliced
2 garlic cloves, chopped

8 *basil leaves*
2 *ounces air-dried fish roe* (bottarga), *thinly sliced*
Salt and pepper, to taste
1 *head leaf lettuce*

Drizzle the sea biscuits with 1 cup water and 1 tablespoon of the vinegar until they soften, place on a large platter, and sprinkle with one tablespoon of the olive oil. Wash and cut up the vegetables, keeping them separate, and set aside. Chop the garlic and basil and set aside. Slice the *bottarga* into thin slices and set aside. Prepare a dressing with the remaining olive oil and vinegar, the chopped garlic and basil, and salt and pepper to taste and set aside. Layer the remaining ingredients on top of the *gallette*: lettuce, tomato, cucumber, and pepper. Sprinkle the dressing over the top and refrigerate for 1 hour. Before serving, add the *bottarga* on top.

PANZANELLA O PAN MOLLE (Bread and Vegetable Salad)

SERVES 4
4 *slices day-old country bread, cut into cubes*
2 *tablespoons white wine vinegar*
4 *tomatoes, cut into cubes*
1 *bell pepper, cut into small pieces*
1 *small white onion, cut into julienne*
6 *tablespoons extra virgin olive oil*
Salt and pepper, to taste
8 *basil leaves, cut into strips*

Drizzle the bread with 2 tablespoons water and the vinegar. Squeeze out excess liquid and place bread in a large serving bowl. Add tomatoes, pepper, and onion. Dress with olive oil, salt, and pepper; toss and add the basil leaves. Refrigerate until ready to serve.

CAPPON MAGRO (Ligurian Seafood Caponata)

This is the original recipe, still used today, for true *cappon magro*, Genoa's traditional Christmas Eve dinner specialty. Today *cappon magro* can be tasted in some Ligurian restaurants, though it usually must be ordered in advance. It is a multi-step recipe, but worth the effort.

SERVES 8

Gallette
8 *sea biscuits (gallette)*
1 *garlic clove*

2 tablespoons vinegar
Pinch of salt

Brush the sea biscuits with garlic and drizzle with 2 tablespoons water, the vinegar, and salt. Squeeze out the excess water and set the biscuits aside.

Vegetables

1 small cauliflower
12 ounces green beans
4 celery stalks
2 carrots
2 bunches red beets
2 potatoes
4 artichokes
½ cup plus 1 tablespoon extra virgin olive oil
3 tablespoons wine vinegar
Salt and pepper, to taste

Cook the vegetables whole, separately, until tender to the fork. Remove from the heat and cool. Peel and slice the beets and potatoes; dice the rest of the vegetables. Prepare a dressing by combining the oil, vinegar, salt, and pepper. Dress all the vegetables separately and set aside.

Fish

1 pound sea bass
1 pound lobster
16 medium shrimp, poached
16 anchovy fillets
16 mushrooms
16 green olives, pitted
2 ounces bottarga of tuna
16 oysters
½ cup extra virgin olive oil
2 tablespoons lemon juice

Poach, bone, and crumble the bass. Poach the lobster, slice, and set aside. Prepare 8 skewers with the shrimp, anchovy, mushrooms, and green olives and set aside. Slice the *bottarga* very thin and set aside. Shell the oysters and set aside. Prepare a dressing with the olive oil and lemon juice. Dress the bass, the lobster, and the skewers and refrigerate.

Sauce

1 bunch parsley
1 garlic clove

1 tablespoon pine nuts
2 tablespoons capers
4 anchovy fillets
2 hard-boiled egg yolks
3 slices crustless bread
6 large pitted black olives
1 cup extra virgin olive oil
6 tablespoons wine vinegar

Place all the ingredients into a food processor; mix well to get a fluid consistency. Set aside.

Assembling the Dish
Take a large round or oval platter and start by layering the sea biscuits flat on the platter. Sprinkle with 4 tablespoons of the sauce; add a few thin slices of *bottarga*.

Next, continue layering all ingredients, taking a little bit of each, placing the vegetables first, then the fish. Add 2 tablespoons of the sauce on each layer and continue until all ingredients are used. As you build it up, the final shape should be like that of a dome or a pyramid.

Decorate with the skewers previously prepared. Circle the base of the platter with oysters topped with the sauce and serve.

LEGUMI
Legumes

FAGIOLI (Beans)

New World (*Phaseolar vulgaris*) beans were first introduced to Europe by the Spaniards and the Portuguese who, in the sixteenth century, imported them from Central America. In archaeological research, Old World beans (*ceci, fave,* and *lenticchie*) have been found to be of common use as early as 4000 to 5000 B.C. Before America was discovered, only one type of bean was known in Italy, the so-called *fagiolo dell'occhio* (eye bean), a small bean already known to both the ancient Greeks and the Romans. In Italy, the first beans of American origin were cultivated in the area around Belluno, north of Venice, by order of a Church dignitary who had been sent a sack as a tribute from the king of Spain.

Today, beans are grown in almost every region of Italy, particularly in Campania, Veneto, Lazio, Tuscany, Lombardy, and Piedmont. The most common bean is *borlotto*, oval in shape with white stripes, of color ranging from white to red, coffee, gray, and dark blue, which turn an even dark brown while cooking.

Another popular variety is *bianco di Spagna*, which is much larger, as long as one to one and a half inches. This bean is white or off-white in color. Finally, the best-known beans are cannellini or *toscanelli*, white or cream-colored and rather small. They are grown almost everywhere, especially in Tuscany.

Beans can be bought either fresh in season or dried all year round. The number of varieties increases often because beans are particularly suitable for genetic crossings. Nearly every region in Italy has its favorite variety of beans.

Dry legumes do age. Check production dates on the package. Buy legumes not older than twelve months old. Generally, the quality of legumes is denoted by the thickness of the skin; the thinner the better. Older legumes have a tendency to lose the skin in the cooking process.

If you are using dried beans, soak them in cold water overnight. Fresh beans are cooked starting with boiling water. In either case, bring the beans to a boil and then cook over medium heat for about 1½ hours for dry beans or 30 minutes for fresh. The ratio of water to beans should be four to one.

CECI (Chickpeas)

These are round, slightly dented, beige seeds. They are only available dried or canned (cooked). If using dried *ceci,* before cooking make sure there are no pebbles mixed in with the chickpeas. *Ceci* can be used in soups, as a side dish for pork, either whole or mashed, or simply boiled and seasoned with oil. Their flavor is enhanced by adding rosemary, bay leaf, and garlic.

FAVE FRESCHE (Fresh Fava Beans)

Fava beans (also called broad beans) are a springtime legume. It is preferable to choose medium-size pods since they have a small seed with a more delicate flavor. If the seeds are too big, you might want to peel them to make them more digestible. If they are very small, you can serve them raw with fresh *pecorino* or salami as an appetizer.

FAVE SECCHE (Dried Fava Beans)

Before cooking dried fava beans, soak them for a day or two. The peel can be removed to make them easier to digest or they can be purchased peeled. Make sure they have no small holes caused by larvae. Throw away any beans with flaws. Dried fava beans are cooked in the same way as other dried beans and are used for soups and side dishes as well as mashed.

LENTICCHIE (Lentils)

Dried lentils are usually served in winter. They are sold in several different types and sizes. The most important variety are lentils from Castelluccio (Umbria). They are tiny in size and tastier. Soak lentils in water for several hours before cooking. Lentils are usually stewed and served with cuts of pork (for example, *zampone* or *cotechino*). Lentils are cooked the same way as other dried beans.

PISELLI FRESCHI (Fresh Peas)

These are green springtime legumes with a green pod containing small round seeds. Depending on their size, fresh peas are ranked as "extra fine," "fine," or "medium." There are two main varieties of peas: those which must be removed from the pod and can be eaten fresh, and those to be consumed whole (see *taccole*, page 112), including the pods. Tender, fresh peas are very sweet and can be braised, steamed, baked, or cooked in water for soups. They make a delicate side dish for white and red meats. Peas should not be shelled until just before cooking or they will dry up and become tough.

PISELLI SECCHI (Dried Peas)

Two kinds of dried peas are sold in Italy: whole peas with the peel intact (also called new peas), and split peas, which are peeled and dried. These can be used in the same way as dried beans but they cook much faster.

TACCOLE (Snow Peas)

This variety of pea is eaten in the pod after cutting off the two ends. The pods should be cooked in boiling salted water, then sautéed in olive oil or butter and served as a side dish. They can also be used in soups.

CANNELLINI ALL'UCCELLETTO (Stewed Beans)

SERVES 10

2 pounds dried white beans (cannellini)
4 garlic cloves, peeled and crushed
8 sage leaves
¼ cup extra virgin olive oil
1 pound tomatoes, peeled, seeded, and diced
Salt and pepper, to taste

Soak the beans overnight. Boil the beans in salted water for 1 hour. Drain and set aside. Brown the garlic with 4 of the sage leaves in 2 tablespoons of oil. Add the tomatoes, cook briefly, add the beans, and mix until well coated. Cover and let simmer gently for 30 minutes. Remove from heat. Place on a serving platter or in a bowl. Salt and pepper to taste, add other 4 sage leaves and the remainder of the olive oil, and serve at room temperature.

CANNELLINI AL FIASCO (Cannellini Beans Stewed in a Flask)

This can be cooked in a glass flask placed in a bain-marie. In Tuscany, where this is a traditional dish, *cannellini* beans are stewed in a cone-shaped terra-cotta pot (*fiasco*) with a wide base and a tight opening on top.

SERVES 6

1 pound dried cannellini beans
2 garlic cloves, peeled and crushed
2 sage leaves
Pinch of rosemary
⅓ cup extra virgin olive oil
Salt and pepper, to taste

Soak the beans in cold water overnight. Drain and put them in an ovenproof casserole dish along with the garlic, sage, rosemary, ¼ cup of the olive oil, and 4 cups of water. Place the casserole, covered, over low heat and cook gently for 2 hours so that the water evaporates. Add more water if necessary. The beans will absorb the oil. Place the beans in a bowl or serving platter and add the remaining oil, salt, and pepper to taste. Serve.

BORLOTTI CON LE COTICHE (Borlotti Beans with Pork Rinds)

SERVES 4

1 pound fresh pork rinds
2 small onions
2 garlic cloves
1 pound borlotti beans, soaked overnight
¼ cup extra virgin olive oil
2 celery stalks, finely chopped
2 small carrots, finely chopped
¼ cup peeled, seeded, and chopped tomatoes
Salt and pepper, to taste
1 cup beef broth (see pages 123–24)

Place the pork rinds, 1 onion (cut into large chunks), and the garlic in a large pot. Cover with cold water, bring to a low simmer, and cook for 2 hours or until the pork rinds are tender.

In a large pot, boil the beans in lightly salted cold water for 1 hour, or until tender. Drain. Prepare a *soffritto* in a casserole with the oil and the remaining onion (finely chopped), celery, and carrots. Cook until tender but not brown. Add the beans and pork rinds cut into 2-inch strips, the tomatoes, and freshly ground pepper. Add the broth and cook for 30 minutes. Adjust salt and serve piping hot.

FAGIOLI ALLA VENETA (Borlotti Beans with Anchovies)

SERVES 4

1 pound fresh borlotti beans, shelled
Salt and pepper, to taste
2 garlic cloves, crushed
2 tablespoons extra virgin olive oil
10 salted anchovy fillets, chopped
1 cup white wine vinegar
1 tablespoon chopped parsley

Boil the beans with a pinch of salt for 30 minutes, or until tender. Sauté the garlic in oil. Remove and discard the garlic when golden brown. Add the anchovies until they blend in with the oil. Add the vinegar and pepper and reduce for 10 minutes. Add the parsley, mix well, and pour this sauce over the drained beans. Adjust the salt and pepper, toss well, and serve.

Note:
Dried beans may be used instead of fresh beans. If so, cook for 1½ hours.

FAVE STUFATE (Braised Fava Beans)

SERVES 4

> *4 pounds fresh fava beans*
> *2 ounces prosciutto, cut into strips (use the fattier part)*
> *2 new or spring onions, finely sliced*
> *1 ounce mortadella, cut thick and diced*
> *2 cups beef broth (see pages 123–24)*
> *Salt and pepper, to taste*
> *6 slices country bread*

Shell the fava beans and set aside. Place the *prosciutto* fat and onions in a casserole and sauté until tender but not brown. Add the fava beans, *mortadella,* and beef broth. Add salt and pepper to taste. Cover the casserole and cook over low heat for 30 minutes, or until the fava beans are tender, adding more broth if necessary. The final dish should be fairly moist. Grill or toast the slices of bread on both sides. Place them on a serving platter and pour the fava beans over the bread. Serve very hot.

FAVE FRESCHE CON PANCETTA (Fresh Fava Beans with Pancetta)

SERVES 4

> *4 pounds fresh fava beans*
> *¼ pound pancetta, diced*
> *1 onion, thinly sliced*
> *1 celery stalk, sliced*
> *2 tablespoons extra virgin olive oil*
> *1 cup beef broth (see pages 123–24), hot*
> *Salt and pepper, to taste*
> *2 tablespoons chopped parsley*

Shell the fava beans, removing the peel if they are very big. Put the *pancetta,* onion, and celery in a casserole. Sauté in the oil, stirring frequently. When the fat of the *pancetta* has melted, add the fava beans, moisten with hot broth, and continue cooking. When the fava beans are completely done, about 30 minutes, add salt and pepper to taste, sprinkle with parsley, and serve.

LENTICCHIE IN UMIDO (Braised Lentils)

SERVES 6

> *1 tablespoon lentils*
> *1 small onion, thinly sliced*
> *2 ounces pancetta, cut into strips*
> *Sage leaves*
> *Salt and pepper, to taste*

Soak the lentils in water overnight. Sauté the onion with the pancetta and a few sage leaves in a casserole. Cook until tender but not brown. Strain the lentils and add them, covering with lukewarm water. Add salt and pepper to taste and cook 1 hour over medium heat, or until the lentils have absorbed all the water. Lentils prepared this way are served as a side dish to *cotechino* and *zampone* (see pages 40–41).

PANIZZA (Chickpea Polenta)

This dish, of Arab origin, is a common preparation in Liguria and Sicily today and lends itself to many different culinary interpretations.

SERVES 8

> *Salt, to taste*
> *7 cups chickpea flour*

Bring 2 quarts of water to a boil, add salt, and start to pour the flour slowly into water, whisking gently so as not to form lumps. Cook for 1 hour, stirring constantly. When ready, pour the cooked mix onto a flat board, about ⅓ inch thick, let it cool and become firm, and cut into squares or desired shapes. Serve as cocktail food, or with salami.

Note:
Panizza can be served hot, that is, soft, onto plates with grated *Parmigiano,* a drizzle of extra virgin olive oil, and chopped scallions.

PISELLI ALL'UOVO (Peas with Egg Drops)

SERVES 12

> *2 ounces pancetta, cut into strips*
> *1 onion, chopped*
> *2 tablespoons extra virgin olive oil*
> *2 pounds shelled fresh peas*
> *3 eggs*

2 tablespoons breadcrumbs
2 tablespoons grated pecorino cheese
Salt and pepper, to taste

Sauté the *pancetta* and onion in olive oil. When tender but not brown, add the peas and 2 cups of water, and cook for 30 minutes over medium heat. In the meantime, in a medium bowl, mix the eggs, breadcrumbs, and *pecorino*. Pour this mixture over the peas, toss gently to allow the eggs to set slightly, and remove from the heat. Adjust salt and pepper to taste and serve.

FUNGHI E TARTUFI
Mushrooms and Truffles

Mushrooms and truffles belong to the same family of vegetables (*Fungi*), the main difference being that mushrooms grow on the surface, receiving their nourishment from the earth, whereas truffles grow underground, feeding through the roots of trees.

Mushrooms are unanimously considered a culinary treat. Whether added to fettuccine or risotto, broiled or sautéed, or in a simple salad, mushrooms have a cherished role in Italian cooking. It is true, though, that they have little to offer from a nutritional point of view—they are made of 80 to 90 percent water, the rest being tiny quantities of minerals such as potassium and iron—but of course we don't eat them so much for sustenance as for our palates' delight.

Although some types of mushrooms, such as porcini and *ovoli*, are delicious alone, others such as *chiodini* and *gallinacci* are better as a complement to other preparations. Finally, others such as pleurotes are better preserved in oil or vinegar. There are many varieties of edible mushrooms in Italy, located mainly in a few regions, as described in the following pages.

We will not attempt here to teach how to distinguish poisonous mushrooms from edible ones. A good field guide can teach you the basics. The best education, however, is to go mushroom gathering with someone experienced and qualified. Buying wild mushrooms from a greengrocer is perhaps the safest way to purchase them.

FUNGHI (Mushrooms)

PORCINI (*Boletus edulis*)

This well-known variety grows mainly in the Appenino Emiliano around Parma, in Valtellina, in the Appennino Toscano (particularly the Garfagnana), in the Piedmont hills, and in the mountains of La Sila and Pollino in Calabria, although they can also be found in other mountain areas.

There are several types and qualities of porcini. The best are the ones picked in chestnut woods. The cap is tan colored and butter-white underneath. Porcini with dark caps are from beech trees or fir trees and, although less tasty, they are more suitable for being preserved. As the mushroom gets older, it turns ochre or green underneath the cap. The cap must be big, round, and fleshy and must be supported by a short round stem. Porcini can be eaten in salads or braised, cooked in a sauce, grilled, sautéed, or baked. They are also preserved in oil or dried for winter or commercial consumption.

OVOLI (*Amanita caesarea*)

It is considered by the experts to be the best of all edible mushrooms. When still young, it is closed and completely white, thus looking a bit like an egg. As it opens up, the cap turns a bright yellow-orange. *Ovoli* may be eaten in salads, seasoned with extra virgin olive oil, lemon juice, salt, and pepper. Once ripe, they can be fried (with or without batter), broiled, sautéed, or braised.

GALLINACCI (*Cantharellus cibarius*)

A yellow mushroom whose fragrance recalls the smell of a peach. They are cooked in sauces or preserved in oil. They are also known as *finferli*. Old *gallinacci* must be disposed of because their flesh is too fibrous and tough.

CHIODINI (*Armillaria mellea*)

These are tiny dark mushrooms with small heads and long thin stems. They are easily found as they grow in large spreads. They can be cooked like porcini, and, in addition, they can be preserved in oil. It is preferable to dispose of the lower half of the stem, since it tends to taste woody.

PRATAIOLI (*Agaricus pratensis*)

The oyster mushroom is white and fleshy with a pleasant scent. It is excellent for many preparations. Light pink and easy to find in open fields, *prataioli* are the classic mushrooms used to prepare *funghi trifolati* (sautéed mushrooms).

CEPPATELLI (*Pleurotus ostreatus*)

Pleurotus mushrooms grow at the bases of trees rather than on the ground; this is why they are called *ceppatelli* (literally "little stumps"). They are light gray in color, have a large cap and a very short stem. They can be cooked either breaded or simply fried.

FUNGHI COLTIVATI (Hothouse Mushrooms)

Hothouse mushrooms do not grow wild but are the hothouse-grown version of several varieties of mushrooms (e.g., *prataioli, ceppatelli, pleurotus*, and others). They can be eaten raw, thinly sliced and seasoned with oil, lemon juice, salt, and pepper. In addition, they may be cooked in various sauces.

TARTUFI (Truffles)

Truffles are plentiful in Italy. The two most distinguished varieties are the white truffles from Alba, Asti, and Cuneo (Piedmont) and Acqualagna (Marche) and the black ones from Norcia (Umbria).

White truffles are in season from October to December. They are more flavorful and have a much more pronounced fragrance than black ones. To find white truffles, truffle hunters use trained dogs (or pigs for the black variety). Both are specially trained to sniff the prized tuber. It is then snatched away before the animal can devour it. White truffles are eaten raw, thinly sliced, to top preparations such as *fettuccine, risotto, scaloppine,* and cheese fondue (*fonduta*).

Truffles should be consumed within ten days of picking and are best kept wrapped in paper towels, which should be changed daily. The larger sized truffles can be kept longer.

TARFUFO BIANCO (White Truffle)

The world-prized white truffle (*Tuber magnatum*) from Alba, Asti, or Cuneo (Piedmont) ripens from October to December. Its main characteristics are deep aroma and flavor. Its yellow-green skin is smooth and its inside, whose color can vary from brown to hazel, is hard and furrowed with thin white veins. The white truffles from Acqualagna, a small town near Urbino (in the Marche region), have also become quite popular in recent years.

TARTUFO NERO (Black Truffle)

Originally from Norcia, black truffles have a delicate aroma and taste. They ripen from November to mid-March. The skin is black and thinly wrinkled, and the color of the pulp is a purplish-black. Black truffles are generally cooked and seldom eaten raw. Black truffles can be farmed.

PORCINI BRASATI (Braised Porcini)

SERVES 2

> 1 pound porcini mushrooms
> 2 garlic cloves, crushed
> ¼ cup extra virgin olive oil
> 2 plum tomatoes, peeled, seeded, and chopped
> Salt and pepper, to taste
> 1 tablespoon chopped parsley

Slice the mushrooms or cut them into quarters if they are very small. Brown the garlic in a saucepan with the olive oil and remove garlic when brown. Add the tomatoes, sauté for 5 minutes, and add the mushrooms. Cook the mushrooms until tender and remove from the heat. Add salt and pepper to taste. Add the chopped parsley and serve.

CAPPELLE DI FUNGHI CON ANIMELLE
(Mushrooms with Sweetbreads)

SERVES 4

    8 medium porcini mushrooms
    1 garlic clove
    1 small onion, diced
    1 anchovy fillet
    3 tablespoons extra virgin olive oil
    6 ounces sweetbreads, poached, deveined, and thinly sliced
    Salt and pepper, to taste
    4 slices white bread
    6 tablespoons breadcrumbs
    1 egg
    1 tablespoon Parmigiano
    2 tablespoons chopped parsley

Preheat the oven to 375°F. Clean the mushrooms, remove the stems, and cut the stems into very thin slices; set the caps aside. Chop the parsley and garlic. Sauté the onion, garlic, and the anchovy in a saucepan with the oil. Add the mushroom stems and the sweetbreads. Add salt and pepper to taste and cook for about 10 minutes, stirring frequently. Remove from the heat and cool. Remove the crusts from the white bread, soften it in warm water, squeeze dry, and combine with the sautéed garlic, onion, and anchovy, egg, cheese, garlic, and parsley. Blend well to achieve a soft filling. Season with salt and pepper to taste. Add some breadcrumbs if the mixture is too soft.

    Fill each mushroom cap with the prepared mixture, place in a baking dish, and sprinkle with breadcrumbs and a small amount of oil. Cook for 20 minutes at 375°F and serve hot.

FUNGHI ALLA GRIGLIA (Broiled Mushrooms)

SERVES 6

    12 mushroom caps, preferably ovoli or porcini, though any type of
        fleshy mushrooms will do
    1 tablespoon chopped parsley
    2 garlic cloves

3 tablespoons extra virgin olive oil
Salt and pepper, to taste

Clean the mushrooms and remove the stems, setting them aside for another use. Prepare a *battuto* with parsley and garlic and mix with 2 tablespoons of the olive oil. Make a cross cut in the inside of each mushroom cap, season with the *battuto*, and grill with the inside up for about 5 minutes until tender but crisp. Remove from grill, and add the rest of the oil, salt, and pepper to taste. Serve very hot.

FUNGHI TRIFOLATI (Sautéed Mushrooms)

SERVES 4
2 pounds mushrooms
4 tablespoons extra virgin olive oil
3 garlic cloves
1 tablespoon chopped mint or nepitella
1 tablespoon chopped parsley
Salt and pepper, to taste
4 slices toast

Clean the mushrooms, slice the caps, and chop the steams. In a skillet over medium heat, warm the oil and add the garlic, removing it when brown. Add the mushrooms and sauté briskly over high heat for 4 minutes. When they are tender but still crisp, remove from the heat, add the chopped mint and parsley, and add salt and pepper to taste. Serve over slices of toast.

Note:
Funghi trifolati can also be served as side dish with roast meat, fowl, or venison.

UOVA AL TARTUFO BIANCO (Eggs in Cocotte with White Truffle)

SERVES 6
¼ cup heavy cream
2 ounces butter
2 tablespoons grated Parmigiano
Pinch of salt
12 fresh eggs
1 ounce white truffle
6 slices toast

Preheat the oven to 450°F. Heat the cream over low heat and mix in the butter. When melted, add the *Parmigiano* and salt and stir continuously. Do not bring to a boil. When this sauce is smooth, remove from the heat and set aside. Butter six 6-ounce ramekins. Divide the sauce evenly among them. Add 2 whole eggs to each ramekin and bake in a bain-marie for 7 minutes. They are done when the top is fairly solid (but not too stiff) and white. Remove the ramekins from the bain-marie, add the white truffle, thinly shaved, and serve immediately with toast. (If you are cooking with the bain-marie on top of a stove, cover the ramekins with aluminum foil.) Cooking time may vary according to size and thickness of the ramekins.

MINESTRE, MINESTRONE E ZUPPE
Soups and Broths

Italian cuisine is rich in soups of all kinds because of the variety of vegetables available and the general use of leftovers from bread, starches, fish, and shellfish. Unfortunately, some people seem to shy away from anything that needs to be eaten with a spoon, thus missing along with the wonderful flavors all the creativity and richness of these simple culinary preparations.

MINESTRE (Soups)

The term *minestra* refers to soup containing a liquid, either broth or simply water, with a starchy food, a vegetable, or a legume added. Any type of pasta can be used for *minestra*. In clear soups, usually small-sized fresh or dry pasta, dumplings, or various other types of ingredients such as bread, eggs, or a combination of both may be used. Most leafy vegetables or legumes are suitable for *minestra*.

BRODO (Beef Broth)

Beef broth is a staple element for making good soup. Broth may also be used as a moistening agent for many preparations. Here is the basic recipe.

MAKES 4 QUARTS
1 pound beef brisket
1 pound shoulder of beef
1 veal shank
Salt, to taste
1 onion, quartered
1 tomato, quartered
1 small bunch of parsley
1 celery stalk, cut up
½ tablespoon black peppercorns
2 carrots, cut in chunks
2 garlic cloves
1 egg white

Place the meat into a large pot with 5 quarts cold water and salt. Cover the pot and slowly bring to a boil. Add all the vegetables and spices and simmer for 3 hours. When ready, remove and reserve the meat (which will serve various uses later), remove and discard all the vegetables, and let the broth cool. Pass through a cheesecloth to further remove excess fat and other particles.

To clarify the broth, mix the egg white with 1 cup of cooled broth. Add the mixture to the pot with the broth. Bring to a boil, whisking constantly. Leave the broth to stand for 20 minutes. The fat will surface; remove it. At this point, the broth should be very clear.

Variations:
To make veal or chicken broth, use same method, replacing beef with veal or fowl.

To make fish broth, replace beef or chicken with fish heads and bones (your fish supplier can provide you with these parts). Gills must be removed from the fish carcasses to avoid making the broth bitter.

PASSATELLI IN BRODO (Bread and Egg in Beef Broth)

SERVES 6
> 2 eggs
> 1 cup finely grated white breadcrumbs
> 6 tablespoons grated Parmigiano
> Salt and pepper, to taste
> Pinch of nutmeg
> 2 quarts lean beef broth (pages 123–24), seasoned

In a medium bowl, whisk the eggs and add the breadcrumbs, softened with water and squeezed dry, and 3 tablespoons of the cheese, a pinch of salt and pepper, and the nutmeg. Knead to achieve a firm but soft mix. In a large pot, bring the broth to a simmer. Place the bread mix into a potato ricer and, as the broth simmers, rice the mixture into the broth, passing the mixture through the larger holes of the ricer. Cook for 3 minutes and serve, adding the rest of the *Parmigiano*.

STRACCIATELLA ALLA ROMANA (Egg Drop Soup)

SERVES 4
> 4 eggs
> 6 tablespoons grated Parmigiano
> Salt and pepper, to taste
> 1 quart beef broth (see pages 123–24), seasoned

In a medium bowl, beat the eggs with 2 tablespoons of the *Parmigiano* and salt and pepper. In a large saucepan, bring the broth to a slow simmer. Pour the egg and *Parmi-*

giano mixture into the broth while whisking vigorously so that the egg turns into solid drops. Remove from the heat. Add the remainder of the *Parmigiano,* mix well, and serve immediately.

Note:
Parmigiano can also be served on the side.

CICORIA, CACIO E UOVA (Chicory, Pecorino, and Egg Soup)

SERVES 4

1 pound green leafy chicory
2 onions
4 tablespoons extra virgin olive oil
3 eggs
4 tablespoons grated pecorino cheese
1 quart beef broth (see pages 123–24), hot

Green chicory has a fairly bitter taste, so wash it well and leave it to stand in cool water for 1 hour; it will lose some of its bitterness. Boil and chop the chicory, squeezing all the water out, and set aside. Cut the onions into a large saucepan and sauté with olive oil; when tender, not brown, add the chicory. Beat the eggs and mix with the *pecorino;* add this mixture to the chicory and sauté briskly for a few minutes and remove from the heat. In a large pot, heat the broth to a simmer. Place the chicory mixture in a large pre-heated soup tureen. Pour the piping hot broth over, stir well, and serve.

MINESTRA CON FIORI DI ZUCCA (Zucchini Blossom Soup)

SERVES 4

1 pound zucchini blossoms
1 small onion, diced
1 garlic clove, minced
1 small celery stalk, diced
¼ cup extra virgin olive oil
1 quart cups chicken broth (see page 124)
Salt and pepper, to taste

Wash the zucchini blossoms and set aside (if they are too large, split them into halves). In a casserole, sauté the onion, garlic, and celery with the oil and continue to cook until tender. In a large pot, heat the broth to a simmer. Add broth to the casserole, then add the zucchini blossoms. Simmer for 30 minutes. Add salt and pepper to taste and serve.

MINESTRA DI RISO CON ASPARAGI (Rice and Asparagus Soup)

SERVES 8

   1 pound fresh, thin green asparagus
   2 quarts lean beef broth (see pages 123–24)
   ¼ cup short- or medium-grain rice, rinsed
   4 tablespoons butter
   3 tablespoons grated Parmigiano
   Salt and pepper, to taste

Clean and wash the asparagus ends, starting from the tips, breaking them by hand into pieces about 1 inch long. In a casserole, bring the broth to a boil and add the rinsed rice. Cook, covered, for 12 minutes, then add the asparagus. Cook for another 3 minutes with the pot uncovered. Remove from the heat and add the butter and *Parmigiano*. Adjust for salt and pepper, stir well, and serve.

Note:

When cooking rice, taste it for doneness, just like pasta. Cooking time depends on rice quality, water, and altitude.

LA MARICONDA (Soup with Bread Dumplings)

SERVES 8

   4 cups breadcrumbs
   1 cup milk
   2 ounces butter
   6 tablespoons grated Parmigiano
   Pinch of nutmeg
   2 eggs
   Salt and pepper, to taste
   2 quarts beef broth (see pages 123–24)

Moisten the breadcrumbs with 1 cup warm milk in a bowl and let stand for about 20 minutes. Squeeze out excess milk. Melt the butter in a small saucepan, add the breadcrumbs, stirring constantly with a wooden spoon, and cook until the breadcrumbs are entirely dry.

   Place the cooled breadcrumbs in a bowl, then add 3 tablespoons of the *Parmigiano*, a pinch of nutmeg, the eggs, and salt and pepper to taste. Mix well. If the mixture is too soft to make dumplings, add more breadcrumbs. Leave it to stand in a cool place for about 1 hour. Shortly before serving, divide the breadcrumb mixture into small dumplings, each about the size of a hazelnut. In a large pot, bring the broth to a boil. Gently add the dumplings. Lower the heat and, stirring carefully, cook 5 minutes over low heat. Serve with the remaining *Parmigiano*.

Variation:

White meat from a boiled chicken or cooked ham (both finely minced) may also be added to the breadcrumb mixture before forming the dumplings.

PASTA E FAGIOLI SPOLICHINI (Pasta with Fresh Borlotti Beans)

Just about every region of Italy has its own version of *pasta e fagioli*. This one comes from Campania.

SERVES 6

  2 pounds shelled fresh beans
  Salt, to taste
  2 ounces pancetta
  1 small onion
  2 garlic cloves
  2 tablespoons chopped parsley
  2 ripe tomatoes, quartered
  7 tablespoons extra virgin olive oil
  1 pound mixed dry pasta
  Pinch of pepper
  ¼ cup grated Parmigiano

Cook the beans in 6 quarts of boiling water for 30 minutes, or until done. Add salt to taste. Finely chop the *pancetta,* onion, and garlic, and sauté in the oil with the parsley and tomato over medium heat until the *pancetta* is crisp and the vegetables are just tender. Set aside. When the beans are done, add the sautéed mixture (*soffritto*). Bring to a boil and add the pasta. Stir and let it cook until the pasta is *al dente* (about 8 minutes). Add more hot water or broth if you feel it is getting too dense. Just before serving, add a pinch of freshly ground pepper and 2 tablespoons of the *Parmigiano*. Serve with the remaining *Parmigiano* on the side.

Variations:

Before adding the pasta, pass about half the beans through a food mill or food processor and return resulting purée to the broth.

  The *soffritto* may be eliminated. While cooking the beans, add the crushed cloves of garlic, the chopped onion, tomato, and parsley, and the olive oil.

Notes:

This soup can be made using other types of beans such as *cannellini,* navy beans, etc.

  If you use dried beans, soak them overnight and cook starting with cold water for 1 hour.

PASTA E PATATE (Short Pasta with Potato Soup)

SERVES 4

> 1 pound potatoes
> ¼ cup olive oil
> 1 onion, cut into julienne
> 4 ripe tomatoes, peeled and chopped
> Salt and pepper, to taste
> 8 ounces short pasta, or long pasta broken up
> ¼ cup grated Parmigiano

Peel and dice the potatoes and simmer in a large casserole with 2 quarts of water until tender. Set aside. Prepare a *soffritto* with the olive oil, onion, and chopped tomatoes. When the vegetables are tender but not brown, add to the potatoes. Add salt and pepper to taste. Place casserole on medium heat and bring to a boil. Add the pasta and cook until *al dente*. Remove from the heat, and add 2 tablespoons of the *Parmigiano*. Let rest for a few minutes and serve sprinkled with the rest of the grated cheese.

Notes:
Add more water or broth if your soup gets too thick while cooking.

Whenever pasta is added to a soup, bring the heat to high until the pasta is cooked.

PASTA E LENTICCHIE (Pasta with Lentil Soup)

SERVES 4

> 1 pound lentils
> 2 quarts cold water
> 2 garlic cloves, crushed
> 1 ripe tomato, coarsely chopped
> 1 celery stalk, chopped
> Salt and pepper, to taste
> 8 ounces spaghetti, broken into 1-inch pieces
> ½ cup extra virgin olive oil

Check the lentils for pebbles and soak for at least 12 hours, discarding the ones that float to the surface. Place the lentils in a large pot with 2 quarts of cold water, the garlic, tomato, celery, salt, and pepper. Cook until lentils are tender, about 20 minutes. When ready to serve, bring the lentils to a boil, add the broken-up spaghetti, and cook until *al dente*. Remove from the heat, drizzle with olive oil, and serve.

Variation:
Start cooking the lentils by themselves and halfway through the cooking discard the original water and replace with boiling hot water or broth. Then add the garlic, celery, and tomato. This must be done quickly so as not to interrupt the cooking process.

MINESTRA MARITATA (Meat and Vegetable Soup)

This soup is traditionally served on the day after Christmas. The word *maritata* means married, because the meats and vegetables are married in one soup.

SERVES 12

   1 prosciutto bone
   ½ pound salami
   ¾ pound pork ribs, preferably small ones
   4 pork sausages
   6 ounces pork rind
   1 pound lean beef round
   2 medium onions
   1 medium carrot
   2 celery stalks
   ½ bunch green leafy chicory
   ½ Savoy cabbage
   ½ bunch curly white endive
   ½ bunch broccoli
   ½ cup Brussels sprouts
   Salt and pepper, to taste
   ¾ cup extra virgin olive oil

In a large pot, starting with cold salted water (2 quarts for every pound of meat) cook all the meats, together with the onions, carrot, and celery. Cook for 2 hours. Remove all the meats from the water, reserving the water, and cool.

In the same water cook all the remaining vegetables until tender. Meanwhile, coarsely dice all the meats, separate the pork ribs, remove any meat from the *prosciutto* bone and dice it. Return all the meat to the pot with the vegetables. Stir well and cook for another 15 minutes. Remove from the heat and adjust salt and pepper, if needed. Warm up a large soup terrine by letting hot water sit in it for a few minutes. Pour the soup into the terrine and serve, drizzled with some of the olive oil. Pass the remaining oil for people to drizzle into individual bowls.

Note:
Add more water if the soup gets too thick.

GRAN FARRO E FAGIOLI (Spelt and Kidney Bean Soup)

SERVES 6

   1 pound, 6 ounces fresh borlotti beans
   6 tablespoons extra virgin olive oil
   2 onions, thinly sliced

¼ *pound prosciutto, finely chopped*
1 *celery stalk, chopped*
2 *garlic cloves, crushed*
3 *to 4 sage leaves*
1 *tablespoon marjoram*
Pinch of nutmeg
½ *pound tomatoes, peeled, seeded, and finely sieved*
Salt and pepper, to taste
½ *pound (one cup) spelt (unshelled farro)*

Cook the beans in a large pot of boiling water until tender, about 30 minutes. Drain the beans, reserving the cooking water. Put beans in a food processor and puree to a smooth cream. Heat 3 tablespoons of olive oil in a large saucepan and add the onions, *prosciutto,* celery, garlic, sage, marjoram, and nutmeg. Sauté gently and when the onions start to brown, add the tomatoes, salt, and pepper and simmer this *soffritto* for about 15 minutes. Add the *soffritto* to the bean puree with a little of its own water and bring to a boil. Add the spelt and cook for about 45 minutes, adding more bean water as the soup thickens. When the spelt is cooked, remove from the heat, place in a large soup terrine, drizzle with the remaining extra virgin olive oil, and serve.

Note:
If fresh beans are not available, use dried beans. Soak the beans overnight, rinse in fresh water, and boil for 1 hour.

MINESTRONE (Vegetable Soups)

Minestrone refers to a soup made with at least three kinds of vegetables and may also include dry or fresh pasta, rice, legumes, or dumplings. Grated *Parmigiano* is always used to season *minestrone* that contains a starch. (In some Italian regions *pecorino*, which is aged sheep's milk cheese, replaces *Parmigiano*); grated cheese is never added to *minestrone* that contains only vegetables. *Minestrone* may be served at room temperature, especially in summer, but never cold, straight out of the refrigerator.

MINESTRONE MILANESE (Vegetable Minestrone with Rice)

SERVES 6
2 *firm zucchini*
2 *celery stalks*
2 *carrots*
2 *ripe tomatoes*
6 *tablespoons parsley*
6 *sage leaves*

2 garlic cloves
1 large onion
4 ounces pancetta, cut into strips
¼ cup extra virgin olive oil
1 pound fresh peas, shelled
Salt and pepper, to taste
1 pound dried borlotti beans, soaked overnight
3 potatoes, diced
1 quarter Savoy cabbage, sliced into strips
8 ounces (1 cup) short- or medium-grain rice
¼ cup Parmigiano
Extra virgin olive oil

Rinse and dice the zucchini, celery, and carrots. Peel, seed, and dice the tomatoes. Finely chop parsley, sage, garlic, and onion. Sauté the *pancetta* in a casserole with 2 tablespoons of the olive oil over medium heat together with the garlic, onion, parsley, and sage. Stir this *soffritto* until the onion is soft but not brown. Add all the vegetables, except for the beans, potatoes, and cabbage, together with 3 quarts of hot water and a little salt. Cover the pot and when it reaches the boiling point, add the beans, cover the pot, and cook for 45 minutes. At this point add the potatoes and the cabbage, cut into julienne. Cook another 30 minutes. Check that the cabbage is tender and as the whole simmers, add the rice; cook for 16 minutes, stirring frequently so that the *minestrone*, which should have thickened by now, does not stick to the bottom of the pot. Be careful not to overcook the rice. If the *minestrone* gets too thick, add some water. Remove from the heat and add the grated *Parmigiano*. Let rest for 15 minutes, adjust salt and pepper, and serve either hot or at room temperature. In either case, drizzle some extra virgin olive oil over the soup just before serving.

Variations:
Rice can be replaced with a kind of short pasta.

For *minestrone genovese*, you may add 3 tablespoons of *pesto* just before serving, and replace half of the *Parmigiano* with *pecorino*, but use pasta, not rice.

MINESTRONE DI VERDURE (Vegetable Minestrone)

SERVES 6
1 pound fresh fava beans
1 pound peas
3 ripe tomatoes, sliced
2 pounds white or yellow onions
1½ pounds zucchini

1 head romaine lettuce
2 pounds fresh green leafy vegetables
Handful of basil leaves
2 tablespoons minced parsley
½ cup extra virgin olive oil
2 quarts beef broth (see pages 123–24)
Salt and pepper, to taste

Shell the fava beans and the peas, keeping them separate. Peel, seed, and chop the tomatoes. Slice the onions. Wash and slice the zucchini without peeling them. Wash and coarsely chop the leafy vegetables. Clean, rinse, and mince the basil and parsley. Place all the vegetables in a pot in this order: first the tomatoes at the bottom of the pot, then the onions on top, the zucchini over them, then the romaine lettuce and the green peas, finally, the rest of the fresh green vegetables sprinkled with half of the parsley. Add the fava beans. Drizzle with oil. Cover the pot and cook over medium heat. Do not stir for about 10 minutes, until the vegetables at the bottom of the pot release their water. Add the broth, a pinch of salt, and a pinch of pepper. Stir, cover the pot, and cook on very low heat for about 1 hour. When ready, add the rest of the parsley and serve. Neither rice nor pasta should be added to this minestrone.

FAGIOLI CON CAVOLO NERO ALLA TOSCANA
(Bean Soup with Tuscan-Style Black Cabbage)

SERVES 6
1 pound dried cannellini beans
1 whole black Tuscan cabbage, cut into large chunks (see Note)
2 carrots, medium size
1 large onion, chopped
2 leeks, chopped
2 celery stalks, chopped
1 tablespoon chopped parsley
3 ounces pancetta, cut into strips
½ cup extra virgin olive oil
2 pounds ripe tomatoes, peeled, seeded, and chopped
Pinch of thyme
Handful of basil leaves
Black pepper and salt, to taste
Extra virgin olive oil, for serving

Soak the beans in water overnight. The next morning, drain, put them in a pot with 3 quarts of lightly salted cold water, and let cook for 1 hour, or until tender. Clean, wash, and slice the cabbage, carrots, onion, and leeks. Prepare a *soffritto* with celery, parsley, and *pancetta* and place it all into a large casserole on the stove with the oil. Sauté over low heat until it begins to get tender, then add the cabbage, carrots, onion, and leeks and bring to a simmer. Add the tomatoes, thyme, and a pinch of black pepper, and continue to cook over low heat, stirring frequently until the cabbage gets tender. Add the cabbage to the beans and their broth, stir well, and let cook for 30 minutes more. Remove from the heat, add the basil leaves, taste for salt and pepper, and let it rest for 1 hour before serving. Serve with extra virgin olive oil on the side.

Notes:
Black cabbage may be replaced with Savoy cabbage.

Add more broth if the soup gets too thick.

INCAPRIATA (Fava Bean Soup with Wild Chicory)

SERVES 8
> 2 pounds dried fava beans
> ¼ cup extra virgin olive oil
> 1 teaspoon ground black pepper
> Salt, to taste
> 1 pound wild chicory
> Extra virgin olive oil flavored with peperoncino, for serving

Soak the fava beans in water overnight. Cook the fava beans for 1½ hours, remove from water, and cool. Retain the water for later use. Place fava beans into a blender with the oil, blend them to a soft puree, add black pepper and salt, and set aside. Boil the wild chicory in water with salt added to taste. Cook till the greens are soft but crisp. Reheat the fava beans. Serve with chicory on the side and *peperoncino*-flavored olive oil.

Notes:
The flavored oil can just be replaced with a very good extra virgin olive oil and *peperoncino* on the side.

The fava beans will thicken as they stand on the side. Add some of the fava bean water if the puree is too thick. When served, it should be a soft puree.

ZUPPE (Soups with Bread)

***Zuppa* refers to soup with a semi-liquid consistency obtained by cooking meat, fish, shellfish, seafood, legumes, or herbs in water and then pouring the broth over slices of bread.** Sometimes the bread is toasted and served on the side, or it may be baked with the vegetables and broth. For this preparation it is best to use crusty country-style bread, preferably slightly stale bread (3 to 4 days old) but not very dry; the bread should still be a little soft, or it will not absorb the broth properly.

ZUPPA VALDOSTANA (Cabbage and Cheese Soup)

SERVES 4

   1 small Savoy cabbage (about 1 pound)
   ½ pound fontina cheese
   2 ounces butter
   4 slices of 2-day-old country bread, ½ inch thick, toasted
   Salt and pepper, to taste
   2 quarts beef broth (see pages 123–24)

Preheat the oven to 325°F. Clean and wash the leaves of the Savoy cabbage well. Cook them in boiling water for 10 minutes. Drain and cut into julienne. Cut the *fontina* into thin slices. Melt the butter over low heat. In an ovenproof pot (preferably terra-cotta), place 2 slices of bread on the bottom of the pot, then add the cabbage, top with *fontina* cheese, and top it with the rest of the bread. Add salt and pepper to taste. Drizzle the top layer with melted butter. Gently pour the broth over it and bake for about 30 minutes. Serve hot.

Note:

To make a larger quantity of soup, double the recipe and alternate layers of bread and cabbage and cheese, making sure the top layer is bread.

ZUPPA PAVESE (Egg and Bread Soup)

SERVES 4

   4 slices of crusty country bread
   2 ounces butter
   4 eggs, at room temperature
   ¼ cup grated Parmigiano
   1 quart beef broth (see pages 123–24)

In a skillet over medium heat, fry the slices of bread in butter on both sides. Place each slice of bread in an individual bowl. Break 1 egg on top of each bread slice without breaking the yolk. Cover with grated *Parmigiano*. Bring the broth to a boil and pour it slowly over the eggs. The eggs will cook quickly. Serve immediately.

Variation:

Fry the eggs in butter before placing them on the slices of bread, and then cover with hot broth.

RIBOLLITA (Bean Soup Baked with Bread)

Ribollita literally means "reboiled." This does not mean the soup is actually reboiled but rather refers to the use of leftover bean soup to create a distinctive and beloved speciality.

SERVES 10

4 quarts fagioli con cavolo nero alla toscana
10 slices day-old country bread
4 cups beef broth (see pages 123–24)
1 onion, thinly sliced
1 cup extra virgin olive oil

Prepare the minestrone by following the recipe on page 132.

Preheat the oven to 375°F. Alternate layers of bread and soup in a large terra-cotta pot. Add broth as necessary to moisten. Cover the top layer with thinly sliced onion. Sprinkle generously with ½ cup of the olive oil and bake for 30 minutes. Remove from the oven, let the soup rest for 15 minutes, and serve it in the same pot. Drizzle with olive oil, which gives this dish a silky, smooth texture.

ZUPPA VALPELLINENTZE (Savoy Cabbage Soup and Fontina Cheese)

This soup has many variations, depending on which village it comes from. This version is from Valle d'Aosta, a region in northern Italy.

SERVES 10

1 large Savoy cabbage
2 tablespoons extra virgin olive oil
3 ounces pancetta, chopped
12 slices country bread
12 slices prosciutto
Pinch of black pepper
Pinch of ground cinnamon
Pinch of ground nutmeg
½ pound fontina cheese, sliced (at least 12 slices)
1 ounce butter
2 quarts beef broth (see pages 123–24)

Preheat the oven to 350°F. Clean the Savoy cabbage and remove the stem. Sauté the cabbage leaves in a saucepan with oil and pancetta, making sure not to break the leaves. When wilted but still crisp, remove from the heat and let cool. Toast the bread and place in a flat baking pan large enough to hold 6 slices of bread flat. Place a layer of cabbage leaves over the bread, topped with slices of *prosciutto*. Add a pinch of pepper, cinnamon, and nutmeg. Add thin slices of *fontina*. Continue with layers until all the ingredients are used up, making sure the top layer is *fontina*. Dot with butter and generously cover with broth.

Bake for 30 minutes or until top is a little golden brown.

PAPPA AL POMODORO (Tomato and Bread Stew)

SERVES 12

½ cup extra virgin olive oil
4 garlic cloves, chopped
2 bunches basil, chopped
3 pounds ripe tomatoes, peeled, seeded, and cut into large chunks
Salt and freshly ground black pepper, to taste
2 loaves day-old country bread, cubed
1 quart beef or chicken broth (see pages 123–24)
6 basil leaves
Extra virgin olive oil, for serving

Preheat the oven to 375°F. Heat 4 tablespoons of the olive oil, garlic, and half the chopped basil in a saucepan over medium heat. Remove and discard the garlic when brown. Add the tomatoes, adjust for salt and pepper, and cook for 20 minutes. Add the remaining half of the chopped basil and set aside. Coat the bread cubes with olive oil in a baking pan. Add salt and pepper to taste and toast the bread in the oven until golden. Add the tomatoes to the bread and toss well, adding the broth—as needed— to make a thick stew of the bread and tomatoes. You should be able to see broth surrounding the bread. If not, add more. Bake for 20 minutes until most of the broth is absorbed—the consistency should be that of a stew. Serve in individual soup bowls, adding basil leaves and a dash of extra virgin olive oil.

CACCIUCCO LIVORNESE (Fish Stew Livornese-Style)

Cacciucco is a soup traditionally made with various types of fish, such as dogfish, seatoad, scorpion fish, conger eels, gobies, stargazer, etc., most of which are not found in the United States. However, you can use many other sorts of firm-fleshed fish. According to tradition, this soup should contain at least five different sorts of fish.

SERVES 8

2 pounds mixed fish fillets, such as red snapper, rock cod, halibut, bass, monkfish
  (reserve the heads and bones for the broth)
1 pound octopus and squid (optional)
1 medium onion, chopped
1 carrot, chopped

1 *celery stalk, chopped*
1 *tablespoon chopped parsley*
1 *whole peperoncino*
3 *garlic cloves*
⅓ *cup extra virgin olive oil*
1 *cup dry white wine*
½ *pound ripe tomatoes, peeled and seeded*
Salt and pepper, to taste
2 *quarts fish broth (see page 124)*
8 *large shrimp*
6 *slices bread, ½ inch thick, toasted*

Cut the fish fillets into 2-ounce pieces. Cut the octopus and squid into medium-size chunks. Make a *soffritto* with the onion, carrot, celery, parsley, *peperoncino,* and 2 cloves of the garlic. Put it in a saucepan together with the oil and sauté until the onion is golden and the vegetables are just tender. Add the squid and the octopus and cook over low heat for 20 minutes, occasionally moistening with white wine, then add the tomatoes. Add salt and pepper to taste and finish cooking the octopus and the squid, for 15 minutes or more until tender. In another pot, place 2 quarts of water and the heads and bones of the fish. Cook for 90 minutes, stirring every now and then. Cool and pass this broth through a fine sieve and add the broth to the pot with the octopus and the squid.

Bring to a simmer and add all the remaining fish to the pot together with the shrimp. Add the 2 quarts fish broth and finish cooking. (Time is determined by the size of the fish, probably no more than 5 minutes.) Remove from the heat. Rub the remaining garlic clove over the bread slices. Using a large rimmed soup plate for each person, pour the fish broth over the slices of bread, top the bread with the fish, and serve.

Note:
A large bowl for the table may be used. In this case, serve the bread on the side.

ZUPPA DI VONGOLE (Clam Soup)

This delicious soup is served with garlic bread, either placed into the soup just before serving, or on the side.

SERVES 4
4 *pounds very fresh clams, preferably New Zealand cockles or vongole veraci*
4 *slices bread, cut about ½ inch thick*
3 *garlic cloves*
⅓ *cup extra virgin olive oil*
1 *pound ripe tomatoes, peeled, seeded, and chopped*

Pinch of peperoncino
1 cup fish broth (see page 124), if needed
2 tablespoons chopped parsley
Salt and pepper, to taste

Rinse the clams and place in cold salted water for 2 hours without touching them, so that they release any possible remaining sand.

Toast the bread, rub the slices with 1 clove of the garlic, and set aside. Take the clams out of the water and let them drain through your fingers. (Do not drain with a colander to avoid picking up the sand as well.) Brown 2 crushed garlic cloves with the olive oil in a large casserole. When the garlic is lightly brown, remove and discard it. Add the tomatoes and a pinch of *peperoncino.* Cook for about 10 minutes and bring to a simmer, and add the clams. Cover the pot and cook until all the clams are open. Add broth only if you do not have enough liquid.) Remove from heat. Add the chopped parsley and salt and pepper to taste just before serving. Place the bread in individual large soup bowls. Pour the broth and clams over the bread and serve hot.

Variations:

This *zuppa* can be prepared without tomatoes. Replace them with 1 cup of white wine, reduce for 2 minutes, and add the clams. The garlic toast can also be served on the side.

One can use mussels instead of clams.

SOPA COADA (Squab Soup)

SERVES 6

6 squabs or 2 pounds guinea hen
Salt and pepper, to taste
6 tablespoons butter
1 cup white wine
6 cups chicken broth (see page 124)
6 slices bread, cut ½ inch thick
4 tablespoons grated Parmigiano

Preheat the oven to 325°F. Split in half and clean the squabs, generously seasoning with salt and pepper. In a large casserole, brown the squabs in 4 tablespoons of the butter. When they start to get golden brown, add the white wine, cover the pot, and cook slowly over low heat for 45 minutes, or until done. Remove from the heat, cool, and bone the squabs completely, trying to keep the meat as whole as possible. Using the pot that the squabs were in, add the broth and simmer slowly for 15 minutes. Skim off any excess fat and keep warm over low heat. Toast and butter the bread slices. Arrange half the buttered toast in a baking dish and drizzle with the broth. Top with half the squab meat and grated *Parmigiano,* add another layer with the same ingredients, and pour the rest of the broth over it. Bake for 25 minutes.

Note:
This soup can be made with tripe in place of fowl.

BUSECCA (Tripe Soup)

SERVES 8

2 pounds tripe, the curly part (foiolo) already cooked (page 242)
2 onions, chopped
3 sage leaves
4 tablespoons extra virgin olive oil
1 ounce butter
1 carrot, chopped
2 celery stalks, chopped
4 cups vegetable broth
8 slices of bread
6 tablespoons grated Parmigiano
Pepper, to taste

Tripe is sold already cooked, but to make *busecca* it still requires two more hours of cooking before starting with the recipe. When you bring the tripe home, simmer it in water, covered, for 2 hours. Drain and cool. Cut the tripe into a fine julienne. Sauté the onions and sage with olive oil and butter in a casserole. When the onions are wilted but not brown, add the tripe. Sauté for 5 minutes and then add the carrot and celery. Add the vegetable broth and cook for 45 minutes. Place each slice of bread into a rimmed soup plate and pour soup over the bread. Serve grated *Parmigiano* on the side and offer freshly ground pepper.

Variations:
Other versions call for adding sliced potatoes and beans (*cannellini* beans are preferable). The beans are best when cooked separately and then added to the tripe. The proportions of potatoes and beans compared to tripe are: one-eighth as much potatoes and one-quarter as much beans.

PASTA E RIPIENI,
GNOCCHI E POLENTA
Pasta and Stuffings, Gnocchi and Polenta

PASTA (Pasta)

Cereals have been a primary food staple throughout the ages. Since ancient Rome, the basic daily diet in Italy has consisted mostly of starchy foods made with flours (the Latin *pultes*), from ground barley, rye, or spelt *(farro)*.

The creation of bread as we know it today was favored by the introduction of wheat—which originated in the highlands of Ethiopia—and the discovery of yeast. Then, as the use of soft and hard wheat boomed, pasta began to be produced for individual needs first and, later, on an industrial scale. Pasta has become the fundamental feature of the Italian diet. *Spaghetti* and *maccheroni, penne* and *cavatelli, ravioli, tortellini, fusilli,* and the many other pasta varieties belong to an immense family of ingredients, all of poor origins yet offering a surprisingly balanced diet.

Legend has it that Marco Polo brought pasta to Italy on his return from China. This assumption is actually incorrect. The first to produce historical evidence of this is Massimo Alberini, a noted historian who died in Venice in the spring of 2000. A few years before, as he was collecting material for the project of a spaghetti museum, while researching in the city archives in Genoa, he found a will. In the document, witnessed and signed by a public notary on February 2, 1279, Ponzio Bastone, a soldier, mentions among his belongings *una bariscella plena di macaronis* (a barrel full of macaroni). The document is important for two reasons: First, it dates long before the return of Marco Polo from China, and second, the word *macaroni* appears for the first time, clearly to indicate dried pasta, as one cannot imagine that he would leave his heir a barrel full of fresh pasta!

PASTA SECCA (Dried Pasta)

Dried pasta—that is, the pasta you normally find for sale at the market—must be made with hard wheat flour, regardless of size or shape. If it contains a percentage of soft wheat flour, it will take less time to cook but will be sticky and the water in which it cooked will be cloudy. Pasta made solely with hard wheat flour is compact and translucent; its surface feels slightly coarse to the touch. It will snap when it breaks, as if it were made of glass. It will take longer to cook than that made with soft wheat, will considerably increase in size after cooking, will not stick (although it should be stirred occasionally), and the water in which it cooked will stay relatively clear.

The quality of pasta, however, is not measured only by how much hard wheat flour it contains. Other basic factors are the millstone employed in grinding it, the water used, the kind of extruder used, the form, the manufacturer's skill, and last but not least, a careful and thorough drying process, which must be carried out in separate stages over a long period of time and in the appropriate environment.

PASTA ALL'UOVO SECCA (Dried Egg Pasta)

Dried egg pasta is made by adding 7 ounces of egg for each 2.2 pounds of wheat. It may come in short shapes and is best cooked in beef or vegetable broth. Longer egg pasta like *tagliatelle* is served with sauce or *ragù*. Pasta cut into large squares is used for *pasticci* (lasagna) and *timballi* (baked pasta).

PASTA GLUTINATA (Gluten Pasta)

Gluten pasta is particularly recommended for children, convalescents, and the elderly. The gluten, added to enrich the pasta, is a substance rich in protein, found abundantly in hard wheat flour. It is a tenacious, elastic substance that gives cohesiveness to the particles of wheat flour. This kind of pasta is only available in small forms suitable to be cooked in beef or vegetable broth.

How to Cook Dried Pasta

In cooking pasta, it is advisable to use a heavy pot, the kind that allows the water to retain the heat longer, with a wide bottom to let the heat spread evenly, and high sides to avoid the danger of boiling over. A pot like this allows the water to boil more quickly and to reach the boiling point again more rapidly once the pasta has been added. This is very important because if it takes a long time to return the water to a boil after the pasta has been added, the pasta may turn out sticky.

For each ¼ pound of pasta, 1 quart of water and about ½ ounce (1½ teaspoons) of coarse salt are necessary. When the water reaches a full, rolling boil, add the pasta. When cooking short pasta, add it all at once. With long pasta it is better to add it in two or three batches, one right after the other, taking care to spread it out so that it does not stick. If you are cooking *ziti* or *bucatini* (thick spaghetti with a hole), make sure the pasta is fully immersed in the boiling water so that the hole is soaked immediately. After adding the pasta to the water, stir, cover the pot, and turn up the heat if possible so that the water can return to a boil fast. Once the water is boiling, take off the lid immediately. This is crucial; pasta cooked in a covered pot will be sticky. While cooking, pasta must be stirred every now and then to prevent the pieces from sticking to each other and to the bottom of the pot. Stir short pasta with a large wooden spoon and long pasta with a long wooden fork.

Cooking time will vary according to the quality, form, and thickness of the pasta, or even with the hardness of the local water and the altitude. To determine whether pasta is done, taste it repeatedly as it approaches readiness. Remove from the water when still al dente, which means when the pasta has a slightly firm, chewy texture. It is a good habit to drain pasta when it is still a bit undercooked. Drain it thoroughly, but keep some of the water, as you may need it later. If you plan to use a rather liquid sauce, the warm sauce will itself provide the necessary moisture to complete the cooking process. If you are using a heavier sauce, you may need to add some of the cooking water you have kept aside.

The standard way to drain pasta is to pour it into a colander or a strainer, depending on the amount and size. As you do so, the pasta will lose a lot of the starch coating each strand or piece. The optimal way to take pasta out of its cooking water is with a long fork, a skimmer, or any other appropriate utensil.

Pasta is then put into a pan already containing the sauce, which will allow it to be tossed over the hot sauce, or in a tureen with a few tablespoons of the sauce at the bottom. Adding a ladle of cold water to the drained pasta to stop the cooking process is a questionable practice. One might do so only if pasta had been left to cook longer than necessary.

Notes:

Most times pasta is *mantecata* before serving, that is, sautéed briskly in a skillet with the desired sauce and *Parmigiano*.

Seafood sauces for pasta should never have grated cheese added; the cheese is too strong for the delicate taste and texture of a fish sauce.

It is a mistake to think that well-cooked pasta is more digestible. Indeed, the opposite is true. If pasta offers some resistance to chewing, one will instinctively chew longer, hence producing more saliva and more gastric juice to ease digestion.

While one might think that some gourmets exaggerate when they claim that each type of pasta favors a particular type of sauce, it is true that not all kinds of pasta are compatible with a given sauce. A rule of thumb: Use lighter sauces for thin and long pasta and heavier sauces for thicker and short pastas.

Most Common Types of Dried Pasta

PASTA LUNGA (Long Pasta)

Capellini, capelli d'angelo, capelvenere
- Shape: Thread-like (very fine) and round. They can also be found packaged in bundles or "nests." When vegetable coloring is added, green- or red-colored pasta nests result.
- Use: With very delicate sauces and in soups
- Cooking Time: 2 to 3 minutes

- Recommended Sauces: Can be cooked in beef broth, or seasoned with butter, or just with a very good extra virgin olive oil

Spaghettini, spaghetti, vermicelli
- Shape: Long, round strands
- Use: For pasta dishes with sauces
- Cooking Time: 5 to 8 minutes
- Recommended Sauces: *Spaghettini* is best with sauces containing oil, garlic, and *peperoncino* or with light fish sauces, whereas *spaghetti* is suitable with heavier sauces such as tomato, *carbonara,* and fish *ragù. Spaghetti* may also be tossed with just oil or butter and grated cheese.

Bigoli, vermicelloni
- Shape: Long, round, thicker strands
- Use: For pasta dishes seasoned with heavier sauces
- Cooking Time: 10 to 12 minutes
- Recommended Sauces: Meat and game sauces

Trenette, linguine
- Shape: Long, flat strands
- Use: For pasta dishes with vegetable and fish sauces
- Cooking Time: 5 to 7 minutes
- Recommended Sauces: *Trenette* with *pesto* or other vegetable sauces; *linguine* with either oil and vegetable combinations or light fish sauces

Lasagne, lasagne festonate, tagliatelle (also called fettuccine), reginette, tripolini
- Shape: Long, flat, and wide, *tripolini* being narrower than the others. *Lasagne festonate* are called this because of their peculiar festooned edges. The larger types of *lasagne* can also be used for *pasticci.*
- Use: For baking with various sauces and other ingredients
- Cooking Time: 7 to 10 minutes, depending on size
- Recommended Sauces: Game and any type of *ragù*

Bucatini, perciatelli, maccheroncelli
- Shape: Long, tubular, hollow (*bucatini* are thinner)
- Use: For all sauces. Can also be used in vegetable soups (*minestra* and *minestrone*) but then the tubes need to be broken into smaller segments.
- Cooking Time: 8 to 10 minutes
- Recommended Sauces: *Bucatini* or *perciatelli* are very suitable for *amatriciana* and other meat- and vegetable-based sauces.

PASTA CORTA (Short Pasta)

Rigatoni millerighe, penne, sedani, maniche
- Shape: Tubular in shape, varying in size; can be either straight or curved, smooth or grooved (grooved pasta sometimes has spiral patterns)
- Use: The smaller type is suitable for soups, the larger with sauces. May also be baked.
- Cooking Time: 14 to 16 minutes
- Recommended Sauces: The smaller varieties are suitable for light sauces; the larger varieties for tomato and beef *ragù.*

Fusilli, conchiglie, farfalle
- Shape: *Fusilli* look like short, spiral-like spaghetti, *conchiglie* look like sea shells; *farfalle* look like butterflies or bow ties.
- Use: With vegetable sauces, also as cold pasta salads
- Cooking Time: 10 to 13 minutes
- Recommended Sauces: Light sauces with tomato, vegetable soups

Stelline, anellini, alfabeto, risone
- Shape: *Stelline* look like little stars, *anellini* like rings, *alfabeto* like letters of the alphabet, *risone* like grains of rice.
- Use: Mostly for clear soups
- Cooking Time: 5 to 7 minutes
- Recommended Sauces: Liquid sauces and broth, occasionally for molds

CAPELLINI CON SALSA VERDE (Capellini with Green Sauce)

SERVES 6

2 tablespoons chopped basil
2 tablespoons chopped parsley
2 garlic cloves
¼ cup grated Parmigiano
¼ cup extra virgin olive oil
1 pound capellini

Combine basil, parsley, garlic, and *Parmigiano* in a food processor. Start the blender and add olive oil so as to obtain a dense but fluid sauce. Set aside. Boil capellini in plenty of salted water. Be careful as this kind of pasta cooks very quickly. Drain while still *al dente,* reserving about a cup of the cooking water. Toss the pasta with the sauce and serve.

Note:
If the pasta is too dry, add 2 tablespoons of the cooking water.

LINGUINE ALLE VONGOLE VERACI (Linguine with White Clam Sauce)

SERVES 6

2 pounds clams, preferably cockles
6 tablespoons extra virgin olive oil
4 garlic cloves, crushed
Pinch of peperoncino
1 pound linguine
1 tablespoon chopped parsley

Buy clams that are imported—*vongole veraci* are recognizable because they have 2 suckers (they look like little horns). Let the clams sit in cold salted water for at least 1 hour. Steam the clams in a large pot just until they open. Do not overcook or they will get chewy. Remove from the heat and let cool. Remove each clam from its shell. Pass the remaining broth through a fine sieve or cheesecloth. Put the shelled clams in the strained broth and set aside but keep warm.

In a large sauté pan, warm 4 tablespoons of the olive oil. Add the crushed garlic and a pinch of *peperoncino*. Remove the garlic when browned. Add two thirds of the clam broth and reduce by a third. Add the remainder of the clam broth and the clams. Remove from heat. Cook the *linguine* in plenty of salted water. When very *al dente* drain the pasta. Toss briskly with the clam sauce, add the parsley and remove from heat. Put the pasta in a serving bowl, drizzle with the remaining 2 tablespoons of olive oil, and serve.

Variation:
For red clam sauce, add 2 cups of peeled, seeded, and chopped plum tomatoes just after removing the garlic.

SPAGHETTI ALLA PUTTANESCA (Spaghetti Streetwalker-Style)

SERVES 6

6 anchovy fillets
1 pound ripe tomatoes
6 tablespoons extra virgin olive oil
3 garlic cloves, crushed
Pinch of peperoncino
3 ounces pitted olives, preferably Gaeta or niçoise
1 tablespoon capers
Salt and pepper, to taste
1 pound spaghetti
12 basil leaves

Chop the anchovies. Peel, seed, and chop the tomatoes. Pour the oil into a warmed skillet and add the garlic and *peperoncino*. Cook over medium heat until the garlic browns.

Add the chopped anchovies, olives, and capers. Sauté briskly, then add the tomatoes. Stir and cook for about 10 minutes. Adjust for salt and pepper. Cook the *spaghetti* in plenty of boiling salted water until *al dente*. Toss the *spaghetti* with the sauce, add the basil leaves, and serve.

Note:
Spaghettini may be used instead of *spaghetti.*

PASTA CON LE SARDE (Bucatini with Fresh Sardines)

SERVES 6

> 1 onion
> 6 tablespoons extra virgin olive oil
> 8 anchovy fillets
> 1 tablespoon chopped wild finocchietto (see Glossary)
> 1 tablespoon tomato paste
> 1 tablespoon raisins
> 1 tablespoon pine nuts
> Pinch of saffron threads
> 1 pound fresh sardines, cleaned, boned, and refolded
> Salt and pepper, to taste
> 1 pound bucatini
> 1 cup fish broth (if necessary)

Clean and coarsely chop the onion. In a sauté pan over medium heat, brown the onion in olive oil. Add the anchovies, the *finocchietto,* and the tomato paste. Stir briskly until the mixture is homogeneous. Add the raisins, pine nuts, and saffron, stir, and get this sauce very hot. Cook the sardines in this sauce, making sure they do not break up. Remove the sardines when cooked on both sides and set aside but keep warm. Adjust the sauce and sardines for salt and pepper. Cook the *bucatini*. When *al dente,* drain and sauté briskly with the sauce over medium heat for 2 minutes. Add some broth if sauce is too dry. Place the pasta on a serving platter. Arrange the sardines on top and serve hot.

PASTA ALLA NORMA (Pasta with Eggplant and Basil)

SERVES 6

> 1 pound eggplant
> Salt and pepper, to taste
> 1 garlic clove
> ¼ cup extra virgin olive oil
> 1 pound ripe tomatoes, peeled, seeded, and diced

1 pound penne
10 basil leaves
½ cup ricotta salata, grated

Slice the eggplant and place on a surface propped on a slant, cover with salt, and leave under a weight for 1 hour or until the bitter water seeps out. Brown the garlic in the oil. Add the tomatoes and salt. Bring to a simmer over medium heat and continue cooking, stirring occasionally, for 15 minutes. Add a pinch of pepper. Remove from the heat and set aside. Rinse the slices of eggplant and pat dry. Fry in hot oil. Place on paper towels to drain, then coarsely dice and set aside. Cook the *penne* in a large pot of boiling salted water until just *al dente* and drain. Quickly toss the pasta in a large skillet with half of the tomato sauce, the eggplant, a few basil leaves, and half of the grated cheese over high heat, no more than 2 minutes. Put the pasta in a serving dish; cover with the remaining half of the sauce, and the rest of the grated *ricotta*. Sprinkle with a few more basil leaves and serve.

PASTA FRESCA (Fresh Pasta)

How to Make Fresh Pasta

Fresh pasta is made with 2 pounds (7 cups) all-purpose flour, 8 whole eggs, and ½ teaspoon salt. Depending on the region of Italy, less or more eggs are used. In some cases a little water is added; in others, 2 eggs and more water. In other regions, only the egg yolks and a little oil are used. Regardless of these regional variations, the dough must be well kneaded—that is, until little bubbles are visible—before being stretched with a rolling pin.

Procedure: Pour the flour on a pastry board *(spianatoia)* in a cone-shaped mound. Break the eggs into the center of the cone and blend the yolks with the whites, using a fork or fingers, then begin gradually kneading the egg with the flour. When the dough has a thick texture so that it is no longer possible to use a fork, the egg will no longer be liquid and about half of the flour will be incorporated. Continue to work the dough with your hands, pushing it up from all sides and adding in as much flour as possible. Keep on kneading for about 15 minutes. The dough must be thick and rather stiff or it will be difficult to roll out, though it might seem to be the opposite. Wrap the dough with a cloth and keep it under a weight for 30 minutes. This allows the dough (particularly the gluten in the dough) to relax; it will be less elastic and much easier to roll out after a short rest.

Note:
The procedure described below is the most authentic way to make pasta. Mechanical aids may be used instead of manual methods. The result may vary somewhat. It is said that the warmth of the hands gives the hand-kneaded dough a better, more chewy texture.

Green Pasta

Wash ½ bunch of spinach and cook until soft. When ready, squeeze it very tightly between your palms, so that the spinach is as dry as possible, then sieve or put it in a food processor. Add the spinach to the flour and eggs in the basic recipe. You may add or do without an egg depending on the wetness of the spinach.

Red Pasta

Add 3 tablespoons of concentrated tomato paste to the basic recipe.

How to Roll and Cut the Dough by Hand

Put the dough on a pastry board that has been lightly dusted with flour, punch it down flat with your palms, and start rolling it out with a floured rolling pin. To roll it out evenly, start from the center of the dough, rolling in all directions and extending the pressure evenly toward the outer edges of the dough. Fold the dough over occasionally and keep rolling it without pushing too hard with the rolling pin. In the end, the dough should form a large, flat sheet of equal thickness throughout. Sprinkle with a little flour and fold the pasta into a roll. Cut through the roll into ribbons as wide as desired with a very sharp knife, starting from one end. When finished cutting, unravel the ribbons on the board, tossing with more flour. Let the pasta dry for about 1 hour before cooking.

The Most Common Types of Fresh Pasta

Lasagne

1 or 2 inches wide, as long as desired, best baked with *ragù* and other ingredients. For *lasagne* preparation, use whole, square, or rectangular sheets, according to the baking pan being used.

Maltagliati

Irregular cuts of leftover sheets of pasta; used in *minestra* or *minestrone* or with light sauces

Pappardelle

½ inch wide, 6 to 8 inches long, best with game sauces

Quadrettini

Little squares used for clear soups

Tagliatelle

¼ inch wide and long, best with tomato sauce and meat *ragù* (in central Italy, *tagliatelle* are called *fettuccine*)

Tagliolini

$\frac{1}{16}$ inch wide and long, best with light sauces or vegetables

Tagliolini Paglia e Fieno

As above but with a mix of spinach and plain egg noodles

Trenette

$\frac{1}{8}$ inch wide and long, best with *pesto* or fish sauces

Fresh Pasta Cut into Shapes

Farfalle

The Italian word for butterflies or bows, shaped as their name implies

Strichetti

Means "pinched," in this case in the center, thus achieving the same shape as *farfalle*. Both types are cut from a flat sheet of pasta, approximately 2 inches long and 1 inch wide for *farfalle,* and 3 inches long and 2 inches wide for *strichetti*. Pinch the dough in the center of the longer side to form a bow. Make as many as necessary. Both types may be used with light, fluid tomato and vegetable sauces.

Notes:

All fresh pasta can be made with the addition of a vegetable puree for coloring, following the method explained above.

Cooking time varies from 2 to 3 minutes for *paglia e fieno* to a longer time for *farfalle*. A rule of thumb is that when pasta starts to come up to the surface, it is likely to be done. As always, the best test is to try it; it should be slightly firm when you take a bite.

With the addition of grated *Parmigiano* to the basic dough recipe (1 tablespoon for each 3½ cups of flour) and double the eggs, the pasta, cut ⅛ inch wide, is called *tajarin*, a specialty from Piedmont. This pasta is used for broths or boiled and sautéed with butter and shavings of white truffles when in season.

TAJARIN AL TARTUFO BIANCO (Tajarin with White Truffle)

In Piedmont, *tagliolini,* or *tajarin* as they are called in dialect, are prepared using this recipe, which honors the local white truffle as the perfect accompaniment. Sometimes a spoonful of *Parmigiano* is added to the pasta dough. Remember that this thin pasta cooks very quickly. Therefore make sure you prepare the ingredients beforehand.

SERVES 4

4 ounces butter
Pinch of nutmeg
Salt and white pepper, to taste

1 pound tagliolini (see page 149)
¼ cup grated Parmigiano
1 ounce white truffle

Melt and clarify the butter. Add nutmeg, salt, and pepper to taste. Cook the pasta in boiling water for 3 minutes. Drain the pasta, reserving about 1 cup of the cooking water. Toss the *tagliolini* quickly in a large preheated bowl away from the heat, with the butter and the *Parmigiano*. Add a ladleful of the cooking water, toss well, and spoon the pasta onto serving plates. Slice the white truffle over the pasta, using a truffle slicer.

How to Cook Fresh Pasta

All types and shapes of homemade pasta are cooked in plenty of boiling salted water or broth. Pasta should be added all at once, making sure the water (or broth) is boiling rapidly and returns to the boiling point quickly after the pasta has been added. Stir with a wooden fork for long pasta or a big wooden spoon for short kinds. When the pasta starts to come to the surface, try it and drain it when still lightly underdone (al dente). Remember, the pasta will continue to cook when still very hot and during the addition of the condiment.

Pasta must be served as fast as possible after cooking. Add sauce or sauté with the desired condiment. This procedure is called *mantecare*. Serve immediately.

Other Types of Fresh Pasta

In preparing the following pasta dough recipes always follow the basic recipe procedures; just add or delete ingredients as specified.

BIGOLI (Whole-Wheat Spaghetti)

Bigoli, thick whole-wheat *spaghetti*, is a traditional type of pasta from the Veneto. To make *bigoli*, a special kitchen utensil called *torchio* is used.

Mix whole-wheat flour with 2 eggs, ½ cup milk, and 2 tablespoons melted butter for each pound (3½ cups) of all-purpose flour. Work into a hard dough. Pass the dough through a *torchio* and this thick kind of *spaghetti* will come out without a hole. *Bigoli* is traditionally served with an onion sauce slowly cooked in olive oil with a couple of anchovy fillets or in a game or duck *ragù*. This preparation is called *bigoli in salsa*.

CIRIOLE (Twisted Eggless Pasta)

Knead whole-wheat flour with the necessary amount of warm water and a pinch of salt. Knead. Cut the dough into thin strips and pull and twist each piece with your hands until it becomes about 6 to 8 inches long and fairly thin, only about twice as thick as *spaghetti. Ciriole* are usually served with *amatriciana* sauce or with oil, garlic, and *peperoncino.* Cooking time is 12 to 15 minutes.

GARGANELLI (Fresh Quills)

The dough for *garganelli* is prepared with all-purpose flour, eggs, and grated *Parmigiano* (1 tablespoon cheese to 1 pound [3½ cups] of flour), then rolled out very thin and cut into 2-inch squares. The dough is rolled with a wooden stick over a comb-like utensil called a *pettine.* The result is a quill-shaped pasta. Meat *ragù* is the traditional sauce. Cooking time is 7 minutes.

MACCHERONI ALLA CHITARRA (Fresh Spaghetti from Abruzzo)

The dough for *maccheroni alla chitarra* is prepared the same way as fresh pasta but with 60 percent semolina flour and 40 percent all-purpose flour and 4 whole eggs per every pound (3½ cups) of flour. This is a rustic form of pasta, a specialty of Abruzzo, cut into rather thick, long, and squared strings on a utensil called a *chitarra,* a wooden two-sided frame lined with many thin wires stretched across its length, much like the strings of a guitar. (The word *maccheroni* should not mislead the reader because this preparation of pasta resembles much more a long string pasta [e.g., *spaghetti*], but in Abruzzo it is called *maccheroni.*)

The thickness of the fresh pasta, when rolled, should be approximately as thick as the distance between any two wires of the *chitarra.* Lay the sheet of pasta over the wires and cut with a rolling pin, pressing over the *chitarra* wires. Dust the cut pasta with flour, form 4-ounce nests, and set aside until ready to cook. The preferred sauce for *maccheroni alla chitarra* is lamb *ragù,* but it may also be served with other sauces such as tomato and basil. Cooking time varies depending on thickness.

MALLOREDDUS (Tiny Dry Dumplings)

In Sardinian dialect, *malloreddus* stands for "young bulls" or "calves." Make the dough with white wheat flour, warm water, salt, and a pinch of saffron and knead. Stretch the dough to ⅓ inch thick and cut strips of the same thickness. Pinch off pieces of dough the size of a bean and roll them against a non-metal sifter so that the pasta beans will curl when pressed. They will look like tiny dumplings. *Malloreddus* must dry for at least 2 days. It is usually served with a sausage *ragù.* It cooks in 12 to 15 minutes.

ORECCHIETTE (Ear-Shaped Pasta)

This is a specialty of Apulia in the south of Italy, and as its name suggests (in Italian *orecchio* means "ear"), it resembles the shape of little ears. To make *orecchiette,* knead the flour with water to make a stiff dough. Knead the dough into a ½-inch-thick roll, cut it into strips ½ inch wide, and cut the strips into pieces the size of kidney beans. Press down each piece and roll it along the pastry board either with a round-point knife or with your thumb, going from left to right. The dough will first stretch and then roll up. Finally, turn it inside out over the tip of your thumb, thus forming little ear-like shapes. *Orecchiette* may be boiled in water along with vegetables (e.g., broccoli rape, arugula, broccoli, etc.) and drained. Cooking time is approximately 12 to 15 minutes. To prepare *orecchiette,* brown garlic in olive oil with *peperoncino.* Add tomatoes. When the sauce is ready, add cooked *orecchiette,* sauté briskly, and serve immediately.

PIZZOCCHERI (Buckwheat Tagliatelle)

Mix 2 pounds (7 cups) buckwheat flour with 12 ounces (2½ cups) all-purpose flour. Add warm water and knead. Roll the dough out to about ⅛ inch thick and cut into strips ⅓ inch wide. *Pizzoccheri* are typical of Valtellina and are served with vegetables, fresh cheese (*toma* or *bitto,* a local specialty), and plenty of butter.

Variations:

Eggs may be added to the dough, just as in the basic recipe for fresh pasta, and milk can be used instead of water for kneading.

TESTAROLI (Pasta Triangles)

This pasta is typical of Lunigiana, an area between Liguria and Tuscany; its roots are Etruscan. *Testaroli* provide a good example of a food preparation technique inherited straight from our ancestors. *Testaroli* are in fact simple disks of pasta made with water and flour and cooked on a *testo* (from the Latin *testum*), which is a hot flat surface of either terra-cotta or cast iron. Pour 1 pound (3½ cups) of all-purpose flour into 1 quart of water containing 1½ teaspoons of salt and mix well until you have a fluid consistency (like that of a pancake mix). Heat up a *testo* or a cast-iron pan, and make as many thin, flat disks as you can, until you finish up the mixture. As you make the disks of dough, set them aside, one on top of the other, and leave to rest until they cool. Cut the disks into triangular shapes (though any shape will do). Bring a pot of salted water to a boil, turn off the heat, immerse the *testaroli,* cover the pot, turn the heat up again, and cook for 6 to 7 minutes. Once cooked, remove the *testaroli* with a strainer, place on a serving platter, and use classic *pesto* as a condiment. Serve immediately.

TROFIE (Small Twisted Pasta)

Trofie are a specialty of Liguria. Mix together 2 pounds (7 cups) of all-purpose flour, 6 ounces of bran, a pinch of salt, and water. Knead the mixture to obtain a smooth, compact, and elastic dough. Punch down the dough ⅓ inch thick and cut it into ⅓-inch-wide strips. Cut 2-inch-long strips and with the palm of your hand rub the strips across the pastry board, one at a time to make an elongated twisted shape. Dust with flour and set aside. *Trofie* are cooked in plenty of boiling, salted water together with a finely sliced potato and a handful of very thin string beans. Cooking time is 8 to 10 minutes. They are traditionally served with *pesto*.

TAGLIATELLE CON I FUNGHI (Tagliatelle with Mushrooms)

SERVES 4

1 small onion, very finely chopped
¼ cup extra virgin olive oil
½ pound porcini mushrooms (when in season), sliced
Salt and pepper, to taste
1 pound tagliatelle
2 ounces butter
¼ cup grated Parmigiano

Prepare a *soffritto* by sautéing the onion in olive oil. When onion is just tender, add the sliced mushrooms. Sauté for 2 minutes and add salt and pepper to taste. Remove from the heat. Cook the *tagliatelle* in plenty of boiling salted water. When *al dente,* drain the pasta, reserving about a cup of the cooking water. Toss pasta in a large skillet with the mushroom sauce, the butter, and half of the *Parmigiano.* Add a few tablespoons of cooking water if too dry. Dish onto a serving platter and serve with the remainder of the *Parmigiano* on the side.

FETTUCCINE ALLA CARBONARA (Fettuccine Carbonara)

SERVES 6

¼ pound pancetta
2 egg yolks
½ cup grated pecorino cheese
Salt, to taste
1 pound fettuccine
2 tablespoons extra virgin olive oil
1 teaspoon cracked peppercorns

Chop the *pancetta* and sauté over a low flame. When it is golden brown, remove from the heat, discard excess fat, and set aside.

Beat the egg yolks and combine with the cheese and salt to taste. Whisk well. Set aside. Boil the *fettuccine* in plenty of boiling salted water. When *al dente,* drain and put in a large skillet with the olive oil. Over high heat, add the *pancetta,* the egg and cheese mix, and the cracked pepper. Toss well and serve immediately.

Note:

The original recipe requires *guanciale* (smoked pork jowl). It also calls for the use of the discarded excess fat instead of the olive oil.

FETTUCCINE ALFREDO (Fettuccine with Cream)

This recipe comes from Alfredo Di Levio, the owner of the famous Alfredo restaurant in Rome. It is an adaptation of *fettuccine alla doppia creama*, a classic recipe, as prepared in his restaurant. Alfredo liked to calls his double cream *doppio burro* (double butter). The following is the original recipe:

SERVES 4

>   1 pound fettuccine
>   1 ounce butter
>   1¼ cups heavy cream
>   5 ounces grated Parmigiano
>   Freshly ground white pepper
>   Salt, to taste

Have all your ingredients ready before you start. Cook the *fettuccine* with more salt than usual. Drain and remove when *al dente,* reserving a cup of cooking water. Place the pasta in a large skillet with a few tablespoons of cooking water and the butter. Toss well, then add cream and *Parmigiano*. Toss well. The result should be a smooth, velvety sauce. It should not be dry. Add freshly ground pepper and salt. Serve immediately.

Variation:

In *fettuccine al mascarpone*, the cream is replaced with *mascarpone*.

PAPPARDELLE AL SUGO DI LEPRE (Pappardelle with Hare Sauce)

SERVES 8

>   **Marinade**
>   4 cups dry red wine
>   1 celery stalk, cut up
>   1 onion, cut up
>   2 thyme sprigs

1 carrot, cut up
1 bay leaf
1 hare, cut into pieces

Sauce
2 ounces pancetta, cut in strips
¼ cup extra virgin olive oil
Pinch of nutmeg
2 pounds pappardelle
6 tablespoons grated Parmigiano

Prepare the marinade by combining all the ingredients. Pour over the hare and marinate for 12 hours, refrigerated.

The next day, in a casserole, sauté the *pancetta* in olive oil over high heat. Drain the hare, reserving the marinade. Add the hare to the casserole and cook until brown on all sides. Add the marinade and a pinch of nutmeg. Continue to cook until the meat falls from the bone. (The hare can be stewed on the stove over low heat or in the oven at 375°F.) When done, set aside and cool. Remove the meat from the bones. Sieve the cooking liquids and place in a saucepan. Add the shredded hare meat and keep hot. Boil the *pappardelle* in plenty of boiling salted water. Toss with the hare sauce and half of the *Parmigiano*. Serve with the rest of the *Parmigiano* on the side.

Note:
Wild fowl or venison can be used instead of hare.

FARFALLE AL POMODORO FRESCO
(Fresh Bow Ties with Tomato and Herb Sauce)

SERVES 4
¼ cup extra virgin olive oil
1 garlic clove, crushed
Pinch of peperoncino
Pinch of oregano
1 tablespoon chopped parsley
1 pound ripe tomatoes, peeled, seeded, and diced
1 pound fresh bow-tie pasta
4 cups chicken broth (see page 124)
Salt and pepper, to taste

Heat the olive oil in a pan. Add the garlic, *peperoncino,* oregano, and parsley. Sauté over low heat. Add the tomatoes. Cook for 12 minutes with the pot covered over medium heat. When ready to serve, cook the pasta in the sauce rather than boiling it in water: Bring the tomato sauce to a simmer. Add the pasta and stir gently, adding the broth as needed until done. This should not take more than 4 to 5 minutes. Remove from the heat and adjust the flavoring with salt, pepper, and *Parmigiano* if desired.

PASTA RIPIENA (Stuffed Fresh Pasta)

Cappelletti, tortellini, agnolini, ravioli, and *tortelli* are always made with dough containing eggs, usually stretched thinner than that used for *tagliatelle.* The dough for stuffed pasta is stretched out, filled with stuffing, and cut into the desired size and shape. They can be squares, circles, or rectangles and more.

Stuffed fresh pasta is classified into types and varieties according to the different ways it is folded and shaped. Often the same variety goes under different names in different regions of the country.

The stuffing may be made of various meats, vegetables, fish, or cheese and is usually bound with eggs and *Parmigiano.*

To make *ravioli,* for example, the stuffing is placed on stretched dough previously brushed with a beaten egg or water and another sheet of pasta is placed on top of it. It is then pressed down with your hands all around the stuffing, so that little packets are formed. Finally, it is cut into squares of varying sizes with a pastry cutter. Make sure the dough is tightly sealed around the stuffing to prevent air bubbles from forming.

How to Cook Stuffed Fresh Pasta

Stuffed fresh pasta that is to be served with a sauce must be cooked in salted boiling water. Add stuffed pasta all at once, and then gently stir with a spoon or a skimmer. It is important that the water start boiling again very quickly after pasta is added. When the water starts boiling again, turn down the heat, because fast boiling can break up the stuffed pasta (remember that stuffed fresh pasta is thinner than in other preparations). As the pasta floats to the top, try it: If it needs longer cooking time, push it down with a skimmer. Cooking time varies according to the thickness of the dough. Stuffed pasta must be cooked *al dente.* The heat of the sauce will complete the cooking process, so be sure not to overcook. Drain the pasta well by scooping it out with a skimmer (do not use a colander); arrange it in layers in a bowl, and top each layer with hot sauce and *Parmigiano.* If pasta is to be cooked in broth, follow the same procedure outlined above, using a rich beef or chicken broth.

CANNELLONI

Cannelloni are rectangles of boiled fresh pasta stuffed and rolled with a desired filling, covered with a favorite sauce, dotted with butter and grated *Parmigiano,* and baked. Make the pasta dough as in the basic recipe (see page 147). Stretch the dough to ⅛ inch thick and cut into 6 by 4-inch rectangles. Cook the pasta in plenty of salted boiling water, adding 2 tablespoons oil, until *al dente,* strain, and cool with cold water to stop the cooking. Coat with olive oil so that they do not stick together and will be easier to work with. Stuff with the desired stuffing, roll, and arrange in a greased baking pan. Add sauce, dot with butter, and sprinkle with grated cheese. Bake in a preheated 375°F oven for 25 minutes and serve.

Notes:

Any stuffing for *ravioli* is suitable for *cannelloni*—that is, any meat, vegetable, fish, and cheese, and bound with egg and *Parmigiano.* But the stuffing for *cannelloni* should be firmer than that used for stuffed pasta (which is sealed on all sides), or the stuffing will run out of the 2 open ends.

Sauce for *cannelloni* must be more fluid and abundant than usual, to keep the pasta moist, because some of the liquid will evaporate while baking.

Cannelloni are also called *manicotti* in the United States. Sometimes a batter is used to make crêpes, instead of pasta, and then stuffed.

CANNELLONI RIPIENI DI VITELLO E SPINACI
(Cannelloni Stuffed with Veal and Spinach)

SERVES 6

18 cannelloni
¾ pound chopped veal
3 ounces butter
2 pounds spinach leaves
¼ pound ham, chopped
2 whole eggs
Salt and white pepper, to taste
Pinch of nutmeg
6 tablespoons grated Parmigiano
1¼ cups ragù bolognese (page 30)
2 tablespoons extra virgin olive oil

Preheat the oven to 375°F. Follow the basic recipe to prepare the pasta for *cannelloni* (see page 157). Prepare the stuffing: Sauté the veal with 2 tablespoons of the butter. Boil the spinach and chop, squeezing out excess water. Mix the veal and ham with the spinach, eggs, salt, pepper, nutmeg, and 4 tablespoons of the *Parmigiano.* Chop in a food processor to obtain a smooth stuffing. Prepare the *ragù.* Cook the squares of pasta in salted boiling water until the pasta squares surface. Drain and cool and coat with oil. Prepare the *cannelloni* as follows: Pipe on each cooked pasta square the stuffing with a piping bag, about ¾ inch thick. Roll up the *cannelloni.* In a buttered baking dish, line up the rolled *cannelloni.* Pour the meat sauce over and sprinkle with the remaining 2 tablespoons of *Parmigiano.* Dot the top with the remaining butter and bake for 25 minutes, or until the topping is bubbling. Remove from the oven. Let rest for 10 minutes and serve.

CAPPELLETTI (Alpine Hats)

This pasta is shaped somewhat like an alpine hat. Cut the pasta, thinly rolled and brushed with water, into 2-inch squares with a pastry cutter. Place a bit of stuffing in the center of each square, fold a corner edge over, and press around the stuffing. Then, keeping the stuffed area against your index finger, pinch together the 2 far corners of the resulting triangle. While pinching the ends together, lightly push the stuffing upward. The resulting *cappelletti* should not have a hole in the center but should look like an alpine hat.

CRESPELLE (Stuffed Crêpes)

Crêpes are thin pancakes prepared with flour, milk, and eggs. To prepare *crespelle,* use an 8-inch round iron pan. Heat the pan until a drop of water sizzles. Brush the pan with oil. Pour in 3 tablespoons of the mixture. Rotate the pan so that the mix spreads evenly to cover the whole bottom. The crêpe will form very quickly. Brown both sides and make as many as you need. The filling may be similar or more delicate than the stuffing used for pasta but should definitely be softer. Spread the stuffing evenly, then fold each *crespella* twice to form a triangle. Finish the dish following the recipe of your liking.

CRESPELLE CON RIPIENO DI POLLO
(Crespelle with Chicken Stuffing)

SERVES 6

> 18 *crespelle (see above)*
> ¾ *pound boneless white chicken meat, chopped*
> 6 *ounces mozzarella, diced*
> 1 *tablespoon chopped parsley*
> 3 *ounces butter*
> Salt and pepper, to taste
> 1 *cup tomato sauce (see pages 33–34)*
> 2 *tablespoons grated Parmigiano*

Preheat the oven to 375°F. Make *crespelle* as in basic recipe. To prepare the stuffing, combine the chicken, *mozzarella,* parsley, 2 tablespoons of the butter, salt, and pepper. Work to a smooth, soft texture in a food processor.

Spread the stuffing evenly on the *crespelle* and fold them in triangles. Arrange in a buttered baking dish. Pour the tomato sauce evenly over the top. Sprinkle with *Parmi-*

giano and dot with the remaining butter. Bake for 25 minutes. Remove from oven and serve.

RAVIOLI (Stuffed Pasta)

Ravioli are stuffed squares of pasta filled with vegetables, *ricotta,* meat, fish, and so on. Prepare the dough as in the basic recipe (see page 147). Roll 12-inch sheets of dough and brush with water or egg. Place the stuffing onto the dough in small dollops, evenly separated 2 inches from one another. Place a second sheet of dough on top of the first and press down gently in order to allow air to come out. Use a pastry cutter to make 2-inch-square *ravioli.* These are usually served with light sauces, a *ragù,* or simply melted butter, sage leaves, and *Parmigiano.*

ROTOLO DI PASTA (Stuffed Pasta Roll)

Prepare fresh pasta as in basic recipe (see page 147), then stretch dough out to make two ⅛-inch-thick sheets. Cut the sheets into a rectangular form, approximately 10 inches wide and 12 inches long. Once the dough is in sheet form, spread a filling on 1 sheet, making sure not to reach the very end of the dough. Place the second sheet on top of the first and roll them both together. Wrap in cheesecloth. The cooking method is unusual because *rotolo di pasta* must be cooked by steaming it, floating over boiling salted water. For this, it is best to use an oval pot, or a pot that resembles a fish poacher, so that the ends of the cheesecloth can be tied to the handles of the pot. This way, the pasta roll will be suspended over and not sitting in the boiling water. Cooking time can be as long as 2 hours. When done, discard the cheesecloth, and cut the roll into ½-inch-thick slices. Arrange them on a serving platter and serve with melted butter and *Parmigiano.*

ROTOLO DI PASTA RIPIENO (Stuffed Pasta Roll)

SERVES 6
> *3 ounces butter*
> *½ pound chopped lean veal*
> *½ pound chicken livers, diced*
> *2 ounces fresh mushrooms, chopped*
> *¼ pound fresh sausage, crumbled*
> *Chicken broth (see page 124)*
> *2 pounds spinach*
> *4 eggs*
> *¼ cup grated Parmigiano*
> *Salt and pepper, to taste*
> *2 sheets pasta dough, 6 × 12 inches each*

1 yard cheesecloth
2 cups tomato sauce (see pages 33–34)

In a casserole, sauté 2 tablespoons of the butter with the veal, chicken livers, mush-rooms, and sausage. Add a few tablespoons of broth if the mixture is too dry. Cook for about 30 minutes. Remove from the heat and set aside. Wash and clean and chop the spinach, and sauté with the remaining 2 tablespoons of butter for 5 minutes, then cool, squeeze out excess water, and set aside. Combine the meat mixture and spinach with the eggs and 2 tablespoons of *Parmigiano,* salt, and pepper. Grind fine using a food processor to achieve a smooth consistency.

Take 1 sheet of the dough and spread the stuffing, leaving an unfilled ½-inch border. Take the other sheet, place it on top, and roll up the stuffed sheets of pasta. Wrap them in cheesecloth and cook as explained in the basic method of preparation (see page 159). Cook for about 45 minutes. Remove from the pot and cool. Preheat the oven to 375°F. When the *rotolo* is cooled, remove the cheesecloth, slice, and arrange each slice in a buttered baking dish. Pour tomato sauce over the top, sprinkle with the remaining 2 tablespoons of *Parmigiano,* dot with butter, and bake for 20 minutes, or until the *rotolo* is tender to the fork.

Remove from the oven and serve.

TORTELLINI

Legend has it that the man who invented *tortellini* was a cook from Castelfranco, not far from Bologna. It was in his inn that Venus, the goddess of beauty, had stopped for a night's rest. The good cook, curious to see Venus's naked beauty, spied through the keyhole, and afterward remembering Venus's belly button, he attempted to re-create it with dough. Hence, the first *tortellino.*

Tortellini are similar to *cappelletti* (see page 158), except that the edges are straight, not fluted, and they have a hole in the center. Pasta for *tortellini* may also be cut into 2-inch rounds. Also, if you press the 2 ends around the tip of your index finger, *tortellini* will take a slightly tighter shape.

Notes:
Stuffing for *agnolini, cappelletti,* and *tortellini* is generally made with beef, pork, or veal.

Tortelli are like *tortellini,* only larger.

RIPIENO (Stuffing)

RIPIENO PER AGNOLINI ALLA PARMIGIANA
(Stuffing for Agnolini Parmigiana-Style)

MAKES 2 POUNDS, ENOUGH FOR 16 AGNOLINI

1 pound of beef round, or a similar cut such as chuck roast
2 ounces pancetta
2 garlic cloves
6 tablespoons extra virgin olive oil
2 ounces butter
1 large onion, sliced
Salt and pepper, to taste
2 cups beef broth (see pages 123–24)
1 celery stalk, chopped
1 small carrot, diced
Pinch of cinnamon
2–3 cloves
1/2 cup peeled, seeded, and chopped tomatoes
1/2 pound grated Parmigiano
6 tablespoons breadcrumbs
2 eggs

Spike the piece of beef with *pancetta* and garlic. Place in a heated casserole with olive oil, butter, and the onion. Add salt and pepper to taste and cook over a low heat for 10 minutes, or until the meat has browned all over. Add the broth, celery, carrot, cinnamon, a few cloves, and the tomato. Cover and cook very slowly for 4 to 5 hours or until the meat is tender.

Remove the meat and set aside to use as a main course or in any other way. Strain the remaining sauce. Add grated *Parmigiano*, breadcrumbs, and eggs. Adjust the density of the stuffing by adding more cheese and breadcrumbs as needed. Refrigerate stuffing for 24 hours before using.

Agnolini are stuffed and cut into half-moon shapes. They can be served in a capon broth or simply sautéed with butter, sage leaves, and *Parmigiano*.

RIPIENO PER TORTELLINI (Stuffing for Tortellini)

MAKES 1 1/2 POUNDS

1/4 pound pork loin
2 ounces turkey breast
2 tablespoons butter

¼ pound prosciutto
¼ pound mortadella
1 cup grated Parmigiano
2 eggs
Pinch of nutmeg
Salt and pepper, to taste

Chop the pork loin and the turkey breast in chunks and melt the butter in a large saucepan. Add all the meat and brown over very low heat, about 15 minutes. Let cool.

Prepare the stuffing by finely grinding the meat together with the *prosciutto* and *mortadella*. Put the mixture in a bowl, and add *Parmigiano,* eggs, nutmeg, and salt and pepper to taste. Mix all the ingredients well and keep refrigerated for a few hours before using. The most suitable sauce for *tortellini* is *ragù bolognese.*

RIPIENO D'ANATRA (Duck Stuffing)

MAKES 1½ POUNDS
1 pound duck breast, unskinned
1 ounce spinach
4 slices of stale bread
1 cup milk
1 ounce chopped mushrooms
2 scallions, chopped
1 tablespoon extra virgin olive oil
2 ounces bone marrow
1 small bunch parsley, chopped
2 tablespoons heavy cream
Salt and pepper, to taste

Finely chop the duck breast. Rinse spinach and cook in a covered pot without water over low heat until the liquid has evaporated. Remove from the pot, cool, and chop very fine. Trim and discard crusts from bread slices, and dip the white of the bread in milk. Squeeze out excess liquid and mix with the spinach. Sauté the mushrooms, scallions, and the chopped duck breast in oil for a few minutes, until browned, and cool. Next, gather all the ingredients into a food processor, add the bone marrow, parsley, cream, and salt and pepper to taste. Finely grind and bind the whole mixture well. Let cool and refrigerate for a few hours before use. This stuffing is suitable for *ravioli* and *tortelloni.* Sauces may vary from melted butter, sage, and *Parmigiano* to a reduction of duck or beef sauce.

RIPIENO DI CACCIAGIONE (Game Stuffing)

MAKES 2 POUNDS

1 pound game meat, preferably venison
4 sage leaves
2 rosemary sprigs
5 ounces bacon, diced
Salt and pepper, to taste
3 tablespoons extra virgin olive oil
1 tablespoon butter
¼ cup grated Parmigiano
2 eggs
Pinch of nutmeg

Cut the venison into chunks and flavor with the sage, rosemary, bacon, and salt and pepper to taste. Heat the oil and butter in a pan. Brown the venison until it is well done, about 90 minutes, and cool. Place the venison into a food processor. Add the *Parmigiano*, eggs, and nutmeg. Finely grind and bind the whole into a smooth mixture. Keep in a cool place until ready to use. This stuffing can be used for *tortelli* or *ravioli*.

RIPIENO DI CARNE (Meat Stuffing)

MAKES 2 POUNDS

1 ounce butter
1 garlic clove
2 ounces prosciutto, fat part separate
½ pound lean ground veal
½ pound lean ground beef
½ pound ground pork loin
1 cup strong, dry red wine
1 bay leaf
Salt, to taste
Beef broth (see pages 123–24) or water, boiling
¼ pound mortadella
1 cup fresh breadcrumbs
2 eggs
1 cup grated Parmigiano
Pinch of pepper

Brown the butter and the garlic with the finely chopped fat part of *prosciutto*. Cut the veal, beef, and pork into 1-ounce chunks and let brown. Add wine, the bay leaf, and a little salt. Cover and cook over very low heat for about 2 hours. Stir occasionally while cooking. If necessary, add spoonfuls of boiling broth or water. The sauce should be quite concentrated and the meat well browned. Remove the meat and strain the cooking juices.

Finely grind the meat along with the *mortadella* and the lean part of the *prosciutto*. Use the strained cooking liquids to moisten the breadcrumbs. Without squeezing them, add the breadcrumbs to the meat mixture. Add the eggs, *Parmigiano,* a pinch of freshly ground pepper, and salt to taste. Mix and bind the stuffing well. Let it sit in the refrigerator, covered, for a few hours. This stuffing suits all fresh stuffed pasta, particularly the small-size types. Pasta with this filling may be served in broth or with tomato or beef *ragù* or with just butter and *Parmigiano.*

RIPIENO DI FEGATINI DI POLLO (Chicken Liver Stuffing)

MAKES 1 POUND
> ½ *pound spinach*
> ½ *pound chicken livers*
> *3 tablespoons butter*
> ½ *ounce black truffle, sliced (optional)*
> *1 scallion, chopped*
> *2 eggs*
> *Pinch of nutmeg*
> *Salt and pepper, to taste*

Wash the spinach thoroughly, put it in a pot without water, and cook until the liquid has evaporated. Cut the chicken livers into very small pieces and sauté in 2 tablespoons of the butter with the truffle, if using, and scallion until well done. Let cool. Pass it through a food mill with the spinach, then add the eggs, the rest of the butter, nutmeg, and salt and pepper to taste. Mix and bind the mixture into a smooth stuffing. The stuffing is now ready and suitable for *ravioli, tortelli,* and *tortelloni.* The accompanying sauce can vary from butter and sage to a very light tomato sauce. Remember, the sauce must always enhance the taste of the stuffing, not overpower it.

Note:
Spinach can also be cooked in water, as long as it is well strained; this method allows greens to keep their natural bright color. Spinach cooked without water will color the stuffing grayish-green.

RIPIENO DI RICOTTA (Cheese Stuffing)

MAKES 1½ POUNDS
> *1 pound ricotta cheese*
> *2 eggs*

¼ cup grated Parmigiano
Pinch of nutmeg
Salt and pepper, to taste
2 tablespoons breadcrumbs (optional)

Pass the *ricotta* through a sieve; it should not be watery. Beat the eggs in a mixing bowl and while beating, add the *ricotta, Parmigiano,* nutmeg, and salt and pepper. If the stuffing is too soft, add some breadcrumbs. You should have a smooth, consistent stuffing. Refrigerate for a few hours. This stuffing can be used for *ravioli.* Sauces may vary according to your taste; a strained simple tomato sauce is recommended.

RIPIENO DI PESCE (Fish Stuffing)

MAKES 2 POUNDS

Court Bouillon
2 cups dry white wine
1 very small onion, thinly sliced
½ lemon, cut in quarters
3 peppercorns
Salt, to taste

Fish Stuffing
1 pound fish fillets, one type or several
¼ cup extra virgin olive oil
1 very small onion, minced
1 egg
Pinch of salt and pepper, to taste

Make a fish broth as in basic recipe (see page 124), but use white wine, thinly sliced onion, half a lemon, peppercorns, and salt.

Clean the fish and cook it in the court bouillon, about 7 minutes. Let it cool in the broth. Heat the olive oil in a saucepan. Add the onion and cook until brown. Meanwhile, drain the fish, crumble it into small pieces, and add to the cooked onion. Stir and cook over very low heat for a few minutes. Pour the mixture into a bowl and let cool. Mix in the egg, a pinch of salt, and pepper. Blend all the ingredients to get a smooth stuffing. Keep the stuffing refrigerated until needed. This stuffing is best for *ravioli.* A suitable condiment would be a very light and fluid fish or vegetable sauce.

RIPIENO DI SPINACI (Spinach Stuffing)

MAKES 2 POUNDS

12 ounces spinach, cooked
2 tablespoons chopped parsley
1 garlic clove
1 very small onion
2 ounces pancetta
1 ounce butter
½ pound ricotta cheese
1 cup grated Parmigiano
2 eggs
Pinch of nutmeg
Salt and pepper, to taste

Finely chop the spinach. Mince the parsley finely with the garlic, onion, and *pancetta.* Lightly brown the resulting *battuto* in a saucepan with the butter. Add the spinach and salt. Mix well and let cook over low heat until very hot, stirring frequently. Remove from the heat. Sieve the *ricotta* into a bowl. Add the spinach mixture together with the *Parmigiano,* eggs, nutmeg, and salt and pepper to taste. Mix and bind the stuffing well. Let stand in a cool place for several hours before using. This stuffing is suitable for *tortelli, tortelloni,* and *ravioloni.* The most suitable sauce is a strained tomato sauce.

RIPIENO DI ZUCCA (Pumpkin Stuffing)

MAKES APPROXIMATELY 4 POUNDS

3 pounds pumpkin, peeled, seeded, and diced
4 ounces Amaretti di Saronno, crushed
4 ounces mostarda di frutta (see Glossary)
Pinch of nutmeg
1 cup grated Parmigiano
Black pepper, crushed
Salt and pepper, to taste

Preheat the oven to 400°F. Bake the pumpkin until cooked, about 25 minutes. Remove from oven and let cool. Puree the pumpkin pulp using a food mill or food processor. Add half of the crushed *amaretti* and all the other ingredients to obtain a smooth mixture. Place the stuffing in a cool place for a few hours before using. This stuffing is suitable for large *ravioli* or *tortelloni.* The most suitable sauce is butter and *Parmigiano.* When serving the pasta, sprinkle the remainder of the crushed *amaretti* over it just before serving so that the *amaretti* stay crunchy.

Note:
The crushed *amaretti* can also be mixed with grated *Parmigiano.*

PASTICCI E TIMBALLI (Baked Pasta and Molds)

Pasticci and *timballi* are prepared with either dried or fresh pasta, which may or may not be stuffed. For *pasticci* it is better to use dried pasta like *rigatoni* or *tubetti*. For *timballi* fresh pasta and stuffed pasta are used. The pasta is cooked and then mixed with *ragù* and *Parmigiano* and baked. *Pasticci* are prepared in a baking pan; *timballi* are encased with a savory pastry.

To make *pasticcio,* place the pasta of your choice in a greased, shallow baking pan and cover each layer with the various ingredients and the sauce. Bake until a crust forms on top. Let the preparation rest for 15 minutes and serve in the same baking pan.

To make *timballo,* place the pasta in a mold with rather high sides that has been lined with savory short pastry. Cover, seal the pasta with additional pastry, and bake. When done, leave the *timballo* to stand for about 15 minutes, so that it becomes firm, then turn it upside down on a serving dish and serve. You may also use a springform mold, which does not need to be turned upside down. If there is any dough left, it can be used to decorate the top of the *timballo* by cutting it into various decorative shapes (small stars, leaves, and so on) with a pastry cutter. Lay the pastry designs along the outer edge or in the center of the *timballo,* brush them with beaten egg, and bake. Of course in this case, the *timballo* should be baked in a springform mold, so that the decorations are visible.

PASTICCIO DI PIZZOCCHERI (Pizzoccheri with Cabbage and Cheese)

Pizzoccheri, a typical product of Valtellina, a mountain area in northern Italy, are cut into strips very much like *tagliatelle,* but they are made with buckwheat flour. This gives a very distinctive flavor. (See page 152 for more information.) Because of the richness of the dressing—a mix of potatoes, cheese, butter, and cabbage—*pasticcio di pizzoccheri* is a typical winter dish. Local cheese specialties such as *toma* or *bitto* are the traditional cheeses used.

Any semi-aged cheese, such as *stracchino or taleggio,* can be substituted.

SERVES 6

8 ounces butter
4 garlic cloves
4 fresh sage leaves
Salt and pepper, to taste
1 large potato, peeled and diced
4 ounces cabbage, cut into thin strips
1 pound pizzoccheri
¾ pound fresh cheese such as toma, bitto, or another semi-aged cheese

Brown the butter with the garlic and sage. Add salt and pepper and set aside, keeping warm. Bring a large pot of salted water to a boil. Put in the potato and the strips of cabbage. When the potato and cabbage are tender, bring the water to a rolling boil, add the *pizzoccheri,* and cook until just al dente. Drain and place in a heated bowl, alternating layers of *pizzoccheri* and cheese and the browned warm butter mixture. Serve immediately.

PASTA 'NCASCIATA (Pasticcio of Rigatoni with Eggplant)

SERVES 8

    4 medium eggplants
    ¼ cup coarse salt
    6 tablespoons olive oil
    1 garlic clove
    2 ounces chopped lean veal
    2 pounds plum tomatoes, peeled, seeded, and chopped
    Salt and pepper, to taste
    2 ounces chicken liver, chopped
    2 ounces green peas, preferably fresh
    2 pounds rigatoni
    2 ounces aged salami, chopped
    2 ounces mozzarella, chopped
    ½ cup grated pecorino cheese
    2 ounces hard-boiled eggs, sliced
    12 basil leaves, washed and chopped

Slice the eggplants and place them on a chopping board propped on a slant. Sprinkle with coarse salt and leave them under a weight for 1 hour until the bitter water seeps out. Rinse, drain, pat dry, and fry in 4 tablespoons of the olive oil until browned. Set aside. In a casserole, sauté the garlic with the remaining olive oil and remove when golden. Add the veal. When well browned, add the tomatoes and cook for 10 minutes. Salt and pepper to taste. Add the liver and the peas. Cook for 30 minutes. Cook the *rigatoni* just until *al dente,* drain, and cool. Toss the pasta with two thirds of the sauce. Add the salami, *mozzarella,* and half of the *pecorino.* Toss well.

Preheat the oven to 375°F. In a greased baking pan, alternate 1 layer of pasta with 1 layer of eggplant and eggs. The top layer should be pasta. Pour on the remainder of the sauce. Sprinkle the top layer with the remainder of the *pecorino.* Bake for 35 minutes. Remove from the oven and let rest for 10 minutes. Add the basil leaves on top and serve.

LASAGNE DI CARNEVALE
(Lasagne of Meat Ragù with Ricotta and Mozzarella)

SERVES 8

2 pounds lasagne noodles

Meat Ragù
¼ cup extra virgin olive oil
2 ounces prosciutto, sliced and chopped, or pancetta, chopped
2 onions, finely sliced
1½ pound lean beef and pork, chopped
1 cup dry red wine
1 tablespoon tomato paste
2 pounds tomatoes, peeled, seeded, and chopped

Meat Dumplings
¾ pound lean veal or beef
½ cup breadcrumbs, soaked in water and squeezed dry
1 egg
1 tablespoon Parmigiano
1 teaspoon chopped parsley
Salt and pepper, to taste
¼ cup extra virgin olive oil

Other Ingredients
½ pound sausage
2 tablespoons extra virgin olive oil
1 cup ricotta cheese
½ pound mozzarella
6 tablespoons grated Parmigiano
1 ounce butter

Preheat oven to 375°F. Make the fresh pasta following the basic recipe (see page 147), but for this preparation eliminate some of the egg white so that the lasagne turn out a little stiffer. Cut the *lasagne* into ribbons 3 inches wide and 12 inches long or the length of your baking pan.

For the meat *ragù,* make the *ragù* the day before it is to be used so that it is easier to remove the excess fat that will surface. Over medium heat, place the oil and the *prosciutto* in a saucepan together with the onions. Let the onions get tender but not browned and add the chopped meat. Brown on all sides. Add the wine and let reduce by half. Add the tomato paste after diluting it in a cup of water Add the tomatoes and bring to a simmer. Cook for at least 3 hours over low heat with the pot covered. Add some water if the sauce gets too thick. Stir occasionally to make sure the sauce does not stick to the bottom of the pan. Set aside.

For the dumplings, grind the veal. Add the breadcrumbs, egg, *Parmigiano,* parsley, and salt and pepper. Mix all ingredients to get a smooth mixture. Make dumplings the size of a nutmeg and fry in hot oil. Place on paper towels to get rid of excess fat and place in a casserole with 1 cup of the *ragù* and set aside.

Crumble and sauté the sausage with olive oil until well browned. Remove from the pan and set aside. Pass the *ricotta* through a fine sieve and add 2 tablespoons of *ragù,* mix well, and set aside. Dice the *mozzarella* fine and set aside.

Boil the *lasagne* in plenty of salted water, remove when *al dente,* and drain. Cool with cold water to stop the cooking process and grease with a little oil so that pasta sheets do not stick to one another and are easier to manage.

Preheat the oven to 375°F. Butter a large baking pan. Place a little *ragù* on the bottom of the pan. Next, place a layer of lasagne, a thin layer of *ricotta,* a sprinkle of the diced *mozzarella,* the dumplings, the sausage, a layer of *ragù,* and a generous amount of *Parmigiano.* Continue with at least 3 layers. Make sure the ingredients are evenly used throughout the layering. The top layer should be the *ragù,* grated *Parmigiano,* and dots of butter. Bake for 45 to 60 minutes. Let *lasagne* rest for 15 minutes before serving.

TIMBALLO DI TORTELLINI (Tortellini Mold)

SERVES 8

> 2 pounds tortellini
> 2 cups ragù bolognese (page 30)
> 4 ounces butter
> 6 tablespoons grated Parmigiano

Flaky Pastry

> 2 cups all-purpose flour
> Grated zest of 1 lemon
> 5 tablespoons butter
> Pinch of salt
> 3 egg yolks
> 2 tablespoons breadcrumbs
> 1 white or black truffle
> 1 egg, beaten

Preheat the oven to 375°F. Make *tortellini* according to the basic recipe (see page 160). Heat the *ragù.* Cook the *tortellini* just until *al dente,* drain, and place in a bowl. Add the ragù, 6 tablespoons of the butter (diced), and 2 tablespoons of the *Parmigiano.* Mix well and let cool.

Make the flaky pastry and divide it into 2 batches, one twice the size of the other.

Roll out the bigger batch with a rolling pin, making a disk large enough to line a buttered 12-inch springform pan sprinkled with breadcrumbs. Arrange the *tortellini* in layers in the pan, sprinkling each layer with the rest of the *Parmigiano* and very thin slices of the truffle, and dot the top layer with butter. Roll out the second batch of flaky pastry, making a top crust large enough to cover the *tortellini*, lay on top, and seal the edges by pinching them all around. The top may be decorated with pastry leftovers. Brush the pastry with beaten egg and bake the *timballo* for 45 minutes. Let stand for about 10 minutes before serving.

Note:
Tortellini may be replaced with *agnolini* or *cappelletti*.

GNOCCHI (Gnocchi)

Within the Italian tradition, *gnocchi* are simply dumplings, generally made with potatoes and flour. The ratio of potatoes to flour can vary from one region to another, depending on local customs and traditions as well as on the kind of potatoes used. (Baking potatoes are the most suitable for *gnocchi*. Do not choose new potatoes; they are too watery.) *Gnocchi* can also be made with just flour or semolina, *ricotta*, spinach, or breadcrumbs. *Gnocchetti* are usually smaller than *gnocchi*.

GNOCCHI DI PATATE (Potato Gnocchi)

MAKES 2 POUNDS
2 pounds baking potatoes
Salt
1¾ cups all-purpose flour
2 eggs

Wash the potatoes (without peeling) and cook in lightly salted water. It is best to start with cold water. Cooking time depends on potato type and size. A rule of thumb for testing the cooking state is to stick a fork into 1 or 2 potatoes and if it goes in easily, the potatoes are done. When done, drain and cool. Peel and mash the potatoes through a potato ricer (do not use a food mill) and place them on a pastry board or marble surface.

Start to knead by adding the eggs, a small amount of salt, and as much white flour as necessary to make the dough smooth enough not to stick to your fingers. (The ratio of potato to flour should not exceed 4 parts to 1 part.) You don't have to knead the dough too much, just long enough to blend all the ingredients. When the kneading is done, cut a piece of dough and, coating your hands with flour, roll the dough into a long cylinder about the thickness of your index finger. Cut the cylinder into pieces about 1 inch long. Draw the dough lengthwise toward you, pressing against the board with your fingertips. This will make each piece curl up, taking the shape of a little shell. For this purpose you may also use other utensils such as a fork. In this case, the *gnocchi* will be ridged and curled. It is not necessary to give them a particular shape; they may be cut into nuggets of any desired size. Repeat until all the dough is used, trying to handle the dumplings as little as possible. Finally, gently place the *gnocchi* on a flat surface sprinkled with flour without overcrowding. Cook as soon as possible.

A variation to this basic method is to add more eggs to the dough. The eggs will make the mix harder, more consistent. In some cases, this is a desired result, especially if large amounts have to be prepared or if they have to be made long before the final cooking.

How to Cook Gnocchi

Gnocchi should not be prepared too far in advance before cooking. They are best cooked in a large pot with a wide bottom so that the heat underneath can spread properly, allowing the water to rapidly get back to the boiling point after the *gnocchi* have been added.

Add *gnocchi* to boiling water all at once and stir gently. Cook until they float to the top (a few minutes are enough). Lift them out of the water with a skimmer (do not use a colander). Place in a preheated bowl. Toss with the sauce of your choice and add *Parmigiano,* if using, and serve immediately.

Sauces for Gnocchi

There are many sauces for *gnocchi,* and they vary from region to region.

You may use melted butter flavored with sage; tomato sauce; mushroom sauce; *ragù bolognese; pesto,* or one of several meat sauces such as lamb, veal, beef, or pork, as well as the juices from roasting or braising beef; or with *gorgonzola, fontina,* and so on. Sprinkling *gnocchi* with grated *Parmigiano* is a must, regardless of the type of the sauce used, with the exception of fish sauces.

GNOCCHI DI PATATE ALLA BAVA (Gnocchi with Fontina)

SERVES 6
> 1 pound gnocchi (pages 171–72)
> ½ pound fontina cheese, cut into small cubes
> 4 ounces butter
> Salt and pepper, to taste

Preheat the oven to 375°F. Make *gnocchi* as in basic recipe. These *gnocchi* should be prepared right before use. Cook *gnocchi,* and drain. Place *gnocchi* and *fontina* in a buttered baking dish, making sure the top layer is cheese. Dot with butter and bake for 10 minutes. Let rest 5 more minutes. Add salt and pepper to taste and serve.

STRANGOLAPRETI (Neapolitan Gnocchi)

This is the Neapolitan recipe. Although the same name is used for some *gnocchi* preparations in Trentino–Alto Adige, they are quite different dishes.

SERVES 8

2 pounds baking potatoes
4 eggs
1¾ cups all-purpose flour, or less if possible
4 cups tomato sauce (see pages 33–34)
¼ cup grated Parmigiano

Prepare *gnocchi* as in basic recipe, but with twice the amount of egg. The quantity of flour depends on the potatoes' humidity. Make sure the dough is soft and homogeneous. *Strangolapreti* should be cooked as soon as they are ready. If they stand too long, they tend to get tough. Cook in plenty of boiling salted water. When ready, remove with a strainer into a serving bowl. Add tomato sauce and serve with grated *Parmigiano*.

CANEDERLI (Bread Gnocchi)

These are the classic *Knödeln*, a traditional recipe from Trento and Alto-Adige.

SERVES 4

1 pound crustless white bread
2 eggs, beaten
3 tablespoons all-purpose flour, or more if necessary
2 tablespoons grated Parmigiano
Salt, to taste
Sauce of your choice

Soften the bread in water or milk and squeeze it dry. Add the beaten eggs, flour, *Parmigiano,* and salt to taste. Work into a smooth and soft dough. Shape the dumplings the size of a walnut with wet hands and a teaspoon. Dip them in flour and place them on a floured sheet pan. Boil the *gnocchi* in plenty of boiling salted water and remove from the pot with a strainer when they come to the surface. Cooking time is 4 to 6 minutes, depending on the size of the dumplings. Here, several variations are possible with different sauces. The favorite sauce is melted butter with the addition of breadcrumbs and grated *Parmigiano*. Sometimes, *gnocchi di pane* are served as an accompaniment to dishes with a rich sauce. They can also be served in a rich capon broth.

GNOCCHI DI SEMOLINO ALLA ROMANA (Semolina Gnocchi)

SERVES 4

> 2 quarts milk
> 5 ounces butter
> Pinch of salt
> 2½ cups finely ground semolina flour
> 6 tablespoons grated Parmigiano
> 2 egg yolks

Preheat the oven to 375°F. Heat the milk to a boil in a small saucepan with 2 tablespoons of the butter and a pinch of salt. When it starts to simmer, add semolina little by little, stirring all the while. Continue to stir and cook for at least 45 minutes. Turn off the heat. Add 2 tablespoons *Parmigiano* and the egg yolks and stir well. Wet a pastry board or a marble surface and pour out the cooked *semolino*. Spread with a wet spatula to make a layer about ½ inch thick. Let cool. Melt the remaining butter. Cut the layer of *semolino* into round pieces, using a round cutter about 2 inches in diameter. Arrange the *semolino* disks in overlapping layers in a greased baking dish and brush with melted butter and the remaining *Parmigiano*. Bake until top layer is crisp. Serve hot.

MALFATTI (Spinach and Ricotta Gnocchi)

SERVES 6

> 2 pounds spinach
> 1 small onion, minced
> 5 ounces butter
> 1 pound fresh ricotta cheese
> 6 tablespoons grated Parmigiano
> 2 eggs
> 1 egg yolk
> Pinch of nutmeg
> Salt and pepper, to taste
> 1¼ cups all-purpose flour (or as needed)
> 4 sage leaves

Clean, wash, and cook the spinach in the water left on the leaves after washing. Drain, squeeze well, and finely chop. Wilt the onion in 4 tablespoons of the butter, then drain the onion and add it to the spinach. Cook on very low heat, stirring frequently, to allow the spinach to exude more water, then let cool. Sieve the *ricotta* into a bowl. Add the spinach, about 3 tablespoons of the *Parmigiano,* the eggs, the egg yolk, a pinch of nutmeg, and salt and pepper to taste. Mix, adding the flour little by little, as much as necessary to obtain a firm but soft mix. Use a spoon to make dumplings the size of a walnut. Lightly sprinkle *gnocchi* with flour (the amount of flour used to dust them depends on how well the spinach was dried) and set aside on a sheet pan. Bring a generous amount of salted water to a boil in a large pot. Meanwhile, brown the rest of the butter in a saucepan, adding the whole sage leaves. Add the *gnocchi* to the boiling water, stirring gently. As they float to the top, drain with a skimmer and arrange on a serving platter. Pour on the melted butter flavored with the sage and sprinkle with the remaining *Parmigiano*. Serve very hot.

Note:
Instead of sage-flavored butter, you may use a light tomato sauce.

POLENTA (Cornmeal)

Polenta, or cornmeal mush, is traditional and popular throughout northern Italy. The ingredients vary only slightly from region to region. In some areas, *polenta* is made with yellow cornmeal very finely ground, while in other areas it is coarse, and in some others yellow and white cornmeal are blended together. In some cases yellow or white cornmeal is mixed with buckwheat.

The procedures employed to make *polenta* do not vary much. What varies is the thickness of the final product, depending on how and with what it is going to be served.

In order to enhance overall flavor, a harmonious balance in texture between *polenta* and other ingredients is necessary. It is best to use coarsely ground cornmeal to make rather thick *polenta,* while the finely ground type is more suitable for thinner *polenta.* Medium ground cornmeal is suitable for most preparations. Whatever kind of *polenta* is used, make sure it is dry, without lumps, and recently ground. If stored for a long time, it may taste bitter.

Basic Cooking Procedures

The best pot for cooking *polenta* is the traditional *paiolo,* a huge copper pot without a tin lining and with a convex bottom. Stirring is done with a wooden paddle called *tarello.* The pot should only be half full or the water might overflow when you add the cornmeal. The water should be properly salted in order to avoid having to add either salt or water later during cooking. You can also use an aluminum pot and a wooden spoon.

For each pound (3½ cups) of *polenta,* use 2 quarts of water and 1 tablespoon of salt. The water ratio applies to soft *polenta,* which is always served with a sauce or with the addition of other ingredients. If *polenta* is to be baked, grilled, or eaten as a substitute for bread, use 3 parts of water to 1 part *polenta* and the same amount of salt.

Bring the proper quantity of adequately salted water to a boil, then lower the heat. (Be careful of splashing the boiling water.) Add the cornmeal, little by little, stirring constantly. Do not pour directly from the container, but use your hands, pouring a handful at time. After adding all the cornmeal, turn up the heat and cook for 50 minutes to 1 hour, stirring constantly, until it is soft and not grainy. While cooking, the heat should be high enough to cause bubbles to rise and burst on the surface. While stirring, stir the cornmeal off the sides of the pot and from the bottom up. When ready, *polenta* should come off a wooden spoon (*tarello*) and the sides of the pot. It can be served hot immediately with the chosen condiment, or it may be poured out of the *paiolo* onto a wooden board. To do so, smooth the surface of the *polenta* and, with a brisk move, turn the pot upside down and the *polenta* will easily come out. Let it rest for 15 minutes, then cut it with a knife and serve. (*Polenta* is often cut with a piece of thick string stretched tightly between 2 hands.)

Polenta made with finely ground cornmeal forms lumps easily. In order to avoid this, add a fifth of the cornmeal to the salted water while it is still cold, mixing with a whisk. Once the cornmeal is blended with the water, cover in order to prevent the boiling polenta from splashing and let boil for 10 minutes. Then, stirring constantly, add the remaining cornmeal, following the procedures described in the basic method.

How to Serve Polenta

Polenta is often served as a starch in place of bread, especially in rural and mountain areas, together with tiny deep-fried fish, broiled *cotechino,* salami, or cheese. In this case, it is not sauced but is served as a complement to meat, game, and fish dishes cooked in sauces or gravies.

Polenta is also served with cheese (*gorgonzola, toma, fontina*) added in cubes when still very hot. It is delicious when served very hot, dotted with fresh butter, and sprinkled with *Parmigiano*.

It is very good sliced, arranged in layers in a baking dish, covered with slivers of *Parmigiano,* sprinkled with melted butter, and baked for a few minutes. You may add thinly sliced white truffles when in season.

Polenta leftovers may be sliced and fried in oil or lightly grilled over charcoal, then served either as a side dish or, better yet, covered with lard minced with parsley and garlic. *Polenta* may also be prepared by cooking it with other ingredients like beans, cabbage, spinach, and potatoes. In this case, it is dotted with butter or browned lard, sprinkled with *Parmigiano,* and served as a complete meal. *Polenta* is also served soft with a sauce or other condiments.

POLENTA CON FAGIOLI BORLOTTI E CAVOLO
(Polenta with Borlotti Beans and Cabbage)

SERVES 6 TO 8

7 ounces dried borlotti beans
1 small Savoy cabbage (about 1 pound), shredded

Salt and pepper, to taste
2 pounds (7 cups) coarse yellow polenta
2 garlic cloves, crushed
¼ pound pancetta, cut into small cubes
¾ cup all-purpose flour
1 cup olive oil, for frying

Soak the beans overnight, then put them in lightly salted, cold water, and cook over medium heat for 40 minutes. Clean and wash the cabbage and cook until tender. Combine cabbage and beans in the same pot, bring to a boil, add salt and pepper, and start to pour in ground *polenta*. Follow the same procedure to cook *polenta* as in basic recipe (pages 175–76). It will take at least 45 minutes for the *polenta* to cook. Add additional hot water if it becomes too dry. When ready, turn the *polenta* onto a wooden board and let cool. Sauté the garlic with the *pancetta* over low heat and remove when brown. Discard excess fat and set the crispy *pancetta* dots aside. Cut the cooled *polenta* with the cabbage and beans into strips about 2 by 4 inches. Dredge with flour and sauté in a pan with plenty of oil until crisp. Dot with the *pancetta* and serve very hot.

PASTICCIO DI POLENTA CON RAGÙ DI CARNE
(Polenta with Meat Ragù)

SERVES 6
2 pounds (7 cups) medium grind yellow polenta
2 cups meat ragù (see page 30)
½ cup grated Parmigiano
2 ounces butter
2 tablespoons white breadcrumbs

Preheat the oven to 375°F. Make *polenta* as in the basic recipe (page 175–76). Once ready, pour into a large baking dish, previously moistened with water so that the *polenta* does not stick to the sides. Let cool, turn the dish upside down, and remove it. Now the cold *polenta* has the shape of the baking dish. Cut *polenta* horizontally into 4 equal layers with a long knife or colorless twine. Butter the same baking dish and pour in a few tablespoons of *ragù*. Place the first layer of *polenta* at the bottom of the baking dish, spread *ragù* over the layer of *polenta*, and sprinkle with *Parmigiano*. Repeat with the remaining 3 layers *of polenta* in order to rebuild its original shape. End with *ragù*, dot with butter, and sprinkle with the rest of the *Parmigiano* mixed with the breadcrumbs. Bake for about 40 minutes, or until the top is golden brown. Remove from the oven and let rest for 15 minutes before serving.

POLENTA CONCIA (Polenta with Butter and Fontina)

SERVES 6

3½ cups coarsely ground yellow polenta
8 ounces butter
¾ pound fontina cheese, cut into small cubes

Make *polenta* following the basic procedure (pages 175–76) and when it is almost ready, add the butter, cut into small pieces. Blend in the cheese 5 minutes before turning the heat off. Leave to stand for 10 minutes and then turn it onto a wooden board and serve.

Variation:

Replace 1 cup of yellow cornmeal with 1 cup of buckwheat flour and replace *fontina* with *bitto* (see Glossary). This recipe is a specialty of Valtellina, in northern Italy, where it is called *polenta taragna*. When preparing this dish the buckwheat flour is whisked into the water when it is still cold. It is then brought to a boil and yellow cornmeal is added, following the cooking process as in the basic method.

Note:

Polenta taragna is always served with good quality salami thickly sliced by hand, or fresh pork sausage sautéed until brown.

RISO
Rice

Rice is a very old nutrient. We know for a fact that it was grown in India as early as 4000 B.C. We do not know exactly when it spread to Italy. The only documentation we have is a letter dated September 27, 1475, in which the Duke of Milan, Galeazzo Maria Sforza, promises the Duke of Ferrara twelve sacks of rice seeds. It also indicates that cultivation of rice along the Po River was already considered viable. It should be noted that rice was not easily accepted because it was felt that the stagnant waters necessary to grow rice would bring health risks such as malaria.

Today, however, rice is one of the basic elements of Italian cuisine. There are many recipes for rice and risotto. Most of them originate in the main areas of rice consumption, including Piedmont, Lombardy, and the Veneto.

In Piedmont we find the origins of *risotto*. The basic preparation is onion sautéed in butter, finished with butter and *Parmigiano,* and topped with the juice of a roast. In some parts of Piedmont, *risotto* is served with truffles, in other parts with sausage. This region also boasts a rich tradition of *risotto* recipes with red wines, especially in the Barolo production area. In the areas of Pavia, Milan, and Como, *risotto* with freshwater fish is very common because of the many rivers and lakes in that region. Credit for several variations is attributed to the monks from Certosa because their diet called for lean foods such as frog's legs and sweetwater prawns, often enriched with mushrooms.

The most famous Italian rice preparation is *risotto alla milanese*, prepared with saffron. Various legends claim its illustrious beginnings. One of them gives credit to a master glassblower who, on the day of his wedding, added saffron (which he used to color glass) to the risotto so that he could serve a golden *risotto* in honor of his bride. The truth is probably much simpler. *Risotto alla milanese* is none other than a simplified version of the Spanish paella, from the period when Milan was ruled by the Spaniards.

As we move east and south, versions of *risotto* change according to regional ingredients. We find *risotto* with black ink in the Veneto, *sartù di riso* in Naples, and *arancini di riso* in Sicily. These are just a few of many interpretations where the creativity of Italian home cooks and professional cooks played a triumphant role.

Italian rice can be divided into two main types, hard- and soft-grain rice, and four varieties: *comune, semifino, fino*, and *superfino*. Although the *superfino* extra-long variety is by far the most expensive, it should be noted that the nutritional value is the same for all kinds of rice. The difference from one rice to another is due to several factors such as grain size, response to cooking vis-à-vis texture, the year's productivity, and the production method.

Rice is a most genuine and natural foodstuff and the most digestible of all cereals. It cannot be altered and does not undergo any process while cooking that might change its basic structure.

RISO COMUNE (Common Short-Grain Rice)

This rice has small, round grains that tend to disintegrate in the cooking process. It is mostly used in soups (*minestra di riso* or *riso in brodo*). It is rich in starch, partly released in the cooking process, which enhances the flavor of the broth but causes it to be slightly cloudy. It is also suitable for desserts. It cooks in about 10 to 12 minutes.

RISO SEMIFINO (Semifine Medium-Grain Rice)

This rice is medium in size with roundish grains. Its use is the same as for short-grain rice. It cooks in 12 to 14 minutes and is suitable for *timballi, sartù,* and *supplì.*

RISO FINO (Fine Long-Grain Rice)

This rice has long, tapered grains. It is particularly suitable for *risotto* since it has a medium starch content and absorbs seasonings well. It cooks in about 16 to 18 minutes.

RISO SUPERFINO (Superfine Extra-Long-Grain Rice)

This rice is fat and long. It can be used for *risotto* but is more suitable for pilafs. It is low in starch and absorbs less water; it is tastier when eaten plain. It cooks in 12 to 14 minutes.

Some Advice About Rice

Rice must never be washed before cooking. When cooking rice, the pot must be kept uncovered to prevent grains from disintegrating. Don't forget that rice, like pasta, continues to cook after it has been removed from the stove. Rice must, therefore, be served immediately to avoid overcooking, or it must be removed from the heat while still al dente if it has to rest for a few minutes as is the case in most types of risotto preparations.

Single portions of rice range as follows:

- 2½ ounces for a *risotto* rich in vegetables or other ingredients;
- 3 ounces for a regular *risotto*;
- 4 ounces for boiled rice cooked in water.

RICE COOKING METHODS

Boiled Rice

The most suitable type of rice for this simple preparation is extra-long grain. Use 1 quart of water for each 8 ounces of rice. Bring an adequate amount of salted water to a low boil and add the rice. Let cook, uncovered, stirring with a wooden spoon every now and then. Turn off the heat when the rice is still al dente. Strain and retain some cooking water in case the condiment is too dry.

Place the rice in a previously warmed serving bowl, mix the condiment in, and toss well. If the rice is to be merely buttered, let the butter soften before adding it to the rice. *Parmigiano* is used in most rice preparations except those with sauces containing fish.

Risotto

The word *risotto* refers to rice that has been toasted briefly in a *soffritto*, then cooked by gradually adding boiling broth or water, and then *mantecato* (adding butter and *Parmigiano* and stirring before serving). Remember that rice suitable for *risotto* absorbs a quantity of liquid three times the weight of the rice itself. To cook *risotto,* it is preferable to use a medium-height, heavy saucepan with a rather large bottom so that the heat can spread evenly underneath.

RISOTTO

SERVES 4

 1 *medium onion, finely chopped*
 4 *ounces butter*
 ¾ *pound superfine (1½ cups) long-grain rice*
 6 *cups veal or chicken broth (see page 124), hot*
 6 *tablespoons grated Parmigiano*

In a sauté pan over medium heat, cook the onion in 2 tablespoons of the butter. When the onion loses its crunchiness (do not let it brown), add the rice and toast gently over medium heat, stirring frequently with a wooden spoon until the rice absorbs the butter. If the recipe calls for dry white or red wine, add it first and let it almost completely evaporate. Pour a ladle of boiling broth into the pot. Continue to stir and gradually add more broth as the rice absorbs the liquid. It is important to keep the rice simmering constantly, so ladle the amount of broth wisely as you add it to the rice. When the rice is cooked *al dente,* turn off the heat. Add the remaining butter and the *Parmigiano,* and let stand, covered, for a couple of minutes so that the rice finishes cooking. Serve immediately.

Notes:

Risotto should not be too dry but lightly creamy, and each grain of rice should be fluffy.

The broth used for *risotto* should always be rather light and clear, most often made from chicken or veal. The ratio of broth to rice for *risotto* is 3 parts broth to 1 part rice, more broth or hot water for boiled rice. For *risotto* use only imported superfine Italian rice since it is less rich in starch and therefore more suitable for this preparation.

Risotto can be made with ingredients such as meat, fish, vegetables, game, and so on. Some of the most suitable vegetables are asparagus tips, green peas, beans, fava beans, radicchio leaves, artichoke hearts, leeks, zucchini, and mushrooms. Chicken liver and quail are suitable for meat-based *risotto*. For fish-based preparations, the most common ingredients are mussels, clams, baby cuttlefish, shrimp, scampi, crayfish, lobster, and swordfish.

Risotto recipes are often named after the ingredients used, for example *risotto con piselli*, with green peas, *risotto agli scampi, risotto al radicchio.*

Parmigiano is never added to *risotto* with fish or shellfish. There are some exceptions, however, depending on personal taste.

Risotto mantecato

Virtually any *risotto* can be *mantecato*, that is, have butter and *Parmigiano* whisked in with a wooden spoon just before being served. This procedure allows *risotto* to reach its smooth, creamy texture. A few specific recipes, however, provide some exceptions.

Because the quality of extra virgin olive oil has so dramatically improved over the last few years, it is common practice to finish fish *risotto* with olive oil rather than butter. Stir olive oil into the *risotto* just as you would with butter.

Risi

Most regions of Italy have variations on *risotto,* most notably in the Veneto, where such preparations are called *risi.* These are prepared very much like *risotto,* the difference being that they are much more fluid. This is achieved by simply using more broth and removing the rice from the fire while still fluid. Venetians like to say that *risi* must be *all'onda* (wavy), that is, when the rice is poured into the dish, the consistency should be so liquid as to allow the rice to form waves.

RISO IN CAGNONE (Rice with Sage and Parmigiano)

SERVES 6

> *1 pound (2 cups) superfine extra-long-grain rice*
> *4 ounces butter*
> *2 sage leaves*
> *1 garlic clove*
> *6 tablespoons grated Parmigiano*
> *1 rosemary sprig*

Bring 4 quarts of salted water to a boil. Add the rice and cook, uncovered, stirring every now and then. Brown the butter in a large frying pan with the sage and garlic. Remove the garlic when brown and the sage leaves as well. Drain the rice while still *al dente* and pour in a serving bowl. Add the *Parmigiano,* toss well, place the sprig of rosemary in the center, and serve.

Note:
In the Piedmontese version, diced *fontina* is added instead of *Parmigiano.*

RISOTTO ALLA MILANESE (Risotto with Saffron)

SERVES 4
> *2 ounces beef marrow (optional)*
> *4 ounces butter*
> *1 medium white onion, thinly sliced*
> *¾ pound (1½ cups) superfine long-grain rice*
> *½ cup dry white wine*
> *6 cups beef broth (pages 123–24), hot*
> *Pinch of saffron*
> *6 tablespoons grated Parmigiano*

Dip the bone marrow briefly in boiling water. Remove the marrow from the bone. Using a saucepan, melt 2 tablespoons of the butter and add the onion. When the onion begins to get tender, add the marrow, stir briskly, then add the rice and stir until it is lightly toasted and has absorbed the butter. Pour in the wine and let evaporate. Add a ladle of broth and let the rice absorb it, stirring constantly. Continue to add broth, 1 ladleful at a time, stirring, until the rice is almost done. Allow each ladleful of broth to be absorbed before adding the next one, but make sure to maintain a constant simmer. When the *risotto* is almost ready, after 14 minutes, dissolve the saffron in a little broth and add to the rice. Do not add it at the beginning since the saffron should not cook. When the rice is done *al dente,* turn off the heat and mix in the rest of the butter and the *Parmigiano.* Stir the rice well with a wooden spoon until the ingredients are blended thoroughly and the *risotto* is smooth. Serve immediately.

RISI E BISI (Rice and Peas)

SERVES 4
> *2 ounces lean pancetta, chopped*
> *2 tablespoons extra virgin olive oil*
> *1 small onion, finely chopped*
> *6 ounces fresh shelled peas*
> *6 cups beef broth (pages 123–24), hot*

³/₄ pound (1½ cups) superfine long-grain rice
4 ounces butter
6 tablespoons grated Parmigiano
1 tablespoon chopped parsley
Salt and pepper, to taste

Sauté the *pancetta* in a saucepan until it gets crisp. Drain off the liquid fat. Add the olive oil and the onion. Sauté until the onion loses its crunchiness. Do not let it become brown. Add the green peas and a ladleful of broth. Stir and let cook on low heat for about 10 minutes. (If the peas are tough, cook for 5 more minutes.) When the peas are halfway cooked, add the rest of the broth, bring to a boil, add the rice, and simmer over medium heat. Stir frequently, adding more broth if necessary, especially toward the end. Remember that the result should be fluid enough to form a wave on the dish when served. Once *al dente,* turn the heat off, mix in the butter, the *Parmigiano,* parsley, a pinch of pepper, and salt to taste. Serve.

Note:
In the Padua area, this rice is prepared with goose meat preserved in its fat. It is called *risi e bisi con l'oca unta.*

RISOTTO AL NERO DI SEPPIA (Risotto with Cuttlefish Ink)

SERVES 4
½ pound cuttlefish or squid
2 small onions, chopped
1 garlic clove, chopped
½ cup extra virgin olive oil
1 cup dry white wine
¼ pound (1½ cup) superfine long-grain rice
6 cups fish broth (see page 124), hot
Salt and pepper, to taste

Clean the cuttlefish or squid, setting aside three of the ink sacks, and cut it into thin strips (your fish store attendant can do the cleaning and sack removal.) Brown 1 onion and the garlic in 2 tablespoons of the olive oil. Remove the garlic when brown and add the squid. Sauté briskly, then add the white wine and continue cooking the squid for about 15 minutes, depending on squid size and quality, and set aside. In another casserole prepare a *battuto* with the other onion and 1 tablespoon of olive oil. When the onion is soft but not brown, add the ink sacks, stir well, and add the rice. Make the *risotto* following the basic procedure (see pages 181–82) using the fish broth. When *al dente,* remove from the heat and add half of the squid and the remaining olive oil. Stir well, add salt and pepper to taste, and pour the *risotto* into a serving dish. Place the remaining squid in the center and serve.

Notes:

Parmigiano is not required for this risotto.

If the *risotto* needs more binding, add 2 tablespoons butter or very good extra virgin olive oil.

RISOTTO CON LE QUAGLIE (Risotto with Quail)

SERVES 4

Salt and pepper, to taste
4 quail, boned and ready to cook
4 sage leaves
12 very thin slices lard or pancetta
5 ounces butter
1 cup dry white wine
2 tablespoons brandy
1 medium white onion, finely minced
¾ pound (1½ cups) superfine long-grain rice
6 cups beef broth (pages 123–24)
6 tablespoons grated Parmigiano

Preheat the oven to 425°F. Salt and pepper the insides of the quail and insert a sage leaf in each. Wrap the quail with the lard or *pancetta* slices, fastening with toothpicks. Melt 1 ounce of the butter in a saucepan and brown the quail, moistening them with ½ cup of wine and the brandy. Let the alcohol evaporate. Finish roasting for 15 minutes. Cool the quail, strain and deglaze the pan juices, and set aside. Quarter the quail and remove the breastbones. Return the pan juices to the saucepan and add the quail pieces. Complete cooking for another 6 minutes over low heat.

Prepare a *risotto,* using 1 tablespoon of the butter, the onion, rice, and beef broth. When the onion is wilted, add the rest of the wine. When it has evaporated, continue making the *risotto* following the basic procedure (see pages 181–82). When the risotto is done *al dente,* remove from the heat and add the remaining butter and the *Parmigiano.* Stir well with a wooden spoon. Pour the *risotto* into a serving dish and arrange the quail all around, alternating legs and breasts. Drizzle the edge of the *risotto* with the pan juices and serve.

RISOTTO CON LE COZZE (Risotto with Mussels)

SERVES 4

4 pounds mussels
½ cup extra virgin olive oil
2 garlic cloves, crushed
1 small onion, finely chopped
¾ pound (1½ cups) superfine long-grain rice

6 cups fish broth, more if needed (see page 124)
1 tablespoon chopped parsley

Wash and brush the mussels thoroughly. Leave them in salted water for 1 hour to get rid of any residual sand. In a casserole with 2 tablespoons of olive oil, sauté the garlic. When golden brown, remove it. Drain and add the mussels and cook with pot covered until they open. Remove from the heat and let cool. Extract the mussels from the shells, making sure to remove the beards. Set aside. Strain the resulting broth through a very fine sieve or cheesecloth. Add the mussels to the broth and set aside. Sauté the onion with 1 tablespoon of the olive oil. When the onion begins to get tender, add the rice and let it toast to absorb the oil. Add the mussel broth a ladleful at a time to cook the risotto. Use fish broth if necessary. Prepare the *risotto* as in the basic recipe (see pages 181–82). When the rice is *al dente,* remove from the heat and add the parsley and half of the mussels. Stir in the remainder of the olive oil with a wooden spoon. Place the *risotto* in a serving dish and dot with the remaining mussels. Serve.

SARTÙ DI RISO (Neapolitan Rice Mold)

Sartù is a rice pie that is particularly rich. It comes from the aristocratic cuisine of Naples. The word comes from *surtout*, meaning "above all others."

SERVES 12

Ragù
1 small onion, chopped
2 tablespoons extra virgin olive oil
4 sausages, crumbled
3 ounces chicken livers, diced
1 ounce dried mushrooms, reconstituted in lukewarm water, chopped
1 tablespoon tomato paste
2 cups beef broth (see pages 123–24)

Meatballs
½ pound ground beef
1 egg
2 tablespoons grated Parmigiano
2 tablespoons breadcrumbs, soaked in water and squeezed dry
Salt and pepper, to taste
1 cup olive oil, for frying

Rice
2 pounds (4 cups) medium-grain rice
8 ounces butter

4 quarts beef broth (pages 123–24)
6 tablespoons grated Parmigiano

Assembly
4 ounces butter
3 tablespoons breadcrumbs
6 ounces mozzarella, diced
6 ounces peas, steamed

For the *ragù,* sauté the onion in 2 tablespoons of olive oil. When wilted, add the sausages and the chicken livers and brown. Add the mushrooms and sauté for 3 more minutes. Dilute the tomato paste in the broth and add to the casserole. Cook the *ragù* for 30 minutes, remove from the heat, and set aside.

For the meatballs, combine in a mixing bowl the ground beef, the egg, the *Parmigiano,* the breadcrumbs, salt, and pepper. Mix well and make small meatballs the size of a hazelnut. Heat the frying oil and fry the meatballs till they are golden brown. Set aside.

For the rice, prepare the rice as *risotto* using some of the butter and all of the broth (follow the recipe on pages 181–82), but remove from the heat after 12 minutes. Add the remaining butter and the *Parmigiano.* Spread the rice out on a flat pan and let cool.

To assemble the *sartù,* preheat the oven to 375°F. Grease a 12-inch round baking pan with butter and generously dust the pan with breadcrumbs. Place the cooled rice in a mixing bowl and add the *mozzarella,* peas, and meatballs as well as half of the ragù. Pour the rice mixture into the baking pan and dust the top of the rice generously with breadcrumbs and dot with curls of the remaining butter. Bake for 45 minutes. Remove from the oven and let the *sartù* rest for 10 minutes. Remove the *sartù* from the baking pan by turning it upside down onto a round serving platter. Serve in wedges over the remaining *ragù.*

SUPPLÌ ALLA ROMANA (Supplì Roman-Style)

SERVES 10
1 ounce dried mushrooms
2 onions, chopped
6 ounces butter
1 pound (2 cups) semifine medium-grain rice
2 quarts broth (see pages 123–24)
2 tablespoons extra virgin olive oil
2 ounces chicken livers, chopped
3 ounces chopped lean veal
2 ounces pancetta, diced
6 ripe tomatoes, peeled, seeded, and chopped
Salt and pepper, to taste

½ pound mozzarella, cut into strips
2 cups olive oil, for frying
1 cup flour
2 eggs, beaten
6 tablespoons breadcrumbs

Reconstitute the mushrooms in lukewarm water, chop, and set aside. Make a *risotto* with one of the onions, butter, rice, and broth as described in the basic recipe (see pages 181–82), let it cool, and put it in a mixing bowl.

Prepare a *ragù* by sautéing 1 onion in the olive oil. When the onion is soft, add the chopped livers, veal, *pancetta,* and mushrooms. Add the tomatoes and a pinch of salt and pepper and let simmer over low heat for 30 minutes, or until the mixture has reduced to a rather thick *ragù*. Remove from the heat and let cool.

Take a small amount of rice in the palm of your hand, flatten the rice, and place in the center 1 teaspoonful of the *ragù* and 2 strips of *mozzarella*. Close your palm and form a ball twice the size of a walnut. Make sure the filling is securely closed in the center of the ball. To fry, heat the frying oil. Coat each rice ball with flour, dip in beaten eggs, and roll in breadcrumbs. Fry the *supplì* balls until golden brown and crunchy. Place on absorbent paper to get rid of excess fat and serve immediately.

RISO AL SALTO (Crisp Rice Patty)

SERVES 4

6 ounces butter
1 small onion
¾ pound (1½ cups) long-grain rice
4 cups beef broth (see pages 123–24)
Pinch of saffron
¼ cup grated Parmigiano
Salt and pepper, to taste

Prepare *risotto alla milanese* following the basic recipe (see page 183), but remove from the heat after 14 minutes. Add 3 ounces butter and the *Parmigiano*. Remove it from the pan and spread it out in a large flat pan so that it cools. Melt 2 tablespoons of butter in an 8-inch nonstick frying pan, add 6 spoonfuls of cooled risotto, and flatten into a patty that covers the bottom of the pan with a spatula. Cook over medium heat. As the rice patty cooks, the starch remaining in the grains of rice is expelled and makes the rice stick together perfectly. Shake the pan so the patty does not stick to the bottom, flip over the rice patty (or use a plate), and cook the other side. Continue to fry patties until the rice is finished. With this amount of rice, you should be able to do 6 patties of rice. Add salt and pepper to taste.

PESCE
Fish

Throughout the centuries, Italians retreated inland, building villages and towns high up on the hills to protect themselves from barbaric invasions from the sea. Italians, therefore, developed a beef, vegetable, and dairy diet in their homes, relying heavily on home-grown farm products. This situation also affected the seashore populations who, perhaps because of seafood's abundance, considered fish less nutritious than beef. This erroneous perception has changed in recent times, and today the Italian diet relies heavily on the richness of the Mediterranean Sea that surrounds the entire peninsula.

The origins of Italian cooking at the seashore, however, were well established centuries ago. The Romans themselves started the first breeding of moray and gilthead bream for the tables of the rich. Since ancient times, the most prized Mediterranean fish was caught for roasting or broiling. Seashore populations developed a seafood tradition that found its expression in a rich array of fish stews (*zuppe di pesce*), which involved cooking different types of fish together with a few vegetables and one common condiment, olive oil. It is to be noted that recipe books from the fifteenth to the eighteenth century totally ignore fish. It is only in the writing of Vincenzo Agnoletti in 1814 that we find the first hint of "fish broths to pour over slices of bread."

Zuppa di pesce, which takes different names in different regions (*cacciucco, brodetto, ciuppin* and so on), does not have basic preparation rules. This comes as no surprise for a dish born not only out of the necessity to use just about any type of fish, including the least expensive, available at that moment but also out of the inventiveness of last-minute customers who bought whatever was left over from the day's catch.

Over the last century, the consumption of fish has increased considerably thanks to an extraordinary distribution network that allows merchandise to get to the market still very fresh. The fish market in Milan, for example, is the most important in Italy and one of the most important in Europe. It is, therefore, relatively easy to find in Milan, Bergamo, and other locations far away from the sea restaurants that are well known for their fish specialties.

The fish mentioned in this chapter are the most common varieties and the recipes the most popular. *Cacciucco, brodetti,* and *zuppe* are all much the same although the names vary from one village to the other, each claiming its recipe to be the original one. From the immediate consumption of the small fish along the shores to commercially organized fish markets in the larger cities of Milan and Rome, today fish is one of the most important nutrients in the Italian diet.

The quality of fish is primarily determined by its environment: the cleaner and richer in nutritive elements the water is, the better the fish will taste. All fish, including shellfish, must be eaten fresh or perfectly preserved by freezing, smoking, or salting.

How to Recognize Fresh Fish

Fresh fish has virtually no smell or, if it comes from the sea, should smell only of seaweed and saltwater. The body should be stiff, the flesh firm. The skin should not be dry. The scales (if present) should be shiny, tightly connected to each other and to the body. The eyes should be clear, shiny, and not sunken. The gills should be red and wet. The stomach should be firm, neither swollen nor lacerated. The tail should be rigid and the anal orifice completely closed. If you buy fish fillets or steaks, check that the flesh is white or rosy, with iridescent reflections, and feels firm to the touch.

How to Clean Fish

Fish must always be thoroughly cleaned, regardless of how it is going to be cooked. If it has scales, they must be removed. Place the fish on a large sheet of paper. Holding it by the tail (if it is slippery, use a towel), lightly scrape the fish with the back of a knife or one with a dull blade held at an angle, scraping from the tail to the head until all scales are removed. The fins may also be removed. Gut the fish by making a small opening in the stomach to remove the intestines and black membrane (if present) that lines the stomach cavity.

To improve the appearance of fish, remove the guts by inserting your fingers through the gills and pulling them out through this opening. Wash the fish well and let it drain, head down. This procedure is appropriate for most kinds of fish. With spiny fish, it is a good idea to remove the fins first, since they are rather sharp-pointed.

How to Fillet Fish

Clean the fish and lay it on its side on the cutting board. Cut the fish with a sharp knife along the spine line. Cut deeply into the flesh, releasing the fish from the backbone. Make a diagonal cut behind the head and the gills and remove the fillet. Repeat on the other side.

How to Fillet Sole

Slip the point of a knife under the skin near the tail and cut toward the tail to detach the skin. Grab the skin in one hand, hold the tail down with the other, and pull the skin toward the head, peeling it away from the flesh. Repeat the operation on the other side. Then, with a flat, flexible knife, cut the flesh down the center on either side of the backbone. Starting from the center, work toward the edge (along the bones). Remove the fillet with a knife. Repeat on the other side. A big sole will yield 4 fillets.

Cooking Techniques

POACHING LIQUID

MAKES 4 QUARTS
  3 quarts water
  1 quart dry white wine
  2 carrots, quartered
  1 onion, quartered
  2 celery stalks
  1 sprig parsley, chopped
  2 bay leaves
  ¾ teaspoon salt
  8 peppercorns

First prepare the poaching liquid: In a large pot, bring the water, white wine, and all the vegetables and salt to a boil for about 45 minutes over medium heat. Add the peppercorns 10 minutes before the end. When the liquid is ready, let cool, strain, and pour the broth in a poacher. Add the selected fish. Bring slowly to a boil. Reduce to a simmer and cook, uncovered, until the fish is cooked through, usually 5 to 7 minutes. See recipes below for more details about poaching fish.

Variations:

Poaching Liquid with Vinegar: The procedure and ingredients are the same as in the basic recipe except that the wine is replaced with 2 cups of white wine vinegar. Boil the vinegar and reduce it by half before adding it to the water. Cooked in this way, the flesh of the fish will keep its pinkish color. One-half cup of lemon juice may replace the vinegar.

Poaching Liquid with Milk: Use only water and milk (1 quart milk to 1 quart water), 2 bay leaves, 6 white peppercorns, ½ lemon (sliced), 1 small onion, and a sprig of thyme. Add salt to taste. If the poaching liquid is to be used for salt cod, no further salt is needed. Simply bring to a boil and remove from the heat. The poaching liquid is now ready. Bring the poaching liquid back to a simmer before adding the fish.

Poaching Liquid with Water: Mix only water and coarse salt together (1 tablespoon salt for every quart of water), so that the very delicate flavor of the fish is not altered. In coastal areas, fish may be cooked in seawater.

PESCE BOLLITO (Poached Fish)

Saltwater fish is usually cooked in a poaching liquid as described above, although it can be simply cooked in salted water.

Poached fish that takes more than 20 minutes to cook does not need to be cooked in a specially prepared poaching liquid. Simply place vegetables and aromatic herbs on the bottom of a fish poacher.

If cooked whole, fish must be started in a cold liquid. Bring the cold water rapidly to a boil, then turn the heat down and cook slowly. If fish is plunged in boiling water whole, the skin will break and the fish will tend to break apart.

Fish fillets, however, must be started in a boiling liquid. If pieces of fish are cooked in cold water, the flavor and juices will drain from the fish. A hot liquid prevents this by sealing the exposed flesh, thus keeping the juices in.

PESCE IN BRODETTO (Fish Cooked in Broth)

Oil and cover the bottom of a saucepan with finely minced scallions, onion, carrot, and celery. Sauté over medium heat for 5 minutes. Add salt and place the fish on top. Add enough poaching liquid to cover the fish completely. Bring to a simmer and cook until the fish is done to your liking. Remove the fish and place it on a serving platter. Top with its broth and serve.

Note:
The ingredients used for the broth may vary according to taste.

PESCE IN BLEU (Quick-Poached Fish)

This preparation is suitable for small live fish (no more that 20 to 24 ounces), especially freshwater fish. Hit the fish on the head to stun it. Gut and wash the fish without removing the scales. Handle the fish with care to avoid removing the viscous substance. Place on a dish and sprinkle with white vinegar. Soak the vinegary fish in the desired poaching liquid and simmer over low heat. The skin of the fish will tear somewhat and become bluish. Cook until done to your liking. Bring the fish to the table in its own broth, bone it, and serve it with steamed vegetables. Freshwater trout is classically prepared this way.

PESCE IN UMIDO (Moist-Baked Fish)

There are two ways to cook fish in the oven: moist-baking and roasting. Moist-baking is best for small fish (under 5 pounds).

A sauce may be prepared in advance and the fish added and then baked, or the cooking may start with the fish and the vegetables, along with herbs and spices, lightly browned in a skillet on top of the stove. A poaching liquid is added and the cooking is finished in the oven. Temperature and baking time vary according to the fish and the recipe being prepared. This type of preparation can also be finished on top of the stove.

PESCE ARROSTO (Roast Fish)

Use this method only for whole fish, preferably weighing 5 pounds or more. Make diagonal cuts along the body so that the fish can cook evenly. Marinate it in extra virgin olive oil, bay leaves, parsley, and other herbs. Then brown the fish on both sides in a pan on top of the stove over medium heat. Put it in the oven at 375°F, basted with the juices released by the fish or a prepared juice. It is not necessary to turn the fish unless the heat is uneven and the fish is small enough to be handled easily. Remove from the oven when done to your liking and place on a serving platter. Bone and serve.

Note:
Moist-baking is suitable for most fish fillets, while roasting is only suitable for whole fish.

PESCE AL CARTOCCIO (Fish Baked in Parchment or Aluminum Foil)

This method is suitable for small fish fillets. Grease a large piece of parchment paper or aluminum foil and place the fish with desired herbs and spices in the center. Fold up the paper or foil into a tightly closed but loose packet. Bake at 375°F (about 15 minutes for fillets). Make one *cartoccio* per portion. When done place each *cartoccio* on a plate; slit the center, open, and serve.

PESCE SALTATO AL BURRO (Fish Sautéed in Butter)

This cooking procedure is used with small and flat fish or with large fish cut into fillets. Salt the fish and lightly coat it with flour. Cook it in butter on both sides until golden brown. Serve hot, topped with the sauce of your choice, or on its own.

PESCE IMPANATO (Breaded Fish)

This is made in the same way as fish sautéed in butter, except the fish is first dredged in flour, dipped in beaten egg, and then coated with white breadcrumbs. Pat the breadcrumbs tightly on the fillets so they will not form bubbles as they fry. Fry in olive oil until golden brown. A mixture of olive oil and butter can also be used for frying.

PESCE FRITTO (Fried Fish)

Olive oil is the best fat for frying fish. Oil temperature should vary according to the size of the fish being fried: the smaller the fish, the higher the temperature. Fish for frying (either whole or cut into pieces or fillets) should not weigh more than 3 ounces. Except for whitebait, anchovies, and other small fish, which can be directly coated with flour before frying, all fish may be dipped in milk first. After frying, drain off excess frying oil by placing the fish on paper towels. Serve very hot with chopped parsley and lemon wedges. The very popular *fritto misto* is a platter with a variety of fried fish. The combinations of fish served vary according to the region and to what is seasonably available on the market. Never cover fish when frying or it will lose its crunchiness and become steamy.

PESCE ALLA GRIGLIA (Broiled Fish)

Broiled fish is better if it is not scaled or seasoned but simply brushed with olive oil before broiling. When broiling fish without scales, coat it with flour before brushing with oil to prevent it from sticking to the grill. If the fish is rather large, score it diagonally along its body with shallow cuts, so it can cook through more easily. Alternatively, the fish can be filleted or cut across into 1-inch-thick slices. Certain types of fish are more suitable to be cut one way than others. For example, salmon and turbot may be cut across; bass is filleted.

When broiling a whole fish, make turning easier by using a hand grill that folds open like a book. Broiled fish should be turned just once, since too much handling may break it. Check for doneness by piercing the fish with a long-handled fork—the fork should go through the flesh easily. When the fish is cooked, you may brush it with a dressing of olive oil, lemon, parsley, salt, and pepper or serve it plain with a dressing on the side.

SALTWATER FISH

ALICE (Anchovy)

Anchovy is a saltwater fish from the family of *pesce azzurro* (blue fish). It has a short jaw and a tapered body. Anchovies are in season from March through September. They do not have scales. Their color is bluish-green except for the insides and stomach, which are silver. They can be marinated, fried, or baked. They can be preserved whole in salt or, if filleted, in oil, plain or with capers.

BACCALÀ (Dried Salt Cod)

The name *baccalà* comes from the Flemmish *bakeljamo,* which later became the Portuguese *bacalao.* To make salt cod, larger cods are used. The cod is boned and its sides are preserved under salt using wooden barrels, subsequently removed, and air-dried; smaller cods are preserved whole (*stoccafisso*).

Before cooking, salt cod must be soaked in cold water (either under running water or in water that is changed frequently) for at least 18 hours to soften the flesh and remove the salt. It is then cut into pieces, and prepared in the desired manner.

BIANCHETTI (Whitebait)

The spawn of both sardines and anchovies, whitebait are very small fish that can be fried or cooked in *frittate* and fritters. If whitebait is really fresh, it can be simply boiled and drained and served hot with a dressing of olive oil and a few lemon drops. Or it can be marinated and eaten raw as a salad with oil, lemon juice, salt, and pepper.

BRANZINO O SPIGOLA (Sea Bass)

This saltwater fish migrates upstream in the spring and lives in freshwater until the fall. Its exquisite flesh is lean, firm, white, flaky, and delicate, its scales small. It is gray on the back and silver on the sides. The smaller ones are broiled or baked *al cartoccio*, while the larger ones may be poached or boned and filleted and then moist-baked.

CERNIA (Grouper)

In Italy, grouper is considered the venison of the sea. It must be tenderized in the refrigerator for at least 2 days before cooking. Grouper lives in sea coves and is caught by spear hunting. This fish is available in spring and fall. Its back is dark yellow, lighter in the belly area. The lower part of the body has dots that disappear when exposed to the air. Grouper can be cooked whole or sliced starting from the middle or toward the tail. It can be boiled, broiled, or baked. In America, grouper is found in warmer waters. The flesh is much more crumbly, and it must be used immediately after the catch.

DENTICE (Red Snapper)

This saltwater fish has a tapered body and slanted profile. It has 4 sharp-pointed teeth and its color is purple and violet with silver overtones. The American species is similar to the European one but bright red. Snapper is best roasted or baked.

MERLUZZO (Fresh Cod)

This cold saltwater fish can grow very large. It has a broad, more or less elongated body, well-defined head and fins, a large mouth with strong teeth, and a kind of beard. Dorsal color ranges from brown to greenish or yellowish depending on its habitat. The flesh is white and delicate and flakes easily. Larger cod can be sliced. The most suitable ways of cooking cod are baking, poaching, braising, or rolling into croquettes. It is better not to broil cod because it falls apart easily.

MUGGINE (Gray Mullet)

Mullet is in season year-round with the exception of January and February. Its back is dark gray, the stomach silvery white. On its sides are silver and gold parallel lines. Its flesh is white and delicious, although fatty. Its flavor varies according to season, geographical origin, and its diet. Mullet can be boiled, stewed, sautéed, broiled, or baked. Its liver is delicious. In many Italian regions the egg sac is salted and air-dried and is known as *bottarga*.

ORATA (Gilthead Bream)

This saltwater fish can be found on the market almost all year long. The smaller variety is available from October through January. Its body is sky blue with silvery reflections and vertical dark stripes. It has a dark purple spot near the gills. The belly is silvery. Gilthead bream owes its name to the golden yellow line shaped like a half moon between the eyes. Its flesh is lean, white, and delicate and can be prepared in many ways. Small ones can be sautéed, big ones cooked in a poaching liquid or baked or broiled.

PAGELLO O SARAGO (Sea Bream)

This is a beautiful, rather small saltwater fish at its best in spring or summer. It has a tapered oval shape with a slightly slanted head. The mouth is tapered and the eyes and teeth protrude. Its back is shiny blue, shading to silvery white in the belly area. The occasional large ones are reddish in color. Near the pectoral fins, sea bream has a black spot and light bluish dots. Its flesh is lean and delicious. It is best roasted or broiled.

PESCE PALOMBO (Sea Squab)

This fish, which has a delicious flavor and is caught in the Mediterranean, comes from the same family as the shark (*squalo*). It must be skinned before it is filleted or cut for its desired use. It may be moist-baked and grilled in fish stews.

PESCE SPADA (Swordfish)

This is a very large Mediterranean fish especially bountiful near Sicily. Its name comes from the long, thin, sword-like bone protruding from above its mouth. The flesh is delicious, compact, and rosy. It is usually braised, sautéed, or grilled.

RANA PESCATRICE (Angler or Monkfish)

Although this fish is not particularly attractive—its overly large head and mouth make it resemble a large toad—its flesh is very tasty, similar in texture and flavor to lobster. It is most flavorful in the winter months. Since only the tail is eaten, the head can be used to make a poaching liquid. Monkfish may be boiled, stewed, broiled, or baked and may be included in a fish stew.

ROMBO (Turbot)

Turbot may grow to be very large. It is an oval-shaped saltwater fish. There are many varieties, but the best are those that have small green or yellow bony plates that end in hooked points on the back. This variety is called *chiodata* (nailed) and has two eyes on the back. Its flesh is white and tasty, though rather firm. It is preferable to tenderize the flesh by keeping it on ice 1 or 2 days before preparing. When purchasing turbot, check to see that its gelatinous external layer is soft. This indicates freshness. It is best poached or grilled.

SAN PIETRO (St. Peter's Fish)

St. Peter's fish is another rather ugly saltwater fish, dark yellowish in color with thin threads attached to the fins and back. It can be found in spring and summer. Its name comes from the two dark spots on its sides which, according to legend, are said to be St. Peter's fingerprints. St. Peter's fish has firm, white flesh suitable for most preparations. It is usually filleted and can be sautéed, moist-baked, or grilled.

SARDINA (Sardine)

Sardine is a small saltwater fish with very fatty flesh that belongs to the family called *pesce azzurro*. An Italian proverb says that a sardine has 24 virtues, but loses one every hour it is out of the water; that is to say, the fish must be cooked when it is very fresh. Sardines have firm flesh, bright eyes, and red gills. They can be fried or baked. They are used in the classical preparation of *pasta con le sarde*.

SCORFANO (Scorpion Fish)

In season from June to October, this fish is commonly found in the muddy seabed of the Mediterranean. Its flesh is prized and especially good in *zuppa di pesce*. The larger specimens can also be baked.

SGOMBRO (Mackerel)

This rather common fish living in the Mediterranean is inexpensive and quite good when eaten fresh. The flesh is rather fatty. Mackerel is either broiled or baked in parchment or aluminum foil (*al cartoccio*).

SOGLIOLA (Sole)

This is a choice saltwater fish, available on the market all year-round. It is flat. The top-side skin is greenish-black and the belly side white. The best variety comes from the North Sea, particularly in the English Channel near Dover. The flesh is exquisite, lean, and delicate. Sole can be cooked in many ways, whole or filleted, but it is best sautéed. Whatever the cooking method, the skin must always be removed. Dust with flour and sauté in butter and serve with half a lemon per serving.

STOCCAFISSO (Dried Cod)

Stoccafisso is a whole small cod cured in salt and air-dried. This preserving technique goes back to the Vikings. The name comes from *Stockfish*, which in German means "fish as stiff as a stick." The fish are tied by the tail and hung, in a climate that is cold and dry. The best stockfish comes from Northern European countries. Before cooking, dried cod must be softened. Beat it with a wooden stick or a wooden pestle and then soak it in cool water (running water is better) for 4 or 5 days, even longer if possible. The water should be changed at least twice a day. Soaking it for as long as possible is very important or the flesh will be tough and woody regardless of how long it has cooked. It takes about 1½ hours to cook, depending on the recipe.

STORIONE (Sturgeon)

This saltwater fish is caught in spring and summer when it swims upstream to spawn. Its flesh is exquisite but very fatty. It is usually filleted or sliced, boiled, stewed, or baked, occasionally marinated in white wine first. Sturgeon egg sacs are a major source of caviar (*caviale*), and jelly is made from the sturgeon's bladder.

TONNO (Tuna)

Tuna can reach notably large dimensions, sometimes over 13 feet in length and over 1,000 pounds in weight. The most important Italian tuna-fishing areas are located along the Sicilian and Sardinian coasts where tuna fish pause during their mysterious migrations. The tuna egg sac is used to prepare *bottarga*. Its flesh is very prized, partic-ularly in the Japanese market. It can be served raw with just olive oil, salt, and pepper, braised, sautéed, or broiled. It must remain underdone, otherwise the flesh will become woody.

TRIGLIA (Red and White Mullet)

Mullet is among the most prized saltwater fish, despite its many thin bones. Some gour-mets call it "the woodcock of the sea" because, like the woodcock, red mullet, when fresh, can be eaten with its innards. In this case, it is broiled without washing or removing the scales.

This fish has two varieties: red (or stone) mullet and white mullet. Red mullet, fished off rocky bottom coasts, has brilliant red on its back and brighter red with golden stripes on its sides. The breast, throat, and belly are rosy white. The lower jaw is equipped with two pendant barbells on the chin. White mullet is fished in deep waters with muddy bottoms. It has a rosy color with silvery reflections on the sides. Red mullets are more prized than white ones. They are best from May to July, since in these months they are at their largest and the flesh is at its whitest.

Mullets can be cooked in various ways: The smaller ones are best fried, the larger ones moist-baked.

FRESHWATER FISH

AGONE (Fresh Shad)

This lake fish is very common but not a prized variety. The best shads are found in Lake Maggiore and Garda in the north of Italy. Shads are fished in May and June. They may be broiled or left to dry in the sun and wind, then preserved in containers with bay leaves. They are called *missoltitt* (from the name of the container in which they are packed, *missolta*).

ANGUILLA (Eel)

This anadromous fish lives in rivers, swamps, or marshes. Eels go out to sea to spawn during the months of January and February, then swim upstream in the spring. Newborn eels are called *cieche*. For some unknown reason, in Italy they may be found only in the Tuscan coast area between Forte dei Marmi and Viareggio at the mouth of the river Arno. Legend has it that eels go to the Sargasso Sea in the Caribbean to spawn. This legend is supported by the fact that large schools of eels are seen crossing the Strait of Gibraltar during the winter months. Eels are in season from October through May. Their flesh, though fatty, is delicious. It can be cooked in many ways but preferably is roasted or grilled. It is also delicious marinated. Large eels are called *capitoni* and are part of the traditional Christmas Eve and Christmas Day meals in southern Italy.

For most preparations, eels must be skinned. Ask your fishmonger to skin the eel. To do it yourself, cut the eel's skin right behind the head, hang the eel on a hook by the mouth, and pull the skin down. It will peel off as if it were a glove. Then gut and clean. If the preparation requires that the skin be left on, the skin should be scrubbed with ash. If ash is not available, a rough cloth or a pumice stone will do. Wash well after scrubbing.

CARPA (Carp)

This is a common freshwater fish of a rather inferior quality. Its flesh is rosy-white, its back dark, the sides golden yellow, and the stomach greenish white. The best carp are found in clear, flowing waters (in either rivers or lakes). Those raised in swamps have a muddy aftertaste. Swamp carp are recognizable by their darker color and intense smell. If you buy a swamp carp still alive, you can purge it by keeping it in cold running water for 3 days, or by feeding the carp 2 tablespoons of vinegar, then scraping and cleaning well, keeping it in running water for an hour. Make sure the fish is very fresh. Clean, rub with salt, and let rest for half an hour. Rinse off the salt before cooking. Small carp can be fried and then marinated in vinegar with spices, if desired, while larger ones can be broiled or stewed.

LUCCIO (Pike)

This is a big freshwater fish known as "the shark of rivers" for its voracity. Its body is covered with small, greenish scales, the stomach and sides white with green gradations. The head is rather pointed, heavy, and strong; the mouth is enormous. The peak season for pike is September. Its flesh is lean and flaky in texture. It can be cooked whole or sliced, either boiled, broiled, or baked (with or without coating). Since the pike's flesh is rather dry, it is best served with a sauce.

PESCE PERSICO (Perch)

This freshwater fish, which is at its best in May, has a golden, greenish back with 5 to 7 vertical stripes that shade off in the vicinity of the belly. The fins are rosy. It has two dorsal fins, one of which has very sharp points. Its flesh is excellent, compact, white, and delicate. Perch should be gutted immediately after it is caught. One of the most exquisite varieties is the perch trout found in Lombard lakes. Another variety is the *persico sole* (sun perch), recognizable by a shiny black spot near the gills, partly surrounded by a bright red circle. Big perches may be sautéed or boiled in a poaching liquid with vinegar. The smaller ones may be fried and the very large ones can be baked. Perches can also be filleted, floured, and breaded, cooked in butter and sage or other delicate sauces.

TROTA (Trout)

Trout is a freshwater fish of many varieties. Brown trout lives in cold, clear mountain rivers or lakes. Its body is agile and resilient and its color varies according to the environment, though it always has red and black dots surrounded by a small ring of either white or pink. Rainbow trout has a more slender body than that of the brown variety and its head is slightly smaller. Its color varies but its distinctive marks are a rosy stripe on its sides and a thick concentration of black spots. It can be found in mountain streams as well as lowland lakes. Lake trout resembles brown trout. Its back has a dark bluish color which becomes paler blue on the sides and yellowish on the belly. Contrary to popular belief, salmon trout *(trota salmonata)* is not a hybrid between a trout and a salmon but a trout that has lived primarily on a diet of shrimps, thus acquiring its pink-colored flesh. All these varieties of trout have lean flesh. There are many ways to cook trout: the smaller ones should preferably be sautéed or quick-poached; the bigger ones can be baked. Trout is available all year-round, since it is often bred in commercial hatcheries.

Trout is best when poached as in *pesce in bleu* (see pages 192, 205–6).

COSCE DI RANA (Frog's Legs)

Although frogs are not a fish, frog's legs are listed in this chapter. Only the legs are suitable for cooking preparations. Their flesh is white, very tender, and delicate. They may be sautéed, fried in batter, or added to *frittate*. Frog's legs are also excellent with risotto.

CROSTACEI E MOLLUSCHI (Shellfish and Mollusks)

How to Recognize Fresh Shellfish and Mollusks

When buying mussels, clams, or other bivalves, always check to see that the shells are tightly closed. If a shell is open, tap it lightly. If it closes instantly, that means that the shellfish inside is still alive, which means it's suitable for cooking. If the shell is closed, shake the bivalve. If it is alive, you will hear nothing, because the creature inside is tensed up trying to keep the shell tightly closed. Shellfish should be soaked in cold, salted water. Dispense with any floating shellfish because they are either dead or empty. Mollusks (squid, cuttlefish, and octopus), if fresh, should not smell like moss. The flesh should be firm and shiny. The skin should not be dry. The tentacles should not break when pulled.

Lobster, crayfish, and other crustaceans must be bought and cooked while still alive. The flesh of fresh crustaceans is firm and compact. If they have been kept on ice for a long time the flesh may become soft and flabby, the tail may break off from the rest of the body, and the head may have a strong smell.

ARAGOSTA E ASTICE (Spiny Lobster and Maine Lobster)

Spiny lobster belongs to the family Palinuridae. Its body can grow up to 22 inches and it has two antennas. Maine lobster belongs to the family Nephropidae. The body is the same as the spiny lobster, but it has two pincer-like claws. Spiny lobster is commonly found in the waters of the Mediterranean and Adriatic and off the coasts of South Africa, Australia, and New Zealand. The type we call Maine lobster is found from Newfoundland down to the Carolinas.

If possible, choose a female lobster (its eggs are delicious). To recognize a female lobster, turn it upside down and observe the small fins on the abdomen, which look somewhat like a fan. In the female, these are larger and longer than in the male since the female uses these fins to protect the eggs as they are maturing, while in the male the fins barely touch. Lobsters should not have holes in their shell or broken-off limbs. It does not matter if the antennas are damaged because they are very fragile and can break during combat. Lobster can be boiled, steamed, or baked.

CALAMARO (Squid)

Calamari, or squids, are mollusks whose body resembles a sack with a large and flat fin attached to it toward the middle. The extremity of the body has tentacles. Its color when fresh is pinkish with purple-brown spots.

The flesh of *calamari* is more delicate than that of *totani*, a similar mollusk. *Totani* has a triangular, spear-like fin. They are purple when fresh; otherwise, a white color will be predominant. *Calamari* and *totani* should both be cleaned by removing the fin, eyes, beak, and all that is inside. Then they should be skinned and washed several times. The smaller *calamari* are excellent fried; the larger ones may be moist-baked, with or without stuffing.

CANNOLICCHIO (Razor Clam)

The shell of this mollusk is long and tubular, about five inches long, and yellowish-gray of varying intensities in color. The "foot" protrudes from one end of the shell and the siphon from the other. These are excellent when eaten raw with lemon juice but they can also be stewed.

CAPPASANTA (Scallop)

This kind of mollusk has a very large and beautiful shell, and can be eaten either raw (with lemon juice) or cooked. *Cappesante* gathered in winter are particularly good. As is the case with all shellfish, scallops must be alive when cooked. If there are any open shells, insert the tip of a knife. If the scallop is alive, the shell will close instantly. Otherwise, dispense with the scallop. The flesh inside is shaped like a large, flattened cork. This part is known as the *noce* (nut), and attached to it is the red half moon of roe known as the *corallo*. Around the *noce* is a gray muscle, or foot, which must be discarded. To open the shells, put them in a covered pot over low heat for a few minutes.

COZZA (Mussel)

This bivalve can be gathered from either the sea or commercial mussel beds. Mussels are available all year round, though they are bigger in spring and summer. Their shells are purple-black. The flesh varies from pink to coral red. Prior to cooking, the shells should be vigorously scraped under running water to remove all dirt and sludge. Mussels are very tasty and can be used to prepare many dishes. They may be cooked, with or without stuffing; they may also be steamed with wine and garlic. When buying mussels, check to see that the shells are tightly closed. Tap on any open one. If it is alive, the shell will close instantly.

DATTERO (Date Shell)

The shell of this shellfish looks very similar to a date, in both size and color. Date shells are more highly prized than mussels, and the best ones are medium-size, about two inches long.

Date shells live in deep niches embedded in rocks and are difficult to collect. In Italy today, the search for *datteri* is prohibited along the entire seashore line. They are best eaten raw, when very fresh; otherwise, *datteri* are steamed with garlic and parsley.

GAMBERO (Shrimp)

Shrimp belong to the family Decapodi. They have ten feet, five on each side, and do not have claws. They can reach a length of about eight inches. Their color varies from pink to bright red. Shrimp flesh is prized and very popular in the Mediterranean.

In the same family is the *gambero imperiale*. This is a beautiful, rather large sea shrimp (whole, it can be up to six inches long). Its color is red and yellow with dark spots on the tail tips. Its flesh is delicious and delicate. All shrimp can be baked, broiled, fried, or boiled.

GRANSEOLA (Mediterranean Crab)

This exquisite variety of crab is commonly found in the Adriatic and the Mediterranean. It is also found in the east Atlantic and the British Isles. The scientific name is *Maja squinado* and it belongs to the family Majidaee. The body has an ovoid shape with an extremely hard shield full of strong, pointed thorns. Its length can reach a maximum of eight to nine inches. Mediterranean crab has five pairs of legs with two forelegs equipped with claws. *Granseola* is sold fresh and alive. It is generally boiled like lobster; its shield is then removed, the flesh taken out, and the cartilage trimmed. It is dressed with extra virgin olive oil, lemon, salt, and pepper and put back into its empty shell.

LUMACHE (Snails)

Snails are considered land mollusks. They are protected by a spiral shell within which they can remain for many months. The best variety is the *vignarole*, which live on grapevines. They are best from October through March. They must be purged and can be prepared in *guozzetto* (light broth) or with *risotto*.

MOSCARDINO (Bottom Octopus)

Moscardino is a small mollusk similar to octopus. It lives in muddy bottoms, has eight tentacles, and one line of suckers. *Moscardini* should be boiled in salted water lightly acidulated with either vinegar or lemon. They may be served warm or cold with extra virgin olive oil, lemon juice, and parsley; they may also be fried or used to prepare a very good condiment for *spaghetti*.

POLIPO (Octopus)

Octopus is a sea creature found in many varieties. *Polipo verace* (stone octopus) can be recognized by the double line of suckers on its tentacles, whereas the octopus with red and white dots is known as *scorria* or *polpessa* (the name varies from region to region). Prior to cooking, it is advisable to remove the skin of larger octopus. If you do not want to skin it, rub it vigorously with a very rough cloth under running water until foam is no longer produced. Or the skin can be removed after cooking while still hot. Very big octopus must be tenderized before being cooked. To do so, pound the body with a stone or a piece of wood to break down the tough fibers, being careful not to crush the octopus. Octopus is available all year round except in January, May, and August. All kinds of octopus are cooked in the same way, that is, boiled or stewed. *Scorria* or *polpessa* are particularly suitable for *risotto* or pasta dishes, or boiled with a condiment of olive oil, lemon, garlic, and parsley.

SCAMPO (Seawater Prawn)

Prawn is a prized crustacean with two long claws, eight feet (four on each side), a fan-like tail, a large head with white, firm, and delicate flesh. It can be up to ten inches long. It belongs to the family Nephropidae, the same as lobster. (They are often mistaken for shrimp.) Prawns may be cooked in boiling water with aromatic herbs, cooking time varying according to size. They are served with olive oil, lemon juice, and finely minced parsley. Often they are incorrectly called "shrimp scampi."

SEPPIA (Cuttlefish)

Cuttlefish is available year round. The large ones are best between January and June, but medium or small ones are always preferable. The hood, or body, of the cuttlefish is shaped like a rounded sack surrounded on each side by a fringe. Inside, underneath the skin of the hood, there is a large flat fin which must be removed prior to cooking. Its mouth is surrounded by ten tentacles. When fresh, it has a greenish color, with luminous yellow highlights on the belly, and the hood is dark brown with light stripes. The ink sack, which is inside the bag portion of the body, can be used to prepare *risotto al nero di seppia* (pages 184–85) or to season pasta. *Seppia* is cooked like squid, that is, moist-baked, grilled, or stuffed.

VONGOLA (Clam)

These are marine bivalves although, unlike the mussels, the shell is light gray in color. As with all shellfish, clams must be cooked alive. Clams are cooked in various sauces, some of which go well with *spaghetti* or *risotto*. If you want to cook them directly in a sauce, keep them in lightly salted, cold water so that the shells will open, releasing any sand that might be trapped inside. Always drain them with your hands; a colander will not rid the clams of sand.

Vongola verace is indigenous to the Mediterranean. It can be recognized by its two suckers protruding from its main body. This type of clam is prized in Italy, particularly in the south. It is the preferred variety for preparing clam sauce.

ORATA LESSA (Poached Gilthead Bream)

SERVES 4

2 gilthead breams, 2 pounds each
4 quarts poaching liquid (page 191)

Use a fish poacher. If you cook the fish whole, start by placing the fish in cold liquid. If you cook fillets, bring the liquid to a very light simmer (to the point where the surface shimmers or slightly moves) and then add the fish fillets. Cook until done (whole fish should take 6 minutes for each pound, fillets 5 minutes for 6- to 8-ounce portions. A fork will easily pierce the flesh when it is done. Remove fish from the poacher and serve with oil, lemon, chopped parsley, and salt and pepper to taste, or another sauce.

TROTA IN BLEU (Quick-Poached Trout)

SERVES 4

4 trout, 1¼ to 1½ pounds each
½ cup white wine vinegar
4 quarts vinegar-based poaching liquid (page 191)
2 ounces butter, browned
Juice of 1 lemon
1 tablespoon chopped parsley
Salt and pepper, to taste

The trout should be alive, stunned, gutted, and cleaned. Pour white wine vinegar over the fish and marinate for 5 minutes. Using a fish poacher, add the vinegar-based poaching liquid. Bring it to a simmer, then place the fish in the poacher and cook for 4 to 6 minutes, depending on the size of the fish. Remove from the liquid and serve 1 trout per person with steamed vegetables. You may serve with a sauce made with the browned butter, lemon, parsley, and salt and pepper to taste.

Note:

The poaching liquid may be adapted to suit the cook's skill and creativity. It can be 50 percent water and 50 percent white wine. Vegetables may be added or not.

ZUPPA DI PESCE (Fish Stew)

SERVES 4

3 pounds assorted fish, such as gray mullet, turbot, St. Peter's fish, scorpion fish
    (optional), scallops, shrimp, or any fish with a firm texture
¼ cup olive oil
6 crushed garlic cloves
½ pound tomatoes, peeled, seeded, and chopped
Salt and pepper, to taste
2 tablespoons chopped parsley
4 slices of country bread, toasted
1 whole garlic clove

Fillet the fish, reserving the bones and the heads. Bring 2 quarts of water to a boil in a large pot. Add the fish bones and heads, including the shrimp heads. Cook for 2 hours. Cool and strain the broth. Set aside but keep hot.

Prepare a *soffritto* by sautéing the olive oil and crushed garlic. When the garlic is golden brown, add the tomatoes and sauté for 3 minutes. Start adding the fish, one at a time, in order of cooking time: first the scorpion fish, if using, the shrimp, turbot, St. Peter's fish, gray mullet, and scallops. Cook each for 3 minutes. Add 4 cups of broth and bring to a simmer. Adjust with salt and pepper to taste. Finish cooking the fish (2 to 3 minutes) and remove from the heat. Place on a large serving platter, sprinkle the parsley over, and serve with country bread rubbed with the whole garlic clove.

Note:

There are as many variations and as many names for this preparation as there are church bells. Just to mention a few, there are *brodetto, cacciucco*, and *ciuppin*. The type of fish added also varies; some do not include mollusks, while some add bivalves. Some claim that at least thirteen or fourteen different types of fish should be used; others use only one type.

TRIGLIE ALLA LIVORNESE (Red or White Mullets Livornese-Style)

SERVES 4

2 garlic cloves, crushed
10 tablespoons extra virgin olive oil
1 celery stalk, chopped
2 pounds ripe tomatoes, peeled, seeded, and chopped
2 pounds red or white mullets
1¾ cups all-purpose flour
Salt and pepper, to taste
1 tablespoon chopped parsley

Preheat the oven to 375°F. Sauté the garlic in a skillet with 2 tablespoons of the olive oil. Remove the garlic when golden brown. Add the celery. When tender, add the tomatoes and cook for 10 minutes. Remove from the heat and set aside. Coat the fish lightly with flour and fry in a saucepan with 7 tablespoons of olive oil until golden brown on both sides. Add salt and pepper to taste. Grease a casserole with the remaining 1 tablespoon of olive oil, place the mullets in it, and pour the sauce in the casserole over the fish. Bake for 5 minutes. Generously sprinkle the dish with chopped parsley and serve.

Note:
Red mullets should be prepared bone-in; white mullets should be filleted prior to frying.

ALICI IN TORTIERA (Moist-Baked Anchovies)

SERVES 4

2 pounds anchovies
2 tablespoons breadcrumbs
2 tablespoons grated pecorino cheese
1 tablespoon oregano
4 garlic cloves, chopped
6 tablespoons extra virgin olive oil
Salt and pepper, to taste
1 tablespoon chopped parsley

Preheat the oven to 350°F. Remove the heads and split the anchovies open. Remove the bones and the tails, wash, and pat dry. Prepare a *battuto* by mixing the breadcrumbs, *pecorino,* oregano, and garlic. Grease a baking dish with oil and coat it with a thin layer of the *battuto.* Place half the anchovies in the dish, head to tail, leaving no empty spaces. Sprinkle with half the remaining *battuto.* Make a second layer of anchovies, and cover with remaining *battuto.* Drizzle with 5 tablespoons of olive oil. Bake for 6 minutes. Drizzle with 1 tablespoon of oil, add the salt, pepper, and chopped parsley, and serve.

Variations:

Pour the juice of half a lemon over the top, just before serving.

The anchovies can also be prepared bone-in.

INVOLTINI DI PESCE SPADA (Swordfish Rolls)

SERVES 6

　　2 pounds center-cut swordfish
　　1 small onion
　　1 garlic clove, chopped
　　¼ cup extra virgin olive oil
　　½ cup breadcrumbs
　　1 tablespoon capers
　　3 ounces provolone piccante, diced
　　2 eggs
　　2 tablespoons chopped basil
　　Salt and pepper, to taste
　　1 cup salmoriglio (see page 33)
　　2 tablespoons extra virgin olive oil
　　1 tablespoon chopped parsley

Preheat the oven to 375°F. Thinly slice the swordfish, trim the edges, and set the trimmings aside. Chop and brown the onion, garlic, and bits of swordfish trimmings in 2 tablespoons of the olive oil. When done, add the breadcrumbs and capers. Toast for 2 more minutes. Remove from the heat and let cool. Add the diced *provolone,* the eggs, and basil to the mixture. Add salt and pepper to taste. Mix into a smooth filling. Flatten the swordfish fillets slightly with a mallet and place 1 teaspoonful of filling in the middle. Roll up the fillets and close with toothpicks. Grease a baking dish with oil and arrange the rolls of swordfish in it. Drizzle with the *salmoriglio* and bake for 18 minutes. Remove from the oven, sprinkle with the remaining 2 tablespoons of olive oil, add the chopped parsley, and serve.

Note:

You may have more sauce ready to serve on the side.

SARDE A BECCAFICO (Stuffed Fresh Sardines)

SERVES 6

　　2 pounds sardines
　　½ cup extra virgin olive oil
　　4 garlic cloves, crushed
　　5 tablespoons white breadcrumbs

8 anchovy fillets, chopped
2 tablespoons raisins
2 tablespoons pine nuts
1 tablespoon chopped parsley
½ cup grated pecorino cheese
Salt and pepper, to taste
4 bay leaves

Preheat the oven to 375°F. Clean the sardines, remove heads, split open, remove bones, and pat dry. In a skillet with 6 tablespoons of the olive oil, sauté the garlic until brown, then remove. Add the breadcrumbs, anchovy fillets, raisins, pine nuts, and parsley and sauté for 3 minutes. Remove from the heat. When cool, add the *pecorino* and salt and pepper to taste. Mix well. Stuff the split sardines and fold over. Drizzle a baking dish with olive oil and line with the stuffed sardines. Add the bay leaves and bake for 15 minutes. Remove from the oven, place on a platter, and serve.

SARAGO ALLA GRIGLIA (Grilled Sea Bream or Black Sea Bass)

SERVES 4

4 sea breams, each 20 to 24 ounces
¼ cup extra virgin olive oil
Salt and pepper, to taste

Make a few incisions on the inside of each fish, along the bone, in order to ease the cooking process. (Fish this small does not need to be scored on the outside; nor does it need to be scaled when grilled.) Make sure the grill has been thoroughly brushed before placing the fish on it. Light the grill. If possible, use aromatic woods. The fire is ready when the wood has burned completely and has formed a light layer of ash. Simply place the fish on top of the grill. It should take about 25 minutes (12 minutes on each side) to cook the sea bream. When boned, drizzle olive oil over the fish and add salt and pepper to taste. Serve immediately. As an alternative it can be oven-roasted at 375°F.

COUSCOUS CON PESCE (Fish Stew with Couscous)

SERVES 4

1 pound (2 cups) couscous
¼ cup extra virgin olive oil
2 garlic cloves, crushed
1 tablespoon chopped parsley
1 small onion, chopped
2 quarts poaching liquid (page 191)

2 pounds grouper or red snapper fillets, 4 ounces each
Pinch of cinnamon
Pinch of nutmeg
Salt and pepper, to taste

Cook the couscous by pouring it in a fine strainer and placing it, suspended, over boiling water. Take care not to let the steam come out of the sides. This can be done by placing aluminum foil between the strainer and the sides of the pot. It will take at least 1½ hours for the couscous to cook. Warm the oil in a pot and brown the garlic. Add the parsley and onion. When tender but not brown, add the poaching liquid. Bring to a simmer and add the fish fillets. Cook the fish for 6 minutes. Add the cinnamon, nutmeg, salt, and pepper. Place the cooked couscous on a large platter and add as much fish broth as needed to make the couscous fairly moist and loose. Top with the hot, cooked fish fillets and serve.

Note:

This dish, of Arab origin, is very common on the west coast of Sicily between Trapani and Marsala. The couscous is prepared with fish instead of vegetables or mutton as in Tunisia, Algeria, and Morocco.

GAMBERI CANNELLINI ALLA TOSCANA
(Shrimp with Cannellini Beans)

SERVES 4

    1 pound dried cannellini beans, soaked overnight
    6 tablespoons extra virgin olive oil
    1 garlic clove, chopped
    20 large shrimp, peeled and deveined (20 count or larger)
    2 rosemary sprigs
    ½ pound tomatoes, peeled, seeded, and chopped
    Salt and pepper, to taste
    ¼ cup extra virgin olive oil

Cook soaked beans in lightly salted cold water for 1 hour, or until tender, reserving 1 cup of the water. Heat 4 tablespoons of the olive oil in a casserole. Brown the garlic and remove it. Add the shrimps and cook on each side for 3 minutes. Remove from the heat and keep warm on the side. In a separate casserole, add the remaining 2 tablespoons of olive oil, 1 sprig of rosemary needles, the tomatoes, *cannellini* beans, the reserved water, salt and pepper to taste, and simmer for 6 minutes over medium heat. Remove from the heat. Place on a serving platter, with the shrimp on top. Drizzle with extra virgin olive oil, add a sprig of rosemary, and serve. The final dish should be moist, not soupy.

POLIPO ALLA LUCIANA (Octupus alla Luciana)

This preparation is called *alla Luciana* because it is a favorite among the fishermen of Naples, particularly those from Santa Lucia Point.

SERVES 4

2 pounds stone octopus, preferably 4 small ones, 8 ounces each
1 pound ripe tomatoes, peeled, seeded, and chopped
6 tablespoons extra virgin olive oil
1 tablespoon chopped parsley
2 garlic cloves, crushed
Salt and pepper, to taste

Preheat the oven to 425°F. Clean, wash, and put the octopus into a casserole or a terracotta pot with the tomatoes, olive oil, parsley, garlic, and salt and pepper to taste. Cover the casserole and cook in the oven for 45 minutes. (Alternately, the dish can be cooked over low heat on the stovetop.) Shake the pot occasionally, so that the octopus does not stick to the bottom. Remove from the heat. *Polipo alla Luciana* may be presented on the table in the same pot or on a serving platter.

CALAMARI IN ZIMINO (Squid with Swiss Chard)

SERVES 4

2 pounds Swiss chard, outer leaves removed
1 pound tomatoes
1 medium onion, finely minced
1 celery stalk, finely minced
6 tablespoons olive oil
Salt and pepper, to taste
1 pound squid, cleaned and cut into rings
1 tablespoon chopped parsley
Extra virgin olive oil, preferably Ligurian, for drizzling

Wash the Swiss chard and coarsely chop it. Set it aside. Peel, seed, and chop the tomatoes. Sauté the onion and celery in a saucepan in the olive oil until tender but not brown. Add the Swiss chard, the tomatoes, salt, and pepper. Stir, cover, and cook over medium heat until wilted. Add the squid and continue to cook for 20 more minutes over medium heat. Remove from the heat. Add the parsley, drizzle with olive oil, and serve directly from the saucepan.

Note:
This recipe can also be prepared with cuttlefish.

CALAMARI RIPIENI (Stuffed Calamari)

SERVES 6

1½ pounds medium or small squid
2 garlic cloves, crushed
6 pitted brown olives
1 tablespoon capers
Pinch of peperoncino
¼ cup extra virgin olive oil
1 tablespoon breadcrumbs
2 tablespoons grated Parmigiano
1 pound tomatoes, peeled, seeded, and chopped
Pinch of oregano
Salt and pepper, to taste
2 tablespoons chopped parsley

Wash the squid. Remove the tentacles, chop them, and set aside. Sauté 1 garlic clove, olives, capers, and *peperoncino* in 2 tablespoons of the olive oil. When the garlic is golden brown, add the squid tentacles. Sauté for 2 minutes over medium heat. Remove from the heat and cool. Add the breadcrumbs. Mix with the cheese to achieve a smooth stuffing. Stuff the squid with this mixture (do not overstuff or they will burst while cooking). Sew the opening of the sack with a needle and colorless thread or seal it with a toothpick. Sauté the remaining clove of garlic with the remaining 2 tablespoons of olive oil and add the tomatoes, a pinch of oregano, and salt and pepper to taste. Cook for 10 minutes. Place the stuffed squid in the sauce, cover, and cook gently over low heat for another 30 minutes, adding a little water if too dry.

Place on a serving platter, sprinkle with chopped parsley, and serve.

BACCALÀ IN UMIDO (Moist-Baked Salt Cod)

SERVES 6

2 pounds salt cod, softened (see page 194)
1¾ cups all-purpose flour
¼ cup extra virgin olive oil
1 pound onions, chopped
4 anchovy fillets, chopped
1 tablespoon capers
1 tablespoon raisins, softened in lukewarm water
1 tablespoon pine nuts
1 tablespoon chopped parsley

Preheat the oven to 375°. Cut the softened salt cod into 2-ounce pieces. Lightly dust with flour and fry in 2 tablespoons very hot oil until browned all over but not cooked through. Remove excess fat by draining on paper towels. Keep warm. Sauté the onion in a separate baking pan with the remaining 2 tablespoons of olive oil. When tender but not brown, add the anchovies, capers, raisins, and pine nuts. Add the fried cod to the pan. Mix well and cook for 1 hour in the oven. Occasionally baste the top of the cod with the cooking liquids. If it gets too dry, add a few tablespoons of hot water. Remove from the oven, place on a serving platter, add parsley, and serve.

Variations:
Add 2 pounds of peeled, seeded, and chopped tomatoes and 1 cup of pitted black olives, cook for 20 minutes, add the fried cod, and bake in the oven at 375°F for 1 hour.

The raisins and pine nuts can be omitted.

BACCALÀ ALLA VICENTINA (Dried Cod Stewed in Milk)

SERVES 6

2 pounds air-dried cod (stoccafisso)
1 pound onions, chopped
2 garlic cloves, crushed
6 tablespoons extra virgin olive oil
8 anchovy fillets
3 tablespoons chopped parsley
All-purpose flour for dusting
3 tablespoons grated grana padano cheese
1 quart milk, or more as needed
1 teaspoon pepper
Polenta (see pages 175–76), for serving

Soften the cod (see page 194) and cut into small pieces (about 2 ounces). Make a *soffritto* by sautéing the onions and garlic in 2 tablespoons of the olive oil until browned. Add the anchovies and cook over low heat for 2 more minutes. Stir in the parsley. Remove from the heat and set aside. Place the cod in a casserole and dust it with flour and *grana padano*. Sprinkle the *soffritto* over the top. Drizzle with the remaining 4 tablespoons of olive oil and add as much milk as needed to cover the cod. Cover the pot and cook over low heat for 3 hours, or until the milk is completely absorbed by the cod. *Baccalà alla vicentina* is better if left to sit for a few hours after cooking and then reheated. Serve with *polenta*.

Note:
In Veneto, dried cod is called *baccalà* (see page 194), thus creating some confusion as to what type of fish to use. In this recipe, dried cod must be used.

ANGUILLA ALLA BRACE CON ACETO BALSAMICO
(Broiled Eel with Balsamic Vinegar)

SERVES 4

1 eel, about 2 pounds, cleaned but not skinned (see page 199)
2 tablespoons extra virgin olive oil
2 rosemary sprigs
Salt and pepper, to taste
1 teaspoon balsamic vinegar

Cut the eel across into 2-inch lengths, split open, and remove the bone. Marinate for 1 hour in 2 tablespoons of the olive oil and rosemary. To cook the eel, place on a grill or on a baking dish in a broiler, skin down. Broil or grill the fish until tender enough that a fork will go smoothly through. Remove from the heat, add salt and pepper to taste, and brush with balsamic vinegar. Serve immediately.

RANE IN GUAZZETTO (Frog's Legs in Tomato Sauce)

SERVES 4

2 garlic cloves, crushed
1 onion, chopped
2 celery stalks, chopped
¼ cup extra virgin olive oil
1 pound tomatoes, peeled, seeded, and chopped
36 frog's legs
1¾ cups all-purpose flour, for dusting
2 ounces butter
1 tablespoon chopped parsley
Salt and pepper, to taste
6 croutons

In a skillet, prepare a *soffritto* with the garlic, onion, celery, and olive oil. When the vegetables are tender but not brown, add the tomatoes and cook for 12 minutes over medium heat. Wash the frog's legs and pat dry. Lightly dust the frog's legs with flour and sauté in a separate skillet with butter until just brown. Remove the frog's legs from the skillet and add to the tomato sauce. Continue cooking over medium heat for another 8 minutes. Adjust for seasoning and add parsley and salt and pepper. Serve with the croutons.

Note:
If the sauce is too thick, add ½ cup of hot water before adding the frog's legs.

COSCE DI RANA CON UOVA (Frog's Legs with Eggs)

SERVES 4

24 medium-size frog's legs
1¾ cups all-purpose flour, for dusting
6 tablespoons extra virgin olive oil
12 eggs
1 tablespoon chopped parsley
2 tablespoon grated Parmigiano
1 ounce butter

Wash the frog's legs and pat dry. Dust with flour and fry in 4 tablespoons of the oil until they are cooked through. Remove from the pan and place on paper towels to get rid of excess oil. Cool, bone, and set aside. Break the eggs into a bowl. Add the parsley and *Parmigiano* and mix well (do not let the eggs become frothy). Place the butter and the rest of the oil in a 12-inch iron pan. Add the frog's legs. When hot, add the eggs and stir well so that the frog's legs are well spread in the pan. When the eggs start to coagulate, spread them evenly in the pan and cook slowly with the pan covered. When eggs are done, place on a serving platter the size of the pan and serve.

Note:

The eggs can be removed from the pan by placing the platter over the pan and with a quick movement turning the pan over so that the golden brown side of the eggs is on the platter.

LUMACHE

How to Cook Snails

Snails are available frozen or canned, but tradition calls for cooking them when alive. They must be purged before they are eaten. This requires a series of time-consuming but not difficult operations.

Put the live snails into a wicker basket lined with grape or fig leaves (lettuce can be used instead) and some crustless bread previously soaked in water and squeezed. Cover the basket with a towel tied on with a string so that the snails do not escape. Let them purge for 3 days, unrefrigerated. After this time, remove and discard the dead snails (they will be out of their shells) and put the live snails into a deep pot.

Cover with salted water and add a cup of wine vinegar.

Move the snails about with your hands or a wooden spoon. Leave them in this water for 2 hours. The top of the water will become quite foamy and viscous. Then put the snails into another deep pot and repeat the procedure. Continue changing pots and water until no more foam rises to the surface.

Drain the snails and rinse them in running water. Put into a cooking pot and cover with cold water; add salt, and a cup of wine vinegar. Bring slowly to a boil.

Cook for about 15 minutes. Drain the snails, remove them from the shells with a fork, and cut off the black ends. Wash the snails in vinegar and dry with a towel sprinkled with cornmeal. Rinse them again, then put them in a cooking pot with equal parts of water and white wine, enough to cover them. Bring to a boil. Cook over low heat for 3 hours. Drain and prepare according to the recipe. To clean the shells, boil them in water with baking soda, rinse very well, and dry.

LUMACHE ALLA LIGURE (Snails Ligurian-Style)

SERVES 4

 5 salted anchovy fillets
 1 sprig of rosemary
 2 garlic cloves, finely minced
 ¼ cup extra virgin olive oil
 48 snails, purged (see procedure, pages 215–16)
 1 bottle dry white wine
 Salt and pepper, to taste
 12 basil leaves
 4 slices country bread, toasted

Finely mince the anchovies. Sauté them with rosemary needles and garlic in olive oil until the anchovies disintegrate. Add the snails. Stir and moisten with white wine, 1 cup at a time. When the wine evaporates, add salt and pepper and continue to cook for 30 minutes over low heat, moistening with more wine when necessary. Remove from the heat, add the basil, and serve the snails on toasted country bread topped with their own sauce.

Variation:
Finely sliced mushrooms may be added after moistening the snails with wine.

CARNE
Meat

In Italian cooking, the variety of beef preparations is almost endless, and full of creative interpretations. These include the marvelous *bollito misto* and the more traditional preparations of *stufato, brasato*, and *stracotto*, which are subject to countless variation. Cooking meat is full of surprises and, sometimes, contradictions. There is room for improvisation and plenty of opportunity to use leftovers, either raw or cooked. This can easily be noticed in the preparations of *involtini, polpettone*, and *spezzatino* in addition to unique ways to use variety meats such as tripe, liver, and other innards.

Regardless of the recipe, it should be noted that herbs and spices are used to enhance the flavors of the meat. Gabriele D'Annunzio (1863–1938), playwright, novelist, and flamboyant political leader, was also a noted gourmand. He used to peek in his mansion's kitchen and constantly remind his cooks of one thing: "*Non dimenticate i sapori! I sapori!*" That is, do whatever you wish to the food but do not forget flavors! The flavors!

Beef, veal, pork, and lamb are the most common types of meat available in Italy. The various cuts of meat are classified according to four categories: *primo taglio* (prime cuts), suitable for broiling and other quick preparations; *secondo taglio* (choice cuts), suitable for longer cooking; *terzo taglio* (select cuts), used for slow preparations such as boiling, stewing, and braising; finally, *frattaglie* (variety meats, including all innards).

COOKING TECHNIQUES

BOLLITO (Boiled Meat)

Beef and veal as well as poultry can be cooked in water. The following cuts are best for this type of preparation:

Basic Cuts

- *Beef:* brisket, flank, shoulder, tongue, neck, head
- *Veal:* hindshank, foreshank, neck, head, foot, tongue
- *Pork:* shoulder, head, foot

Flavoring

Carrot, celery, onion with a clove of garlic spiked in it, a few cloves, several basil leaves, one bay leaf, and a ripe tomato all add flavor and color. If, however, the vegetables are to be served with the boiled meat, they should be added when the meat is half-cooked or later so that they will not overcook. Onions, leeks, radishes, carrots, celery, and potatoes are served with boiled meat.

The Water

For two pounds of meat, use two quarts of water, with one tablespoon of salt added (further additions can be made to taste). If too much water is used, the meat will taste bland.

The Pot

The pot should be large enough for the meat to be covered with water while cooking. If the pot is too big, the water will not cover the meat; if it is too small, it may boil over.

Cooking Procedure

Bring the water to a boil together with the vegetables. Add the meat, starting with the pieces that need longer cooking such as foot, tongue, and foreshank. Bring to a boil again and reduce the heat, add salt, and continue to cook over a very low flame until all the meat is cooked. It will need at least two hours. For a more flavorful broth, put the meat into cold water and slowly bring to a boil. If the meat is too fatty, skim the fat occasionally. Often a marrow bone is cooked together with the meat, to add flavor. If marrow is used, wrap the bone in a piece of cheesecloth and tie with string to prevent the marrow from dispersing in the broth while cooking. Add the marrow bone halfway through cooking.

While cooking the meat, it is not necessary to remove the foam; in fact, if the foam is incorporated in the broth, the result will be richer in albumin. To get a clear broth, follow this procedure after the meat and herbs have been removed: While the broth is still warm, beat one egg white, add to the broth, and return the broth to a simmer until the egg white has coagulated and risen to the surface. Cool the broth and gently remove the raft. The egg white will have absorbed most or all of the fat and impurities. Drain the broth very carefully and return the lean meats to the broth, but keep the fattier part very warm.

ARROSTO (Roast Meat)

Basic Cuts

- *Beef:* T-bone, tenderloin, rib, rib-eye, strip loin
- *Veal:* chuck, loin, rack, rib-eye
- *Pork:* loin, rack, leg, whole (when small)

Seasonings

Rosemary, sage, and garlic.

Roasting Utensils

Roasting can be done on the stove, on a spit, or in the oven. Roasting on a spit is prefer-able; in the absence of a spit, roast the meat in the oven on a rack using a roasting drip pan (*leccarda*), so that the juices from the roast can be collected for later use and the meat can cook without soaking in its own fat.

The Oven

If you are using an oven, make sure it is preheated to the desired temperature before putting in the meat; high heat will sear the meat, sealing in the juices. As soon as the meat is browned on all sides, lower the heat and continue to cook. If the oven is equipped with a spit, do not preheat.

Preparing the Meat for Roasting

When roasting certain cuts of meat (always check the recipe), it is common practice to wrap leaner cuts of meat (except pork) with thin slices of lard or *pancetta*. This pro-vides the meat with the necessary fat for browning, enhances its flavor, and protects it from extended exposure to high temperature. Secure the slices of fat with string. It is preferable not to add salt in advance because it draws out the juices. Salt and pepper may be added about ten minutes before cooking is completed. In Italy, where meat is generally rather lean, it is sometimes rubbed, spiked, or marinated with herbs and left to stand a while prior to roasting.

Roasting Procedure

If you are using a spit, make sure that it goes through the center of the meat or the spit will not turn properly. If using an oven, place the roast on a rack and place it in a casse-role or a drip pan large enough to catch the liquids. Occasionally baste with the drippings from the roast. Do not use liquids such as milk or wine because the steam produced prevents the meat from forming the desired outer crust. About halfway through cooking, basting should be stopped since the crust now formed around the meat will prevent the fat from penetrating the meat. If the piece of meat is large, thus requiring longer cooking, cover with aluminum foil halfway through to prevent the outside of the meat from becoming too dry. Roast to the desired temperature and let the meat rest for ten minutes before serving. (Roast temperature may be tested with a meat thermometer.)

Roasting Pork

The procedure for roasting pork is slightly different from the one outlined above. Pork should never be cooked wrapped with slices of fat because it is already fatty enough. Some pork recipes allow for roasting in its own fat. Pork must be well done but not dry.

Roasting on Top of the Stove

The meat should be brushed with olive oil and browned, then cooked in the oven at 425°F to the desired temperature.

How to Serve Roast Meat

Roasts can be served with broiled vegetables, roast potatoes, braised greens or onions, and are often accompanied by a green salad.

BRASATO (Marinated Braised Beef)

The term *brasato* (braised) derives from the word *brace* (charcoal) because of an ancient cooking method in which the pot containing the meat was placed in, and covered with, the embers. Braising is very common in Italy, particularly in Piedmont and Lombardy.

Beef for braising is marinated in wine, herbs, and spices. The braising starts by browning the meat on all sides, brushing it with olive oil or other fats, then cooking it slowly in the liquids used for the marinade for at least two hours. For braising, it is necessary to use a large and deep pot with a heavy bottom. It can be stainless steel, aluminum, clay, or stainless steel–lined copper. The liquid should cover the meat only halfway, never entirely. Leave the cover slightly ajar. Braising requires careful attention and long cooking time.

How to Serve Braised Meat

When *brasato* is ready, drain the braising liquid and reduce it slightly. Arrange the meat (sliced or whole) on a preheated serving dish; top with the reduced liquid and serve with pureed or boiled potatoes, potato *gnocchi,* or *polenta.* It is preferable to let *brasato* stand for at least two hours before serving.

STRACOTTO (Oven-Braised Meat)

Meat for *stracotto* can be either beef or veal; it is not marinated. It must be a whole cut of at least 4 to 5 pounds. The ingredients are very similar to the beef *brasato,* although it is cooked much longer with the pot covered and the oven at a medium temperature.

STUFATO (Stewed Meat Chunks)

Stewing meat is very popular in Italy. **The meat is cut into small pieces and cooked slowly with other ingredients** such as onions, potatoes, peas, tomatoes, and more. Stewing can be done on top of the stove or in the oven.

SALTARE (Sautéed Meat)

Sautéing is a way of cooking thin cuts of meat or poultry in as small amount of fat as possible. Since this cooking technique requires high heat, a pot with a heavy bottom is necessary. It should be shallow to allow any steam to evaporate quickly. All the meat should be in direct contact with the bottom of the pan so that no pieces overlap. Usually olive oil is used for red meat, while butter is used for white meat. A mix of olive oil and butter can also be used.

Procedure: Heat a small amount of the desired fat in a sautéing pan. (The quantity of fat should be small or the meat would be fried and not sautéed.) When the fat is hot, arrange the meat in the pan and cook over high heat. Cooking time will vary according to how thick the slices or other cuts are. Turn with a spatula or flip the meat over with a brisk movement of the pan and finish cooking. Salt and pepper should be added only after the meat is cooked. Unless a specific recipe says otherwise, the meat should not be allowed to cook in the sauce, or it may turn steamed and stringy.

GRIGLIARE (Broiled Meat)

If possible, broiling should be done over charcoal made from aromatic wood such as oak, juniper, and chestnut or grapevine cuttings. (Do not use resinous wood.)

Commercial charcoal may be used if aromatic wood is not available.

The fire is ready when the red-hot charcoal is covered with a light layer of ash (there should be a good quantity of charcoal in order to ensure adequate heat to complete cooking). The area of the charcoal layer should be bigger than that of the grill. These two points are important because you cannot add more charcoal midway. If the heat is too high, sprinkle the burning charcoal with some hot ashes. Do not use cold ash because it will extinguish the charcoal. Some sprigs of herbs (sage, rosemary, or bay leaves) may be added to the coals and the meat will absorb the aroma.

The Grill

The grill should be very clean, or the meat will adhere to it. Before broiling, the grill should be greased with oil, then heated very hot. This procedure will prevent the meat from sticking.

Cooking Procedure

The meat should be lightly marinated in oil and the desired herbs before placing it on the grill. While cooking, it should be basted occasionally with a brush or a rosemary sprig; this will prevent it from becoming too dry. If the outside dries too quickly, the heat will not penetrate the meat, resulting in uneven broiling. Before turning, the side that has been exposed to the heat should be well cooked. Use a spatula or tongs to turn the meat; a fork would break the seared surface of the meat, causing it to lose its juices. Cooking time varies, of course, depending on the degree of doneness desired. In general, a one-inch-thick slice of meat cooked rare takes about five or six minutes to cook on each side. Add salt and pepper only when the meat is cooked.

Note:
While broiling, fat drops from the meat may fall into the fire and flare up, leaving burns on the food and causing it to smell of burnt fat. In order to prevent this, Tuscan cooks, the masters of *bistecca alla fiorentina*, like to throw handfuls of coarse salt onto the charcoal to curb the flames without reducing the heat.

VITELLO (Veal)

The term *vitello* is used in Italian to refer to the meat of both the male and the female calf. Calves are butchered from one month old until one year. If the calf has been raised on proper food (milk and selected fodder), both its meat and fat will be very white. If it was fed badly and butchered at the wrong age, its meat will be darker in color and will be lean, watery, tasteless, and low in nutritive value.

SCALOPPINE AL LIMONE (Veal Scallops in Lemon Sauce)

SERVES 4

2 ounces butter
12 veal scallops, thinly sliced and pounded flat
All-purpose flour, for dredging
Splash of dry white vine
Juice of 1 lemon
Salt and white pepper, to taste
1 tablespoon chopped parsley
1 lemon, thinly sliced into 12 slices

Melt 2 tablespoons of the butter in a shallow pan. Dredge the veal with flour and sauté briskly for 30 seconds on each side. Remove from the pan, place on serving platter, and set aside in a warm place. Melt the remaining butter in a clean skillet. When hot, add a splash of dry white wine, let reduce quickly, then add the lemon juice, salt and pepper to taste, and parsley. While very hot and foaming, pour the sauce over the veal. Place a thin slice of lemon with a pinch of parsley on each scallop and serve.

SALTIMBOCCA ALLA ROMANA (Veal Scallops with Prosciutto and Sage)

SERVES 4

12 slices prosciutto
12 veal scallops, thinly sliced and pounded flat
12 sage leaves
White pepper, to taste
2 tablespoons extra virgin olive oil
2 ounces butter
All-purpose flour, for dusting
¼ cup Marsala

Place a slice of *prosciutto* over each slice of meat with a sage leaf in the center and add white pepper to taste. Roll the veal scallops up and close them with a toothpick as you would with a safety pin (it should not go across the roll but make a stitch along the sides). Put the oil and butter in a saucepan. Lightly dust the *rollatine* with flour and sauté over high heat for 2 minutes. Add the Marsala and let it reduce for 1 more minute. Remove from the heat and arrange the veal on a serving platter. In the same skillet, let the cooking juices reduce for 1 minute, then pour over the veal. Serve immediately.

Notes:
Saltimbocca can also be sautéed flat rather than rolled.
White wine may be used instead of Marsala.

COSTOLETTA ALLA MILANESE (Veal Chop Milanese-Style)

SERVES 4

4 veal chops, bone-in
2 cups milk
Salt and pepper, to taste
2 eggs, beaten
⅓ cup white breadcrumbs
3 ounces butter

Pound flat the veal chops to about ⅓ inch thick. Dip them in milk and refrigerate for 30 minutes. When ready to cook, drain the chops, add salt and pepper to taste, and dip them in beaten egg and then in breadcrumbs, pressing the crumbs onto the meat with the palm of your hand. Melt the butter in a frying pan and sauté the breaded chops over medium heat for 3 minutes on each side. Turn only once. The crust should be golden brown and the meat should be pink. If you feel you want the meat more cooked, finish in the preheated oven at 425°F. for 5 more minutes.

COSTOLETTA ALLA VALDOSTANA (Veal Chops with Fontina)

SERVES 4

4 veal chops, bone-in, butterflied
¼ pound fontina cheese, sliced into 4 slices
Salt and pepper, to taste
2 eggs, beaten
1 cup breadcrumbs
2 ounces butter
30 grams white truffles (optional)

Preheat the oven to 425°F. Flatten the chops slightly and place slices of *fontina* in between the butterflied chops. Add salt and pepper, fold each chop, and pound the edges together with a mallet. Dip each chop in the beaten egg and then roll in the breadcrumbs. Melt the butter in a skillet. When hot, cook the chops over medium heat for 3 minutes on each side, then cook for 7 more minutes in the oven. Remove from the oven and place on a serving platter. Add a shaving of white truffles (optional) over the veal chops and serve.

VITELLO ALL'UCCELLETTO (Veal Sautéed with Sage)

SERVES 4

1½ pounds top round or veal tenderloin bits
1 ounce butter

¼ cup extra virgin olive oil
6 bay leaves
6 sage leaves
2 garlic cloves, crushed
2 tablespoons white wine
Salt and pepper, to taste

Cut the beef or the veal into irregular strips about 1 to 2 inches long. Put the butter and the oil into a large skillet; add bay, sage leaves, and garlic. Remove garlic when brown and, when very hot, add the veal. Sauté briskly over high heat for 2 minutes. Add the wine and reduce by two thirds. Add salt and pepper to taste and serve.

OSSOBUCO CON GREMOLATA (Ossobuco with Gremolata)

SERVES 4
4 pieces veal shank, cross-cut, each about 12 ounces
All-purpose flour, for dredging
2 ounces butter
¼ cup dry white wine
Salt and pepper, to taste
Pinch of nutmeg
4 cups veal or chicken broth (see page 124)

Gremolata
Grated zest of 1 lemon
1 garlic clove, finely chopped
1 rosemary sprig
1 tablespoon chopped parsley

Dust the veal shanks with flour and brown them in a casserole in hot melted butter over medium heat. When browned, splash the meat with white wine. Let evaporate and add salt and pepper to taste with a pinch of nutmeg. Braise over low heat, adding broth occasionally, until the meat begins to come off the bone, about 2 hours.

To prepare the *gremolata*, chop together the lemon zest, garlic, rosemary needles, and parsley very finely and sprinkle over the veal when almost ready.

Cook for another 10 minutes with *gremolata* and serve. *Ossobuco* may be served with *risotto alla milanese*.

Variation:
After having browned the veal shanks, add 1 pound of ripe tomatoes, peeled, seeded, and chopped, with some chopped celery and carrots and then continue with the recipe.

Note:

The best part of this famous Lombard dish is the bone marrow. It is scooped out with a thin, elongated, narrow spatula called a *scavino*, which in Milanese dialect also refers to the tax man (scrapes you to the bone).

VITELLO TONNATO (Veal in Tuna Sauce)

SERVES 6

2 pounds veal butt or tenderloin
3 cups dry white wine
1 celery stalk, chopped
1 carrot, chopped
1 small onion, chopped
2 cloves
7-ounce can tuna in oil
6 anchovy fillets
2 tablespoons capers
2 hard-boiled egg yolks
Juice of 1 lemon
1 tablespoon white vinegar
2 cups extra virgin olive oil
1 lemon, thinly sliced

Preheat the oven to 375°F. Let the veal marinate in the wine, celery, carrot, onion, and cloves for 2 hours. Remove the meat from the marinade, and place in an oval pan just large enough to hold it. Pour the marinade over and cook slowly in the oven for about 1 hour. Remove from the oven and let the meat cool in its cooking juice.

Degrease and filter the cooking liquid. Blend the liquid in a food mill with the tuna, anchovies, 1 tablespoon of the capers, and egg yolks. Dilute the sauce with the juice of one lemon and vinegar and whisk in the oil in a steady stream until the texture is velvety, similar to mayonnaise. Slice the veal; arrange on a serving platter as follows: Spread a few tablespoons of the sauce on the platter. Add a layer of veal and cover with sauce. Sprinkle with the remaining capers and decorate the rim of the platter with the sliced lemon. Serve.

Note:

Another method is to combine the veal roasting juice with the tuna and to whip it with mayonnaise.

CIMA ALLA GENOVESE (Stuffed Veal Breast Genoa-Style)

SERVES 8

1 ounce dried porcini mushrooms
6 slices white bread, crusts removed

4 pounds veal breast with pocket
¼ pound lean veal
3 ounces calf's head
3 ounces calf's brain
½ pound veal sweetbreads
2 ounces butter
2 tablespoons pistachio nuts, shelled
2 tablespoons pine nuts
2 tablespoons grated Parmigiano
6 eggs, beaten
¼ cup shelled peas
Pinch of marjoram
1 garlic clove, chopped
Salt and pepper, to taste
Pinch of nutmeg
1 carrot, chopped
1 celery stalk, chopped
1 small onion, diced
6 quarts veal broth (see page 124)

Soak the mushrooms in warm water for a few minutes and chop them. Soak the bread in cold water and squeeze to remove excess water. Make an incision in the veal breast, thus creating a pocket closed on 3 sides. To prepare the stuffing, brown all the meat except the veal breast in butter, then grind it coarsely. Mix the meat with the pistachio nuts, pine nuts, *Parmigiano,* eggs, mushrooms, peas, marjoram, and garlic. Add the bread to the meat mixture. Add salt, pepper, and a little grated nutmeg and mix well, to achieve a smooth filling.

To stuff the breast, fill the veal breast with the stuffing. It should not be more than two-thirds full. Sew the opening closed with a needle and colorless thread and prick the meat with a large needle so that it does not burst while cooking. If possible, wrap the meat tightly in cheesecloth and sew it closed. Place the carrot, celery, and onion in a large pot with the broth. Turn on the heat but do not boil. Add the meat to the pot and cook over low heat for about 3 hours. Add salt halfway through the cooking. Remove the stuffed veal breast and place it on a chopping board. Place a plate with a heavy weight on top of the meat and let cool completely. Let it rest for at least 6 hours. Serve the meat sliced with a salad or other cold meats. *Cima alla genovese* keeps for a few days in the refrigerator.

VITELLO IN FRICANDO (Oven-Braised Veal Shoulder)

SERVES 8

2 thick slices of prosciutto, about 4 ounces
2 pounds veal shoulder

2 ounces butter
2 onions, thinly sliced
3–4 cloves
1 carrot, cut into pieces
1 bunch parsley
2–3 celery stalks
1 cup dry white wine
Salt and pepper, to taste
Veal broth, if needed (see page 124)

Preheat the oven to 450°F. Remove the fat from the *prosciutto,* dice, and set aside. Cut the lean part of the *prosciutto* into strips. Lard the veal by making small cuts in it and inserting the *prosciutto* fat. Place the butter, the lean *prosciutto,* the onions, and cloves in a casserole. Let brown lightly, then add the veal and brown on all sides. Add the carrot, parsley, and a few stalks of celery tied together. Turn the oven heat down to 325°F. Pour the wine over the veal, add salt and pepper to taste, cover the casserole, and roast over low heat, turning frequently. Moisten with broth if the meat gets too dry. Cook for 1 hour. Slice thin, adjust for seasoning, and serve with finely sieved roast drippings.

BUE/MANZO (Beef)

Often the terms *bue* (ox) and *manzo* (beef) are employed in the same way. They both refer to a castrated male of the same breed. *Bue* is an animal 1½ years old. *Manzo* is an animal older than a *bue.*

Vitellone (baby beef) is an animal slaughtered between 14 and 16 months old; its meat is tougher than veal and somewhat more tender than beef.

Torello (young bull) is an uncastrated male raised for slaughter, usually slaughtered when two years old. Its meat is excellent, leaner but tender, and flavorful like beef. *Torello* is butchered and cooked the same way as *manzo.*

BOLLITO MISTO (Mixed Boiled Meats)

This dish is a true triumph of Italian cuisine. The meats used to prepare a good *bollito misto* are fowl, beef, veal, and fresh sausage such as *cotechino* and *zampone* (see pages 40–41).

The larger the cuts of meat used, the more flavorful the *bollito* will be. One can readily see that if *bollito* is for several people, larger cuts of meats can be used; the dish will therefore be more flavorful.

SERVES 8
1 bunch parsley, chopped
1 carrot, chopped

1 onion, chopped
2 celery stalks, chopped
1 pound brisket of beef
1 pound veal breast
½ pound veal tongue
½ pound pig's foot
½ pound pig's jowl
Salt and pepper, to taste
½ capon
1 fresh cotechino

Start the meats except the *cotechino* in boiling water, 1 quart for every pound of meat, to seal in the juices. If you start in cold water, you will obtain a good broth, not a good *bollito*.

In a large pot, bring water and the chopped vegetables to a boil. Add the beef and the veal parts, the pig's foot and jowl. Add salt and pepper to taste. Cover the pot, lower the heat, and cook for 1½ hours. Cook the *cotechino* in salted water in a separate pot, pricking the sausage so the casing does not burst. When the *cotechino* is soft (it normally takes about 1½ hours), add it to the other meats. Add the capon and cook for another 30 minutes. Remove from the heat. Remove the meats from the broth, skim and strain the broth, and return the meats to the broth until ready to serve. Ideally, boiled meats should be presented in their broth and sliced at the table.

Notes:
The various cuts of meat may also be cooked separately.

Bollito misto can be served with boiled potatoes, zucchini, and carrots. It may be accompanied by several types of sauces, such as *salsa verde* (page 38), or *mostarda di frutta* (preserved spiced fruit), or *cipolline in agrodolce* (scallions in sweet-and-sour sauce), pickled vegetables, or minced raw pepper with oil and vinegar, salt and pepper.

Leftovers from *bollito misto* may be served in various ways: as a salad with capers, anchovies, gherkins, or aromatic herbs mixed in oil and vinegar; or with a sauce of tomato sauce and onions (in which case it is served hot). It may also be ground for *polpettone* (meat loaf).

BRASATO AL BAROLO (Braised Beef with Barolo Wine)

SERVES 8

Salt and pepper, to taste
2 pounds top round beef
1 bottle Barolo wine
2 garlic cloves, crushed
2 carrots, chopped

2 celery stalks, chopped
2 onions, chopped
1 teaspoon peppercorns
3–4 cloves
1 rosemary sprig
2 tablespoons extra virgin oil
All-purpose flour, for dredging

Salt, pepper, and marinate the meat in the wine with the garlic, vegetables, peppercorns, cloves, and rosemary for 12 hours, covered, in the refrigerator.

Preheat the oven to 375°F. Drain the meat. Heat the oil in a large casserole or a terra-cotta pot. Dust the meat with flour and brown on all sides over high heat. Add the marinade. Cover and cook gently in the oven for 3 hours. Remove the *brasato* from its cooking juice, set aside, and keep warm. Pour the cooking juices through a fine sieve. Adjust for seasoning. Reduce by one third, slice the *brasato*, arrange on a preheated platter, and serve with potato *gnocchi,* soft *polenta,* or mashed potatoes.

Note:
The meat can also be larded or spiked with herbs and *pancetta* before marinating.

STRACOTTO (Oven-Braised Beef)

SERVES 6
2 pounds lean beef round
6 small garlic cloves
Salt and pepper, to taste
6 tablespoons extra virgin olive oil
2 pounds onions, thinly sliced
1 celery stalk, chopped
3 small carrots, diced
1 bunch basil, chopped
1 cup dry red wine
1 pound ripe tomatoes, peeled, seeded, and chopped
Beef broth (see pages 123–24), as needed

Preheat the oven to 375°F. Spike the meat with the garlic and adjust for salt and pepper. Tie it with a string to keep it in form. Place in a casserole with 3 tablespoons of the olive oil and roast for 20 minutes, turning frequently so that it browns evenly on all sides. Sauté the onions, celery, carrots, and basil in a separate pot with the remaining 3 tablespoons of olive oil and cook over low heat for 30 minutes. Add the red wine and tomatoes and cook for another 15 minutes. Remove from the heat and pass the cooking juices through a fine sieve. Place the beef in a terra-cotta pot. Add the sieved vegetable mash and cook in the oven over low heat for 4 hours, turning occasionally. Add small quantities of broth if it gets too dry. Adjust seasoning and serve sliced, topped with its own sauce.

Note:
Beans or *polenta* may be served as a side dish.

STUFATO/RUSTISCIADA (Mixed Stewed Meat with Onions)

SERVES 6
> 2 pounds mixed lean meats (beef, veal, and pork)
> 2 garlic cloves, crushed
> 6 tablespoons extra virgin olive oil
> 3 medium onions, finely sliced
> 1 cup dry white wine
> 6 ounces calves' liver, cut into 1-ounce strips
> Salt and pepper, to taste
> Polenta, for serving

Preheat the oven to 325°F. Coarsely cut the meats into 1-ounce pieces. Brown the garlic with the olive oil in a casserole. Remove the garlic when brown and add the onions. When tender but not brown, add the meat and let it brown evenly. Add half of the white wine and let reduce. Transfer the casserole to the oven and cook slowly for 45 minutes. Add the liver and continue to cook for 5 more minutes, basting with more white wine as the meats get dry. Add salt and pepper to taste. Remove from the heat and serve with polenta.

CODA ALLA VACCINARA (Stewed Oxtail with Celery)

Alla vaccinara means "butcher style" in Roman dialect. This dish was originally prepared at the inns and restaurants near the city's slaughterhouses.

SERVES 6
> 2 pounds oxtails
> 3 ounces lard, chopped
> 1 bunch celery, finely diced
> 1 garlic clove, crushed
> 1 onion, finely sliced
> 1 bay leaf
> 1 carrot, finely diced
> Salt and pepper, to taste
> Pinch of peperoncino (crushed red pepper)

2 cups beef broth (see pages 123–24)
1 cup dry red wine
1 pound tomatoes, peeled, seeded, and chopped
Gnocchi di semolino alla romana (page 174), for serving

Cut the oxtails across into pieces 1½ inches long. Place the oxtails into a pot, cover with cold water, and let rest for 30 minutes. Change the water, bring to a boil, and simmer for 5 minutes. Drain, dry, and set aside. Melt the lard in a casserole, add half of the celery, the garlic, onion, bay leaf, carrot, salt, pepper and *peperoncino*. Cook until wilted and then add the oxtails. When brown, add the broth, wine and tomatoes. Braise on top of the stove with, pot covered over medium heat for about 4 hours. Moisten occasionally with wine as needed. When the oxtails are tender, remove them and set aside. Strain the braising juice, degrease, and adjust for seasoning. Return oxtails to sauce and bring it back to the simmer. Add the remaining celery to the oxtails. Serve the oxtails with *gnocchi*.

INVOLTINI DI MANZO (Braised Beef Rollatine)

SERVES 4
1 pound boneless beef round
1 carrot, cut into pieces
1 celery stalk, coarsely chopped
1 onion, cut into quarters
2 garlic cloves, crushed
1 bay leaf
1 cup dry red wine
12 slices pancetta, thinly sliced with a slicer
2 tablespoons extra virgin olive oil
2 ounces butter
Salt and pepper, to taste
Polenta or mashed potatoes, for serving

Slice the meat thin, like scallops, and pound it flat with a wooden mallet. Place in a baking pan. Marinate with the carrot, celery, onion, garlic, bay leaf, and wine for 1 hour in the refrigerator. Remove the slices of meat from the marinade, pat dry, and cover each with a slice of *pancetta*. Roll each slice, with the *pancetta* on the inside, and tie the *rollatine* with kitchen twine or keep in place with a toothpick. Drain all the vegetables, put them in a casserole, and sauté with the olive oil and half the butter. When tender but not browned, add the *rollatine* and brown quickly. In a separate saucepan, reduce the marinade by half its volume. Pour it over the meat, add salt and pepper, cover, and cook over very low heat for 30 minutes. When ready, remove the twine or toothpicks and place the *rollatine* on a warm platter. Drain the cooking liquid. Add the remaining butter without allowing the sauce to boil. Pour the sauce over the *rollatine* and serve hot with *polenta* or mashed potatoes.

POLPETTONE (Meat Loaf)

SERVES 6

> 2 pounds ground beef
> 1 ounce lard, chopped
> 2 eggs
> 2 tablespoons grated Parmigiano
> 1 cup breadcrumbs
> Juice of 1 lemon
> Salt and pepper, to taste
> ¼ cup milk
> ¼ cup extra virgin olive oil
> 1 ounce butter
> 2 onions, cut in julienne
> 1 cup beef broth (see pages 123–24)

Preheat the oven to 375°F. In a mixing bowl combine the ground beef, lard, eggs, *Parmigiano,* 2 tablespoons of the breadcrumbs, the lemon juice, salt, and pepper. Add a few spoonfuls of milk and mix well. The mixture should be fairly solid but moist. Shape the meat into a loaf and coat with the remaining breadcrumbs. Heat the olive oil in a large pan and brown the meat evenly on all sides. (This will prevent the loaf from breaking while it bakes.) In a large casserole, melt the butter and brown the onions. Place the loaf over the onions and cook in the oven for 1 hour. Keep the bottom moist, with hot water if necessary, to prevent the onions from burning. Remove *polpettone* from the pan onto a serving platter. Add the broth to the pan drippings and reduce by half. Pass through a fine sieve and serve this sauce hot with the meat.

Variations:
Polpettone can be prepared with other kinds of meat, leftovers, or a mixture of meats.

Mashed potatoes, crustless white bread, or chopped greens can be added to the mixture.

BISTECCA ALLA FIORENTINA (Broiled T-Bone Steak)

SERVES 4 TO 6

> 2 T-bone steaks, 2 pounds each
> 2 tablespoons extra virgin olive oil
> Salt and pepper, to taste
> 2 garlic cloves, crushed
> 2 rosemary sprigs

Brush the meat with oil, salt, and pepper, add the garlic and rosemary, and marinate the meat in the refrigerator overnight. Broil the meat on aromatic wood, including olive tree wood if possible. Follow the basic procedure (see pages 221–22) for broiling meat.

Cook 12 minutes on each side, turning it only once. Remove from the heat when the meat has reached the desired temperature, slice, and serve.

Notes:
The meat may also be broiled without marinating. Simply brush with oil before broiling. Add salt and pepper just before serving.

The meat may also be broiled in a kitchen broiler.

The T-bone may be seared on both sides in an iron pan and the roasting finished in an oven at maximum temperature.

FILETTO DI BUE ALLA PIZZAIOLA (Beef Pizzaiola)

SERVES 6

2 pounds beef filet
2 garlic cloves
¼ cup extra virgin olive oil
1 pound tomatoes, peeled, seeded, and chopped
1 teaspoon oregano

Slice the beef into ½-inch thickness (8 slices) and set aside. Brown the garlic in 2 tablespoons of the olive oil, add the tomatoes, and bring to a simmer. Turn down the heat and cook for 15 minutes. Remove from the heat, strain the tomato sauce, and set aside. In a separate pan, sauté the meat slices in the remaining oil briskly on both sides to the desired temperature. In a skillet, heat the tomato sauce and place the cooked meat into the sauce with the oregano. Bring to a simmer, remove from heat, and serve.

MAIALE (Pork)

The pork commercially available today in Italy is considerably leaner than that of the past due to refined techniques for raising pigs. Rosy colored, with iridescent reflections, pork is indeed very tasty. Its meat usually has a lot of fat (even if the hog was raised according to new farming methods). The meat of a young pig is rosier in color, contains more water and less fat, and is more digestible. The meat of an older pig is tastier since it contains less water and more fat. Piglets or suckling pigs are only a few weeks old and have been fed only milk, preferably from their mother. They are generally roasted whole in the oven or on a spit.

All the meat that the pig yields is used one way or another. *Testa* (the head) is used together with other ingredients to prepare *soppressata* (head sausage). The cheek or the temple can be either boiled, smoked, or stewed. The jowls are cured in the same manner as *pancetta* and are called *guanciale* (this part is sweeter and used for *amatriciana* sauce). The neck is preserved in salt and, after adequate aging, made into a sausage called *bondiola*.

Piedini (the feet) are primarily boiled, though they may also be broiled, following the same procedure as for the tail. Boning the front feet up to the ankle provides the casing for *zampone*, a raw sausage for boiling and a specialty of Modena.

Coscia (the leg) is a prime cut and can be roasted when it is from a freshly killed pig. If the leg comes from a freshly killed young pig, it may also be braised, boiled, or cooked in slices. Through a special curing process, it is made into *prosciutto*, which, together with *culatello* and salami, is the pride of Parma farming products.

When taken from a freshly killed pig, the *spalla* (shoulder) should be cooked like the leg. The best part of the shoulder, boned, cooked, and cured, is used to make ham.

Lonza or *lombata* (the loin) is a long, rectangular section of meat, located on top of the fillet in the lumbar region along the spine. It can be cooked in many ways, either whole or sliced. When roasted it is called *arista*.

Cutting the top part of the *lombo* (the loin) into chops yields choice chops, and the terminal part, extending toward the tail, yields the saddle. It can be roasted as a whole piece (either boned or with the bone in).

PORCHETTA (Roast Whole Pig)

SERVES 60 OR MORE
1 whole pig, 50 to 60 pounds or larger, boned
1 cup wild fennel seeds (finocchiella)
24 rosemary sprigs
Salt and pepper, to taste
16 garlic cloves, crushed
1 tablespoon coriander
1 teaspoon nutmeg
1 tablespoon peperoncino
1 cup extra virgin olive oil
Potatoes and onions, for sautéing

Season the pig with wild fennel seeds, 20 of the rosemary sprigs, salt, pepper, a fair amount of garlic, coriander, nutmeg, and *peperoncino*. Roll it up like a large sausage, securely tie it with kitchen twine, and roast it whole in a wood-burning oven or on a spit over charcoal made from aromatic wood for about 6 hours. Cooking time varies according to the size of the pig. If the pig is too big for your oven it may be cut across into 2 pieces.

Baste the pig frequently with a bundle of rosemary sprigs dipped in oil. The juice and fat that collects in the drip pan can be used to sauté potatoes and onions, which may be served with the *porchetta*.

Notes:
Adjust the ingredients according to the size of the pig.

Porchetta is always boned, seasoned, and roasted. It is generally served sliced, at room temperature. In Rome, it is used as *companatico*, for sandwich filling with a bread roll called *rosetta*, which is crusty outside and empty inside and with the sliced *porchetta* makes a great sandwich.

ARISTA DI MAIALE CON CANNELLINI (Pork Loin with Cannellini Beans)

SERVES 6 TO 8

 4 pounds pork loin, bone-in
 2 garlic heads, each cut in 2 pieces
 2 rosemary sprigs
 3–4 cloves
 6 tablespoons extra virgin olive oil
 Salt, to taste
 1 pound dried cannellini beans, soaked overnight
 Freshly ground black pepper

Preheat the oven to 350°F. Spike the meat through the center with a *battuto* prepared with garlic, rosemary, and cloves. Brush the meat with oil, add salt to taste, and set aside for 1 hour. Boil the soaked *cannellini* beans in slightly salted water for 1 hour. Set aside but keep warm. Place the pork in a greased baking pan; roast in the oven for 2 hours, turning the meat frequently in its own fat. When the *arista* is ready, the meat will fall off the bone. Remove from the cooking pan, slice across, and arrange on a serving platter. Drain the beans from their water and serve dressed with olive oil, salt, and black pepper. *Arista* is also very good served cold.

Note:
Often the cooking juices from the meat are used to sauté broccoli rape or black cabbage, which is then served with the *arista*.

BRACIOLE DI MAIALE ALLA NAPOLETANA
(Pork Loin with Raisins and Pine Nuts)

SERVES 8

 1 pound boneless pork leg or shoulder
 4 garlic cloves
 2 tablespoons raisins
 2 tablespoons pine nuts
 1 ounce capers
 2 tablespoons extra virgin olive oil
 1 pound tomatoes, peeled, seeded, and chopped
 Salt and pepper, to taste
 1 tablespoon chopped parsley

Slice the pork and flatten it with a wooden mallet. Chop 2 cloves of garlic very fine; mix with the raisins, pine nuts, and capers. Place a small amount of this mix on each slice of pork and roll up the slices. Tie with kitchen twine or secure with toothpicks. Brown the remaining garlic in olive oil. Remove when golden. Add the pork rolls, brown on all sides, and add the tomatoes. Add salt and pepper to taste and cook for 35 minutes over low heat. Add the parsley, remove from the heat, and serve.

Note:
Braciola can be added to a *ragù*.

SALSICCE CON I BROCCOLI (Fresh Sausages with Broccoli Rape)

SERVES 4
   2 pounds fresh sweet pork sausages (at least 12 pieces)
   6 tablespoons olive oil
   ½ cup water
   6 bunches broccoli di rape
   4 garlic cloves
   Pinch of peperoncino
   Salt, to taste

Prick the sausages with a fork so they don't burst while cooking. In a saucepan, heat 1 tablespoon of the olive oil and sauté the sausages over medium heat. When they are well browned, add the water and continue to cook for 12 minutes. Remove from the heat and set aside. Clean the broccoli rape, discarding the stems and the larger leaves. Wash thoroughly and leave the greens in water until ready to cook. Heat the remainder of the oil in a large casserole. Add the garlic and *peperoncino*. Remove the garlic when brown and add the broccoli rape, removing it from the water without drying. Sauté over medium heat for 20 minutes with the casserole covered, stirring occasionally. It will take 15 minutes for the broccoli to become tender. When almost done, add the sausages, lower the heat, and cook for another 5 minutes, with the pot uncovered. Remove from the heat. Add salt to taste, place the broccoli rape on a serving platter with the sausages on top, and serve.

AGNELLO E CAPRETTO (Lamb and Goat)

Lamb, which is raised on the highlands or the Apennines (the spiral mountain chain that runs throughout most of Italy), plays a major role in the kitchen in some Italian regions, especially in the spring. From the typical *abbacchio arrosto* (roast baby lamb) to the *testina di capretto* (baked kid's head), lamb and goat are considered a delicacy. The lamb available commercially is classified into three categories, according to age. Lamb killed before its fourth week is called *abbacchio*. This indicates a milk-fed lamb weighing 14 to 20 pounds. Lamb killed when about 3 months old (while still suckling) is called *agnello di latte* (baby lamb) and weighs about 22 to 30 pounds. The meat is white and tender. Older lambs weighing 30 pounds and up at the time of slaughter are also quite tender, though their meat is redder than that of younger animals.

Capretti (male kids) are slaughtered between 6 and 8 weeks old; the females are usually kept for milk production. The meat is similar to the meat of milk-fed lambs, only it is redder in color and tastes gamier. Goat is generally roasted or prepared in any of the ways suitable for lamb.

ABBACCHIO ALLA CACCIATORA (Baby Lamb Cacciatora)

SERVES 8

> 4 pounds baby lamb, combination of leg, shoulder, and ribs
> 4 anchovy fillets
> 1 rosemary sprig
> 3 garlic cloves, chopped
> ¼ cup good white wine vinegar
> ¼ cup extra virgin olive oil
> 2 ounces lard, finely chopped
> Salt and pepper, to taste

Cut the lamb into equal pieces, each about 2 ounces. Rinse them to remove bone splinters and dry thoroughly. Wash and fillet the anchovies, if necessary. Remove the rosemary needles and discard the stem. Combine with one clove of garlic and prepare a *battuto*. Place the *battuto* into the vinegar, mix well, and set aside. Sauté 2 cloves of garlic in the oil and lard in a saucepan large enough to contain all the pieces of lamb in a single layer. Discard the garlic when golden brown. Add the pieces of lamb, turning the meat until all sides are evenly brown. When the meat is browned, add a small amount of salt (remember that anchovies are salty) and pepper, moisten with the *battuto* and vinegar mixture, and continue to cook over medium heat for 30 minutes. When the lamb is ready, arrange the meat on a preheated serving platter together with its cooking juices and serve.

AGNELLO BRODETTATO (Braised Lamb with Eggs)

SERVES 4

> 2 pounds baby lamb shoulder
> 1½ lemons
> 1 ounce lard
> 2 ounces prosciutto, chopped
> 1 onion, chopped
> Salt and pepper, to taste
> 1 cup dry white wine

3 egg yolks
1 teaspoon chopped parsley
Pinch of marjoram

Rub the lamb with half a lemon. Wash, dry, and cut the meat into 2-ounce pieces. Melt the lard in a saucepan; add the *prosciutto* and onion. When the onion is wilted, add and brown the lamb. Add salt and pepper. When the lamb is evenly brown, splash it with white wine. Cook till tender, for about 1 hour, over low heat, adding a few spoonfuls of hot water if necessary. Beat the egg yolks in a bowl with the chopped parsley and marjoram, 1 teaspoon of grated lemon zest, and the juice of a whole lemon. When the lamb has finished cooking, turn off the heat and pour the egg mixture over it. Stir and let the eggs coagulate but do not let them set too hard. Dish out onto a serving platter and serve.

TESTINA DI CAPRETTO AL FORNO (Baked Spring Kid's Head)

This dish is considered a delicacy, especially in central and southern Italy.

SERVES 6
3 spring kid's heads
2 ounces pancetta
3 garlic cloves, chopped
6 rosemary sprigs
6 tablespoons white breadcrumbs
Salt and pepper, to taste
½ cup extra virgin olive oil
1 cup dry white wine

Preheat the oven to 475°F. Clean and split the kid's heads. Remove any visible cartilage. Prepare a *battuto* with the *pancetta,* garlic, rosemary needles, breadcrumbs, salt, and pepper. Spread the *battuto* over the heads, pressing lightly so the mixture adheres tightly. Cover the brain portion with aluminum foil so it does not burn while cooking. Oil a baking pan, add the kid's heads, and bake for 2 hours, basting occasionally with white wine. Lower the oven temperature after 30 minutes to 375°F.

Note:
Although this is not a recipe of common use, the writer includes this recipe as a curiosity item for the reader. The same applies to the next recipe, *pastissada de caval.*

CARNE DI CAVALLO (Horsemeat)

In Italy, horsemeat is sold in special butcher shops *(macellerie equine)* since it is very delicate and subject to stringent sanitary regulations. Horsemeat must not be allowed to age for too long, since it spoils more quickly than beef. Today, commercial horsemeat is obtained from young horses that have been raised on farms and have never been used as work animals. Horsemeat may be used for braising and stewing and can be cooked like beef. Colt meat can be compared to veal, although it is more flavorful. Horsemeat butcher shops also sell donkey meat. If the donkey is young, its meat is very similar to horsemeat. Donkey meat is used to make *tapulone*, a Piedmontese specialty.

PASTISSADA DE CAVAL (Horseman's Stew)

Legend has it that this landmark in Veronese cuisine dates back to the time of King Theodoric in the early Middle Ages. Following a particular bloody battle in which a great number of horses were killed, the meat was given to the citizens of Verona who had been starving because of a famine. It was in these unhappy circumstances that, quite by chance, it was discovered how to cook this delicious dish. Since then the recipe has been handed down over the centuries. Even in those times, using horsemeat aroused uncertain feelings (perhaps more so than today), in that men had developed a rather affectionate relationship with horses, so that it seemed unnatural to eat their meat.

SERVES 6 TO 8

> 4 pounds horsemeat
> 1/4 cup extra virgin olive oil
> 2 ounces butter
> 1 pound onions, chopped
> 2 pounds mashed tomatoes, peeled, seeded, and chopped
> Salt and pepper, to taste
> 2 cups dry red wine, preferably Amarone, Bardolino, or Valpolicella
> Polenta or potato gnocchi, for serving

Tenderize the meat by pounding it with a mallet and cut it into pieces of about 1 ounce each. Heat the oil and butter in a pan and brown the onions. Add the tomatoes, meat, salt, and pepper and cook for about 30 minutes. Pour in the wine, cover, and cook over low heat for at least 3 hours. Serve with *polenta* or with potato *gnocchi*.

Note:
Pastissada is better reheated the next day.

FRATTAGLIE (INNARDS)

The term *frattaglie* refers to the innards or organ meats of all animals, regardless of species. The U.S.D.A. also calls them "variety meats" or "edible by-products."

ANIMELLE (Sweetbreads)

These are the thymus glands of veal and lamb. Tender and delicate, veal sweetbreads are divided into 2 parts: The choicest portion is round and full, often referred to as the nut or *noix*; the other, less desirable part has a more tapered shape and is taken from the throat. They may be fried (either whole or cut into pieces) or cooked in delicate sauces. *Animelle* must always be purged and blanched first.

To blanch and purge, place the sweetbreads in a pot with cold water, changing the water every hour for three hours. Put them in cold water again and bring the water slowly to a boil. Simmer for 5 minutes and place in cold water again for another 20 minutes. Drain and remove all the fat and cartilage parts. Leave the skin on. Wrap the sweetbreads in a cloth and place under a weight for 1 hour. This method will allow the meat to be more compact when it is sliced.

CERVELLA (Brain)

This is choice organ meat. Beef, veal, lamb, and goat brains may be fried, cooked in a delicate sauce, or made into fried dumplings. Brains must also be purged and blanched before cooking.

Blanch by placing under cold running water for 2 hours. Remove from the water and skin. Put back in the cold water so that any residual blood is eliminated or the brain will become dark when cooked.

CORATELLA (Mixed Innards)

A popular Roman speciality, this is a combination of all of the innards of lambs and goats (heart, kidneys, liver, etc.) and is cooked either stewed or sautéed by itself or with artichokes. See also pages 24 and 245–46.

FEGATO (Liver)

Liver varies in texture, size, and color according to the size and feed of the animal it comes from. If a calf has been properly fed, the liver's color will be light pink; if not, it will be darker red. Liver must always be fresh. It may be fried, sautéed, cooked with wine, or either roasted or braised as a whole piece. Always remove the membrane that surrounds it, as it is tough. To keep the liver from toughening, it should be cooked very fast on brisk heat, only until it changes color.

LINGUA (Tongue)

Both veal and pork tongue are sold commercially. They are either boiled or stewed. Beef tongue may also be pickled, preserved, and then boiled before consumption. Tongue may be eaten warm or cold.

RETE (Caul Fat)

This is the fatty, net-like membrane that encloses an animal's stomach. The pig's caul fat is most frequently used to wrap meats for roasting or broiling. This method allows the wrapped meat to absorb the fat of the membrane, which makes it tastier.

ROGNONE (Kidney)

Veal and beef kidneys have the same knobbed, oval shape, but they differ in size and tenderness. Kidneys must always be cooked fresh and must never smell of ammonia. They must be purged before cooking (unless they are from a spring veal).

The simplest method to purge kidneys is to remove the fat and slice them or cut them in half and soak in hot water 3 or 4 times. Place them in a colander, add some salt, and let rest for 3 to 4 hours. Drain, rinse, and dry. Kidneys can be broiled, sautéed, or thinly sliced and cooked in oil, garlic, and parsley (*trifolati*).

TRIPPA (Tripe)

Tripe is the stomach and the top part of the intestine of cows, hogs, and lambs. It is divided into 4 parts:

- *Rumine:* a thick, spongy tissue
- *Reticolo:* a part which is shaped like a beehive and textured like a honeycomb
- *Centopelle* or *foiolo:* the part that has thin, overlapping, parallel strips
- *Ricciolotta:* the fattest, very curly part of the tripe

Tripe is rich in protein and low in fats, minerals, and vitamins. It is sold cleaned and parboiled, but requires another 2 hours of cooking. Each region of Italy has different recipes for tripe. In most preparations, all parts are used; in others, just one part.

ANIMELLE IN PANGRATTATO CON CARCIOFI
(Breaded Sweetbreads with Artichokes)

SERVES 6

1½ pounds sweetbreads
¼ cup breadcrumbs
2 eggs, beaten
Salt and pepper, to taste
4½ tablespoons extra virgin olive oil
All-purpose flour, for dredging
3 ounces butter

8 baby artichokes, cut into thin slices
2 garlic cloves
1 parsley sprig, minced
Salt and pepper, to taste

Blanch the sweetbreads. Sift the breadcrumbs. Beat the eggs in a bowl together with salt, pepper, and 1 teaspoon of the oil. Cut the sweetbreads into even pieces; dredge with flour; dip them in eggs, and then in breadcrumbs. Fry the sweetbreads in 4 tablespoons of the butter in a very hot pan. Drain on paper towels to get rid of excess fat and set aside, warm but not covered. Put the artichokes in a saucepan with 4 tablespoons of olive oil, the garlic, parsley, salt, and pepper. Cover the saucepan and cook over medium heat for 6 to 7 minutes. Remove from the heat, add the remaining 2 tablespoons of butter, stir, and remove from the heat. Arrange the artichokes on a preheated platter, place the sweetbreads on top, and serve.

CERVELLA IN CARROZZA (Fried Brains)

SERVES 4
1 pound brains
2 ounces butter
6 tablespoons extra virgin olive oil
1 small onion, finely sliced
1 cup milk
¼ cup all-purpose flour
1 egg, separated
Salt and pepper, to taste
12 slices of bread (crust removed)
1 tablespoon parsley, chopped

Blanch the brains and slice into 12 even pieces. Heat the butter and 2 tablespoons of the olive oil and add the onion. When the onion is brown, add the brains and sauté 1 minute on each side. Remove from heat and set the pan aside. Prepare a batter by putting milk in a bowl and slowly adding in the flour. Whisk well and add the egg yolk, salt, and pepper. Whip the egg white and fold into the batter. You should get a thick batter. Place a slice of brain with the onion on each slice of bread and dip into the batter. Fry in remaining oil. Drain the brains on paper towels; sprinkle with salt and chopped parsley. Serve very hot.

FEGATO CON CIPOLLINA DORATA (Liver with Onions)

SERVES 4
2 medium onions, finely sliced
2 ounces butter

¼ cup extra virgin olive oil
1 tablespoon parsley
1 pound calves' liver, cut into ¼-inch-thick slices
Salt and pepper, to taste
2 tablespoons dry white wine

Sauté the onions in 2 tablespoons of the butter and 2 tablespoons of the oil in a covered skillet over low heat. When the onions are cooked and the liquid is reduced, add some parsley. Set aside this *soffrito* and keep it warm. Season the slices of liver with salt and pepper. Sauté the slices of liver on each side very quickly in the remaining 2 tablespoons of butter and the remaining 2 tablespoons of oil over a high heat, turning with a wooden spatula. Sprinkle with the wine and remove from the heat. Arrange the liver on a preheated serving platter, top with the onion *sofritto*, and serve.

FEGATELLI DI MAIALE (Pork Liver with Laurel)

SERVES 4
4 pork livers
2 caul fat membranes
12 bay leaves
¼ cup extra virgin olive oil
Salt and pepper, to taste

Clean the livers, remove the skin, and keep whole. Place the caul fat in water for about 1 hour so that it softens, and then cut into 4 pieces. Wrap each piece of liver with 3 bay leaves in the caul fat. Heat the olive oil and fry the wrapped liver to brown it on all sides. Continue to cook, over medium heat, covered, for 10 more minutes. Remove from the pan, add salt and pepper to taste, and serve immediately with toasted country bread.

ROGNONE AL MARSALA (Kidneys with Marsala)

SERVES 4
1 pound veal kidneys
3 ounces butter
¾ cup veal broth (see page 124)
1 tablespoon Marsala
Salt and pepper, to taste
1 tablespoon chopped parsley

Purge the kidneys (see page 242) and cut into 1-inch strips. Melt half the butter in a saucepan. Add the kidneys and sauté for 1 minute. Remove the kidneys from the saucepan and set aside. In a casserole wide enough to accommodate the kidneys in

1 layer, prepare a sauce with the remaining butter. When it begins to color, add the broth. Reduce briskly by 50 percent, then add the kidneys. When the kidneys are very hot, add the Marsala wine, and reduce for 2 minutes on high heat. Remove and add salt, pepper, and chopped parsley. Serve.

TRIPPA CON FAGIOLI (Veal Tripe with Beans)

SERVES 12

4 pounds tripe (foiolo)
2 medium onions
2 celery stalks, chopped
1 bay leaf
¼ cup extra virgin olive oil
½ pound carrots, thinly sliced
2 sage leaves
8 ounces ripe tomatoes, peeled, seeded, and chopped
1 cup beef broth (see pages 123–24)
1 pound dried borlotti beans, presoaked and cooked for 1 hour
Salt and pepper, to taste
6 tablespoons grated Parmigiano

Buy the tripe from your butcher. This is already cooked, but you must still wash and cook the tripe in plenty of boiling salted water for 2 hours. Remove, cool, and cut the tripe into thin strips, about 2 inches long. Cook over medium-high heat in plenty of salted water with 1 onion, quartered, celery, and the bay leaf for 1 hour. Drain the tripe and set aside. In a casserole, sauté the other onion, thinly cut, with the olive oil, carrots, and sage. Sauté until well browned. Add the tomatoes and cook for 5 minutes. Add the broth. When it simmers, add the tripe and cook for 20 minutes. Add the beans and mix well. Add salt and pepper to taste. Cook for 5 more minutes and remove from the heat. Mix in the grated *Parmigiano* and serve.

CORATELLA CON CARCIOFI (Stewed Innards with Artichokes)

SERVES 4 TO 6

1 pound lamb innards (heart, kidney, and liver)
6 artichokes
Juice of 1 lemon
¼ cup extra virgin olive oil
Salt and pepper, to taste
1 tablespoon chopped parsley

Slice the kidney and the liver and dice, rather small, the heart. Remove the outer leaves and chokes from the artichokes and cut them in thin slices; keep in water with half of the lemon juice added. Heat 2 tablespoons of the oil in a large skillet and add the heart. When it is well browned and tender, after about 5 minutes, add the kidney and liver and cook for another 2 minutes. In another pan, sauté the drained artichokes with the remaining 2 tablespoons of olive oil. When tender, add to the innards. Add salt and pepper and the remaining lemon juice. Sauté the combined innards and the artichokes and, when very hot, place on a preheated serving platter, decorate with the parsley, and serve.

POLLAME E CACCIAGIONE
Poultry and Game

In Italian cooking, poultry has always been more prominent than beef. With the exception of Piedmont, Maremma, and Val di Chiana, the breeding grounds for much-prized beef, on the peninsula cows were mostly valued for their milk and oxen were mostly used for working the land. Cows were butchered and eaten only after their milk productivity was exhausted. Oxen were butchered when they had lost all their strength to work the land. Farmyard animals such as chickens, ducks, geese, guinea hens, turkeys, and rabbits, on the other hand, were grown to satisfy everyday eating needs. In Renaissance cookbooks, recipes mention farmyard animals much more than game because hunting was a sport practiced by the nobility only.

Today, however, the large consumption of farmyard animals has led to industrial farm breeding, which has given us a product of higher nutritional value but less flavor than the chickens our fathers ate. With time and the ever-growing demand for higher quality food, large-scale production is improving, while free-range poultry is available once again. Among farmyard game, we must not forget rabbit. Its meat is white and tasty but can be stringy if the animal is old. Rabbit is often cooked just like chicken. At one time, wild game was the only meat that could save people from starvation. Today the strong smell and taste of wild game is only reluctantly accepted. As a growing number of game farms are starting to produce a milder-tasting product, game will continue to gain the popularity it deserves.

POLLO (Broiler Chicken)

This chicken is 3 to 5 months old, usually weighing 2 to 3 pounds. It is suitable for roasting, frying in sauce, or boiling, with or without stuffing.

POLLASTRA (Pullet)

A pullet is a female chicken, 5 to 7 months old, that is, a chicken that has not yet started to lay eggs, weighing roughly 3 to 4 pounds. It should be boiled or poached, with or without stuffing.

POLLO NOVELLO (Spring Chicken)

This is a 3-month-old chicken (either male or female). Cleaned, it usually weighs 1½ to 1¾ pounds. It can be broiled, roasted, or fried.

CAPPONE (Capon)

The capon is prized for its choice meat. It is a castrated male chicken, usually killed when about 10 months old. It can weigh 4 pounds and can be boiled, roasted, or braised, with or without stuffing.

GALLINA (Hen)

This is a mature female chicken that has already laid eggs. It is allowed to mature because it is kept to produce eggs and to brood chicks. It is often used to make broth.

GALLETTO (Rooster)

Young roosters are suitable for the same preparations as spring chickens. If the rooster has reached mating age, its meat will be tough; in this case, it should be used only to make broth.

ANATRA (Duck)

Duck can be cooked in various ways, including roasted, jugged, and braised. Always choose young ducks, especially if they are to be roasted. Duck can also be used to prepare excellent sauces for pasta or polenta. *Germano* (wild duck) is smaller and more flavorful than domestic duck and is usually stewed. Duck sauce is used as a condiment for pappardelle noodles.

OCA (Goose)

Geese are usually available in winter, particularly in December. Some are extremely fat (their liver is highly prized) and their average weight (cleaned) is about 9 pounds. The best geese are those less than 10 months old with white or faintly pink skin and underdeveloped breastbones. Goose is cleaned like chicken and can be roasted or cooked in various other ways. It should be cooked with only a small amount of fat since it is rather fatty. To de-fat the bird, place it in a warm oven (225°F) for about 1 hour and discard the residual fat before cooking. In some regions, goose is cooked and preserved in its own fat.

TACCHINO (Turkey)

Both tom and hen turkeys are available commercially. These are rather large birds and are cooked like chicken. They can be roasted in the oven at low temperature, basted frequently with the cooking juices because the meat tends to be dry. If cooked on top of the stove, it is necessary to split the turkey into pieces suitable for different preparations such as fried, stewed, or cooked in a sauce. For these preparations, a young turkey is preferable. The breast meat can be used in most recipes intended for veal.

FARAONA (Guinea Hen)

Originally a wild hen, it was introduced again in the fifteenth century by Portuguese sailors, who brought the birds from the Guinea Gulf, hence the name guinea hen. This bird has delicate, delicious meat considered by some to be even superior to pheasant. If available, a 6- to 8-month-old guinea hen is preferred. Cleaned, it will weigh 2 pounds at most. It may be roasted or cooked like a pheasant. If roasted, cover the breasts with thin slices of lard.

PICCIONE (Squab or Pigeon)

These are farm-grown birds with delicate, lean meat. The best ones are less than 7 months old, with tender, almost white meat. Older birds have tough meat, which must be cooked at length. It can be fried, stewed, breaded (as cutlets), roasted, broiled, and baked. If roasted, it is best to wrap the bird with slices of *pancetta*.

QUAGLIA (Quail)

Quail are small birds with delicate and delicious meat. The best time for wild quail is October, although farms provide domestic quail all year round. In buying quail, choose the fatter ones. In some Italian cities they are sold on skewers, wrapped with slices of pancetta, ready to be cooked. Quail are cleaned like chicken and can be cooked in various ways: baked, broiled, stewed with mushrooms, or sautéed. Quail can also be used to prepare mouthwatering *risotto*.

PERNICE (Partridge)

The most common varieties of partridge are the gray- and the red-legged partridge. Baby partridges are hunted in September. You can tell a baby partridge by looking at the first wing feather: it will be pointed (in an adult partridge, the wing is rounded). The beak will be rather hard and almost black. The legs (which have not grown spurs yet) will be gray. The eye will be surrounded by a small red circle. A partridge is plucked like chicken, just before cooking. If you wish to roast the partridge, it is preferable to cook the bird when freshly killed. If the bird is to be cooked in a sauce, it is best to use an adult bird. Partridges can be jugged, cooked in a casserole, roasted, and so on. A partridge for roasting should be larded or cooked in vine leaves. It is frequently stuffed or served with grapes. A large partridge can serve two.

TORDO (Thrush)

This is a small bird from the blackbird family, with a very delicate flavor. Various types can be found in Italy. Thrush meat is very delicate and may taste different according to what the bird has been eating. Smaller thrushes have the most delicate meat, whereas larger ones can be slightly bitter. Thrushes are usually prepared like quail: roasted, broiled, or as an ingredient in pâtés and terrines.

PASSERO (Sparrow)

These are the most common birds in Italy. The meat is particularly suitable for serving with *polenta* (a typical dish from Veneto is *polenta e osei*, where *osei* means "birds"). Usually they are not gutted, but cooked directly on the spit or in a pan, wrapped in *pancetta* and flavored with sage and broth, which can be used later together with the drippings from the roasting to prepare a sauce.

FAGIANO (Pheasant)

This is regarded as the most delicious of the game birds. It is available on the market during the winter season. If possible, select a 12- to 14-month-old pheasant. Although the male pheasant has prettier plumage than the female, the meat of the female is more delicate. The male has rather pointed spurs, the bigger the spurs, the older the pheasant.

If you yourself have to prepare the pheasant for cooking, this is the procedure to follow. Pheasant meat must be hung to mature. In addition to making the meat more tender, hanging enhances the flavor of the bird. The bird, unplucked, must be hung by the beak from a hook in a cool, airy place until well matured. It is impossible to say how long it will take, but certainly no more than 4 days, depending on the climate and the age of the pheasant. The bird is ready to cook when, if you blow on the feathers, the visible skin is a bluish (not greenish) color. Check the bird after it has been hung to mature for 2 days and each day thereafter.

Put it into the refrigerator for a couple of hours before plucking. When cooking, do not use strongly flavored ingredients, since these would overpower the taste of the pheasant. A good pheasant is always under 2 pounds; the female pheasant will weigh a little less. Young pheasants can be roasted on the spit, or larded with pancetta and roasted. The meat should be cooked until pink. The older and fatter birds can be cooked in *salmì*, fricasseed, or used as ingredients for pâtés and terrines.

BECCACCIA E BECCACCINO (Woodcock and Snipe)

A most prized variety of game with gourmets, woodcock is a migratory bird that flies to warmer climates in late fall. Its meat is delicious, succulent, and nutritive. It is always better to buy the bird ready to cook, but if you have to prepare it for cooking yourself, follow this procedure. The bird must be hung to mature with the feathers on for about 5 days or until greenish shimmers appear on the abdomen (if the shimmers are purple, the bird has been hung to mature too long). Pluck only just before cooking. Singe the bird and clean well with a wet cloth. Cut off the legs, turn the bird on its back, turn the head around, and tuck the beak inside the body. The woodcock should be either roasted in the oven or on the spit; in either case it must be larded with lard or *pancetta*. Snipe is a marsh-like bird similar to woodcock, only a little smaller. It is cooked like woodcock.

CONIGLIO (Rabbit)

Rabbits no more than 5 or 6 months old are the best for roasting. They should be larded with lard or *pancetta* to keep the meat moist. Rabbit can also be boned and cooked with stuffing *"in pancetta."* Usually the legs and thighs are roasted, while the front part (saddle), which has less meat, is either stewed or used to prepare a sauce for pasta. The liver is also used for making *ragù*.

LEPRE (Hare)

Hare may look like wild rabbit, but it has stronger hind legs and can weigh 8 ounces more and up. Winter is the best season for hare. If kept in a cool place, the meat keeps fresh 5–6 days before cooking. Hares that are 10 to 12 months old are best. Hare should be marinated before cooking, although marinating should nsot be excessively long (12 to 24 hours at most). Hare can be cooked in many ways: roasted, in *salmì*, and in sauce that is served with *pappardelle*. Hare is customarily served with *polenta*.

CAMOSCIO, CERVO, CAPRIOLO E DAINO
(Chamois, Deer, Roebuck, and Fallow Deer)

These large animals are usually sold in pieces. The meat has a gamy taste, even after about a week's hanging, generally on a bed of mountain grass, and must be marinated at length. The taste will be improved if the meat is larded before cooking. Younger animals, not older than 2½ years, are preferable for cooking.

CINGHIALE (Wild Boar)

Boar is a sizable animal, related to the pig, with hard bristles and large tusks protruding from its snout. Its meat is delicious, especially if the animal is young (about 6 months old). When older, the meat becomes tough and requires long marinating. If it is 3 to 6 months old, the baby boar (or milk-fed boar) can be hunted and need not be marinated; it can simply be rubbed with oil and kept in the refrigerator for 3 or 4 days. Chops from young boar should be simply seasoned with salt and pepper, then sprinkled generously with lemon juice and left to marinate for a couple of hours before cooking. Wild boar can be cooked in *salmì* like hare, or roasted. The chops can be broiled. The legs can also be salted and dry-aged for *prosciutto*.

POLLO ALLA DIAVOLA (Split Roast Chicken)

SERVES 2
>1 young chicken, about 1½ pounds
>6 tablespoons extra virgin olive oil
>2 rosemary sprigs
>Salt and pepper, to taste
>Juice of ½ lemon

Preheat the oven to 375°F. Wash and dry the bird. Cut it open along its back and remove the breastbone. Turn it over and pound the breast with a meat mallet without crushing it. Cut 2 holes in the skin beside the chicken's tail and insert the ends of the leg bones into them. Sprinkle 2 tablespoons of oil on both sides, and rub with the rosemary and salt and pepper, to taste. Place a weight over the chicken and refrigerate it, keeping it flat for at least 6 hours. Place the chicken with 3 tablespoons of olive oil in a cast-iron skillet over medium-high heat until the chicken is well browned on both sides. Then place it in the oven and roast for 25 minutes. Baste often with oil, using a brush or a rosemary sprig. Remove chicken from the oven and serve, allowing one-half chicken per person. Just before serving, squeeze the half lemon over the 2 servings.

Note:
For this preparation you may use *galletti* (small roosters). In that case, use 1 bird per person.

POLLO ALLA CACCIATORA (Chicken Cacciatora)

SERVES 4
>2 pounds chicken parts
>1 small carrot, chopped
>1 celery stalk, chopped
>1 onion, chopped
>1 garlic clove
>6 tablespoons extra virgin olive oil
>Salt and pepper, to taste
>1 bay leaf

Juniper berries
1 cup dry white wine
1 ounce dried mushrooms, reconstituted in warm water
1 pound tomatoes, peeled, seeded, and chopped
½ cup chicken broth (see page 124)
1 tablespoon chopped parsley

Wash the chicken parts and pat dry. Sauté the carrot, celery, onion, and garlic in olive oil. When tender but not crisp, add the chicken parts, salt, pepper, bay leaf, and a few juniper berries. Let brown over high heat. Add the wine and, when it has evaporated, add the mushrooms, tomatoes, and broth. Cook for about 1 hour over medium heat. Remove from the heat and arrange on a preheated serving platter. Sprinkle with parsley and serve.

Note:
Cacciatora is a word that indicates a family-style dish with hearty seasoning. Besides chicken, rabbit, lamb, and even rice (according to a recipe handed down to us by Pellegrino Artusi) can be called *cacciatora*.

ANTRA ALLE OLIVE (Duck with Olives)

SERVES 4
1 young duck, about 2½ pounds
5 ounces black olives, Gaeta or niçoise
2 ounces pancetta or prosciutto, chopped
1 small carrot, chopped
1 celery stalk, chopped
1 garlic clove
3 tablespoons extra virgin olive oil
1 medium onion, thinly sliced
1 rosemary sprig
½ cup dry white wine
2 bay leaves
4 anchovy fillets, chopped
½ cup tomatoes, peeled, seeded, and chopped
Salt and pepper, to taste
1 tablespoon chopped parsley

Clean and cut the duck into 8 parts. Pit the olives and mince half of them. Prepare a *battuto* in a large saucepan with the *pancetta,* carrot, celery, minced olives, and garlic in the oil. Add the onion and rosemary and cook for 4 to 5 minutes. Add the duck parts and let brown, moistening with wine. When the wine has evaporated, add the bay leaves, anchovies, and tomatoes. Add salt and pepper, cover the saucepan, and cook over very low heat, turning the pieces of duck occasionally, for about 1 hour. Add the rest of the olives and cook for another 10 minutes. Remove from the heat and place the duck on a preheated serving platter. Strain the sauce and pour over the duck. Add the parsley and serve.

FARAONA AL CARTOCCIO (Bagged Guinea Hen)

SERVE 4

> 2 guinea hens
> 2 tablespoons extra virgin olive oil
> 3 garlic cloves, crushed
> 8 sage leaves
> Salt and pepper, to taste
> 1 piece caul fat
> ¼ pound pancetta, sliced

Preheat the oven to 375°F. Clean the guinea hens, then wash and pat dry. Brush the inside and outside with olive oil. Put the garlic, 4 sage leaves, and salt and pepper inside and outside the birds. Scald the caul fat in boiling water, drain, and spread on a kitchen towel to dry. Wrap the birds in *pancetta* and the remainder of the sage leaves and then wrap the whole in the caul fat. Grease a sheet of parchment paper with oil and wrap the birds in it. Seal by twisting the edges of the paper onto themselves. Cook in the oven for about 1 hour. Remove from the heat, open the bagged hens, carve, and serve with the cooking juices left in the *cartoccio*.

CAPPONE CON LE NOCI (Capon with Walnuts)

This is a specialty from Lombardy, traditionally prepared in the Christmas season. The broth is excellent and can be used to cook small ravioli to serve as a first course.

SERVES 4

> 1 capon, about 4 pounds or larger
> 4 slices white bread, crusts removed
> ¼ cup heavy cream
> 1 ounce butter
> 20 walnuts, shelled and chopped
> 3 egg yolks
> ¼ cup grated Parmigiano
> Salt and pepper, to taste
> Pinch of nutmeg
> 2 celery stalks
> 1 small carrot, cut into 4 pieces

Clean and bone the capon, except for the legs, and leave it in its natural shape. Soak the bread in the cream. Soften the butter and mix with the walnuts. Beat the egg yolks with the *Parmigiano* and the soaked bread. Blend the mixture well with a wooden spoon and combine with the butter and walnuts. Mix to achieve a soft but consistent stuffing, adding more bread or cream if necessary. Add salt and pepper and nutmeg. Fill the capon with the stuffing. Sew and tie the bird closed. Bring a large pot of water to a boil. Add the celery and carrot, lower the heat, and cook the stuffed capon in this broth over low heat for 1½ to 2 hours, adding salt halfway through. Serve the capon carved with some of the stuffing.

Note:
This dish is often accompanied by preserved spiced fruit *(mostarda di frutta)*.

PICCIONE RIPIENO (Stuffed Squab)

SERVES 4

4 squabs
¼ pound top round of veal
¼ pound pancetta
¼ pound prosciutto, diced
¼ pound cooked pickled tongue, diced
½ onion, chopped
1 small carrot, chopped
1 small celery stalk, chopped
4 ounces butter
Salt and pepper, to taste
½ cup Marsala
2 tablespoons grated Parmigiano
1 piece caul fat, blanched
Bay leaves
2 cloves
Roast potatoes, for serving

Preheat the oven to 450°F. Bone the squabs, except for the legs. Wash, and pat dry. Chop the veal and *pancetta* and mix with the *prosciutto* and tongue. Brown the vegetables in half the butter. Add salt and pepper and all the meats except caul fat. Cook for 15 minutes over medium heat. Add the Marsala and *Parmigiano,* mix well, remove from the heat, and let cool. Fill the squabs with the stuffing and secure with caul fat so that the stuffing will not fall out. Place them in a greased baking pan with the remaining butter, a few bay leaves, the cloves, and salt. Start to cook in the oven at 450°F. After 15 minutes, lower temperature to 375°F and roast for about 30 minutes, turning frequently. Remove the caul fat, arrange on a serving platter, and serve with roast potatoes.

CONIGLIO ALL'ISCHITANA (Rabbit Stew)

This is a traditional recipe from the island of Ischia, off the coast of Naples.

SERVES 4
1 rabbit, 2 pounds
4 garlic cloves
6 tablespoons extra virgin olive oil
1 cup dry white wine
4 cups peeled, seeded, and chopped tomatoes
Salt and pepper, to taste
8 basil leaves

Cut the rabbit into pieces. In a terra-cotta pot, sauté the garlic in the olive oil until golden brown and discard. Add the rabbit pieces to the hot oil and cook until they are well colored, and add the wine. When the wine has evaporated, add the tomatoes, salt and pepper to taste, and cook for 30 minutes with the pot covered. Remove from the heat, add the basil leaves, place on a preheated serving platter, and serve.

Note:
The sauce is very good as a condiment for pasta *(bucatini)*.

CINGHIALE ALL'AGRODOLCE (Wild Boar in Sweet-and-Sour Sauce)

SERVES 6
½ cup wine vinegar
2 cups dry red wine
4 bay leaves
1 thyme sprig
1 teaspoon peperoncino
3 cloves
2 onions, chopped
1 carrot, chopped
1 celery stalk, chopped
3 pounds wild boar fillet
2 ounces butter
2 tablespoons bitter cocoa
1 tablespoon sugar
½ cup dried prunes, softened and chopped
2 tablespoons candied orange peel
1 tablespoon raisins

1 tablespoon pine nuts
Salt and pepper, to taste

Prepare a marinade by boiling the vinegar and wine with the bay leaves, thyme, *peper-oncino,* cloves, 1 onion, carrot, and celery. Pour into a large pot and let cool. Place the boar fillet into the marinade and refrigerate for 48 hours. When ready to cook, preheat the oven to 425°F. Chop the remaining onion and brown in butter, in a large roasting pan. Add the cocoa, sugar, prunes, candied orange peel, raisins, and pine nuts. Sauté for 5 minutes over medium heat, then add the boar meat (reserving the marinade) and roast on all sides. Pass the marinade through a sieve, and add to the meat. Add salt and pepper, to taste. Continue cooking in the oven for at least 2 hours, or until the meat is very tender and the sauce thick. Serve with *polenta,* potatoes, or potato *gnocchi.*

ANATRA SELVATICA CON PAPPARDELLE
(Wild Duck with Broad Noodles)

SERVES 4

1 wild duck
1 celery stalk, chopped
1 carrot, chopped
1 small onion, chopped
4 tablespoons extra virgin olive oil
1 ounce butter
3 ounces prosciutto, cut into strips
2 tablespoons dry white wine
1 pound ripe tomatoes, peeled, seeded, and chopped
Salt and pepper, to taste
1 teaspoon fennel seeds
1 pound fresh pappardelle

Wash and dry the duck and cut into equal pieces. Brown the celery, carrot, and onion in oil, butter, and *prosciutto* in a saucepan. Add the duck and brown well, then splash with wine. When the wine has evaporated, add the tomatoes. Add salt and pepper and cook slowly for 1½ hours. Add the fennel seeds and cook for another 20 minutes. Remove the pieces of duck and keep them warm. Strain the sauce, return it to the pan, and add the duck. Heat through. Cook the *pappardelle* in boiling salted water, drain, and serve with the sauce. The duck meat can be served on top of the pasta or as a second course.

SCOTTIGLIA (Mixed Meat Stew)

This is a Tuscan specialty also called *cacciucco di carne.* The dish requires the widest possible variety of meats. The ones taking longer to cook should be added first.

SERVES 6

1 *onion, minced*

1 *garlic clove, minced*

4 *tablespoons olive oil*

3 *pounds various cuts of meat, such as veal round, beef chuck, chicken, rabbit, pork shoulder, 1 squab cut in quarters, ½ pound of each of all the other meats cut in cubes or bite-size pieces*

1 *cup dry red wine*

1¼ *pounds ripe tomatoes, peeled, seeded, and chopped*

Salt and pepper, to taste

1 *cup beef or chicken broth (see pages 123–24)*

1 *tablespoon chopped parsley*

8 *basil leaves*

Brown the onion and garlic in oil in a large saucepan. Add the meats, one at a time, tougher meats first, so that they will all be ready at the same time. Splash occasionally with red wine. When the meat is browned, add the tomatoes. Add salt and pepper and continue cooking for at least for 1 hour, adding broth if needed. Cook until the meats are tender to the fork, add parsley and basil, and serve with country bread toasted and rubbed with a clove of garlic.

LEPRE IN SALMÌ (Hare in Salmi Lombard-Style)

The term *salmì* denotes the slow braising of game, which produces a thick and flavorful sauce that can be used as a condiment for pasta. The best-known *salmì* is prepared with hare. Hare can also be identified as wild rabbit.

SERVES 4

2 *hares, about 1 pound each*

1 *bottle Barbera wine*

3 *onions, chopped*

1 *carrot, chopped*

1 *celery stalk, chopped*

1 *garlic clove*

Pinch of peperoncino

1 *teaspoon juniper berries*

Minced thyme

Minced marjoram

2 *bay leaves*

1 *tablespoon salt*

1 *ounce butter*

2 *ounces pancetta*

4 tablespoons lard, chopped
¼ cup grappa
3¼ ounce bittersweet chocolate
Polenta, for serving

Cut the hare into small pieces and marinate in wine, 1 onion, carrot, celery, garlic, *peperoncino,* juniper berries, minced herbs, whole bay leaves, and salt. Marinate for 12 hours in the refrigerator, turning the hares in the marinade from time to time.

When it is time to prepare the *salmì,* use a large pan to hold the hares. Heat the butter and *pancetta* and brown 2 onions. Add the hares and brown well. Add the marinade and cook over high heat for 1 hour. Take the hares out of the casserole and keep warm. Sieve the liquid into another casserole. Bring to a simmer, add salt to taste, the pieces of lard, grappa, and chocolate, and reduce for another 2 hours. Add the hares and continue to cook for another 15 minutes. Serve with *polenta.*

Note:
If the sauce is being used for *pappardelle* in the popular Tuscan specialty called *pappardelle alla lepre,* do not remove the hare from the casserole. Instead, continue cooking until the meat falls off the bone.

FORMAGGIO
Cheese

Italy boasts hundreds of varieties of cheese. A catalog published in 1977 mentions as many as 451 different varieties, thus making it extremely difficult to cover them all in this volume. It may be enough to consider that, throughout the peninsula, wherever there is a herd there is a copper pot to make whey and a cellar where cheese such as *caciotta, robiola*, or *caciocavallo* rest on wooden boards. This chapter will discuss a selection of the best-known Italian varieties.

Storage

Cheese is best kept in a dark, humid, ventilated room at a constant temperature of 45 to 50°F. If it has to be refrigerated, it is advisable to store it in the vegetable section, wrapped loosely in porous paper or cheesecloth to allow air in.

Serving

The basic rule is that cheese must be served at room temperature. Cheese can be served with fruit or vegetables. For instance, *pecorino romano* is traditionally served with fava beans, and goat cheese is often served with radishes. Bread, of course, is a most important element in serving cheese. Large crusty country loaves, olive bread, walnut bread, and bread with sesame seeds are all appropriate. Many types of cheese are suitable to be served cooked, especially the soft, fresh types such as *mozzarella, ricotta,* and *fontina*. Honey or *saba* can also be used as an accompaniment to cheese; the sharp and sweet characteristics of the two products complement each other.

FORMAGGI FRESCHI (Fresh Cheese)

Fresh cheese is sent to market after a very brief period of ripening. Its nature and nutritional value, therefore, are not significantly altered. It should be consumed shortly after it is purchased. Although not "real" cheeses, *ricotta, mascarpone,* and *mozzarella* can be included in this category. In Italy, fresh cheeses are called *latticini;* all other cheeses are called *formaggio*.

CAPRINO

Despite its name (literally translated as goat cheese), it was made only with cow milk at one time. Today, however, we find cheese named *caprino* that is made with either cow or goat milk. Sometimes these are combined; at other times 100 percent cow milk or 100 percent goat milk is used. At all times *caprino* denotes soft cheese in small cylindrical shapes.

CASATELLA

This is a soft cheese made with whole cow milk. It is traditionally made in Veneto. It is aged for six days and is best when used fresh.

CRESCENZA

This is a product from Lombardy. It is an uncooked milk product, soft-textured, and high in fat content, made from whole, pasteurized cow milk, and ripened for 15 days. *Crescenza* is white, with a buttery consistency, rectangular in shape, with no crust and no holes.

MASCARPONE

This is not really a cheese but rather a very rich substance made from cream that has been soured with fermenting bacteria. It is a regional specialty of Lombardy. It is sold by weight and usually used to prepare desserts such as *tiramisù*.

MOZZARELLA

Originally from southern Italy but now produced all over the country, *mozzarella* is made from cow or *bufala* whole milk. *Bufala* is a breed of cows originally from the eastern countries. It has no resemblance to the American buffalo. *Mozzarella* is uncooked with a stringy consistency, very white, soft yet solid, and high in fat content. *Mozzarella* is sold in various forms: 10- to 12-ounce braids, 4- to 14-ounce round balls, and 2-ounce bite-size pieces. Not long ago, *mozzarella* was sold without a wrapper, but a new law makes it obligatory to wrap it. Nowadays *mozzarella* shapes are sold in individual plastic bags with a small amount of whey to keep the cheese fresh. If it is necessary to store *mozzarella* without whey, it can be put in a covered cup in a salt and water solution. Whether in whey or water, it must be stored in an airy, cool place. It should not be refrigerated.

RICOTTA

Ricotta is technically not a cheese, but a cheese by-product. *Ricotta* is obtained by re-heating the leftover whey at the end of the cheese-making process. *Ricotta* literally translated from Italian means "reheated," hence the name. There are various types of ricotta. The best known is *ricotta romana,* made from sheep milk and formed in spherical wicker baskets. The other is *ricotta piemontese,* made from cow milk and shaped in pyramids. Ricotta can also be salted and aged, a practice more popular in the south of Italy, particularly in Sicily.

ROBIOLA

Robiola is made from whole cow milk and shaped into pieces weighing about 1 pound. It is an uncooked cheese, high in fat, with a slightly piquant taste, yellowish in color, with a few little holes. It is not really ripened but is kept in the dairy until a light, yellowish-red crust forms. In Emilia-Romagna, *robiola* is also made with sheep milk or mixed sheep and cow milk. It is eaten fresh or within a month of production.

SCAMORZA

This is an uncooked cheese, high in fat, with a stringy and soft consistency. It is made with whole cow milk. It is formed in slightly leaning pear shapes weighing about 12 ounces and aged for about 2 weeks.

STRACCHINO

This cheese is made with whole milk from "tired cows" (*stracc* is dialect for "exhausted") who have traveled from the Alpine pastures down to the plains in the fall. It is similar to *crescenza* but with a slightly more solid consistency.

TOMINO

This is made with partly skimmed cow milk. Its consistency is hard and compact, and it is white, with practically no crust. It has a sweet taste. Each shape weighs about 10 ounces. It is ready 2 weeks after production. *Tomini* are sold fresh wrapped in paper but can also be sold marinated in oil with hot pepper or other aromatic herbs.

FORMAGGI INVECCHIATI
(Aged Cheese)

Cheese aged for less than a year is made with the addition of special microbes (molds and bacteria). After curdling, the mixture is cooked.

ASIAGO

Asiago is a compact, yellowish cheese made from whole cow milk; it is therefore high in fat content. It has small to medium-size holes, and a smooth, even, and elastic crust. The wheels weigh between 20 and 25 pounds and are aged for 6 months before they are ready for consumption.

BITTO

This is a specialty of Valtellina made of whole cow milk, sometimes mixed with sheep milk. The wheels weigh between 6 and 15 pounds. The cheese is cream-colored with tiny holes and has a very delicate taste after aging for about 40 days. Sometimes it is left to ripen a little longer, in which case the color deepens and the taste becomes more marked. *Bitto* is used in many regional recipes, but since it is not easily available, it is often replaced with *fontina*.

CACIOCAVALLO

Originally from southern Italy, this cheese is now produced all over the country. Its name ("horse cheese") comes from the way it is aged. Two pieces of cheese are tied together and then draped over a stick to age, as if they were on horseback. *Caciocavallo* is made from whole cow milk and has a soft, stringy consistency. It is compact and yellowish with a thin, smooth yellow crust. It is formed in the shape of a melon or a salami and weighs about 10 pounds. The aging process lasts 3 months for normal consumption.

CACIOTTA

This name is given to a wide range of cheeses produced both industrially and in daries. Made of sheep or cow milk or a mixture of both, sold in round wheels weighing less than 2.2 pounds and only slightly ripened, *caciotta* generally has a delicate flavor, few or no holes, and is white or yellowish in color. The crust is thin and ranges from light to darker yellows.

CASTELMAGNO

This is a cheese made with cow milk at an altitude of 3,500 feet. The cheese takes the name of the village in which it is made. *Castelmagno* is whitish with light green streaks; the taste is delicate and grainy but creamy. It is aged from 4 to 6 months.

FONTINA

Fontina is a specialty of Valle d'Aosta and owes its name to the fact that it melts easily (*fondare* means to melt). It is a hard cheese made from whole cow milk and is high in fat, semicooked, light yellow in color, elastic, with few holes. The crust is thin and compact and stamped with the logo *Fontina della Valle d'Aosta*. The wheels weigh 4 to 8 pounds and are aged for about 4 months.

GORGONZOLA

Gorgonzola is made from whole cow milk, uncooked, and high in fat. The cheese is very soft, sometimes creamy (if there are thin stripes throughout the cheese it is not the best quality), white or yellowish in color with green areas, and has a strong taste. The crust is reddish and rough, and it is wrapped in aluminum foil with the producer's name on it. It is a speciality of Lombardy and is sometimes called *erborinato* (from *erbor*, parsley in Milanese dialect). Its characteristic green streaks come from specially selected mold cultures (*Penicillin glaucum*) added during the production process. The wheels weigh about 20 pounds and are ripened 3 to 5 months. After the first month, *gorgonzola* is pierced with long copper needles to allow the air in and to favor the growth of mold. Nowadays there is a sweeter version of this cheese, called *panerone*, which has a softer consistency.

MONTASIO

This cheese is made with cow milk, partially skimmed. When making this cheese from yesterday's milk, the milk is skimmed; from today's milk it is whole. It is best used when two months old—when it ages it becomes saltier. *Montasio* is also used to prepare *frico*, a specialty from Friuli.

PECORINO

Pecorino is a hard, wholly cooked, grayish-white cheese with a strong taste, made from whole sheep milk. The crust is hard, thick, and darkened with oil.

The wheels are not even in size and can vary from 12 to 40 pounds. They must be aged for at least 8 months. Fresh *pecorino* is eaten directly, whereas the aged variety is used for grating. Among the many varieties of *pecorino,* almost all of which are produced in small dairies, the best ones are *pecorino romano, sardo,* and *siciliano,* which is made in a basket with grains of black pepper.

QUARTIROLO

This cheese owes its name to the fact that the milk comes from cows fed on the fourth cutting of grass (*quartirola* grass). *Quartirolo* is similar to *taleggio* but is lower in fat content.

TALEGGIO

Taleggio takes its name from a valley in the Bergamo area. It is a raw cheese made with whole cow milk and is high in fat content. Its consistency is very soft, almost creamy, when very ripe. *Taleggio* is white or yellowish in color and has a relatively strong taste. The crust is thin, soft, and reddish. The forms are rectangular and weigh about 4 pounds. *Taleggio* is aged 40 days.

TOMA

This is a specialty from the region of Piedmont. The cheese is made in July, August, and September in every valley of the countryside. *Toma* made at higher altitudes is better. *Toma* is made with cow milk, skimmed to various degrees, depending on who makes it and where. For example, *toma* made in Biella is lightly skimmed, while the one made in Sordevalo is totally skimmed. The aging varies according to the degree of skimming: from 1 month for cheese made with whole milk to 6 months for *toma* made with skimmed milk.

FORMAGGI INVECCHIATI OLTRE UN ANNO
(Cheese Aged for Over a Year)

GRANA

This is a generic name for cheeses that have a grainy texture like *Parmigiano-Reggiano, grana padano,* and others. They are made with cow milk. All types of *grana* can be used in similar ways.

GRANA PADANO

This cheese is similar to *Parmigiano,* but it is produced year-round in the area north of the Po River with whole milk from cows that are fed on hay. It is a wholly cooked, hard, semifat cheese, yellowish in color, with a delicate taste. The crust is hard, occasionally dark, and oily. The wheels weigh between 50 and 75 pounds and are aged 1 to 2 years. *Grana padano* is used in the same way as *Parmigiano*.

PARMIGIANO-REGGIANO

This is a *DOC (Denominazione di Origine Controllata)* cheese. This means that its production is carefully controlled and regulated by the local government through a consortium to ensure its quality. Produced in the provinces of Parma, Reggio Emilia, and Moderna, and part of the province of Mantova, *Parmigiano-Reggiano* is made from April 1 until mid-November, with whole milk from cows fed on fresh grass, and it is known as *Maggenger*. The *grana* produced in the winter is known as *Vermengo*. Both are hard, wholly cooked, compact cheeses, light yellow in color, with a strong but not piquant taste. The crust is very hard, oily, the words *Parmigiano-Reggiano* pricked all over the surface. The wheels weigh about 60 pounds and are aged from 18 months to 5 years. *Parmigiano* is excellent grated, but is also eaten in chunks chipped off the wheel with a specially shaped knife. It is used in a vast number of Italian recipes.

PROVOLONE

Provolone is made with whole milk and must have a fat content of at least 45 percent. It is shaped into cylindrical forms that are later immersed in brine and hung in warm, smoky chambers for a period of time, which varies depending on their size (10 to 80 pounds or more). Aged for at least 3 months, *provolone* has a fairly compact texture when young, getting slightly veined and sharper as it ages. The color is a light straw yellow. This cheese is produced all over Italy with the exception of Piedmont, Tuscany, Umbria, and Sardinia.

FONDUTA (Fonduta)

SERVES 4
> 1 pound fontina cheese
> 2 cups milk
> Salt
> 4 eggs yolks, beaten
> 8 ounces butter
> White truffles (optional)

Cut the *fontina* into small cubes, drop it in a double boiler, and add 1 cup of milk. When the cheese starts melting, add a pinch of salt and stir constantly. Meanwhile, warm the rest of the milk in another saucepan. Add the beaten egg yolks and the butter and stir. When both mixtures are creamy, combine them together. Stir constantly to get a creamy thick mixture. Serve hot and with white truffles, when in season.

MOZZARELLA IN CARROZZA (Fried Mozzarella Sandwich)

SERVES 4

8 slices of thinly sliced bread, crusts removed
1 cup milk
1 pound mozzarella
3 eggs
Salt and pepper, to taste
1 cup flour
Oil, for frying

Moisten the bread with a small amount of milk. Cut the *mozzarella* into 4 slices. Insert each slice of *mozzarella* between 2 slices of bread. Cut the sandwiches in 2 triangles and set aside. Mix the eggs with the rest of the milk and beat well. Add salt and pepper to taste. Lightly dust the *mozzarella* triangles with flour and soak them in the egg and milk mixture. Fry in a skillet with plenty of oil. Remove from oil when golden brown, place them briefly onto an absorbent paper to soak up excess oil, place on a platter, and serve.

PROVATURA ALLA SALSA DI ACCIUGHE
(Mozzarella Toast with Anchovy Sauce)

SERVES 4

1 pound provatura or mozzarella
Salt and pepper, to taste
8 slices bread (soft crust)
8 ounces butter
6 anchovy fillets, chopped
¼ cup milk

Preheat the oven to 375°F. Slice the *provatura* and sprinkle with salt and pepper. Cut the bread the same size as the cheese slices. Place a slice of cheese over a slice of bread. Repeat until you have used up all the cheese. Place the slices in a buttered baking dish and cook in the oven for about 20 minutes, brushing occasionally with butter. Meanwhile, sauté the anchovies with the remaining butter until they melt. Stir in the milk. Season with salt and pepper. Remove the dish from the oven, and transfer the slices to a warm plate. Pour the anchovy sauce over the toast and serve immediately.

RICOTTA DI BUFALA FRITTA (Fried Buffalo Milk Ricotta)

SERVES 6

1 cup frying oil
2 eggs, beaten
Salt and pepper, to taste
1 pound ricotta romana
1 cup fresh breadcrumbs

Start with a large skillet with plenty of frying oil. Beat the eggs, adding salt and pepper. Slice the *ricotta romana* and dip it into the beaten eggs and then coat with breadcrumbs. Fry in hot oil on both sides until golden. Season with salt and pepper.

Note:
This can be served plain or with fresh strained tomato sauce.

DOLCI
Desserts

Italians are not big dessert eaters. The consumption of cakes is very much tied to religious holidays and private celebrations such as name days, birthdays, and weddings, and to certain local specific dates and traditions. Although these traditions are slowly fading, the climate is probably the main reason Italians have been such poor eaters of sweets. Italy's mild Mediterranean climate does not harmonize with the powerful calorie contents of most desserts. Over the last twenty to thirty years, though, following a remarkable change in Italian eating habits, the consumption of cakes has grown. In part, this is due to the fact that dessert making has become less complicated in today's modern kitchens. Plus, innumerable raw ingredients, such as fruit pulp, are becoming more and more common in Italy, making it possible to create lighter desserts.

Piccola pasticceria (small sweet pastry), *panettone* (Christmas cake), *biscotti* (cookies), and *gelati* (ice creams) hold center stage among Italian sweets. Perhaps this is because these desserts are consumed outside the main meal; Italians consider many desserts too heavy after a full dinner.

AMARETTI (Almond Cookies)

MAKES 24 COOKIES
4 cups almonds
1 cup granulated sugar
1 teaspoon vanilla extract
10 egg whites
¼ cup confectioner's sugar

Preheat the oven to 350°F. Blanch and toast the almonds. Peel and chop them very fine or crush them in a mortar with the sugar. Add the vanilla. Beat the egg whites until stiffened, then fold in the almonds. Spoon the batter into a pastry bag fitted with a plain tip. Pipe 2½-inch-wide rounds about 1½ inches apart on a buttered baking sheet and flatten them a bit. Sift the confectioner's sugar over the tops and let stand at room temperature 1 to 2 hours. Bake for about 20 minutes. Remove from the oven and let cool. Amaretti may be kept in a sealed box for several days.

BABÀ AL RUM (Babà with Rum)

Babà was invented by a Polish king in disgrace who was an avid reader of the story of "Ali Baba and the Forty Thieves." In order to improve on a local dessert similar to kugelhopf, the royal highness immersed it in cognac and called this innovation Ali Baba. Later it became known as just babà, probably by the Neopolitans during the Bourbon occupation in the seventeenth century. The Neopolitans also changed the cognac to rum since it was less expensive.

SERVES 10

Dough
1 ounce brewer's yeast
½ cup warm milk
3½ cups all-purpose flour
Pinch of salt
8 eggs
½ cup sugar
8 ounces butter, melted

Syrup
2 cups sugar
4 cups water
½ cup Jamaican rum

Preheat the oven to 375°F. Dissolve the yeast in the warm milk and 4 tablespoons of the flour. Work into a dough. Place the dough in a bowl, cover, and let stand in a warm place for 30 minutes, or until it doubles in size. Make a *fontana* (fountain) on a pastry board with the remaining flour, a pinch of salt, the eggs, sugar, butter, and fermented dough. Work the dough until you have a smooth, soft dough. Put the dough, covered with a cloth, in a warm place and let it double in size. Now place the dough into a large buttered ring mold and let rise again in a warm place for about 1 hour. Bake for 45 minutes.

Prepare a syrup by dissolving the sugar in the water over low heat. Bring to a boil and reduce for 7 minutes and cool. Add the rum. Unmold the babà while still warm. Soak with the warm rum syrup for 30 minutes. Serve with whipped cream or an orange sauce.

Note:
Small babà are made the same way, except the dough is divided and baked in smaller molds.

CANNOLI CON RICOTTA (Ricotta-Stuffed Cannoli)

SERVES 10 TO 12

1¾ cups all-purpose flour
1 tablespoon unsweetened cocoa powder
1 tablespoon ground coffee
Pinch of salt
½ cup granulated sugar
1 ounce butter, softened
1 cup white wine
1 cup ricotta
½ cup confectioner's sugar
1 tablespoon orange flower water
2 tablespoons candied orange and citron peel, diced
2 tablespoons candied cherries, diced
1 ounce chocolate, grated
1 tablespoon cocoa powder
2 tablespoons almond oil or olive oil
1 egg white
Corn oil, for frying
2 tablespoons confectioner's sugar

Mix the flour, cocoa, coffee, salt, and granulated sugar on a pastry board. Make a *fontana* (fountain). Add the butter and enough white wine to work into a moderately firm dough. Knead for a few minutes. Shape the dough into a ball. Wrap it in a cloth and let stand for 1 hour in a cool place.

For the filling, sieve the ricotta. Add the confectioner's sugar and orange flower water. Mix well. Add the diced candied fruit and divide the resulting cream into 2 equal portions. Add the chocolate and cocoa to one half. Store both halves in a cool place.

Coat a few tin pipes (*cannoli* molds), 5 inches long and 1 inch in diameter, with almond oil. Roll the dough to ⅛ inch thick and cut into 4-inch disks. Fold the dough around the molds, overlapping the two ends, and seal with a bit of egg white. Fry in hot oil. Gently drain them and place on paper towels. Cool them for a few minutes. Gently remove the molds and let cool thoroughly.

Fill the *cannoli* with the ricotta cream through one end, and cocoa cream through the other. Dust with confectioner's sugar and serve.

Notes:
Cannoli shells can be prepared in advance, but the cream should be added just before serving or the shell will become soggy.

Cannoli shells are also known as *scorze*.

CASSATA ALLA SICILIANA (Sicilian Cassata)

This cake, a specialty of Sicily, should not be confused with the ice cream dish of the same name. In Erice, *cassata* is made with a citron jam filling and is covered with stretched almond pastry dough.

SERVES 8 TO 10

Sponge Cake
5 egg yolks
1 cup confectioner's sugar
4 egg whites, whipped stiff
¾ cup all-purpose flour
1 dash vanilla extract
2 tablespoons butter

Filling
1 cup sugar
2 cups ricotta
4 ounces chocolate
2 cups mixed whole candied fruit
1 teaspoon vanilla extract
1 teaspoon ground cinnamon
2 tablespoons maraschino liqueur or orange liqueur
1 tablespoon pistachio nuts

Decorating
½ cup apricot jelly

Fondant
1 cup sugar
½ cup water
1 teaspoon glucose
½ cup pistachio nuts, ground to a paste
½ cup maraschino or orange liqueur
1 ounce orange flower water

For the sponge cake, preheat the oven to 375°F. Whip the egg yolks with the sugar to a stiff consistency. Add the egg whites, place in a mixing bowl, and gradually mix in the flour, mixing until smooth. Add the vanilla, mix again, and pour into a buttered 8-inch round baking dish. Bake at 375°F for 45 minutes.

To assemble, line the bottom and sides of a 10-inch-diameter cake mold with thin slices of sponge cake. Dissolve the sugar in a small amount of water over low heat. Sieve the ricotta and mix it with the dissolved sugar. Cut the chocolate into small chunks and dice half of the candied fruit. Add them to the ricotta together with the vanilla, cinnamon, liqueur, and the pistachio nuts. Put the ricotta in the mold, level off the top, cover with slices of sponge cake, and let cool for several hours. Unmold on a platter and finish the cassata.

For the fondant, over medium heat, melt the sugar with water and then add the glucose. Stir the fondant and add pistachio paste, liqueur, and orange flower water. The texture should be of a semifluid icing with a light green color. Spread the top of the *cassata* with apricot jelly. Cover with the fondant, and garnish with the rest of the candied fruit. The fruit should be of various colors and the decoration can be very imaginative.

Variation:
The above glaze is the classical, but you may wrap the *cassata* with almond paste (marzipan), and decorate with the candied fruit the same way.

Marzipan
1 cup almonds, peeled
⅓ cup orange flower water
1 cup confectioner's sugar

Grind the almonds to a paste. Add the orange flower water. Over medium heat, cook the almond paste and the sugar until the sugar is melted and incorporated into the almond paste. Cool and roll it out with a rolling pin. Cover the *cassata* with it.

CASTAGNACCIO (Chestnut Crust)

SERVES **8**
3½ cups chestnut flour
¼ cup sugar
Pinch of salt
4 cups cold water
3 tablespoons olive oil
1 tablespoon grated orange zest
4 tablespoons raisins, soaked and squeezed
2 tablespoons pine nuts
2 tablespoons walnuts, coarsely chopped
1 cup warm milk or as needed
Rosemary needles

Preheat the oven to 425°F. Sift the chestnut flour. Add the sugar and salt. Add the cold water in a thin stream, beating constantly with a whisk so as not to form lumps. Add the oil, orange zest, raisins, pine nuts, and walnuts. Gradually add the warm milk until you have a stiff consistency. Pour the batter into a greased shallow baking pan large enough for crust to be ½ inch thick. Drizzle some oil, add the rosemary needles, and bake for 1 hour. Serve warm or cold.

Note:
The crust can also be served with whipped cream.

CHIACCHIERE (Puff Pastry Strips)

SERVES 10 TO 12
3½ cups all-purpose flour
5 tablespoons sugar
Pinch of salt
1 teaspoon vanilla extract
3 eggs
1 tablespoon dry white wine, or more if needed
Corn oil, for frying
2 tablespoons confectioner's sugar

Mix the flour, sugar, salt, and vanilla on a pastry board, making a *fontana* (fountain) in the center. Break the eggs into the *fontana* and add the wine. Knead about 10 minutes, moistening with an additional spoonful of wine if needed. Wrap the dough in a cloth and let rest in a cool place for about 1 hour. Knead it again for a short while and then make a ⅛-inch-thick sheet.

Cut the dough with a pastry wheel into 3-inch-wide and 4-inch-long pieces, and make 3 vertical incisions on each piece with a pastry wheel. Deep-fry the pieces of dough. Drain of excess oil on paper towels. Place on a platter, dust with confectioner's sugar, and serve.

COLOMBA PASQUALE (Easter Dove)

1 ounce brewer's yeast
4¾ cups all-purpose flour
6 egg yolks
7 ounces butter, softened
½ cup confectioner's sugar
1 teaspoon grated lemon zest
Pinch of salt
⅓ cup warm milk
4 ounces candied lemon and orange peel, diced
3 ounces almonds, blanched
1 teaspoon granulated sugar

Preheat oven to 375°. Dissolve the yeast in some warm water and mix it with ¼ cup flour. Make a rather stiff dough and make a cross-like incision on the top. Roll the dough in flour and put it into a bowl with 1 cup warm water for 30 minutes. Occasionally turn the dough when it floats to the surface.

Knead the remaining flour separately with 5 of the egg yolks, 4 ounces butter, the confectioner's sugar, the lemon zest, salt, and warm milk. Add the leavened dough and knead until the dough is smooth and rather compact. Let the dough rise in a warm place until increased by a third in size. Knead the dough once more, adding half of the remaining butter in pieces. Put the dough back in the bowl to rise until doubled in size. Put the dough on the pastry board once more and knead in the remaining butter and the candied peel. Shape the dough like a dove, or place it in a dove-shaped mold, and let rise for 30 minutes.

Preheat the oven to 375°F. Brush the dough with the remaining egg yolk, top the surface with almonds, pressing them in slightly, and then sprinkle with granulated sugar. Bake for 30 minutes. Lower the heat to 325°F and bake for another 20 minutes.

Colomba pasquale can be served for breakfast as a coffee cake.

COTOGNATA (Quince Preserve)

MAKES 4 CUPS
   2 pounds whole quinces
   1 pound sugar
   Juice of 1 lemon

Remove the cores of the quinces and cook in boiling water until very tender to the fork. Drain and cool. Peel and sieve the pulp and add the sugar and lemon juice. Cook this mixture over medium heat for 15 minutes, stirring occasionally.

Pour the mixture into a flat sheet pan. Let it dry in a cool and airy place. When a light film of sugar has formed on top, turn it over so that it can dry on the other side. This will take 2 days.

Note:
Cotognata is a typical Sicilian dessert. It is customary to prepare it in small molds of various shapes, but it is made in many other regions of Italy.

CROSTATA DI FRUTTA (Fruit Tart)

SERVES 8
   3½ cups all-purpose flour
   1 cup sugar
   Grated zest of 1 orange
   8 ounces butter, softened

1 tablespoon honey
3 egg yolks
1 tablespoon butter for greasing tart pan
1 tablespoon granulated sugar for dusting the tart pan
2 cups fruit preserves or marmalade

Preheat the oven to 350°F. Mix the flour with the cup of sugar and the orange zest. Knead in the softened butter in pieces, the honey, and 2 of the egg yolks. Knead just enough to make a firm dough. Let the dough rest for 1 hour in a cool place. Use two thirds of the pastry to line a buttered, sugar-dusted tart pan. Spread the fruit preserves or marmalade over the pastry. Brush the remaining dough with a beaten egg yolk. Use this dough to make strips. Lay them over the tart in a criss-cross pattern. Bake for about 35 minutes, or until the top is golden brown.

GUBANA (Pastry and Candy Roll)

Puff Pastry
5¼ cups all-purpose flour
Pinch of salt
½ cup cold water
2 tablespoons grappa
8 ounces butter, at room temperature

Filling
4 tablespoons raisins
1 cup Marsala
5 ounces walnuts, shelled and chopped
4 tablespoons almonds, shelled and chopped
4 tablespoons pine nuts
2 ounces candied lemon and orange peel
1 tablespoon breadcrumbs
2 tablespoons butter
Grated zest of 1 orange
Grated zest of 1 lemon
2 egg yolks
1 egg white
Butter for greasing pan
1 tablespoon sugar for dusting pan

Mix the flour, salt, water, and grappa until the dough is soft and elastic. Let the dough rest for 20 minutes, wrapped in a kitchen towel. Remove dough from the towel, and roll it into a ¼-inch-thick square. Place the butter in the center of the dough. Fold each side of the dough over the center. Roll the dough out again. Wrap it again and let it rest for 15 minutes in the refrigerator. Remove, fold the dough, and roll it out again, always rolling in the same direction.

Repeat this operation three times, refrigerating in between. After the last roll, chill the dough for at least 15 minutes before proceeding.

Preheat the oven to 375°F.

While the pastry is resting, make the filling. Soften the raisins in the Marsala and squeeze out the excess liqueur. Put the walnuts, almonds, pine nuts, raisins, and candied peel into a bowl. Fry the breadcrumbs in 2 tablespoons butter and combine with the nuts and the grated orange and lemon zests. Mix well, then add 1 egg yolk and a stiffly beaten egg white. Roll out the puff pastry into a thin rectangle. Spread the filling on top of it. Roll and fold in the filling. Place the rolled-up dough in a buttered and sugar-dusted baking pan. Brush with the remaining egg yolk and sprinkle with sugar. Bake for about 50 minutes, or until it is golden brown.

Variation:

This specialty from the northeast of Italy can also be made with leavened dough. In some Friuli provinces, *gubana* is a simple crust made with melted butter, water, and flour.

PANETTONE (Panettone)

Almost every region in Italy has its own Christmas cake, but this Milanese specialty is by far the most famous—and the most difficult to make. *Panettone* is available in both a high, dome-shaped and a flat version. Natural yeast (that is, leavened dough) is essential to making real *panettone;* if the cake is made directly from brewer's yeast, its flavor is less delicate. The process of letting the dough rise must be carried out according to very specific instructions so that the result has a soft and airy texture. Rising time depends on many factors, including room temperature, the season, and the length of the mixing process. The timing given in the recipe can therefore only be approximate. Follow each step carefully for best results.

SERVES 8 TO 10

1 ounce natural yeast (see above)
¾ cup all-purpose flour
Warm water, as needed
3½ cups all-purpose flour
7 tablespoons sugar
1 egg
5 egg yolks
Salt
4 ounces butter, melted

6 tablespoons raisins
2 ounces candied orange and lemon peel, diced
1 tablespoon butter

Mix the yeast with the flour and as much water as necessary for the dough to be elastic. Wrap in a towel and put into a warm draft-free place (an unlit oven, for example) until doubled in size, about 30 minutes, and the surface is uneven. Make a small *fontana* (fountain) with 4 tablespoons of the flour and the crumbled fermented dough, add ½ cup warm water, and knead until the dough is elastic. Let rise in a warm place for 3 hours. Punch down the dough and then knead in another 4 tablespoons flour with as much warm water as necessary. Place the dough in a warm place to rise for 2 hours. Combine the sugar, egg, and egg yolks. Whisk well together, using a double boiler so that the mixture becomes light and airy. Let cool.

Make another *fontana* with the remaining flour. Put in the middle a pinch of salt, the risen dough, the butter, and the egg mixture. Knead energetically for 20 minutes. When the dough is smooth and elastic, add the raisins and candied peel. Grease and flour a sheet of wax paper and place the dough in the center. Place it into a round mold about 8 inches in diameter and 6 inches high and let rise in a warm place for at least 6 hours, or until the dough has doubled in size.

When the dough has risen, preheat the oven to 400°F. Cut a cross on top of the cake with a sharp knife and put 1 tablespoon butter in the middle. Bake the *panettone* for 40 to 45 minutes. The cake is ready when a skewer inserted in the center comes out dry. Let cool in the mold. *Panettone* can be used as a sweet bread for breakfast or as a coffee cake.

PANFORTE DI SIENA (Siena Fruit Cake)

This specialty from Siena is usually served in the winter, especially at Christmas and New Year's Eve. This cake is flatter and denser and more chewy than the fruitcake we know in the United States.

MAKES A 10- TO 12-INCH CAKE
2 teaspoons ground cinnamon
1½ cups all-purpose flour
4 peppercorns
½ teaspoon cloves
1 teaspoon coriander seeds
Pinch of nutmeg
1 ounce candied orange peel
8 ounces candied melon rind
4 ounces walnuts
8 ounces almonds, blanched and roasted

1 cup sugar
1 tablespoon honey
Wafers, to line mold

Preheat the oven to 350°F. Mix 1 teaspoon of cinnamon with 2 tablespoons of flour (a mixture known as *polverino*). Set aside. Pound the peppercorns, cloves, and coriander seeds. Mix the resulting powder with the remaining cinnamon and nutmeg (this mixture is locally known as *droghe*). Dice the candied fruit and mince the walnuts and mix with the whole almonds. Sift in the remaining flour and combine all the ingredients (except the *polverino,* water, honey, and wafers) together. Set aside. Cook the sugar with 2 tablespoons water in an unlined copper pan until browned and caramelized. Knead the previously set-aside mixture into the cooked sugar and add the honey until you get a smooth mixture. Butter and dust with flour a 10-inch round cake mold. Cover the bottom with thin, flat wafers and pour in the mixture (it will probably be about ¼ inch thick), sprinkling generously with the *polverino*. Bake for 30 to 40 minutes. Let set and cool in the mold. Remove *panforte* from the mold and serve. The cake may be kept for 2 to 3 weeks.

PASTIERA NAPOLETANA (Easter Cheese and Grain Pie)

This is a Neapolitan specialty and is traditionally made for Easter.

MAKES A **12-INCH PIE**

Filling
4 cups wheat berries
6 cups milk
Grated zest of 1 lemon
1 teaspoon ground cinnamon
1 teaspoon vanilla extract
Salt
2 cups sugar
3 cups ricotta
10 eggs, separated, whites beaten
3 ounces candied orange and lemon peel, diced
2 tablespoons orange flower water
2 tablespoons butter
2 tablespoons confectioner's sugar

Pastry
3½ cups all-purpose flour
8 ounces butter, chilled

1 cup sugar
3 egg yolks

For the filling, soak the wheat berries in water for about 1 week, changing the water every day. Drain and boil with fresh water for 15 minutes. Drain and put back in a pot with the milk, lemon zest, cinnamon, vanilla, a pinch of salt, and 1 tablespoon of sugar. Bring to a boil, lower the heat, and cook over low heat until the milk is absorbed.

Preheat the oven to 375°F.

For the pastry, knead the flour, butter, sugar, and egg yolks together quickly. Make a ball of the dough and let rest in the refrigerator for at least 1 hour.

Remove and discard the lemon zest. Sieve the *ricotta* into a mixing bowl. Add the rest of the sugar and whisk until creamy. Add 9 of the egg yolks, the wheat berries, diced candied peel, and orange flower water. Fold in the beaten egg whites. Grease a 12-inch baking pan with butter and dust with sugar. Line with three quarters of the pastry. Add the filling. Roll out the remaining dough and cut into strips. Arrange the strips over the filling in a lattice design. Brush the dough with the remaining egg yolk. Bake the cake for 40 minutes, or until the filling has set and the crust is golden brown. Sprinkle with confectioner's sugar before serving.

Notes:

Pastiera is best if eaten a day after it is cooked. It keeps in the refrigerator for 1 week.

Wheat berries are also sold pre-cooked and softened, sealed in plastic bags.

SFOGLIATELLA RICCIA (Seashell-Shaped Flaky Ricotta Pastries)

MAKES 6

1 cup water
Salt
⅞ cup semolina
½ cup all-purpose flour
6 ounces butter, melted
Pinch of salt
½ cup ricotta
½ cup confectioner's sugar
Pinch of cinnamon
3 ounces candied orange peel, diced
1 egg yolk

Bring the water to a boil. Add a pinch of salt and pour in the semolina, stirring so as not to form any lumps. Cook for about 8 minutes, stirring constantly. Let cool. Make a *fontana* (fountain) with the flour. Put half of the butter, a pinch of salt, and as much water as necessary to knead the dough to a smooth and elastic consistency. Wrap the dough in a towel and let rest for 1 hour. Sieve the *ricotta*. Mix with the *semolina,* 6 tablespoons confectioner's sugar, a pinch of cinnamon, and the candied orange peel. Roll out the pastry with a rolling pin to obtain a 25 by 18-inch rectangle, 1/16 inch thick. Cut the pastry vertically into 4 strips and place one on top of the other, brushing each one with melted butter. Let rest for 30 minutes and then roll up the stack of dough.

Preheat the oven to 375°F. Slice the roll into 10 equal pieces with a very sharp, floured knife. Place the pieces on the pastry board and roll them gently with the rolling pin, first vertically, in an upward direction, and then in a downward direction, to give them an oval shape. Turn the oval disks over, place a bit of *ricotta* filling in the middle of each one, brush the edges with egg yolk, then fold the dough over and press to seal. Brush the *sfogliatelle* with melted butter and place on a parchment paper greased with butter. Bake for 20 minutes. Remove from the oven. Brush with melted butter again, lower the temperature to 325°F, and bake for another 20 minutes. Let cool, sprinkle with confectioner's sugar, and serve.

STRUFOLI (Honey Balls)

MAKES 1 POUND

Dough
3 1/2 *cups all-purpose flour*
4 *eggs*
2 *egg yolks*
1 *ounce butter*
1 *tablespoon sugar*
Grated zest of 1/2 *lemon*
Pinch of salt
Corn oil, for frying

Topping
1 *cup honey*
4 *ounces finely diced candied orange and lemon peel*

Make a *fontana* (fountain) with the flour on a pastry board. Add the eggs and the egg yolks, butter, sugar, lemon zest, and pinch of salt. Knead into a smooth but firm dough. Cut the dough into pieces. Roll them into long cylinders 1/2 inch in diameter and cut each of these into 1/4-inch nuggets. Use up all the dough and place the nuggets on a floured surface. Fry the *strufoli* in hot oil, a few at a time. When golden, drain them well and dry on paper towels to drain of excess oil. Put the honey in a saucepan (preferably with a concave bottom) and bring to a boil. Simmer until the foam subsides and the honey turns golden. Turn the heat down very low and add the *strufoli* with the candied orange and lemon peel. Mix well, coating all the *strufoli* evenly. Place on a dish and mold them into the desired shape (flat, round, or cylindrical) with wet hands. Always serve at room temperature. Do not refrigerate.

TIRAMISÙ (Tiramisù)

SERVES 8

3 egg yolks
6 tablespoons sugar
12 ounces mascarpone
1 cup strong espresso
2 tablespoons brandy
3 dozens ladyfingers
2 tablespoons cocoa
6 tablespoons amaretti, crushed

Beat the egg yolks with 4 tablespoons of the sugar. Add the *mascarpone* and continue to beat very well until the mixture is smooth. Add the remaining sugar, ½ cup of *espresso,* and the brandy. Mix well to achieve a smooth consistency. Moisten the ladyfingers with the remaining *espresso.* Line the sides of an 8-inch mold with the ladyfingers. Pour the *mascarpone* mixture into the mold. Refrigerate for about 2 hours. Just before serving, mix the cocoa powder with the crushed *amaretti* and sprinkle evenly over the top. *Tiramisù* should be served cool, but not frozen.

TORRONE (Nougat)

⅓ cup sugar
6 tablespoons water
2 tablespoons honey
4 egg whites
1 cup shelled hazelnuts, lightly toasted
1 ounce candied orange and citron peel
Grated zest of 2 lemons
Large unleavened wafer sheets

Cook the sugar with water until it reaches the hard-ball stage and set aside. Cook the honey in a double boiler, stirring constantly until foamy. Whip the egg whites until stiff. Fold them into the honey and then add the cooked sugar. Continue mixing until the mixture begins to harden. Add the hazelnuts, candied peel, and the grated lemon zest. Mix thoroughly. Line a shallow rectangular baking pan with the thin sheets of wafer. Pour in the mixture, making an even layer. Top with another layer of wafers. Cover with a wooden board and weight the board down. Let stand for 30 minutes. Turn the baking pan over onto a board. Let it rest for another 30 minutes. The *torrone* is now ready. You can cut it into any shape you wish. Stored at room temperature, *torrone* keeps for a long time, wrapped in wax paper or aluminum foil.

TORTA DI CAROTE (Carrot Cake)

MAKES A 10-INCH CAKE
½ pound small carrots
5 eggs, separated
1 cup sugar
8 ounces blanched almonds, ground
Grated zest of 1 lemon
1 teaspoon cornstarch
2 tablespoons rum
1 ounce butter

Preheat the oven to 350°F. Wash and peel the carrots. Grate them onto a cloth. Cover with another cloth and let stand for about 1 hour to dry. Whip the egg whites and all but 1 tablespoon of the sugar to a stiff meringue. Fold in the carrots, almonds, lemon zest, and cornstarch. Whip in the egg yolks, one at a time. Add the rum, stirring gently. Butter and dust a 10-inch cake pan with the remaining sugar. Pour in the mixture. Bake for about 40 minutes. Let cool before serving.

TORTA SABBIOSA (Sandy Cake)

MAKES A 10-INCH CAKE
3 ounces butter
6 tablespoons confectioner's sugar
3 eggs, separated
⅔ cup all-purpose flour
Pinch of baking soda
3 tablespoons potato starch
Pinch of salt

Preheat the oven to 350°F. Whip the butter with the sugar until it reaches a creamy consistency. Add the egg yolks, one at a time. Sift in the flour, baking soda, potato starch, and a pinch of salt. Beat the egg whites until stiff and add to the batter. Mix well and put it into a 10-inch cake pan lined with buttered parchment paper. Level the top. Bake for about 30 minutes. Remove from oven and cool.

Notes:
This cake is best if eaten the day after baking.
    It will keep for several days if wrapped in aluminum foil and refrigerated.

TORTELLI DI CARNEVALE (Puffed Tortelli)

SERVES 6

1 cup water
Pinch of salt
8 ounces butter
8 ounces all-purpose flour
4 eggs, separated
Grated zest of 1 lemon
¼ cup sugar
Olive oil, for frying
3 tablespoons confectioner's sugar

Bring 1 cup of water to a boil in a small saucepan. Add salt and butter. When the butter is melted, turn the heat off and add the flour all at once. Mix well with a wooden spoon. Turn on the heat again and cook, stirring constantly, for 10 minutes or until the mixture separates from the sides of the pan and begins to sizzle. Turn the heat off and let cool. When the mixture has cooled, beat the egg yolks into the batter, one at a time. Add the lemon zest and the sugar. Mix well. Beat the whites until stiff. Fold them into the batter. Let stand for 1 hour. Heat a good quantity of oil. Drop the batter by the teaspoonful into the oil. The resulting *tortelli* will swell. If there is enough oil they will turn by themselves. Once cooked, drain on absorbent paper and keep in a warm place. Arrange the *tortelli* into a pyramid on a napkin-lined serving dish. Sprinkle with confectioner's sugar and serve.

ZABAGLIONE (Eggnog with Marsala)

SERVES 4

4 egg yolks
¼ cup sugar
4 tablespoons Marsala

Warm the egg yolks and the sugar in a double boiler over low heat and then whip them with a wire whisk. Pour the Marsala into the yolks, drop by drop, and keep beating. The mixture will begin to foam and then swell into a light, soft cream. Do not overcook or it will collapse.

Note:
Cinnamon and grated lemon zest may be added before pouring in the Marsala.

Marsala can be replaced with a high-quality white, sweet, dry, or sparkling wine. Brandy or cherry brandy may also be used.

ZEPPOLE (Sweet Fritters)

Every region of Italy has its own fritter variation. This one comes from the Neapolitan region and it is traditional for the feast of St. Joseph on March 19.

MAKES 24

2¼ pounds potatoes
7 ounces butter, melted
8 eggs
1 teaspoon salt
¼ teaspoon vanilla extract
½ cup sugar, plus more for coating cooked zeppole
Grated zest of 2 lemons
½ cup lukewarm milk
1½ ounces yeast
2½ cups flour
Corn oil, for frying

Boil, cool, peel, and rice the potatoes. Make a well in the center; add butter, eggs, salt, vanilla, sugar, and lemon zest. Proof the yeast with the lukewarm milk, and add it to the potato mixture. Work the mixture gently, adding as much flour as necessary to achieve a smooth dough. When done, form the *zeppole*. Cut the dough into equal parts; roll each piece out to form a cylinder about ½ inch thick. Cut into 5-inch-long pieces and overlap the two ends. Flour a sheet pan and place each *zeppola* on it. Let the *zeppole* rise until doubled in size. Fry them in corn oil until golden brown, then drain them on absorbent paper. Have a container ready with granulated sugar; roll each *zeppola* in the sugar while still hot. Place on a platter and serve.

ZUPPA INGLESE (Italian English Trifle)

SERVES 8

1 quart milk
8 eggs, separated
1 cup confectioner's sugar
½ vanilla bean
1 tablespoon flour
1 sponge cake (see page 272)
2 tablespoons Curaçao or Grand Marnier liqueur
2 tablespoons rum
3 tablespoons raspberry preserves

Warm the milk; add the egg yolks, ¾ cup of the sugar, vanilla, and flour. Keep mixing over low heat until you get a smooth cream, but do not allow it to boil. Cut the sponge cake into slices about ½ inch thick and 1 inch wide. Arrange a layer of sponge cake in a deep serving dish; sprinkle with half of the liqueur to moisten. Spread with 1 tablespoon of raspberry preserves. Pour one-third of the cream over the preserves. Repeat the layers 2 more times, sprinkling the last layer with rum. Whip the egg whites until foamy. Add the remaining sugar and whip until stiff and glossy. Cover the cake with the meringue. Brown the meringue with a blowtorch or in the salamander.

Notes:
Zuppa inglese can be round and flat or egg-shaped. It may also be prepared in a bowl.

The cream may be divided into 2 flavors such as vanilla and chocolate.

In Italy, this dish is prepared with the liqueur Alchermes, but it may be substituted for with Curaçao or Grand Marnier, as indicated in the recipe.

GELATO (Ice Cream)

Gelato has ancient origins. It is believed that the Arabs introduced it to the western world through Sicily. The Greeks and the Turks were also known to prepare lemon-based mixtures that resembled *sorbetto* (sherbets).

It was Caterina de' Medici who brought a Sicilian ice cream maker (whose name has been lost) to the court of Henry II in France in 1533. It was another Sicilian, Procopio dei Coltelli, who opened the famous Café Procope in Paris, opposite the Comédie Française. It was patronized by actors, nobles, and scholars such as Voltaire, who made enthusiastic remarks about the café's sherbets. Procopio's specialties were made with fruit juice mixed with shaved ice and flavored with jasmine or rose.

Sherbets were thought to have a beneficial effect on the nervous and digestive systems. They were usually served between main courses, actually after the first few meat and fish dishes, at sumptuous eighteenth- and nineteenth-century banquets. It was only later that richer ingredients such as egg yolks, sugar, milk, and cream began to be used for what is known today as *gelato alla crema* (ice cream).

Gelati are classified according to the ingredients used.

GELATO (Ice Cream)

Ice cream made in an ice-cream machine. It contains cream or milk, sugar, and egg yolk. A fruit-based sherbet is also called *gelato* in Italy.

SORBETTO (Sherbets)

Sherbet contains fruit juices or crushed fruit and sugar, with the occasional addition of wine or liqueur.

CASSATA E BOMBA (Ice Cream Molds)

Molds are made of *gelati* of two or more flavors. Often the molds can be lined with ice cream and filled with chilled creams. Molds may be flat, round, or heart-shaped, flowers, or geometrical figures. The forms are filled, closed tightly, and frozen. The dessert is removed from the mold when ready to eat.

TORTA GELATO (Ice Cream Cake)

Any round mold can be used to prepare ice cream cakes, but it must be lined with parchment paper and chilled in the freezer before using. Using a springform mold is easiest. More than one flavor of ice cream can be used as long as the flavors are complementary. Meringue disks, candied fruit, sponge cake, or ladyfingers are often used in preparing these cakes, which must then be frozen for several hours. Once the cake is ready, it is removed from the mold, placed on a serving dish, and garnished with whipped cream, candied fruit, or other desired toppings.

SEMIFREDDO (Chilled Cream)

A typical Italian dessert, chilled cream is prepared with an egg-based custard and whipped cream. No ice-cream machine is needed to make *semifreddo;* the basic mixture can be poured directly into the mold and put in the freezer for a few hours.

Semifreddo is also called *spumone.* All *semifreddi* or *spumoni* may be served with an appropriate sauce. These range from simple fruit sauce to the richest vanilla cream.

GRANITA (Flavored Ices)

This is a very light, frozen slush, using juice, fruit pulp, or coffee with sugar and (optional) liqueur added. Unlike ice cream or sherbet, *granita* must be frozen in a pan of plastic or stainless steel. It should be stirred from time to time so that the sides and the top do not freeze solid. If it is frozen solid, churn before serving so as to yield a granular texture. The sugar and/or liqueur will keep the *granita* from freezing solid. *Granita* is served in a long-stemmed glass. Some flavors go well with whipped cream.

GELATI ALLA CREMA (Ice Cream)

GELATO (Ice Cream)

MAKES 1½ QUARTS
   1 *quart whole milk*
   Grated zest of 1 lemon

Pinch of salt
10 egg yolks
1 cup sugar

Bring all but ½ cup of the milk to a boil in a stainless steel saucepan (do not use aluminum), adding the lemon zest and a pinch of salt. Remove from heat. Whip the egg yolks with the sugar in a bowl. Add the cold ½ cup of milk. Add the hot milk a little at a time. Put the mixture in a pot over very low heat and cook for 20 minutes, stirring constantly. Do not let it come to a boil. When the mixture starts thickening, pour it into a bowl and cool. Stir frequently. Strain through a fine sieve. Once entirely cooled, the mixture can be used as a base to churn a flavored ice cream.

Note:
Churning time to make ice cream varies depending on the ice-cream machine used. An ice-cream freezer holds the temperature just below freezing.

GELATO AL CIOCCOLATO (Chocolate Ice Cream)

MAKES 2½ QUARTS
8 ounces bitter chocolate
1 quart milk
1 quart heavy cream
12 egg yolks
1½ cups sugar

Break the chocolate into chunks and melt over low heat. Prepare the ice cream base following the same procedure as in basic recipe (pages 287–88). Add the melted chocolate when the ice cream is taken off the heat. Stir well. When the mix is cool, strain through a sieve, if necessary. Put in an ice-cream machine and churn.

GELATO ALLA VANIGLIA (Vanilla Ice Cream)

MAKE 1½ QUARTS

Use the same ingredients, except substitute vanilla beans for the lemon zest. Proceed as in the basic recipe (pages 287–88). Use as much vanilla as needed to achieve the desired flavor.

GELATI ALLA FRUTTA O SORBETTI (Sherbets)

GELATO AL LIMONE (Lemon Sherbet)

MAKES 2 QUARTS

1½ cups granulated sugar
4 cups water
10 lemons
10 cubes lump sugar
Juice of 2 oranges
2 egg whites

Make a syrup with the granulated sugar and water over low heat until the sugar has entirely dissolved. Reduce by a third, remove from the heat, and set aside. Wash the lemons and rub them with the lump sugar until all the sugar is thoroughly scented with lemon. Add the lump sugar to the syrup and cool. Squeeze the juice from the lemons and the oranges. Add to the syrup, mixing well. Strain the resulting juice. Whip the egg whites thoroughly. Gently fold them into the mixture and churn. Keep sherbet in the ice-cream freezer until ready to serve.

GELATO ALL' ARANCIA (Orange Sherbet)

MAKES 2 QUARTS

Use the same ingredients and procedure as in the recipe for Lemon Sherbet, but add 6 tablespoons orange liqueur or substitute blood-orange juice made with 10 oranges and 2 lemons for the 10 lemons and 2 oranges to give the *gelato* a brighter color.

GELATO AL MANDARINO (Tangerine Sherbet)

MAKES 2 QUARTS

Use the same ingredients and procedure as in the two preceding recipes, substituting 10 tangerines and 2 lemons for the 10 lemons. Halfway through preparing the ice mixture, add 6 tablespoons tangerine liqueur.

GELATO ALLA FRAGOLA (Strawberry Sherbet)

MAKES 2 QUARTS

1 quart water
¼ cup sugar
3 vanilla beans

1 pound strawberries
Juice of ½ lemon
Juice of ½ orange

Bring the water to a boil in a stainless steel saucepan. Mix in and dissolve the sugar. Add the vanilla and let cool. Meanwhile, wash the strawberries in ice-cold water. Pass them through a non-metal sieve or a food mill. Mix the resulting puree with the strained lemon and orange juice. When the sugar syrup has cooled, add the strawberry purée. Mix well and churn the mixture in an ice-cream machine.

GELATO AL MELONE (Watermelon Sherbet)

MAKES 3 QUARTS
2 pounds watermelon pulp
4 tablespoons jasmine flower water or orange flower water
3 cups sugar
7 ounces chocolate, finely minced
3 ounces pistachio nuts, shelled and chopped
7 ounces finely diced candied pumpkin
1 tablespoon ground cinnamon

Sieve the melon. Mix the resulting puree with the jasmine water and 1½ cups sugar. Pour the mixture into the ice-cream machine and churn. Mix the resulting sherbet with the chocolate, pistachio nuts, candied pumpkin, 1 teaspoon of the cinnamon, and the remaining sugar. Stir gently and pour the mixture into a round mold, preferably lined with greased paper. Cover and freeze for at least 2 hours. Remove the sherbet from the mold and sprinkle with cinnamon before serving.

Note:
If possible, decorate with jasmine flowers or lemon leaves.

CASSATA E BOMBA (Ice Cream Molds)

To make a *cassata* or *bomba*, you'll need a special mold with removable top and bottom covers. *Bombe* consist of one or more varieties of *gelati*. In the past they were prepared and stored in spherical molds; today a semi-spherical mold is used. Generally, molds are made with ice cream on the outside and a light and fluffy chilled cream or custard on the inside. Candied fruit, hazelnuts, pralines, and cookies soaked in liqueur are often mixed into the filling. To remove from the mold, immerse the mold in warm water up to its rim for a few seconds. Shake the ice cream out onto a serving dish and cut into 2-inch slices to serve.

BOMBA FANTASIA (Southern Ice Cream Mold)

SERVES **12**

1 tablespoon pistachio nuts
4 tablespoons almonds, chopped
4 figs, chopped
4 dates, chopped
2 tablespoons Curaçao
1 quart sweetened heavy cream, whipped
2 pints vanilla ice cream, softened

Combine the nuts, dried fruit, and Curaçao. Mix this with the whipped cream. Line a spherical mold with vanilla ice cream and fill the center with the whipped cream mixture. Freeze for at least 2 hours. Remove from freezer 1 hour before serving and place in the refrigerator. Unmold just before serving. Slice and serve.

CASSATA GELATO AL PISTACCHIO (Pistachio Ice Cream Mold)

MAKES 1½ QUARTS

2 pints pistachio ice cream
3 ounces mixed candied fruit, chopped
2 tablespoons rum
⅔ cup heavy cream
4 tablespoons caramel-coated almonds
2 egg whites
4 tablespoons confectioner's sugar

Put a semi-spherical mold into the freezer to chill. Soften the ice cream just until spreadable. Line the inside of the mold, leaving the center empty. Put the mold back into the freezer. Soften the candied fruit with rum and drain. Whip the cream. Stir in the candied fruit and the almonds. Beat the egg whites and sugar until stiff. Add to the whipped cream. Fill the center of the mold with this mixture. Put the mold back into the freezer for at least 2 hours. Follow the same procedure as for *bomba fantasia,* above.

Note:
Cassate can also be made in round cake molds.

SEMIFREDDO ALLO ZABAGLIONE (Eggnog Chilled Cream)

SERVES **6**

8 egg yolks
1 cup sugar

1 cup dry Marsala
1 pint heavy cream, whipped stiff
1 pound ladyfingers, as needed

Whip the egg yolks with the sugar in a saucepan. Add ¼ cup of Marsala, a tablespoon at a time. Place the saucepan over a bain-marie and continue whipping until the mixture is foamy. Pour the mixture in a bowl and let cool. Fold in the stiff whipped cream. Pour the mixture into a mold lined with ladyfingers moistened with Marsala. Freeze for at least 5 hours and serve.

ZUCCOTTO (Chocolate and Curaçao Chilled Cream)

This is a specialty from Florence.

SERVES 8
1 sponge cake (see page 272)
4 ounces chocolate, minced
1 quart whipped cream
⅓ cup confectioner's sugar
1 teaspoon vanilla extract
¼ cup Curaçao
3 ounces mixed almonds and hazelnuts, roasted and minced
2 tablespoons cocoa powder

Cut the sponge cake into strips and use it to line a spherical mold. Melt half of the chocolate in a double boiler over medium heat. Pour the whipped cream in a mixing bowl; add the confectioner's sugar, vanilla, half the Curaçao, and minced nuts. Lightly moisten the sponge cake with liqueur. Spoon in half of the whipped cream. Mix the remaining whipped cream with the minced chocolate. Scoop this into the mold, filling it to the top. Seal with more sponge cake strips and moisten with liqueur. Put the *zuccotto* in the freezer for about 4 hours. Make a funnel of wax paper. Fill it with melted chocolate. Make small disks of chocolate on another piece of wax paper and let harden. Remove the *zuccotto* from the freezer 1 hour before serving. Unmold it onto a serving dish, sprinkle with sugar, and garnish with chocolate disks and cocoa powder. Slice and serve.

GRANITA (Ices)

GRANITA AL LIMONE (Basic Lemon Ice)

SERVES 4
2 cups lemon juice
1 cup water
2 tablespoons sugar

Stir together all the ingredients, making sure that the sugar is completely dissolved. Strain the syrup into a flat pan and place in freezer. Scrape occasionally while freezing and churn before serving.

GRANITA AL CAFFÈ (Coffee Ice)

SERVES 6

12 cups espresso
2 tablespoons sugar
1 pint heavy cream, whipped

Follow the recipe for Lemon Ice. Serve topped with whipped cream.

GRANITA AL CIOCCOLATO (Chocolate Ice)

SERVES 4

2 cups plus 6 tablespoons water
2 tablespoons cocoa powder
3 cups sugar
2 tablespoons chocolate liqueur
1 pint heavy cream, whipped

Bring 6 tablespoons of water to a boil and stir in the cocoa. When dissolved, add 2 cups of water and the sugar. Let cool. Follow the basic recipe. Add the liqueur. Serve topped with whipped cream.

GLOSSARY OF WORDS
AND EXPRESSIONS

The following terms, currently in use in Italian cuisine, can be found throughout this book. They form an essential vocabulary for those interested in Italian food.

Abbacchio: Milk-fed baby lamb slaughtered before it is weaned.

Acciugata: Salted anchovies seasoned with olive oil, garlic, chopped parsley, and lemon and left to marinate for an hour or two. It is served as a sauce with pan-broiled or roast beef.

Aceto balsamico: Balsamic vinegar, a specialty of Modena, made from the fermentation of *mosto* (must) aged at least 10 years. In the past it was produced only in a family attic and the recipe was passed from one generation to the next. Today it is also commercially produced.

Acqua di fiori d'arancia: Essence made from orange blossoms and leaves. Used in making desserts such as *pastiera napoletana.*

Acquacotta: Country soup made of onions, celery, and tomato browned in oil and diluted with water. It is served with hot pepper and toasted country bread.

Affettato misto: A term that indicates that various types of sliced salami and *salumi* are offered in the same dish.

Agliata: Sauce made of pounded garlic, oil, and crustless bread.

Agnolini or *Anolini:* Fresh stuffed pasta. In the Parma area, *agnolini* are made with the reduced cooking juices of braised meats. They are usually served in broth.

Agnolotti: Square-shaped egg pasta, filled with meat and vegetables, served either in a broth or with a sauce.

Agone: Freshwater shad, a fish quite common in northern lakes of Italy.

Agresto: The juice from green or unripe grapes, used to make a sauce of the same name, widely used from the fourteenth to the sixteenth century.

Agrodolce: Sweet-and-sour sauce. A very old sauce made of vinegar and sugar or of any other two contrasting ingredients.

Al dente: Pasta cooked *al dente* should have a somewhat chewy texture and should not become mushy when mixed with the desired condiments.

Al fiasco: Cooked in a glass flask or flask-shaped terra-cotta pot. A cooking method used especially with beans.

Al salto: A term used to describe a *risotto alla milanese* cooked, cooled, and then panfried with butter over high heat. The starch expelled from the grains of rice allows the rice to form a crunchy golden crust.

Al telefono: A term used to describe fritters with *mozzarella*. When bitten into, the fresh cheese in the fritters forms long strings like a telephone cord.

Alice: Fresh anchovy.

Alchermes: Liqueur of Arabic origin, perfected in Italy (also known as Alchermes of Florence). It is used almost exclusively in pastries, especially in *zuppa inglese*, for which it is an indispensable ingredient. It is illegal in the United States because it contains a colorant from an insect called cochineal (in Italian, *cocciniglia*).

All'onda: A Venetian term used to describe risotto that is cooked until creamy but semi-liquid in texture (wavy) when poured into a dish.

Amaretto: Cookie made of almonds, sugar, and egg white, crunchy outside and soft inside. Also, an almond liqueur.

Amatriciana: Hot sauce for *spaghetti* or *bucatini* made with *guanciale*, white wine, tomato, and *peperoncino*. It comes from the town of Amatrice in Lazio.

Anguilla: Eel. Eels live in fresh waters; they swim to the sea to spawn and then go back up rivers and lakes.

Anicino: Hard cookie made of flour, baking powder, eggs, sugar, and anise seeds.

Animelle: Sweetbreads.

Antipasto: Appetizer or hors d'oeuvre. *Antipasto* literally means "before the meal."

Appassire: A culinary term meaning to sauté over low heat so that the vegetables soften but do not brown. It may also mean sun-dried.

Appiattire: To flatten a steak or a piece of meat by pounding it with a mallet so as to break the tough meat fibers.

Aragosta: Spiny lobster. This crustacean is equipped with two antennas, no claws.

Aranciata: Sardinian *torrone* made with orange peel, honey, and almonds. In common Italian, it also means orangeade.

Arancino: Rice ball with or without a filling of meat *ragù,* peas, and cheese. *Arancini* are served as *antipasti*. In home kitchens they are made with leftover *risotto*.

Arista: Half saddle of pork roasted in the oven in its own fat. A traditional Tuscan pork preparation.

Arsella: A kind of small clam.

Artusi, Pellegrino: Banker and epicure from Emilia-Romagna who wrote *La Scienza in cucina e l'arte di mangiar bene (Science in the Kitchen and the Art of Eating Well)* in 1891.

Astice: Maine lobster, a crustacean with two large claws.

Babà: Neapolitan dessert made from leavened dough, soaked in syrup and liqueur; it may be topped with whipped cream or served with an orange sauce.

Baccalà: Large cod fillets preserved in salt and air-dried.

Baci di dama: Literally, "lady's kisses." Cookies made with two cookies stuck together with a filling of chocolate or cream.

Bagna cauda: In Piedmontese dialect, "warm dip." Typical Piedmontese sauce made of oil, garlic, and anchovies offered hot as a dip for raw vegetables.

Bagnet verd: The Piedmontese name for *salsa verde*. A sauce for boiled meats made of parsley, garlic, anchovies, crustless bread, and oil. It is used also for *bollito misto*.

Bagnomaria: Bain-marie. A double boiler.

Baicoli: Dry, crumbly cookies; a Venetian specialty to dip in wine or hot chocolate.

Ballotta: Chestnut boiled in its peel and flavored with bay leaves or fennel seeds. *Ballotte* are eaten plain or with wine as a snack.

Bamborino: Beef flank.

Barba de' frati: Literally, "monk's beard." Slightly acidic, long, thin string of a grass-like vegetable.

Barbagliata: Milanese beverage made of milk and chocolate.

Battuto: Herbs, most often parsley and garlic, finely minced together to be added to a finished dish. When sautéed in oil, with or without other minced vegetables, it is called *soffritto*.

Batù d'oca: Boned and salted goose, preserved in its own fat.

Bava: In dishes prepared *alla bava*, the cheese in the recipe melts to form elastic strings when eaten.

Bensone: Sponge cake covered with ground almonds.

Berlingozzo: Sweet, ring-shaped anise-flavored cake, a Tuscan specialty made during the *Carnevale* festival.

Bianchetti: Sardine and anchovy spawn.

Bianchi di Spagna or *spagnoni:* Large, white, kidney-shaped beans (much like Great Northerns in the United States).

Bianco: *In bianco* generally indicates a boiled food with no or very little condiment.

Bigoli: Large rustic fresh *spaghetti* made with a *torchio*.

Bisato: Term used for *anguilla* (eel) in the Veneto.

Biscottato: Said of bread re-baked to a crunchy consistency throughout. It may also refer to a cookie being baked the same way.

Bistecca alla fiorentina: Thick slab of beef cut from the rib with the filet still attached. Similar to a T-bone steak, it should be at least two inches thick and large enough for two to three people. It is usually broiled without fat.

Bitto: Soft, flavorful cheese from Valtellina. If aged, it hardens and can be grated.

Bocconotti: Puff pastry stuffed with chicken livers, sweetbreads, and truffles. It is served as an *antipasto*.

Boero: Liqueur-filled chocolate with a cherry in the center.

Bollito misto: A mix of boiled meats such as beef, veal, pork, and fowl. It is traditionally served with *salsa verde* or *mostarda di frutta*.

Bomba: Dome-shaped ice cream mold.

Bondiola: See Coppa.

Borlotti: Fat, pulpy, medium-sized beans, light brown in color, speckled with darker brown. The nearest U.S. equivalent is cranberry or pinto beans.

Bottarga: The ovary sac of either tuna or gray mullet. After removal from the fish, the sac is placed under a weight to discharge its liquids. It is then hung and air-dried.

The finished *bottarga* is coated with wax for better preservation. Gray mullet *bottarga* is milder than tuna. *Bottarga* is eaten thinly sliced, coated with extra virgin olive oil, and accompanied by a variety of food, as an *antipasto,* or chopped with *spaghetti.*

Braciola or *Braciolina:* Pork *involtino* stuffed with pine nuts and raisins used for *ragù napoletano.*

Brasato: Marinated cut of meat braised in its own marinade.

Bresaola: Cured meat from Valtellina made of very lean, cured dried beef. It is served very thinly sliced with lemon, oil, and freshly ground pepper as an *antipasto.*

Broccoletti di rape: Bitter winter green that grows in clusters on long, slender leaves with firm stems. This vegetable becomes *cime di rapa* when small yellow flowers or tiny green buds grow in the center of the leaf clusters. It is also known in the United States as broccoli rape.

Brodetto: Fish stew from Venice and the upper Adriatic made by cooking larger fish in a broth made with small fish.

Brosones: Fresh Piedmontese cheese preserved in a jar and fermented in vinegar, grappa, or other spirits.

Bruschetta: Slices of a large crusty loaf, toasted and rubbed with garlic cloves and seasoned with extra virgin olive oil and salt and pepper to taste. Chopped tomatoes may be added.

Brutti ma buoni: Literally, "ugly but good." Very simple, flat cookies made with almonds, sugar, and egg whites.

Bucatini: Thick spaghetti with a hole through the middle.

Buccellato: Leavened cake shaped like a round mold.

Bufala: The female of a breed of cattle from the Far East that have been in Italy since the Roman Empire. Today they are bred according to the most advanced technology to maximize milk production for *mozzarella di bufala.*

Burida: A classical fish stew from Genoa. *Burida* may also refer to a stew made with *stoccafisso* (stockfish) only.

Burrata: Fresh cheese from Apulia. On the outside it is stringy like *mozzarella* but inside it is filled with a mixture of creamy butter. In Andria (Bari), the outside is like *caciocavallo.*

Burrida: A Sardinian fish preparation. Using firm-fleshed fish such as catfish, the fish is boiled and covered with a condiment that contains walnuts and pine nuts. The preparation is then cooled and served at room temperature.

Busecca: Milanese term for a typical tripe recipe made with Spanish white beans and plenty of celery and carrots.

Busecchina: Milanese dessert of pureed fresh chestnuts combined with white wine and heavy cream and then baked.

Bussola: Traditional leavened sweet bread made with liqueur. A richer version has candied fruit, almonds, chocolate, and spices. It can also translate as "compass."

Cacciagione: Game.

Cacciatorino: Small, finely ground pork and beef salami.

Cacciucco: Thick Tuscan fish stew made with several types of fish and shellfish, vegetables, and garlic and served over sliced bread.

Caciocavallo: A cheese, made from cow milk, that has a mild, slightly salty flavor and firm, smooth texture when young. As it ages, the flavor becomes more pungent and the texture more granular.

Caciotta: This name is given to a wide range of cheeses produced both industrially and in dairies. Made of sheep or cow milk or a mixture of both, it is sold only slightly ripened. This cheese is white or yellowish, with a few or no holes, and generally has a delicate flavor. The crust is thin and ranges from light to darker yellow.

Caffè valdostano: Coffee served in the typical style of the Valle d'Aosta mountaineers. It is brewed in a special squat and short pot with at least four spouts. Then lemon peel and grappa are added, and it is flamed. It is drunk very hot straight from the spouts.

Cagnone (in): Term used to describe boiled rice served with butter and *Parmigiano.*

Calcioni: Little cookies with fresh *pecorino* filling. The dough is cut on the top so that some of the cheese seeps out during cooking.

Caldarroste: Hot, roasted chestnuts, preferably over coals. Before roasting, the chestnut shells should be punctured so that they do not burst.

Calzone: One of the most famous Neapolitan specialties, *calzone* is a disk of *pizza* dough filled with *prosciutto, mozzarella, ricotta,* and *Parmigiano,* folded over into a crescent shape, and baked in a *pizza* oven.

Cannellini: Small white beans, slightly elongated and arched in form. They are very common in Tuscany, where they are also prepared *al fiasco.*

Cannelloni: Cylindrical rolls of fresh egg pasta. They are boiled, stuffed with meat, vegetables, and/or cheese, and then baked.

Cannoli: Sicilian crunchy pastry shells filled with *ricotta,* sugar, and candied fruit.

Cantucci: Crunchy Tuscan cookies made with flour, sugar, eggs, almonds, and pine nuts. They are eaten dipped in *vin santo* (a Tuscan dessert wine).

Capelli d'angelo: Literally, "angel's hair." Very thin spaghetti usually cooked in broth. Fried and sweetened with honey, they are a Sicilian dessert.

Capitone: A term used in the south of Italy for a large freshwater eel.

Capocollo: See Coppa.

Caponata: Combination of cooked vegetables, capers, olives, and anchovies drizzled with oil and vinegar. It is a Sicilian specialty, served cold as an *antipasto.*

Cappellacci: Large *ravioli* filled with vegetables.

Cappelletti: Fresh egg pasta filled with meat or a mix of cheese, eggs, and spices. They are rather small and shaped like alpine hats.

Cappello da prete: Literally, "priest's hat." A kind of sausage made of pork skin, lard, and spices stuffed into the lower part of the pig's foot, then sewn into a triangle. It must be cooked before eating.

Cappon magro: Elaborate Ligurian seafood and vegetable salad.

Cappone: Fattened, castrated male chicken (capon).

Caprese: Salad made of tomatoes, *mozzarella,* basil, and olive oil.

Caprino: Cylinder-shaped goat and cow milk fresh cheese.

Carbonara (alla): Spaghetti sauce made of browned *pancetta* and raw egg yolks mixed with *pecorino* cheese and cream.

Carpaccio: Very thin slices of lean, raw beef or fish seasoned with oil, lemon, salt, and pepper, or other sauces. This dish was served for the first time at Harry's Bar in Venice and named after a Venetian painter.

Carpione (in): Fried fish marinated in vinegar, oil, herbs, and spices.

Carrettiera (alla): Spaghetti served with a sauce made of browned parsley, onions, garlic, and breadcrumbs.

Carrozza (mozzarella in): Slices of *mozzarella* between two slices of bread. It is floured, dipped in egg, and fried.

Carta da musica: Sardinian bread made of very thin, crunchy dough disks (literally, "music sheets"). It can keep a long time.

Casalinga (alla): Home-style cooking.

Casareccio: Traditional large country bread.

Casatiello: An Easter bread from Naples made with lard and plenty of black pepper.

Casonsei: Ravioli filled with sweet-and-sour stuffing. They are typical of the Bergamo area.

Cassata: Sicilian cake made with two or more flavors, sometimes filled with custard, cream, or *ricotta.*

Cassoeula: A traditional Milanese dish, prepared with pork ribs, salami, and other parts of the pig cooked with cabbage.

Castagnaccio: Traditional Tuscan dessert made of chestnut flour, raisins, and pine nuts and served with whipped cream.

Cavolo nero: Black cabbage with long, dark, narrow leaves. It is very common in Tuscany, where it is used for *ribollita* and other soups.

Ceci: Chickpeas: round, slightly dented, beige seeds sold only dried. *Ceci* can be used for soup, either whole or mashed as a side dish for pork, or simply boiled and seasoned with oil.

Cenci: Another name for *chiacchiere.*

Ceppatelli: Mushrooms often found growing on tree stumps, they are light gray in color with broad, flaring caps and slender stems. Those found on the market are often cultivated in hothouses.

Chiacchiere: Typical *Carnevale* preparation made of strips of sweet dough cut into various shapes and fried in oil. *Chiacchiere* are eaten as a dessert or a sweet snack.

Chiodini: Common variety of small, brown mushrooms that grow in clusters. *Chiodini* means "little nails" since they have tiny round caps and very thin stems.

Chisolini: Rhomboid-shaped pastry dough made with flour, *strutto,* and baking powder. They are fried and served with salami.

Chitarra: Literally, "guitar." A rectangular, wooden frame with evenly spaced wires stretched across, used for cutting sheets of pasta dough into *spaghetti.*

Chizze: Pasta similar to *chisolini,* but the dough is cut and folded like *ravioli* and filled with slices of *Parmigiano.*

Ciacci: Fritters of *ricotta,* flour, and baking powder made by using a utensil similar to a waffle iron. They are served with salami.

Cialzone: Typical *ravioli* made in Friuli. The simple version is made with meat, egg, and a cheese filling, whereas the sweet-and-sour version has raisins, chocolate, and candied fruit.

Ciambella: Baked, round mold of sweet or savory dough.

Cibreo: Scalded chicken giblets, browned in butter, and blended together with flour, lemon juice, and broth.

Ciccioli: The bits of fried pork fat left over when making *strutto.* Either fresh or dried, they are eaten with bread or *polenta.*

Cicerchiata: Dessert from Umbria similar to *strufoli.*

Cicoria: Long, thin green lettuce with a large white vein, chicory is also known in Italy as *catalogna, cicoria cimata,* or *cicoriella.*

Cieche: Just-spawned eels found in Versilia (the coastline from Forte dei Marmi to Viareggio, Tuscany) and Spain. They are usually floured and fried.

Cima: Stuffed veal breast. Traditional Ligurian dish. It is served cold.

Cime di rapa: See Broccoletti di rape.

Cipollacci: See Lampascioni.

Ciriola: A term used in Lazio for a small eel. *Ciriole* are also *tagliatelle* served with browned garlic, oil, and *peperoncino. Ciriola* is also a small, long roll from Rome.

Civet: Piedmontese stew made of game marinated in its own blood, with red wine, herbs, and spices.

Colatura: Liquid that results from salting anchovies. It may be used to season pasta.

Colomba: Leavened Easter cake baked in the shape of a dove and covered with sugar and almonds.

Coltello per tartufo: Truffle slicer. A cutting utensil similar to a spatula; it has an adjustable blade to vary the slices' thickness.

Concia: Another word for marinade. The name *concia* is also used to describe a kind of *polenta* dressed with cheese such as *toma* and *fontina.* Melted butter is poured on just before serving.

Conserva di pomodoro: Dried and pureed tomatoes. This very concentrated mixture is used in small amounts to flavor many dishes.

Conservare: To save, to preserve.

Coppa: Sausage made from deboned pork neck salted and marinated in wine. It is aged, though not allowed to harden.

Corallo: Red shellfish roe as in Maine lobster, scallops, and sea urchins. It is used for stuffings or to color and flavor hot or cold sauces and to make buttery garnishes for fish courses.

Coratella: The innards of a slaughtered lamb or goat.

Costoletta: Chop pounded flat with the bone still attached.

Cotechino: Fresh pork sausage.

Cotenna: Pork rind. Before it is cooked, it is scorched, scraped, and scalded to remove the bristles and some of the fat.

Cotognata: Quince preserve.

Cotoletta: Boneless slice of of veal or pork usually taken from the leg, pounded flat, breaded, and sautéed in butter or a combination of butter and oil. *Cotolette* can also be used to make *involtini.*

Cozze: Mussels.

Cremolata: A kind of granita made like a sherbet.

Cremona: Lombard town where one of the best fruit mustards is produced.

Cren: See rafano.

Crescenza: White, uncooked cheese with a buttery consistency, soft in texture and high in fat. Made from whole, pasteurized cow milk and ripened for 15 days. It has a rectangular shape with no crust and no holes. A typical produce of Lombardy.

Crespelle: Thin pancakes made with flour, milk, and egg. They are prepared like crêpes.

Croccante: Caramel with almonds or hazelnuts, made by spreading the candy out on a cold, greased work surface and cutting it before it hardens.

Crosetti or *Corzetti:* Ligurian fresh pasta made with flour and many eggs. The dough is cut, pressed into little molds with figures carved into them, dried, and then served with a meat or cheese sauce.

Crostino or *Crostone:* A slice of bread, cut into different shapes depending on what it is meant for, and fried in either olive oil or butter or toasted in the oven.

Crumiri: Dry cookies made of flour and cornmeal.

Cuccia: Sicilian dish that can be either sweet or savory. The sweet version is made of wheat berries softened, boiled, and then mixed with *ricotta,* sugar, candied squash, and chocolate. The savory version is simply wheat berries seasoned with oil.

Cugna: A preserve made from a reduction of quince, wine, and sugar, a Piedmontese specialty.

Culatello: Highly prized salami. Unlike *prosciutto, culatello* is aged in a casing. Only the best part of the pig's leg is used.

Cumino: Typical Mediterranean plant. Cumin's aromatic seeds are used both to enrich the flavor of cakes and bread and to produce a liqueur called *kummel.*

Diavolicchio: Another name for hot chili peppers in Abruzzo.

Dolceforte: Sauce with a base of mustard and sugar or any of two contrasting spices, e.g., *peperoncino* and honey.

Droghe: Combination of spices used to prepare *panforte di Siena.*

Erbazzone: Savory pie from Emilia-Romagna filled with young chard or spinach, *pancetta,* eggs, and *Parmigiano.* A sweet version without *pancetta* has the greens mixed with *ricotta,* almonds, and sugar.

Erbette: Tender chard-like green leaf.

Erborinato: A term used for the greenish streaks caused by the natural fermentation of cheese such as *gorgonzola*.

Estrazione: The extraction of olive oil from crushing olives.

Fagioli: Beans.

Falsomagro: Large roll of beef stuffed with chopped meat, whole hard-boiled eggs, *prosciutto,* cheese, and crumbled sausage and cooked in tomato sauce.

Farinacei: Starchy foods, e.g., pasta, rice, dumplings, etc.

Farinata: Chickpea flour diluted with water and oil, then baked in the oven with rosemary. Cut into triangles, it is eaten warm as a snack.

Farro or *Spelta:* A type of wheat grown in mountain areas. It has been used in Italy since the Romans; today it is grown in Liguria, Tuscany, and Apulia. The berry is used for soups and other preparations.

Fave del morti: Cookies made of flour, sugar, almonds, pine nuts, and egg whites.

Felino: A type of salami that takes its name from a village just outside Parma in Emilia-Romagna.

Fettucccine: Ribbon-shaped egg pasta.

Fiasco: A glass or terra-cotta flask, used to cook *cannellini* beans.

Filascetta or *Fitascetta: Focaccia* covered with onions browned in butter, fresh cheese, and sugar.

Finanziera: Garnish or condiment of chicken livers and giblets, olives, sweetbreads, mushrooms, and truffles.

Finocchiella: Fennel seeds, combed from a wild plant.

Finocchietto: A perennial plant that grows wild in Sicily and Sardina.

Finocchio: A celery-like vegetable with a delicate anise flavor. It may be eaten raw or cooked in various ways such as braised, fried, or boiled.

Focaccia: A Ligurian term for a flatbread, which may be topped with onion or rosemary or just olive oil.

Foiolo: The curly part of the upper intestine (tripe).

Fonduta: Fluid and creamy liquefied *fontina* cheese melted slowly in milk and cooked in a bain-marie while gently mixing in some egg yolks.

Fontana: A method of placing the flour on a pastry board in the shape of a fountain or a volcano so that eggs can easily be broken into the cavity on top and folded in with the flour without sticking to the board. It is the typical Italian way of making pasta dough and other dough.

Fontina: Rich, mellow, flavorful cheese from Valle d'Aosta. It is delicious eaten either plain or melted.

Formaggio: Cheese.

Frantoio: Machine to crush olives to extract olive oil. It consists of two large granite wheels that turn. *Frantoio* can also be the name given to the factory where olive oil is made.

Frappe: Another name for *chiacchiere.*

Frattaglie: The innards or organ meat of all animals.

Frico: Fried *montasio* cheese, a specialty from Friuli.

Frisedda: Typical bread from Apulia shaped into a circle, baked, and then cut in half and baked again until dry and crisp. It is served plain or soaked in water and seasoned with oil, fresh tomato, oregano, and salt. It keeps for a very long time.

Frittata: Flat omelet. It may contain vegetables, meat, or cheese.

Fritto (il): An assortment of fried foods that may include vegetables, meat, and fish.

Frutta alla Martorana: Sicilian marzipan molded into pretty fruit shapes.

Frutti di mare: Seafood. The term refers to any type of shellfish as in *insalata di frutti di mare.*

Fugazza: Venetian leavened sweet dough enriched with lots of eggs, liqueur, vanilla, various spices, orange peel, and (when available) iris root.

Funghetto (al): Vegetables thinly sliced or diced, sautéed, and flavored with parsley, garlic, and tomato.

Funghi: Mushrooms.

Fusilli: Short pasta twisted into a spiral.

Galani: Venetian dialect word for *chiacchiere.*

Galantina: Cooked salami made with veal, *pancetta,* pistachio nuts, and spices.

Galletta: Sea biscuit. Made without yeast and shaped like a bagel, *gallette* are generally used in *cappon magro.*

Gallinacci: Also known as *cantarelli* (chanterelles). Pale yellow-ochre mushrooms with upturned, flared caps, and slender, short stems.

Gambero: Shrimp. A crustacean without claws. It can reach a length of 10 inches. The shell can range from pink to bright red; the meat is a delicate pink.

Garganelli: Small quills made of fresh pasta with some *Parmigiano* mixed into the dough. They are shaped by curling fresh pasta dough around a special utensil called *pettine.*

Garum: Very popular fish innards sauce in ancient Rome. Its origins are Greek but in Turkey there is a fish sauce called *gharos* still today. Samples have been found in the ruins of Pompeii, near Naples, and in the south of Spain and wherever there were salt beds. The sauce was made with fatty fish such as mackerel and sardines. The fish was cleaned and left to marinate in terra-cotta containers in alternating layers of mint, oregano, celery, fennel, dill, coriander, and salt. It was left for 7 days in the sun and then mixed every day for 21 days. This mush was saved to use as a sauce for dressing meats cooked on the spit like suckling pig on the spit. For home consumption, it was diluted with water, wine, or vinegar to prepare various condiments.

Gatto: Baked pie of mashed potatoes with the addition of *mozzarella,* hard-boiled eggs, and salami.

Gelato al melone: Watermelon ice made with watermelon pulp, chocolate, and orange flower water.

Giardinetto: Vegetables or *sottaceti* laid out on a plate in such a way as to resemble a garden in bloom.

Giardiniera: Various vegetables marinated in water and vinegar and preserved.

Gnocchi: Small dumplings made of boiled potatoes, egg, and flour.

Gnocchi alla romana: Semolina *gnocchi* usually cut in round disks and baked with butter and grated cheese.

Gola: The tapered, less choice part of sweetbreads.

Gramolatura: The process used to stir olives after the crushing and before pressing to extract olive oil.

Grana padano: Similar to *Parmigiano-Reggiano,* this cheese is made outside the specified Parmigiano production areas. Unlike *Parmigiano,* it can be made all year round. It can be eaten on its own, used as an ingredient, or grated.

Granita: Light slush-ice made with sugar syrup and either fruit juice or coffee.

Granseola: Venetian dialect word for spider crab.

Gremolata: Battuto made of garlic, rosemary, parsley, and lemon peel used on *ossobuco.*

Grissini: Breadsticks made of dough with oil or some other fat. The most traditional ones are those from Turin (*grissini stirati torinesi*), pulled by hand, very long and irregular in shape.

Grolla: Wooden bowl that can also have the shape of a goblet. A typical product of the Valle d'Aosta craftsmen. A similar bowl is also known as *coppa dell'amicizia* (the friendship cup). It is short and wide, with a series of spouts circling its radius, and a cover. This bowl is filled with hot coffee, grappa, and sugar and then flamed. When the flame has consumed most of the alcohol, the bowl is passed around with everyone drinking from a different spout.

Guanciale: The fattest part of the hog jowl, lightly salted and smoked. Used like pancetta, *guanciale* is said to have a better, sweeter flavor than *pancetta.* It is used to prepare *amatriciana.*

Guardaporta: Literally, "doorman," nickname given to *ragù napoletano* because a doorman, supposedly having nothing else to do but watch the main entrance, could look after the slow cooking of the *ragù* as well.

Gubana: Dessert from Friuli made of sweet, leavened dough filled with mixed dried fruit, nuts, and liqueur, rolled and baked. It is served sliced and soaked in grappa.

Impepata di cozze: Mussels opened by steaming them in a covered pan with olive oil, garlic, parsley, and black pepper.

In porchetta: A culinary word that indicates any meat that has been seasoned with herbs, rolled, and roasted.

Insaccato: Meat, fat, and spices more or less finely ground, put in either natural or synthetic casings, and preserved. There are three kinds of *insaccati:* precooked (e.g., *mortadella*); those which must be cooked before eating (e.g., *cotechino, zampone*); and raw, which may be eaten dry-aged (e.g., *salame di Milano*).

Insalata di rinforzo: A Christmas salad from southern Italy made with cauliflower, olives, preserved vegetables in vinegar, anchovies, and capers and dressed with oil.

Intingolo: Sauce or a condiment in which bread, *polenta,* or vegetables may be dipped.

Involtino: Lean meat, pounded flat and rolled with filling and/or spices. These are most often made from fish, veal, or pork. It can also be called *rollatina*. In the south, when this is made with pork, it is called *braciola*.

Iota or *Jota:* Bean soup from Friuli made with fermented turnips and *polenta* or with potatoes, sauerkraut, pork stew, and ribs.

Knödeln: Classic bread dumplings from Alto Adige.

Lampascioni or *Lampagioni:* From the onion family, small, squat, and hard bulbs with a pleasantly bitter taste. They are used in Apulia, boiled and served as a salad, as a side dish for meat, in *frittata*, or baked with potatoes.

Lardo: Lard or fatback preserved by salting or smoking. It is then used as a condiment or thinly sliced and eaten on crusty bread.

Lasagne festonate: Lasagna with curly edges.

Latte di mandorle: The juice of almonds made by pounding the almonds into a paste and then adding water.

Lattemiele: Lombard name for whipped cream.

Latteria: A dairy.

Latticello: The whitish, acidulous liquid in which *mozzarella* is kept.

Lattonzolo: Unweaned piglet.

Lattughino: Lettuce that grows in small bunches with a few tiny, ruffled leaves. The Italian word for lettuce is *lattuga*.

Lattume: The seminal liquid of a male tuna. The entire sac is removed from the fish and air-dried. This is very rare and cannot be considered a common product. It is eaten in the same manner as *bottarga* with greens and extra virgin olive oil.

Leccarda: Dripping pan for roasts on the spit.

Lievitare: To leaven by adding either beer yeast or natural yeast.

Lingua: Tongue. Also, cooked salami made of calves' tongue.

Linguine: Long, flat dried pasta about ⅛ inch wide.

Luganiga or *Lucanica:* Long, thin, and seasoned pork sausage.

Maccheroni: Dried, short, smooth, or ribbed tubular pasta.

Magro: Literally "lean" in cookery. It may also refer to a vegetable filling.

Malfatti: Spinach dumplings made with cheese, spices, and egg yolk. They can be boiled or baked; they are usually served with a dressing.

Malloreddus: Tiny Sardinian dry dumplings made of flour, water, and saffron.

Maltagliati: Pieces of leftover fresh pasta used in soup.

Mandorlato: An Easter preparation made mostly with almonds.

Mangiatutto: Thin asparagus, all of which may be eaten, including the stems. Snow peas (*taccole*) are sometimes given this name.

Manicotti: A term used in the United States for *cannelloni*.

Mantecato: Pasta or rice dish sautéed with butter and cheese just before it is served.

Margarina: Margarine, a less expensive butter substitute.

Mariconda (la): Soup with bread dumplings.

Marinata: Marinade used to preserve, flavor, or tenderize meat. Marinades can be raw or cooked, quick or long.

Maritata: Neapolitan soup of vegetables (cabbage, escarole, etc.) and meats (sausage, pork ribs, veal parts, etc). The word *maritata* implies the two are married (the vegetables and the meat), and mated well in this preparation.

Maritozzo: Sweet bun filled with raisins, pine nuts, and candied fruit.

Marrone: Variety of large and tasty chestnuts obtained by grafting chestnut trees.

Marzapane: Marzipan, almond pastry.

Mascarpone: Rich, dense, fresh, triple-cream cheese made from cow milk. Very fresh *mascarpone* (seldom seen in the United States) is vaguely sweet. It is used in both desserts and savory dishes.

Mattarello: Rolling pin. A heavy, cylinder-shaped wooden stick for rolling out any kind of dough.

Meino or *Pom di mei:* A sweet bun made of cornmeal, flour, baking powder, and eggs. Round and squat in shape.

Meloarancio: Old Tuscan dialect word for orange.

Mesciua: Soup made of chickpeas, beans, and wheat and seasoned with oil, salt, and freshly ground pepper.

Messicani: Veal rolls stuffed with sausage, eggs, and *Parmigiano.* Two or three are skewered onto wooden sticks and cooked in butter, sage, and Marsala.

Mezzaluna: Crescent-shaped knife with one handle at each end used for mincing vegetables, meat, and other foodstuffs.

Migliaccio: A special kind of baked, sweet blood sausage made into a cake. The ingredients are pig's fresh blood, breadcrumbs, lard, raisins, and pine nuts.

Minestra: Broth served with the addition of fresh or dried pasta, rice, small dumplings, vegetables, or eggs and grated *Parmigiano.*

Minestrone: Soup made of various vegetables, rice, or pasta, or a legume.

Missolta: Tin can, in which *agone* (see page 199) is stored after drying.

Missoltitt: Dried and preserved *agoni.*

Misticanza: Mixed salad made of radicchio, watercress, endive, arugula, and other types of field lettuce.

Mitili: Another name for mussels.

Mocetta: Salami from Valle d'Aosta made with meat from chamois or deer.

Morsa: Cradle designed to hold a whole bone-in *prosciutto* to facilitate slicing it by hand.

Mortadella di Bologna: Large, cooked salami made of pork and usually mixed with other meats, seasoned with pepper and pistachio nuts. It is easily recognizable by its broad pink slices with chunks of white fat and pistachio nuts.

Mortadella di fegato: Cooked salami made with liver, *pancetta,* spices, and wine.

Mortaio: A marble, wood, or iron bowl used to crush herbs, nuts, and more, with a wooden pestle.

Mostarda di frutta: Spicy preserve of whole pieces of fruit in sugar syrup and mustard oil. It may include pears, peaches, apricots, watermelon, and pumpkin. Intended as the classic accompaniment to *bollito misto*, it is also mixed into the filling for sweet and savory *tortelli*.

Mosto: Must. Grape juice not yet fermented into wine.

Mozzarella: Fresh cheese from southern Italy, mainly from the Campania region. The best-quality *mozzarella* is made with *bufala* milk (a breed not to be confused with the American buffalo). In other parts of Italy, this same cheese is made with cow milk, and known under the name *fior di latte*. The *mozzarella* produced with *bufala* milk is higher in fat content and much more nutritious. *Mozzarella* has a soft and elastic texture, oval-round shape, and white color. Its taste is sweet and milky. It is sold in various shapes: braids, balls, and bite-size pieces.

Musciame: Dolphin fillet, air-dried. It is eaten thinly sliced and was indispensable at one time in the preparation of *cappon magro*, a typical Ligurian fish salad. Dolphin fishing is forbidden at this time.

Necci: Sweet crêpes made with chestnut flour and served with fresh cheese such as *pecorino* or *ricotto*.

Nepitella: Catmint. Belonging to the same family as mint, it grows wild and is commonly used in salads or to flavor white meats or roasts. The aroma is similar to mint with hints of sage. It should not be confused with wild mint.

Nervetti: *Antipasto* made of boiled calves' foot, deboned and sliced into thin strips. It is seasoned with oil and raw onion and eaten cold.

Noce: The eye or nut of the round, a large, single cut taken from the leg of beef or veal. The choicest veal *scaloppine* are taken from this cut. *Noce* literally translated is walnut.

Nocetta or *Nocciola:* Portion-sized, deboned saddle or rack of veal, lamb, or beef.

Nocino: Alcoholic beverage made from green walnuts and alcohol, marinated for 60 days and aged in bottle for about a year.

Nodino: Loin chop, either veal or pork, cut from the saddle. It is served with or without the bone.

Offelle: Oval cookies made of sweet short pastry.

Olive all'ascolana: Large pitted olives stuffed with cooked chopped meat mixed with *mortadella, prosciutto, Parmigiano,* and eggs, and then breaded and fried.

Orci: Terra-cotta jars glazed inside for storing olive oil.

Orecchiette: Fresh pasta made of only flour and water and shaped into a curl.

Ossobuco: Veal shank cut across into thick slices, braised, and usually served with *risotto alla milanese*.

Ovoli: One of the rarer varieties of mushrooms. *Ovoli* (still closed) are completely oval, pure white, often speckled with brilliant orange.

Pagliata or *Pajata:* The content of the upper part of milk-fed lamb intestines, used in Roman cooking.

Paiolo: Heavy, unlined copper pot with a convex bottom, used for cooking *polenta*.

Pala: Flat shovel used to slide *pizza* into a brick oven.

Palombaccio: Wild pigeon.

Pan de frizze: Sweet buns made with cornmeal, flour, *ciccioli*, and sugar; a specialty from Friuli.

Pan giallo: Sweet bun made with raisins, nuts, candied peel, honey, and chocolate, and iced with chocolate; a specialty from Lazio.

Pan molle: See Panzanella.

Pancetta: The salt-cured belly fat of a pig. *Pancetta* has deep pink stripes of flesh (similar to American bacon) and is used to lard meats and to flavor sauces, soups, or other dishes.

Pandolce: Sweet bread packed with candied fruit; a specialty from Genoa.

Pandoro: Sweet bread made with leavened dough, eggs, butter, and confectioner's sugar; a specialty from Verona.

Pane: Bread.

Pane frattau: Sardinian soup made of layers of *carta da musica* (thin layered crisp bread), sprinkled with grated cheese, and covered with broth.

Pane speziale: A type of bread from Emilia-Romagna similar to *panforte*.

Panettone: Sweet bread made with leavened dough, raisins, and candied fruit; dome-shaped or flat.

Panforte: Sweet bread made with flour, candied fruit, spices, almonds, and sugar; baked on paper-thin wafers; and sprinkled with confectioner's sugar; a specialty from Siena.

Paniscia: Thick soup made with sausage, rice, beans, and plenty of freshly ground pepper.

Panissa or *Paniccia:* Polenta made with chickpea flour and seasoned with oil and chopped onions.

Panpepato: (peppered bread). A sweet bread made of flour, sugar, almonds, pine nuts, orange peel, and plenty of freshly ground pepper.

Pansotti: Typical triangular *ravioli* from Genoa, stuffed with *preboggian*, greens, ricotta, borage, eggs, and cheese. They are usually served with a walnut sauce.

Panzanella: Salad of roasted bread softened in water and vinegar. The salad is made with ripe tomatoes coarsely chopped and dressed with oil and vinegar.

Panzerotti: Disks of leavened dough stuffed with *mozzarella* and a little tomato sauce, folded in half, sealed and fried, served as an *antipasto*. The term also refers to potato croquettes with a piece of *mozzarella* in the center.

Papero: Florentine word for duck.

Pappa al pomodoro: Tuscan soup made of stale, crusty country bread, fresh tomatoes, garlic, basil, pepper, and oil.

Pappardelle: Long, wide strips of fresh egg pasta.

Parmesan: Parmigiano-Reggiano. The word *Parmesan* is now protected in Europe, as it can only be used when referring to *Parmigiano-Reggiano* cheese.

Parmigiana (alla): A food term that refers to preparations from the Parma area. In southern Italy, the term indicates a dish consisting of fried slices of eggplant layered with tomato sauce and *mozzarella* and then baked.

Parmigiano-Reggiano: Parmigiano is a cow milk hard cheese made in the region around Parma. *Parmigiano-Reggiano* is produced under the strictest regulations: It must be made with milk produced between April and November 11 in the provinces of Parma, Reggio, Modena, Mantova, and Bologna. It is a hand-made cheese aged at least 18 months before it is sold. Authentic Reggiano has the words *Parmigiano-Reggiano* etched in a continuous pattern of small dots around the entire circumference of the rind. It is eaten on its own, used in cooking, and for grating.

Parrozzo: Loaf-shaped cake from Abruzzo made of flour, almonds, sugar, and eggs and then iced with chocolate.

Pasqualina (torta): Savory Ligurian artichoke pie made with lots of very thin layers of pastry.

Passatelli: Mixture of eggs, bread, and grated *Parmigiano* passed through a ricer and dropped directly into broth.

Pasta: Spaghetti and *maccheroni, penne* and *cavatelli, ravioli, tortellini, fusilli,* and so on, belong to a huge family of food of poor origins, all having in common the characteristic of offering a surprisingly balanced diet.

Pasta al forno: Baked pasta dressed with *ragù* and other ingredients.

Pasta alla Norma: Spaghetti with fried eggplant, tomato, and grated aged *ricotta salata.*

Pasta 'ncasciata: Pasticcio of *maccheroni* and meatballs seasoned with meat sauce and layered with hard-boiled eggs, salami, *caciocavallo,* peas, and other ingredients, covered with more meat sauce, baked till golden brown, then removed from its mold and served.

Pasta per sigillare: Dough made with flour and water and used to seal the cover of a pot in order to minimize heat dispersion.

Pasta reale: Another name for marzipan. An almond dough used in sheets to cover *cassata siciliana,* or used to make fruit-shaped confections.

Pastella: Batter.

Pasticcio: Pasta layered with several ingredients and baked.

Pastiera: Sweet, short pastry filled with *ricotta,* cooked wheat berries, candied fruit peels, and orange flower water.

Pastissada de caval: Horseman's stew prepared with horse meat.

Pecorino: Sheep milk cheese (*pecora* is Italian for sheep), *pecorino* can be mild or sharp in flavor and of soft or hard consistency (the latter is used for grating). The most common type is *pecorino romano,* typical of the Rome area. In Italy, another two common types are *pecorino sardo,* made in Sardinia, and *pecorino toscano,* from Tuscany.

Peoci: Another name for mussels.

Peperonata: Dish made of sweet peppers sautéed in oil, and finished with a *soffritto* of onion, tomatoes, capers, and olives. *Peperonata* is an excellent side dish for meats and is better eaten warm or at room temperature.

Peperoncino: Thin, long, and pointed pepper, either red or green. It can be slightly or extremely hot. It may be dried whole or more or less finely ground.

Peposo: Pork shank cooked with tomatoes, wine, herbs, and freshly ground pepper.

Perciatelli: See Bucatini.

Persicata: Solid peach jam made in the same way as *cotognata.*

Pesce: Fish.

Pescestocco: Another name for *stoccafisso.*

Pesto: Ligurian sauce made of basil, garlic, *Parmigiano, pecorino,* and oil. It is used on *trenette, gnocchi,* and *minestrone.*

Pettine: Utensil used in Romagna to shape pasta dough into short quills *(garganelli).*

Peverada: Sauce for roasted or boiled meats made with bread, beef marrow, *Parmigiano,* broth, salt, and pepper.

Pevere: An old Venetian word for pepper.

Pezzo duro: A kind of molded ice cream.

Piadina: Unleavened *pizza* dough made of water, flour, and *strutto.* It is baked on a *testo* and served hot with salami and cheese or folded over with sautéed leafy greens.

Piatto: Plate, dish; also course as in *primo piatto* (first course).

Picagge: Ligurian dialect word for *fettuccine.*

Piccata: Veal scaloppine sautéed very quickly in a pan with butter, lemon juice, or other ingredients.

Picchiettare: To insert spices such as cloves, cinnamon, or bay leaves in pieces of meat so that flavor can better spread while cooking.

Piedini: Calves' feet boiled and used for a salad called *nervetti.* They can be served as an *antipasto.*

Piemontese: Inhabitant of the region of Piedmont. *Alle piemontese* indicates a dish made in the style of Piedmont.

Pignata: Another name for a large pot.

Pignolata: Large *amaretti* covered generously with pine nuts.

Pignoli: See Pinoli.

Pinoccate: Tiny cakes with a base of sugar and pine nuts; they are commonly wrapped in colored paper.

Pinoli: Pine nuts.

Pinza: Cake made of flour, cornmeal, fennel seeds, raisins, dried figs, and other dried and candied fruit.

Pinzimonio: Dip for raw vegetables made of olive oil, ground pepper, and salt. By extension, the raw vegetables served with this sauce are also called *pinzimonio.*

Pisarei e fasoi: Soup of tiny dumplings made with breadcrumbs, flour, and milk typical of Emilia-Romagna. They are boiled and then tossed briskly with cooked beans with a *soffritto* of *pancetta,* onions, and tomatoes. *Pisarei* are the dumplings and *fasoi* are the beans.

Pissaladeira: A kind of pizza covered with onions, anchovies, black olives, and tomato.

Pistum: Dumplings made of bread, eggs, herbs, sugar, and raisins, boiled in pork broth.

Pitta: Calabrian name for *pizza. Pitta chicculiata* is covered with tomato sauce, oil, and *peperoncino; pitta maniata* is two disks of dough stuffed with slices of hard-boiled eggs, cheese, salami, and *peperoncino.*

Pizza: A disk of dough topped with tomato and cheese, herbs, and various other ingredients, baked in a brick oven heated to at least 650°F.

Pizzaiola (alla): A term used to describe stews and sauces made with tomatoes, capers, oregano, and anchovies.

Pizzoccheri: Tagliatelle made of buckwheat flour and cooked with potatoes, cabbage, and other vegetables, sautéed with plenty of butter and slices of *bitto* (a traditional cheese from Valtellina, a mountam area in northern Lombardy).

Polenta: Yellow cornmeal, either fine or coarsely ground, cooked with water and seasoned with butter and *Parmigiano. Polenta* may vary from soft to a solid consistency depending on its use. In some regions of Italy, white cornmeal or buckwheat flour is used instead of yellow cornmeal.

Polenta concia or *Pasticciata:* Casserole *polenta* layered with sauce, cheese, and butter and then baked.

Polenta taragna: Polenta made with one-half buckwheat flour and one-half yellow cornmeal with the addition of *bitto.* Its name comes from a Lombard word, *tarello,* the stick used to stir *polenta.*

Polpetta: Meatball. A mixture of minced meat, bread, herbs, and cheese shaped into balls, fried, and then added to tomato sauce. Often they are made with meat and vegetable leftovers.

Polpettone: Meat loaf made with the same mixture as meatballs.

Polverino: The floury mixture sprinkled over *panforte* before it is baked.

Porchetta: The word refers to the preparation of a whole pig the Roman way, that is, bound, seasoned, rolled closed, and stitched. It is then roasted in a large wood-burning oven to a crisp. It is served sliced like a salami. The expression *in porchetta* refers also to game and other meats prepared the same way prior to roasting or baking, although the seasoning may be different.

Porcini: Wild mushrooms with large, meaty brown caps slightly rounded on top. The stems are fleshy and wider at the bottom.

Porrata: Sauce prepared in the same manner as *agliata* but substituting leeks for garlic.

Potacchio: Term used to describe food stewed with herbs, white wine, and *peperoncino.*

Prataiolo: White and fleshy mushroom with a pleasant aroma. It can also be hothouse cultivated.

Preboggion: Bundle of wild herbs, used in Ligurian cuisine. The herb combinations change with the season.

Prescinsoeua: Ligurian preparation similar to sour cream.

Prosciutto: Pig's leg, salted, aged, and dressed according to local usage.

Provatura: Fresh cheese from Lazio, made with *bufala* milk, very similar to *mozzarella.*

Provolone: Aged cheese with a pungent, somewhat salty flavor. It can also be mild.

Punta di petto: Brisket of beef.

Puntarelle: Budding tips of a type of chicory cut halfway lengthwise and soaked in cold water until they curl up, they are served as a salad, dressed with oil, vinegar, garlic, and chopped anchovies.

Puttanesca (alla): Pasta sauce made of tomato, black olives, anchovies, capers, *peperoncino,* and basil.

Quadrucci: Fresh or dried pasta, usually made with eggs, cut into little squares and added to soups or broth.

Quaglia: Quail.

Quagliette: Little balls of leftover stuffing wrapped in scalded cabbage leaves and fried.

Quartirolo: Soft, sweet-tasting cow milk cheese shaped into a square.

Radicchio: The red and white leaf chicory of the Veneto region. *Radicchio di Treviso* or *trevigiano* is grown in the Treviso area. It has tender, large leaves with white ribs and red edges. *Radicchio di Castelfranco* grows in small heads with wide, tightly cupped leaves (similar to iceberg lettuce), with white ribs and red edges.

Rafano: Horseradish.

Ragù: Sauce made of meat or fish chopped finely or coarse, cooked slowly with desired herbs and spices.

Ramerino: Rosemary.

Ravioli: Disks or squares of fresh egg pasta stuffed with vegetables or cheese or meat. The larger ones are generally served with butter, sage, and *Parmigiano.* Smaller ones (*raviolini*) are served with various condiments or in broth.

Rete: Caul fat. The membrane surrounding the inner organs of veal and pork, used for wrapping lean meats to be roasted.

Ribollita: Literally, "re-boiled," this soup it is made by using leftovers of Tuscan black cabbage and bean soup baked with stale bread, thinly sliced onion, and extra virgin olive oil.

Ricciarelli: Oval cookies made of almonds, flour, and sugar. A specialty from Siena.

Ricotta: A milk product obtained from acidulated whey, heated to 82°F, when making cheese. It has the texture and consistency of farmer's or pot cheese and is used in both sweet and savory dishes. *Ricotta romana* is made with sheep milk. There is also a salted version which can be aged and used grated (*ricotta salata*).

Rigaglie: Giblets from a chicken or any other bird, in addition to its comb.

Rigatino: Tuscan *pancetta* made with the leanest part of the hog's belly, covered with black pepper, and cured flat.

Rigatoni: Medium-size ribbed *maccheroni* (dried pasta).

Ripieno: Stuffing.

Risi e bisi: A soft *risotto* from Veneto made with rice and fresh peas.

Risotto: A term that refers to a classic Italian rice preparation.

Risotto al nero di seppia: Black risotto made with squid ink.

Robiola: Fresh, soft, whole cow milk cheese with a very delicate taste.

Rocciata: A specialty of Assisi, similar to *panforte,* but shaped in a folded triangle.

Rognosa: Frittata made with salami and grated *Parmigiano* mixed with eggs.

Rollatina: See Involtino.

Rombo: Turbot, a fish common in the Mediterranean and North Atlantic. It is oval, almost rounded, and it may reach a length of 16 inches.

Rossetti: The newborn of red and white mullet. Excellent floured and fried.

Rustisciada: Sliced sirloin and pieces of sausage cooked in sauce of tomato, wine, and onion.

Saba or *Sapa:* Grape must that is cooked until it is reduced by two-thirds; it is used to make desserts and sweet-and-sour dishes or with cheese. Also known as *vino cotto.*

Salama da sugo: Cooked salami made of ground pork, innards, wine, and spices stuffed into a pig's bladder. It must be cooked before eating.

Salam d'la duja: Salami from Piedmont kept soft in a typical ceramic jar (*duja*) filled with melted fat.

Salame: Ground meat seasoned and packed into a casing and aged.

Salame di Milano: Aged, very finely ground salami.

Salame napoletano: Aged sausage with plenty of *peperoncino.*

Salamelle: Small salami similar to *cotechino.* It must be boiled or broiled before eating.

Salamini della verza: Small sausages used to prepare the Milanese *cassoeula.*

Salamoia: Brine.

Salmì: Stew of wild game that has been marinated in wine, herbs, and spices and cooked in the marinade. The sauce is strained and the dish served with *polenta.* Sometimes the sauce is used for *pappardelle.*

Salmoriglio: Warm sauce for roast meats and broiled fish, especially swordfish. It is made with lemon juice, oil, parsley, and oregano emulsified in a double boiler.

Salnitro: Salt of potassium used to preserve food.

Salsiccia: Pork meat in casing. It may be consumed fresh, pan-fried, or cooked in a sauce. It may also be dry-aged.

Saltimbocca: Veal *scaloppine* with *prosciutto,* briskly sautéed in butter, sage, and white wine. It may be rolled like an *involtino* or sautéed flat.

Salumi: Whole cuts of meat cured in salt and dry-aged or cured in brine (*salamoia*) and then cooked and preserved.

San Daniele: Village near Udine, Friuli, where they produce the famous *prosciutto di San Daniele*, a choice variety of cured ham.

Sanguinaccio: Custard made of pig's blood mixed with cocoa and milk.

Sansa: The solid part of the olives left over after the pressing.

Saor: A milder version of *carpione* (*saor* is the contraction of *savor,* which in Venetian dialect means "flavor"), it is a sauce made with fried onions, vinegar, sugar, pine nuts, and raisins. It is used to marinate fresh fish, especially sole and sardines.

Sargassi: Legend has it that eels come to spawn in the Sargasso Sea from the Mediterranean. That portion of the Atlantic Ocean northeast of the Antilles owes its name to a particular alga called *sargasso.*

Sartù: A Neapolitan rice dish baked in a mold.

Savoiardi: Ladyfingers often used in the preparation of ice cream cake or *tiramisù.*

Savor: "Flavor" in Venetian dialect. Also, a preserved fruit cooked in must. It is used to accompany meats or used for various kinds of stuffing.

Sbrisolona: Traditional cake from Mantova made with flour, cornmeal, almonds, sugar, and eggs.

Scacciata: Savory pie made of two layers of leavened salted dough filled with meat, vegetables, and cheese. There is also a sweet version filled with *ricotta,* sugar, and coffee.

Scaloppina: Scallop, that is, a thin slice of lean veal from the center cut of the leg, rib, or loin, or square-cut chuck that has been lightly pounded flat.

Scamorza: Stringy, semi-aged cheese similar to *caciocavallo.*

Scampo: A prawn with claws and 12 legs. It is mostly found in the Mediterranean.

Scapece: Vinegar and mint marinade for vegetables and fried foods.

Scavino: The utensil used to scoop the marrow out of the bone in *ossobuco.* It is a thin, elongated, and narrow spatula jokingly called "the tax man," referring to the fact that it scrapes the marrow to the bone.

Schiuma di mare: Antipasto of small, just spawned, raw anchovies seasoned with oil, lemon, and pepper.

Scorzonera: A bitter root known in America as salsify.

Scottadito: Broiled finger-burning lamb chops, broiled quickly and eaten while still very hot.

Scottiglia: Mixture of various kinds of meat stewed together.

Scripelle: Crêpes cooked in chicken broth, a specialty from Teramo, Abruzzo.

Scrofa: Sow. An adult female pig.

Seadas or *Sebadas:* Large, sweet Sardinian *ravioli* filled with fresh cheese; fried and covered with honey.

Semifreddo: Chilled cream prepared with egg-based custard and whipped cream. The chilled creams may be used as filling for *cassate* and *bombe* or can be prepared with fruits, syrups, and chocolate.

Seppia: Cuttlefish.

Sfinciuni: Rather thick *focaccia* covered with tomato sauce, anchovies, onions, cheese, oregano, and oil. It can be served as an *antipasto,* main course, or snack.

Sfogliatelle: Puff pastry made with many layers of curled pastry filled with *ricotta* and candied fruits. It has a ridged look and the shape of a large seashell.

Sformato: Savory mold bound with eggs and baked in a bain-marie. It may contain vegetables, meat, or fish.

Soffritto: A sauté of one or more vegetables (such as onions, carrots, celery, or parsley) generally used as a start-up for many recipes in Italian cuisine. Various fats may be used (olive oil, *pancetta,* or butter) according to the desired preparation. Sautéed onion as a base for *risotto* is also called *soffritto.*

Soncino: Small, oval-leafed lettuce that grows in small bunches.

Sopa coada: A broth made with squab. The broth and boneless squab is then poured over slices of bread and baked. A specialty from Friuli.

Soppressata: Cooked and aged salami made with meat taken from the pig's head, lard, spices, and pistachio nuts.

Sorbetto: Sherbet usually made with the juice and pulp of fruit.

Sottaceti: Diced or whole vegetables marinated in vinegar or water and then preserved in vinegar in jars. They are served as an *antipasto* or as a side dish for meat.

Sott'aceto: A way of marinating and then preserving food, especially vegetables, in vinegar.

Sottofiletto: The short loin of beef, generally used for *scaloppine.*

Sott'olio: A way of preserving food in oil, especially vegetables and mushrooms.

Spalla: Shoulder.

Speck: Cured, dried, aged pork thigh. A specialty from Alto Adige.

Spezzatino: Cubed or diced meat stewed or sautéed with or without tomatoes and/or other vegetables.

Spianatoia: Rather large, wooden board, perfectly smooth and without knots, generally used to roll fresh pasta.

Spongata: Roll of sweet pastry filled with honey, dried fruit, nuts, and candied fruit.

Spuma: Sweet or savory mousse.

Spumone: Spumone can also be called *semifreddo.* All *semifreddi* or *spumoni* may be served with an appropriate sauce. These range from a simple fruit sauce to vanilla cream.

Steccare: To insert pieces of *pancetta,* lard, or spices through a piece of meat ready to be roasted.

Stecchi: Ligurian brochettes of veal, brains, *Parmigiano,* vegetables, and herbs, breaded and fried. *Stecco* is also the name of the wooden skewer holding the meat.

Stocco or *Stoccafisso:* Known as stockfish, it is prepared with smaller cod, air-dried till it becomes as hard as a wooden stick.

Stracciatella: Soup made by mixing eggs beaten with *Parmigiano* into boiling broth.

Stracotto: Beef braised with herbs, vegetables, and spices and then cooked very slowly and for a long time on top of the stove or in the oven. *Stracotto* is never marinated.

Strangolapreti: Literally, "priest chokers," these dumplings are made of potatoes, flour, cooked greens, and *ricotta* boiled and served with melted butter and *Parmigiano* or with a *gorgonzola* sauce.

Strufoli: A Neapolitan Christmas treat, *strufoli* are small balls of dough that are first fried and then bound together with chopped candied citrus peel and a honeyed syrup to form a wreath or mounded on a platter. They are almost always then sprinkled with colored candy *confetti.*

Strutto: Melted animal fat rid of all meat particles and preserved in soft form. It is used as fat for many preparations.

Stufato: Chunks of meat covered with wine and herbs and stewed over low heat for several hours.

Sugna: See Strutto.

Supplì: Rice balls with *mozzarella,* herbs, and spices in the center. The rice is cooked like *risotto* and is then breaded and fried.

Svezzato: Weaned baby lamb or newly born pig.

Taccola: Snow pea, a kind of pea also called *mangiatutto* ("eat all").

Tagliapasta: Pasta knife in the shape of a small wheel made of tin. It comes in different sizes and can either be grooved or not.

Tagliatelle, Tagliatelline, or *Tagliolini:* Fresh egg pasta rolled out and cut in various widths. *See also Tajarin.*

Tagliere: Chopping board.

Taglio: Cut of meat: *Primo taglio* refers to the choicest cuts; *secondo* and *terzo taglio* indicate less choice cuts.

Tajarin: Piedmontese name of *tagliolini* prepared with at least 20 eggs to 2 pounds of flour. Some add grated *Parmigiano* to the dough. *Tajarin* are made specially to be dressed with white truffle.

Tapulone: Ground donkey meat cooked in wine.

Taragna: See Polenta taragna.

Tarello: Wooden stick used to stir *polenta.*

Tartufo: Very rare aromatic tuber. It can be white or black. The best white truffles are found in the hills near Alba, Asti, and Cuneo in Piedmont. The best black truffles can be found in Norcia (Umbria). The term *tartufo* also indicates rich chocolates or vanilla and chocolate ice cream with candied fruits in the center shaped into a ball and covered with chocolate. *Tartufo* can also be a kind of clam.

Tellina: Tiny variety of clam.

Tenerume: The piece of beef consisting of muscles and tissue where the ribs end.

Testina: The calf's head. It is cooked as part of *bollito misto* or served in a salad cut into julienne with a dressing of oil, lemon, salt, and pepper. Also goat's head, split, breaded, and baked.

Testo: Special flat, round, edgeless cooking utensil with a handle, used for cooking *testaroli.* It can be made of terra-cotta or cast iron.

Tiella: A small iron or terra-cotta casserole. By extension, dishes cooked in this kind of pan.

Tigella: Similar to a *piadina,* it is served hot with lard, garlic, and rosemary.

Timballo: Baked pasta, rice, or *polenta* in a pastry shell.

Tiramisù: Cold dessert made with layers of sponge cake or ladyfingers soaked in coffee and covered with *mascarpone.*

Toma: Soft-ripened cheese, creamy in texture and high in fat content, shaped round and flat. It can be eaten fresh or preserved in oil with herbs or *peperoncino.*

Tomacelle or *Tomaxelle:* Veal *rollatine* stuffed with meat, mushrooms, pine nuts, and herbs and cooked in sauce.

Torcetto: A biscuit made with leavened dough in the form of a doughnut.

Torchio: Utensil used to wind, pull, or stretch pasta. It is especially used to prepare *bigoli.*

Torcolo: Doughnut with candied citrus, raisins, pine nuts, and anise seeds mixed into the dough.

Torrone: Nougat made of sugar, honey, and hazelnuts. In addition to the traditional crunchy variety, there is also a chewy, chocolate-covered version.

Torta: A cake generally made with sponge cake and the desired cream or decorations.

Torta pasqualina: See Pasqualina.

Tortelli: Sweet fritters or *ravioli* stuffed with vegetables, pumpkin, and/or cheese.

Tortellini: Stuffed pasta similar to *cappelletti* but shaped into a closed ring.

Tortelloni: Large *ravioli* usually stuffed with vegetables and/or cheese.

Tortiera: Cake pan, round and of varying sizes, either simple or springform. The term *tortiera* is also used to describe something cooked in this pan.

Toscanelli: Small, brown beans used in dishes such as *pasta e fagioli*. The same beans are also called *fagioli dell'occhio* in Tuscany.

Totano: Mollusk from the same family as squid *(calamaro)* with a triangular fin attached to the bottom of the sack.

Trattoria: Rustic restaurant that serves traditional regional cuisine.

Trenette: Long, flat, dried or fresh pasta.

Trifolare: Refers to the way of slicing meat or mushrooms very thinly and sautéing them briefly, most often in butter.

Trippa: Tripe. The stomach and upper part of the intestines of cow, pigs, and lamb. It is a part of *frattaglie* (innards) and is sold cleaned and parboiled.

Trippate (Uova): Frittata cut into thin strips and served with tomato sauce. The curly strips resemble *trippa* (tripe), hence the name.

Trofie: Little twisted pieces of pasta made with just flour and water. They are a Ligurian specialty traditionally served with *pesto*.

Truscello: Layers of beef meatballs alternating with a mixture of *ricotta, Parmigiano,* and eggs. It is a specialty of Messina.

Uccelletti scappati: Skewers of pork or beef rolls wrapped in *pancetta* and sautéed in oil and sage. They are served with *polenta*.

Uccelletto (all'): Diced or julienned veal or beef browned rapidly in oil and sage, splashed with white wine, and served immediately.

Uova: Eggs.

Vaccinara (alla): Roman dish usually containing oxtail that originated in the Roman slaughterhouse district.

Valdostana: Veal chop sliced open like a pocket, stuffed with fontina, and then breaded and pan-fried in butter.

Valigine: Literally, "little suitcases," cabbage rolls stuffed with meat or vegetables.

Valtellina: Alpine valley by the river Adda in the province of Sondrio, Lombardy. It borders Switzerland to the north, the province of Como to the west, Bergamo to the south, and Bolzano to the east.

Ventresca: Another name for *pancetta. Ventresca* may also refer to the fatty belly flesh of a tuna, a choice cut.

Vermicelli or *Vermicelloni:* Another word for *spaghetti* in the Neapolitan region.

Vincisgrassi: Fresh *lasagne* made with flour and semolina, boiled, then drained and layered with stewed giblets, sweetbreads, brains, *prosciutto,* herbs, and béchamel sauce. It is then baked.

Vino cotto: Must (freshly pressed grapes) cooked for many hours until it is as thick as honey. It is used instead of honey in some desserts. *See also Saba.*

Virtù: Typical soup from Abruzzo made by cooking dried legumes left over from the winter and adding fresh spring vegetables.

Vitello tonnato: Cold dish of veal with tuna sauce. Lean veal is marinated and cooked in white wine, then thinly sliced and covered with a cold sauce of tuna, anchovies, and capers.

Vongola verace: The most prized clam, peculiar for the two horns that protrude from its body. The term *verace* originates in the Neapolitan region. *Vongola verace* translated means "real clam."

Zabaglione or *Zabaione:* Eggnog made with egg yolks, Marsala, and sugar, beaten in a double boiler until fluffy, and served warm or cold with or without fruit.

Zafferano: Saffron is the stamen of a flower originally from Asia Minor. Today it is widely grown in Italy also. It is used for coloring and flavoring.

Zampetto: Pig's trotters (hooves). They are usually stewed, sometimes along with other parts of the animal. They can also be boiled as part of *bollito misto* or by themselves and served with *salsa verde.*

Zampone: Completely boned pig's foot, stuffed with ground pork, pork fat, skin, and herbs. It is traditionally eaten on New Year's Eve with lentils for good luck.

Zelten: Leavened Christmas bread made with rye and white cake flour mixed with candied fruit and iced with honey.

Zeppole: Fritters made of potato, flour, eggs, and yeast. They can be used plain, sprinkled with sugar, or filled with cream.

Zimino: Sauce made with very finely minced beets or spinach, parsley, and garlic blended with oil. It is usually served with fish.

Zimino di ceci: Soup of boiled chickpeas with browned onion, garlic, celery, greens, tomatoes, and dried mushrooms in oil.

Ziti or *Zite:* Long, cylindrical, dried *maccheroni.*

Zuccotto: Semifreddo (chilled cream) made in a dome-shaped mold with layers of sponge cake sprinkled with liqueur and filled with whipped cream and chocolate.

Zuppa: Semi-liquid soup made by cooking meat, fish, shellfish, dried beans, or vegetables in water. *Zuppe* are usually served with slices or cubes of toasted or leftover country bread.

Zuppa inglese: Italian version of English trifle; sponge cake soaked in Alchermes and layered with vanilla cream, chocolate, and fruit preserve.

Zuppa pavese: Hot broth poured over buttered or plain toasted bread with one or two eggs on top.

BIBLIOGRAPHICAL NOTE

In compiling this book, and in many years of work in the restaurant profession, I have read and consulted a large number of excellent publications. The ones I've found most useful are listed below.

HISTORICAL WORKS

1300s: Anonimo toscano del Trecento, *Libro della cucina* (manuscript in the University Library of Bologna), Bologna 1863.

1400s: Maestro Martino da Como, *Liber de arte coquinaria* (manuscript in the Congress Library, Washington, D.C.), Venice 1516, under the name of Giovanni de' Rosselli and the title *Epulario*; Bartolomeo Sacchi, known as Platina, *De Obsoniis ac de honesta voluptate et valetudine*, Rome 1474.

1500s: Bartolomeo Scappi, *Opera*, Venice 1570; Cristoforo di Messisburgo, *Banchetti, composizioni di vivande et apparecchio generale*, Ferrara 1549.

1600s: Bartolomeo Stefani, *L'arte di ben cucinare*, Mantua 1662.

1700s: Jacopo Vittoreli, *I maccheroni*, Venice 1773; Vincenzo Corrado, *Il Cuoco galante*, Naples 1773; Francesco Leonardi, *L'Apicio moderno*, Rome 1790.

1800s: Ippolito Cavalcanti, duca di Buonvicino, *Cucina teorico-practica*, Naples 1837; Pellegrino Artusi, *La Scienza in cucina e l'arte di mangiar bene*, Florence 1891.

CONTEMPORARY WORKS

Among the books that I have consulted more often during the compilation of this volume are Massimo Alberini, *4000 Anni a tavola*, Milan 1972; *Storia del pranzo all'italiana*, Milan 1966; Massimo Alberini and Giorgio Mistretta, *L'Italia gastronomica*, Touring Club Italiano, Milan 1984; Vincenzo Buonassisi, *Il Codice della pasta*, Milan 1973 (English Edition, *Pasta*, Wilton, 1976); Luigi Carnacina and Luigi Veronelli, *La Cucina regionale*, Milan 1974; Riccardo Di Corato, *2214 Vini d'Italia*, Milan 1975, *451 Formaggi d'Italia*, Milan 1977, and *928 Conditmenti d'Italia*, Milan 1978; Fernanda Gosetti, *In Cucina con Fernanda Gosetti* and *il Dolcissimo*, Fabbri, Milan 1984; *The Food of Italy*, Waverley Root, New York 1977; Luigi Veronelli, *Bere giusto*, Milan 1971; *Grande Enciclopedia della gastronomia,* Selezione del Readers Digest, Milan 1990.

ENGLISH INDEX

pasta with fresh *borlotti* beans, 127
pasta with lentil soup, 128
rice and asparagus soup, 126
short pasta with potato soup, 128
soup with bread dumplings, 126–27
spelt and kidney bean soup, 129–30
veal broth, 124
zucchini blossom soup, 125

soups (with bread), 133–39
bean soup baked with bread, 135
bread and egg in beef broth, 124
cabbage and cheese soup, 134
clam soup, 137–38
egg and bread soup, 134
fish stew Livornese-style, 136–37
Savoy cabbage soup and *fontina* cheese, 135–36
squab soup, 138–39
tomato and bread stew, 136
tripe soup, 139

soups (vegetable), 130–33
bean soup with Tuscan-style black cabbage, 132–33
fava bean soup with wild chicory, 133
vegetable *minestrone*, 131–32
vegetable *minestrone* with rice, 130–31

spices, 20–21
cinnamon, 20
cloves, 20
mace, 20
mustard, 21
nutmeg, 20
pepper (white or black), 20
saffron, 21
vanilla, 21

truffles, 119
in *antipasto,* 24
black truffle, 119
eggs in cocotte with white truffle, 121–22
eggs with white truffle, 83
fried eggs with polenta and truffles, 83
tajarin with white truffle, 149–50
white truffle, 119

veal, 222–28
ossobuco with *gremolata,* 225–26
oven-braised veal shoulder, 227–28
stuffed veal breast Genoa-style, 226–27
veal chop Milanese-style, 224
veal chops with *fontina,* 224
veal in tuna sauce, 226
veal sautéed with sage, 224–25
veal scallops in lemon sauce, 223
veal scallops with *prosciutto* and sage, 223
See also meats

vegetable dishes, 89–99
artichokes, sautéed, 91
artichokes braised with mint, 90–91
broccoli rape Roman-style, braised, 89–90
broccoli rape with garlic and *peperoncino,* Neapolitan-style, 90
chicory sautéed with *pancetta,* 92
eggplant, 93
eggplant, sautéed, 94–95
eggplant and tomato stew, 95
eggplant *Parmigiana,* 93–94
eggplant stuffed with *caciocavallo,* 96–97
fennel with *fontina* cheese, 93

pearl onions, sweet-and-sour, 92
peppers sautéed with oil and capers, 95–96
peppers stuffed with bread, 97
Savoy cabbage rolls, 91–92
tomatoes stuffed with bread and herbs, 98
tomatoes stuffed with rice, 97–98
zucchini, baked, 96
zucchini stuffed with cheese, 98–99
See also soups (vegetable)

vegetables, 85–89
in *antipasto,* 24
artichokes, 86
asparagus, 85
broccoli rape, 85
cabbage, head, 89
cabbage, Savoy, 89
cardoons, 86
celery, 88–89
chicory, 86
eggplant, 87
fennel, 87
gourd squash, 89
leek, 88
muscari bulbs, 87
pepper, 87
red beets, 85
squash and zucchini blossoms, 87
Swiss chard, 86
tomato, 88
turnip, 88
zucchini, 89
See also greens; salads

vinegar, 12–14
aromatic vinegar, 12
balsamic vinegar, 13–14
common vinegar, 12
decolored vinegar, 12
honey vinegar, 14
wine vinegar, 13

ITALIAN INDEX

ABOUT THE AUTHOR

As one of the nation's most respected restaurateurs, Tony May has worked diligently for four decades to elevate the image of Italian cuisine in America. He serves on the boards of Gruppo Ristoratori Italiani (Club GRI), Distinguished Restaurants of North America (DIRONA), and Trustee Emeriti of the Culinary Institute of America (CIA), where he was active in establishing the Caterina de Medici Restaurant and a course of study on authentic Italian cooking for American students. He is currently the President of the Italian Culinary Institute for Foreigners (ICIF) in Costigliole D'Asti, Piedmont, Italy, a school for culinary professionals located in a historic medieval castle.

For years, first as General Manager and then as owner, Tony May operated and re-established the dancing policy at New York's Rainbow Room in Rockefeller Center (1964–1986). In 1981, he received his first IVY Award. In 1986, he opened the restaurant Palio, which attracted critical acclaim throughout the world. Two years later, he followed with San Domenico NY, the flagship restaurant of the Tony May Group that has garnered international praise. San Domenico NY was the first Italian restaurant in the United States awarded three stars by the *New York Times*.

In 1989, Mr. May was chosen by a distinguished panel of his peers to be included in the prestigious *Who's Who of Cooking in America*, and in 1990, he was selected as the Silver Plate recipient in the *Independent Restaurant Operator* category by the International Food Service Manufacturers Association (IFMA). In 1992, he received his second IVY Award in recognition of his restaurant San Domenico NY. In May 1992, Mr. May was awarded the Silver Spoon by *Food Arts* magazine for his achievements over the past twenty-five years as a restaurateur and a leader in the food service industry. In 1993, he was inducted into *Nation's Restaurant News* "Fine Dining Hall of Fame."

Ready for expansion and bringing quality Italian cuisine to more casual dining, Mr. May opened Gemelli at New York's busy World Trade Center in 1997. With its back-to-basics Italian cuisine and a relaxed countryside-style atmosphere, Gemelli quickly became one of the area's favorites. In March 1998, Tony May introduced PastaBreak, a fast-food establishment offering quick, inexpensive restaurant-quality food on the concourse of the World Trade Center.

On September 11, 2001, both Gemelli and PastaBreak were destroyed in the attack on the World Trade Center. Mr. May worked tirelessly to help feed the rescue workers, as well as to help his displaced employees. He opened a new PastaBreak in the E-Walk complex in Times Square on October 7, 2002, rehiring many of his downtown employees.

As a result of his lifelong endeavors, he was invested as a *Cavaliere* and subsequently as *Commendatore dell'Ordine al Merito della Repubblica Italiana* for his efforts on behalf of his native country's gastronomy. In 1996, his restaurant San Domenico NY was one of only twenty-four restaurants throughout the world to receive the first *Insegna del Ristorante Italiano* from the president of the Republic of Italy, an award denoting the finest Italian restaurants outside of Italy.

Tony May resides in New York City with his wife, Halima.